Literary Trails of the North Carolina Mountains

NORTH CAROLINA LITERARY TRAILS

is a project of the North Carolina Arts Council,

an agency of the Department of Cultural Resources

PROJECT DIRECTOR: Debbie McGill, Literature Director,

North Carolina Arts Council

literary trails

of the North Carolina Mountains

A GUIDEBOOK

Georgann Eubanks

Photographs by **DONNA CAMPBELL**

The University of North Carolina Press *Chapel Hill*

© 2007 The North Carolina Arts Council

All rights reserved

Designed by Richard Hendel

Set in The Serif and Scala Sans types

by April Leidig-Higgins, Copperline Book Services

Manufactured in Canada

The paper in this book meets the guidelines for
permanence and durability of the Committee on
Production Guidelines for Book Longevity of the
Council on Library Resources.

Library of Congress Cataloging-in-Publication Data
Eubanks, Georgann.
Literary trails of the North Carolina mountains:
a guidebook / by Georgann Eubanks; photographs
by Donna Campbell.
      p. cm.
Includes bibliographical references and index.
ISBN 978-0-8078-3137-3 (alk. paper)
ISBN 978-0-8078-5833-2 (pbk.: alk. paper)
1. Literary landmarks—North Carolina—Guidebooks.
2. Authors, American—Homes and haunts—North
Carolina—Guidebooks.   3. North Carolina—In
literature—Guidebooks.   4. North Carolina—
Intellectual life—Guidebooks.   I. Campbell, Donna,
1951–   II. Title.
PS144.N63E93   2007
820.9—dc22   2007019453

Unless otherwise noted, the photographs are by
Donna Campbell. The maps are by Michael T. Southern.

Acknowledgments of permissions appear in a section
immediately preceding the index.

11 10 09 08 07   5 4 3 2 1

CONTENTS

PREFACE

Every book is a journey, carrying us into worlds unknown and worlds familiar. Through books we learn about ourselves and others—the culture of whole communities, the poetry of place, and the daily chores, observances, and surprises of life among characters imagined and real.

Now suppose you combined the journey of a book, many books, even, with an actual trip—say, a statewide tour of the places, people, and events described by those curious creators of books, in this case North Carolina's poets, playwrights, novelists, biographers, and essayists. Throughout history, our state's native and visiting writers have been a talented lot. Connecting their work and lives to actual places in North Carolina worth visiting is the idea behind this series of guidebooks.

In this volume, covering western North Carolina, we will visit the mountain range where mysterious lights inspired an entire novel by science fiction writer Jules Verne, though he never traveled to North Carolina from his home in France.

We'll climb the ridge that poet and novelist Robert Morgan favored as a place to go parking as a young man and visit the hotel room where a despairing F. Scott Fitzgerald once fired a pistol, pretending to commit suicide. We'll stand on the porch of the boardinghouse run by Thomas Wolfe's mother, where she bluntly told Fitzgerald that she would not rent a room to him with alcohol on his breath.

We'll meet Sequoyah, the man who invented the first Native American alphabet, and we'll read an excerpt from our state's first novel—a story of the Cherokee people written by U.S. senator Robert Strange and published in 1839.

We'll drive by the shores of the ice cold lake where novelist Elizabeth Spencer got goosebumps as a girl during summer camp. We will stop to admire the magnificent stone home on an Asheville hilltop where the young songwriter Nina Simone took piano lessons as a teenager and where Zelda Fitzgerald and her husband Scott came to a private performance by the Hungarian composer Béla Bartók.

We'll dig into correspondence between Gilded Age novelists Henry James and Edith Wharton as they compared notes on their separate visits to Asheville's Biltmore House in 1905 and explore how their relationships with the Vanderbilts influenced their writing.

We'll encounter the dark story of mountain bride Frankie Silver, who murdered her drunken husband—a tale taken up by a range of writers over the decades, including Manly Wade Wellman, Sharyn McCrumb, and Perry Deane Young.

We'll stand beside the sagging cabin where Hemingway stayed during a hunting trip in Tryon, not far from the neighborhood where playwright and actor William Gillette cooked up the quirky characterization and iconic props for his stage adaptation of Sir Arthur Conan Doyle's *Sherlock Holmes*.

We'll learn some tips on how to cook spicy possum from Horace Kephart, the librarian-turned-writer/naturalist who came from St. Louis in 1905 to the Great Smokies. Kephart lobbied hard over his lifetime to have his beloved mountains protected as a national park, a measure he did not live long enough to witness.

Throughout, we turn again and again to the work of the late Wilma Dykeman, whose family dates back to the eighteenth century in these mountains. Perhaps more than any other book from the region, her landmark volume *The French Broad* (1955) presents the richness of tale and tradition here. Meanwhile, Dykeman's 1966 novel, *The Tall Woman*, today in its fortieth printing, foreshadows Charles Frazier's *Cold Mountain* as a story of post–Civil War women and their hardscrabble strength and will to survive.

This literary guidebook (and its two companion volumes about the Piedmont and Coastal Plain) are finally books about books, a way to read your way across North Carolina. Each half- or whole-day tour will steer you to the spots that inspired both our state's native-born writers and the many literary visitors who also found their muse here.

As such, this narrative goes beyond the literature itself. It requires a deeper imagining—to see what these authors have seen, to breathe the air in the places where they have lived and worked and written, to consider their aspirations, fears, and struggles.

Writers have always been celebrities of a sort, characters in their own right who often spark a reader's curiosity about how they worked and where—with what kind of pencil or typewriter or computer—and about how they managed to harness their considerable gifts. This guide offers some of that back story.

The featured excerpts from these authors are intended to enhance your appreciation of what you are seeing, or in some cases, what you are *not* seeing because of the march of "progress." Many of the sites across the state included in the three volumes are not as they were when a particular writer lived or worked there.

Despite these changes, however, everywhere you turn in this state there are amazing stories. Of course that is true anywhere, if you pay attention. But in North Carolina there is something particularly rich in the *sound* of stories as they are told by Tar Heels—the cadence and the color, the shoulder-to-shoulder intimacy of tragedy and humor—all offered in accents and a syntax as variable as the geography of this 600-mile-wide landscape. North Carolina is bursting with extraordinary settings and authentic characters just waiting to tell their stories if you bother to stop and ask a few questions while you're passing through town.

North Carolina is still predominantly a state of small towns, mostly rural, with people profoundly connected to the land and rooted in a long genealogy of stubborn, self-reliant, and resilient families—Native American, African American, and European American. More recently, the state has added the voices of peoples with Hispanic and Asian backgrounds, newcomers who seem to seek the same self-sufficiency and independence as their neighbors in this place where there is still plenty of room to stretch and live your way into new stories to be told and retold.

North Carolina's many Indian tribes (more Native Americans live here than in any state east of the Mississippi) are the oldest practitioners of narrative. Then, with the arrival of white people came the abiding mystery of the Lost Colony—North Carolina's first European settlement, which disappeared from the coast after John White's departure from Roanoke Island in August 1587, thereby setting another long-told tale in motion. This story eventually led, in the twentieth century, to the invention of an art form—the outdoor drama, a theatrical genre offered here first and now all across the nation as a tourist attraction and lively history lesson.

North Carolina must also admit to a long lack of literacy—a deficit that has paradoxically strengthened our oral traditions and ensured the conveyance of local history and wisdom across generations. Sadly, literacy is still low in this state so rich in stories and with more than its share of successful writers.

In the hope of fostering literacy and expanding our fascination with North Carolina writers, we invite you and your children to take some time with the excerpts offered here. They are intended to be read aloud as you tour. Many sites beg for a long picnic, a reading or two, and a contemplative hour to witness the comings and goings in a landscape, homesite, or crossroads. You may also want to try your hand at writing about the places you visit.

Some authors included along these trails are very well known; others may have works that have fallen out of print; and some may be only locally or little known. The excerpted works have been selected for their connection to a specific place, for their historical significance in the state's literature, or for the bit of local color or culture they evoke.

A great many distinguished writers who have significant bodies of work that reach far beyond the confines of North Carolina are included here. However, to give a full accounting of these writers' contributions is well beyond the bounds of this project. The reader is encouraged to delve deeper when an excerpt inspires curiosity. Ultimately, any effort to be all inclusive of the state's writers is impossible; new works are coming out every day. However, the North Carolina Arts Council, the sponsor of this project, will continue to update the trails by means of its website, listing new and notable books.

We hope the literary hors d'oeuvres offered here will entice you to the full feast—the novels, poetry collections, memoirs, and creative narrative histories that have a North Carolina connection. We have taken care to include works from well-established publishers that should be readily available in each trail's region (if not statewide). Out-of-print works can be found at libraries, and some may be available at used bookstores and through online vendors that specialize in finding these volumes.

We have also included information on long-running creative writing workshops, university programs, seasonal festivals related to literature, and regular readings hosted by writers' groups, public libraries, and schools. Of course, we don't expect you to follow every trail completely and thoroughly—each covers a vast amount of real estate—but we invite you to choose among them according to your interests and proximity.

Some tours may involve hiking or biking as you are so inclined and also offer opportunities for bird watching, wildflower identification, whitewater rafting, fishing, photography, camping, and other forms of sightseeing.

Let North Carolina literature be your starting place. Carry a journal. Write your own poem. Invite the stories of those you meet along the way. We can't begin to tell it all here.

Georgann Eubanks

trail one

The Southern Mountains : Place

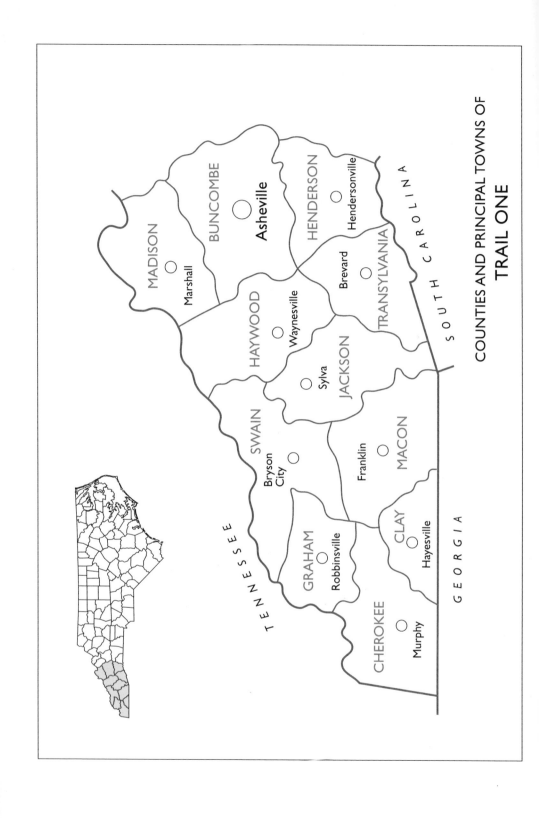

COUNTIES AND PRINCIPAL TOWNS OF
TRAIL ONE

Let these peaks have happened.

The hawk-haunted knobs and hollers,
The blind coves, blind as meditation, the white
Rock-face, the laurel hells, the terraced pasture ridge
With its broom sedge combed back by wind:
Let these have taken place, let them be place.

And where Rich Fork drops uprushing against
Its tabled stone, let the gray trout
Idle below, its dim plectum a shadow
That marks the stone's clear shadow.

In the slow glade where sunlight comes through
In circlets and moves from leaf to fallen leaf
Like a tribe of shining bees, let
The milk-flecked fawn lie unseen, unfearing.

Let me lie there too and share the sleep
Of the cool ground's mildest children.

—From *Source*, by Fred Chappell
  (Baton Rouge: Louisiana State University Press, 1985), 5.

Trail 1 is full of superlatives—the oldest mountains (the Appalachians), the highest town (Highlands), the oldest inn (Woodfield), one of the oldest rivers (the French Broad), and the largest house (Biltmore). You can see a replica of the size thirteen shoes of Thomas Wolfe, retrace the excesses of F. Scott Fitzgerald and Horace Kephart, imagine the giants of Cherokee lore—Judaculla, Tau-keet-ta —and stand humbly under the massive trees in Joyce Kilmer Forest.

The scale and proportion of North Carolina's westernmost mountains and the demands of surviving among them have prompted grand actions, tall tales, and large living. Traveling by car over these roads that were once washboard trails, it is impossible not to be impressed by the small footprint of our human presence beside the swiftness of so many rivers, the enormous walls of rock, the thickets of laurel, the milky morning fog. That this land has such a rich storytelling tradition speaks to the extremes of living here—the hardships and the glories, too. Becoming familiar with the poetry and prose of the region enriches the traveling experience tenfold.

Black Mountain : Montreat : Swannanoa

The area in this tour inspired the edgy and irreverent literary avant garde of the 1940s and early 1950s at Black Mountain College while also serving as home to the world's most famous evangelist, Billy Graham, and his wife, poet Ruth Bell Graham, who in turn served as a mentor to contemporary mystery writer Patricia Cornwell. Explore the source of this incredible literary variety among the charming villages of Black Mountain, Montreat, and Swannanoa.

Writers with a connection to this area: Patricia Cornwell,
Robert Creeley, Fielding Dawson, Ed Dorn, Robert Duncan,
Ruth Bell Graham, Francine du Plessix Gray, Jill Jones,
Alfred Kazin, Charles Olson, Joel Oppenheimer, Mary Caroline
Richards, Elizabeth Spencer, Peter Turchi, Ellen Bryant Voigt,
Jonathan Williams

■ BLACK MOUNTAIN COLLEGE

We begin our literary tour of North Carolina in this village where a major confluence of visual art, music, dance, and literature occurred in the twentieth century. Say the words "Black Mountain" to writers, painters, dancers, musicians, and educators today, and most know what an extraordinary constellation of forces began to gather here in the 1930s.

In 1933, John Andrews Rice, a disgruntled classics professor from Florida's Rollins College, chose Black Mountain as the place to launch a progressive experiment in liberal arts education. Rice believed that college students would learn best in a communal environment where they lived alongside faculty, shared meals with them, and readily crossed the boundaries of traditional academic disciplines in their collaborative quest for new ideas. Abstract German painter Josef Albers and his wife Anni, a weaver, were among the first faculty members hired to teach at Black Mountain College. Albert Einstein also

tour 1

TOUR 1: BLACK MOUNTAIN - MONTREAT - SWANNANOA

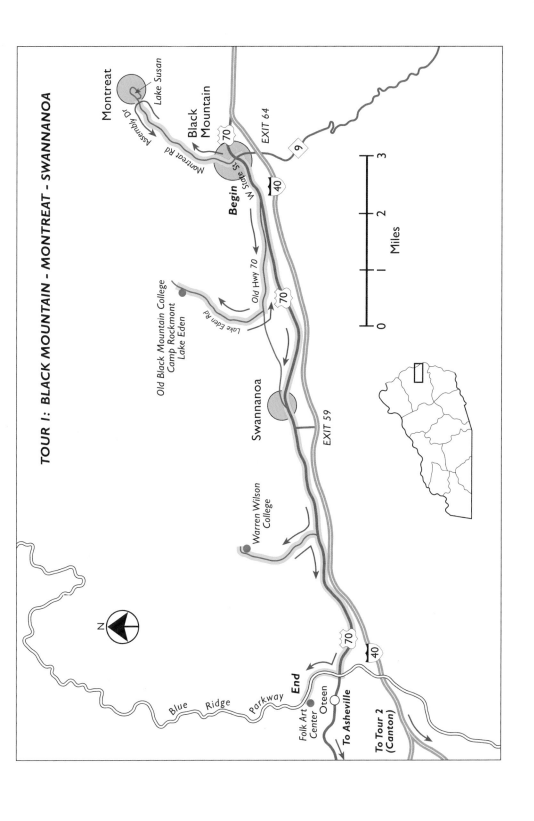

The Studies Building is one of the few remaining campus structures from Black Mountain College, located on the grounds of Camp Rockmont, home of the Lake Eden Arts Festival.

spent time here and served on the school's board, and inventor Buckminster Fuller, who taught engineering to the Black Mountain students, built his first geodesic dome on the campus. Though John Andrews Rice left in 1938, Black Mountain College lasted until 1956 and attracted some 300 faculty members over the period, some of whom had first been students here.

Beginning in 1944, during the inviting summer months, Black Mountain hosted special institutes in the arts. These events drew many of the most innovative composers, painters, dancers, and poets of the era. Painters Jacob Lawrence, Willem de Kooning, and Robert Motherwell taught a student body that included such notable future artists as Robert Rauschenberg. Merce Cunningham, working alongside composer John Cage, launched his dance troupe here. With these extraordinary collaborations across disciplines, some would suggest that Black Mountain was the birthplace of what we now call "performance art."

Black Mountain College also had a significant impact on literature, spawning the careers of dozens of nationally acclaimed writers. Charles Olson, called the "father" of the Black Mountain School of poets, helped to shift the institution's focus on visual art to literature during its last years in the 1950s. Among his students were novelist Francine du Plessix Gray; poets Robert Creeley, Fielding Dawson, Ed Dorn, and Robert Duncan; longtime *Village Voice* columnist Joel Oppenheimer; and publisher and poet Jonathan Williams. Robert Creeley eventually taught at Black Mountain himself and launched the *Black Mountain Review*, a little magazine that published work by Jorge Luis Borges, Allen Ginsberg, C. G. Jung, Jack Kerouac, and William Carlos Williams. Faculty member Mary Caroline Richards and her students started the Black Mountain Press, which issued Richards's first poetry collection and a number of other literary publications. Literary critic Alfred Kazin taught here, and John Dewey, Thornton Wilder, and Henry Miller visited or gave lectures at the school.

Among the many stellar writers and artists influenced by the college, Fielding Dawson was one of the most prolific in writing about his campus experiences. He went to Black Mountain College in 1949 to study painting alongside fellow students Robert Rauschenberg and Kenneth Noland, but he ended up being profoundly influenced by Charles Olson's poetry classes. Dawson stayed until 1953, when he was drafted into military service. In his lifetime, he published more than twenty books and many other smaller volumes. The last was a collection of stories, *The Land of Milk and Honey* (2001).

In the 1980s, Dawson taught writing to prisoners at Sing Sing and Attica and was appointed by American PEN president Larry McMurtry to chair the organization's Prison Writing Program. In the 1990s Dawson hosted a radio show on New York's WBAI in which he presented writing by inmates on the air. His own writing reflects the free-flowing, playful style he developed at Black Mountain:

Black Mountain was freedom.

And within that freedom I and others developed a discipline in drawing and writing that involved listening and seeing with such continuous intensity, it became my way of life. As much an influence on me today and every day, as it ever was. Black Mountain was not something you grew out of. Like freedom, you grew into it.

The pure open space we lived every day, was a lot like Paradise: not involved in the accepted world, the understood geopolitical sense of reality. Black Mountain was the people who were there, which explains its sudden changes. From 1950, or for sure '51, it was [Charles] Olson's until it closed. Very different than Albers'. . . .

   We had to go to classes or face the wrath of the teacher: there wasn't any kidding around. . . . Classes were tough, we couldn't miss them—homework, heavy as it was, then doubled . . . it may have been free of academic rules and regulations, but that made it worse, the whole burden on us, and the faculty maybe getting plastered with us the night before no matter, we had to produce.—From *The Black Mountain Book*, rev. ed., by Fielding Dawson (Rocky Mount: North Carolina Wesleyan College Press, 1991), 7, 205.

The Black Mountain legacy continues through the work of its many students and their students working today. Jonathan Williams's Jargon Press, headquartered in Winston-Salem, is the primary heir to the Black Mountain tradition in North Carolina. Just down the road from Black Mountain in Swannanoa, Warren Wilson College—where many students earn their way, deferring tuition by helping to grow, prepare, and serve food in the dining hall and perform other tasks to keep the college running smoothly—partly reflects the early influence of Black Mountain College. Other progressive colleges around the country—including Bard, Goddard, and Antioch—were likewise influenced by the Black Mountain model.

   It is still possible to visit the old campus and imagine what it might have been like to study there more than fifty years ago. Initially the college leased space from the Blue Ridge Assembly—today a YMCA camp south of I-40 that is used year-round by religious and other nonprofit groups. The assembly's Lee Hall, now on the National Register of Historic Places, was almost large enough to accommodate the entire college in its early years.

   Anticipating the expiration of its lease, the college bought a summer camp in 1937 called Lake Eden, approximately five miles northwest of town. Painter Josef Albers contacted his German colleague architect Walter Gropius, who, like Albers, had fled Nazi Germany and come to the United States in the early 1930s. Gropius had coined the term "Bauhaus" to describe the innovative architectural style he had established in Berlin. Albers enthusiastically commissioned plans for a new Black Mountain campus from Gropius and his associates at Harvard. As it turned out, the design was far too ambitious for the college's meager resources.

   The college then turned to Lawrence Kocher, a former managing editor of the *Architectural Record*. He joined the faculty at Black Mountain in 1940, just before the college moved to Lake Eden. Kocher designed the Studies Building for the new site. Students and faculty built the facility, which opened in 1944. Other original buildings, including the dining hall, the Round House (where musicians practiced), two lodges, and the Quiet House (built to commemorate two accidental deaths), are still in use by today's Camp Rockmont, though the dining hall and Quiet House have been modified.

DIRECTIONS

Whether you are coming from the east or west on I-40, take exit 64 and follow NC 9 less than 0.5 miles north across the railroad tracks to the intersection with State Street (US 70). Straight ahead is the road to Montreat. If you turn right, you'll find the Black Mountain Visitor's Center one block down on the left at the traffic light at West Street. If you go left, you'll be in the middle of Black Mountain, with its quaint shops and cafés.

To Lake Eden: Follow State Street (US 70) west out of Black Mountain toward Swannanoa. In less than a mile, look for a fork to the right marked "Old Highway 70" just before Duke's Hot Dogs. Take this fork. On Old 70 West, you'll pass the Veterans Cemetery, the Black Mountain Center, and the Grove Stone Quarry, all on your right. Look for signs to Owen High School and the Presbyterian Children's Home and turn right on Lake Eden Road. Continue past the high school and residential areas. Here the road is flanked by graceful old white pines, a handsome split-rail fence on your left, and large boulders on the right. Pass the first entrance to Camp Rockmont, and the old Black Mountain College Studies Building will soon appear on your left on the far side of the lake. The second entrance to the camp, on your left, leads into the old Black Mountain grounds. No tours are available.

■ THE TOWN OF BLACK MOUNTAIN

Easily explored on foot, Black Mountain's downtown area is also worth a few hours of your time if you enjoy crafts, antiques, art, and jewelry. Black Mountain is home to a lively music scene that draws heavily on old-time music and the area's Celtic roots. Jerry Read Smith, North Carolina's distinguished hammered dulcimer player and maker of these elegant instruments, has a shop on West State Street.

The literary tourist will definitely want to duck into Black Mountain Books at 103 Cherry Street. A favorite of local novelist Jill Jones, Black Mountain Books is one of those shops where you can browse for ages without noticing the passage of time. With its stock of nearly 18,000 titles, this store specializes in several categories of books—southern literature, southern Americana, church history, literature by women, and modern first editions. It also has a remarkably comprehensive collection of volumes documenting the history of Black Mountain College, including past volumes of the *Red Clay Reader* (founded by editor Charlene Swansea in 1964) and the now-scarce Black Mountain tribute issue of the *North Carolina Literary Review* (1995) published by East Carolina University.

You'll find several shelves of books about North Carolina and novels by writers from the early to middle twentieth century; most are out-of-print collectors' items. A glass case near the front of the store protects a precious number of signed first editions that the store also lists on eBay. At the time of our visit, several copies of Patricia Cornwell's first book, a biography of poet Ruth Bell Graham, signed by both the author and her subject, were selling for more than $200, along with first editions of Thomas Wolfe's *Look Homeward, Angel* and Seaboard, North Carolina, novelist Bernice Kelly Harris's *Janey Jeems*. The store also sells locally handcrafted oak bookcases.

Black Mountain Books proudly promotes the work of local writer Jill Jones. Her novel, *Emily's Secret* (1995), is a fantasy based on the premise that novelist Emily Brontë had a secret lover on which she later based her character Heathcliff in *Wuthering Heights*. In *Bloodline* (2000), Jones invents a contemporary reincarnation of Jack the Ripper, the legendary London killer who was also the topic of *Portrait of a Killer: Jack the Ripper—Case Closed* (2002), written by former Montreat resident Patricia Cornwell.

For more information on Black Mountain, see <http://www.visitblack mountain.com>.

■ MONTREAT

Montreat is distinguished as the home chosen by the prolific writers Ruth Graham and her evangelist husband, Billy. It was also the childhood home of their friend Patricia Cornwell.

The name Montreat is actually a contraction of "Mountain Retreat Association," a partnership that was formed in 1898 to purchase a failed sheep farm of 4,500 acres up the road from Black Mountain, at the base of Graybeard Mountain. The initial investors—a resident of Asheville and a Congregational minister from Connecticut—convinced fifteen others to help them buy the land that is now Montreat. They set about to create "first of all and chiefly a place for health and rest for Christian people and secondly for religious and educational purposes."

Plagued throughout its history by periods of near financial collapse, Montreat was rescued for the first time when the Presbyterian Church (usa) agreed in 1906 to take over the secluded valley, with its collection of thirty-some rustic cabins and cottages, a hotel, a post office, and a church/school building.

Soon, more lots were offered with a ninety-nine-year lease to an enthusiastic group of mostly Presbyterian newcomers. Meanwhile, the day-to-day administration of Montreat was turned over to a financially savvy Presbyterian minister from Gastonia, Robert C. Anderson.

Anderson launched a normal school for the training of teachers that eventually became Montreat College in 1916. He raised funds for the building of the Assembly Inn—a 200-room edifice that was considered a luxury hotel by its first guests in the inauspicious year of 1929. (Anderson also later secured much-needed funding to renovate the inn by leasing it to the U.S. government for the internment of Japanese and German families during World War II.) For the complete story, see Elizabeth Maxwell's *A Flowing Stream: An Informal History of Montreat* (1997).

Over the years, Montreat has served as a seasonal retreat, a conference facility, and a continuing education resource for Christian groups. It has hosted summer camps for girls and boys for more than a century, creating the kind of indelible memories described here by Chapel Hill fiction writer Elizabeth Spencer in her autobiographical essay, "Heading for the Hills":

Often, at night, the camp director, a really pretty widow, would come up and talk to us about her religious beliefs, speaking with utter sincerity and simplicity. She always prayed for us aloud before we loaded up in the truck bed and went caroling away on one of our Saturday trips to the Biltmore Estate or some other place too distant for hiking to. She would read a Psalm about the Lord preserving our going out and our coming in for now and evermore. It is easy to see that she lived with the worry that someone might fall off a mountain or get snake bit. A tragic accident was about all that was needed to upset her precarious financial balance. She could often be observed in her rooms with her bright head of hair bent down over account books. At any rate, the Lord heeded her: we all lived.

In the middle of this sojourn, so kindly conceived of as the place I was to improve my health, meet new people, gain weight, have fun, a letter arrived announcing that my mother, brother, and two aunts were on the way. A terrible pretender, I had written glowing letters home about how wonderful everything was, but another, truer message had somehow got through between the lines of the awkwardly written missive. I was

Lake Susan, where the young Elizabeth Spencer "cooled off"
during summer camp at Montreat.

thought to be homesick. The idea! I replied. Nevertheless, when, a week later, the family car pulled up the twisting road from the lake, I felt the key strike the prison door. No more ice water or wearisome clambering over slimy moss. No more shouting songs with silly words. No more scheduled play. Liberation was at hand.

It may be that my mother and aunts had invented the whole plan of my rescue from homesickness in order to get to North Carolina. At any rate, I joined the party, and the mountains took on another aspect entirely, as the view was now something not demanding to be hiked through. My mother and aunts would never have dreamed of climbing anything beyond the steps with balustrades, and my brother never mentioned it either. We were tourists in a beautiful land, which I could see for the first time without thinking how not to cry. Little Switzerland was a day trip, and Chimney Rock another; the camera was often out. The mountain air they delighted in became wonderfully breathable to me as well, "pure ozone," as they called it, and we followed twisting roads both up and down, dizzy with daring and danger, hoping the car would make it and the radiator would not explode.

These then, that summer, were the Smokies, my first mountains. I came back to say good-bye to my friends at camp and be present at the closing night banquet where many tears flowed freely from those parting with such dearly loved friends. I wonder how much of this outpouring was not simply the adolescent need to have as many emotions as possible. I loved everybody there the minute I didn't have to see them any longer. . . .

It was the mountains that lingered with me. Their lofty outline against evening skies, the rosy corona the sunset left as it faded, seemed when I withdrew from it irreplaceable. Surprising myself, I longed to return, to have it back once more. For both air and atmosphere are singularly differ-ent up there in that region around Asheville. And Asheville itself grew im-portantly larger for me as I read more and found one afternoon, absorbed beneath the trees in the front yard in Mississippi, how a young man named Thomas Wolfe had grown up there, lived along its streets, known its people and climbed into the sunlit mountain stillness hand in hand with his first love. —From *Close to Home: Revelations and Reminiscences by North Carolina Authors*, ed. Lee Harrison Child (Winston-Salem: John F. Blair, 1996), 48–50.

Montreat has also been home to many retired clergy and church mission-aries and their children (known as "PKs," or preacher's kids, and "mish kids"). Notably, Montreat was the retirement destination in the early 1940s for Nelson and Virginia Bell, the late parents of poet Ruth Bell Graham. Ruth and Billy Graham were married at Montreat Presbyterian Church in 1943, just two years after Ruth's parents left their medical missionary work in China, where Ruth was born and raised. Wanting to stay close to her parents, Ruth moved with her new husband into a modest house in Montreat, and they began their family.

As Billy Graham's fame as a preacher grew, Montreat became a tourist destination, with many travelers hoping to get a peek at the Grahams. In self defense, the mischievous Graham children actually set up road blocks on the single, narrow road leading into Montreat and extracted tolls from travelers, just as, in those days, the Montreat gate required a fee from people coming into the community — a practice long since suspended.

Ruth Graham's longing for privacy and retreat from this onslaught of tourists was detailed in *A Time for Remembering: The Story of Ruth Bell Graham* (1983), the first book published by Patricia Daniels Cornwell. Cornwell is better known, however, as the first woman in the United States to receive the Gold Dagger, England's highest crime-writing award.

In 1997, Cornwell updated the biography that she wrote when she was twenty-four, now entitled *Ruth, A Portrait: The Story of Ruth Bell Graham*. As she writes in the preface:

> I met Ruth through her parents, Nelson and Virginia Bell, whom I grew to love shortly after my mother moved my two brothers and me from Miami to Montreat in 1963, when I was seven. Homesick for my own grandmother, I visited Mrs. Bell several times each month, entering without knocking through the screened-in back porch that led into the warm, fragrant kitchen. Beneath a layer of wax paper on top of her refrigerator there were always cups of homemade custard, generously sprinkled with nutmeg and deliciously moist. — From *Ruth, A Portrait: The Story of Ruth Bell Graham*, by Patricia Daniels Cornwell (New York: Doubleday, 1997), 7.

Patsy Daniels, as she was called then, went to school with the Grahams' youngest son, Ned. At one point in her troubled life, Patsy's mother drove the children up to the Grahams' secluded homestead and tried to convince Ruth to take in the Daniels children and raise them for her. (Patsy's mother had been abandoned by her husband before leaving Miami and was struggling as a single parent.) Instead, Ruth befriended Patsy and encouraged her to develop her gifts as a writer.

Cornwell visited Ruth Graham many times during her years at Davidson College and after her rise to international prominence as a crime writer. Once, the story goes, Cornwell landed a private helicopter on the tennis courts at Montreat and took Graham up for a dizzying ride over her beloved mountain cove.

In her biography of Ruth Graham, Cornwell describes the genesis of the Grahams' house:

> In early 1954, the Grahams had been offered a good deal on a 150-acre cove, located two miles from their house [in Montreat] between two ridges,

or hogbacks, on one of the Seven Sisters. The land was occupied by two mountain families who grew corn on one slope and culled timber on another. The people decided to sell out and the cove was offered to the Grahams for a mere forty-three hundred dollars....

Billy surveyed the property with skepticism, but Ruth felt her blood race at the potential.

"I leave it up to you to decide," he said just before he left for the West Coast.

She borrowed the money from the bank and bought the cove while he was gone. When he returned he was incredulous.

"You *what?*" he asked.

After he recovered from his initial shock, they began making plans, deciding they would build behind the tall bank of white pines.... Billy wanted to cut the evergreens to afford them a view of the valley. Ruth believed that no tree should be cut unless it was absolutely necessary. They compromised by deciding to build farther up the ridge....

All but the frame of the new house was built of old wood, most from log cabins Ruth discovered in the mountains. Dressed in blue jeans and an Army jacket, she would drive her Jeep through western North Carolina, stopping at gas stations to leave her telephone number with attendants in the event they heard of cabins for sale. Six months after her first inquiry, she began receiving calls. She bought a two-story cabin for four hundred dollars. A dog-trot, or two cabins connected by a breezeway, she picked up for a hundred and twenty. Most cabins sold for about fifty dollars, and when she didn't buy the entire building, she would pay several dollars per wormy chestnut, oak or yellow poplar log....

Ruth furnished her home with castoffs, hunting in such unlikely places as the town dump, where the workmen found a heavy slab of wood that had once been Lake Susan's diving board. It soon became the fireplace mantle in the Grahams' living room, carved with "Eine Feste Burg Ist Unser Gott" (or "A Mighty Fortress Is Our God").—From *Ruth, A Portrait*, by Patricia Cornwell, 133–34, 136–37, 138.

When the Grahams finally moved up the mountain in 1956, they named their homestead Little Piney Cove. Today the home still sits boldly on the ridge where Ruth Bell Graham wrote volumes of verse and her memoirs. Her writing reflects her spiritual life and her engagement as the mother of five and the caretaker for her own parents in their last years. Her 1994 children's book, *One*

Wintry Night (also coincidentally the title of a popular holiday recording by Black Mountain musician Jerry Read Smith), is one of the best-selling Christian gift books of all time.

DIRECTIONS

To reach Montreat, begin at the intersection of State Street (US 70) and NC 9/Broadway in Black Mountain. Here NC 9 becomes Montreat Road as it heads due north toward the mountains and Montreat. In a few miles you'll come to the stone entrance to Montreat. Here Montreat Road changes to Assembly Drive. This road carries you past the following sites:

Billy Graham Evangelistic Association Montreat Headquarters is on the corner of Louisiana and Assembly Drive but is not generally open to the public. It houses an office full of memorabilia from Billy Graham's years of international ministry. The small home where Ruth and Billy Graham first lived in Montreat is nearby, as is the original home of Ruth Graham's parents, Nelson and Virginia Bell.

Farther down the road on the right is Lake Susan, the chilly pond that has given goose bumps to thousands of youngsters, including writer Elizabeth Spencer, throughout the long history of Montreat's summer camps.

The Assembly Inn is directly across the road from Lake Susan. It is the larger of the two hotels in the Montreat facility and worth seeing.

Chapel of the Prodigal was designed to present Ben Long's biblically based fresco of the prodigal son (Luke 15) in the best light. Long, a Statesville, North Carolina, native, is one of only a few fresco masters working on the planet today. (His cousin, Robert Long, is a nationally recognized poet and was the first executive director of the North Carolina Writers' Network.) Ben Long's work can be seen in several other parts of the state, including Morganton (Tour 15), Glendale Springs and West Jefferson (Tour 18), and Crossnore (Tour 17), and in Charlotte and Statesville. Long, who also studied creative writing with novelist Reynolds Price, taught at Montreat College as the Hamilton Guest Artist in Residence while working on the fresco. Upstairs on the chapel balcony is the Ruth Bell Graham Prayer Room.

You may also want to have a peek in Montreat Presbyterian Church, the historic church where Ruth and Billy Graham were married, and then stop by Moore Center, where you will find the Montreat bookstore, featuring literature pertaining to the area and Montreat's history.

Finally, there are several popular hiking trails that run from Montreat up to remarkable vistas from Graybeard Mountain and Lookout Mountain. Ask for details at the Assembly Inn or the bookstore in Moore Center.

Warren Wilson College in Swannanoa has a low-residency graduate program in creative writing.

■ SWANNANOA

Warren Wilson College, the largest institution in Swannanoa, has a distinctive undergraduate curriculum and one graduate level program—in creative writing. Designed and initiated by Ellen Bryant Voigt at Goddard College in 1976, the Master of Fine Arts (MFA) in creative writing at Warren Wilson was the first low-residency graduate program in writing in the country. "Low residency" means that adult professionals can earn their degrees while keeping their day jobs. Every six months creative writing students gather on the Warren Wilson campus to study with distinguished authors who regularly teach at other colleges and universities across the county. For ten days, MFA candidates work intensively in groups, hear faculty lectures that are open to the general public, give readings of their work, and plan their next six months' work with their primary faculty adviser, work that will be discussed by correspondence.

It was no coincidence that this innovative format for graduate study in creative writing came to Warren Wilson. Pioneering pedagogy has always been a part of the school's culture. In 1893, even before the Presbyterians assumed ownership over at Montreat, the Women's Board of Home Missions of the Presbyterian Church purchased the land where the college is now located. The churchwomen wanted to provide educational opportunities to young people who were growing up in isolated mountain communities where public services were practically nonexistent. The Asheville Farm School, as it was initially called, graduated its first class in 1924. The school emphasized vocational training with the idea of helping its students learn trades and skills that would serve them for a lifetime in their rural environment.

Always open to innovation, the school moved toward an admissions policy that was unusual for the times. At the height of American xenophobia in 1941, the school admitted its first Japanese American student. Its first African American student came to campus in 1952, two years before the *Brown v. Board of Education* decision.

In 1957, the school discontinued its high school program, adopted a junior college curriculum, and eventually became a four-year liberal arts college in 1966, named for Warren Wilson, a Presbyterian clergyman who wrote one of the first studies on the sociology of rural life in America.

Most undergraduates here subsidize their tuition by taking various jobs on the 1,100-acre campus that includes a working farm, a managed forest, and extensive organic gardens. Warren Wilson is also home to the North Carolina Outward Bound School.

DIRECTIONS

To reach Swannanoa from Black Mountain, proceed on either I-40 or US 70 West. From I-40, take exit 59 and turn right onto Patton Cove Road. In 0.2 miles, turn left onto US 70. In 2.1 miles turn right at the sign directing you toward the Warren Wilson campus. If you are coming in on US 70, simply watch for the sign directing you to Warren Wilson. The campus is 1.2 miles ahead on your right.

■ LITERARY LANDSCAPE

Black Mountain Center for the Arts
225 West State Street
Black Mountain, NC 28711
828-669-0930
admin@blackmountainarts.org
<http://www.blackmountainarts.org/>

This nonprofit organization hosts exhibits, workshops, and classes in music, visual, and literary arts. Local fiction writers, poets, and singer/songwriters are faculty for the writing workshops and also serve as judges for the center's annual short-story competition. Occasionally the center will host a Reader's Theater, and it also sponsors "Stories & Songs of the Swannanoa Valley," a local folk play based on oral histories collected from the community that has been presented each summer for several years.

Swannanoa Valley Museum

223 West State Street
Black Mountain, NC 28711
828-669-9566
swannavalleym@bellsouth.net
<http://www.swannanoavalleymuseum.org/>

Housed in the town's old firehouse, this regional museum offers an eclectic collection of artifacts that document the history of the region from the Stone Age through the rise of Native Americans to white settlement and the coming of the railroad to western North Carolina. Exhibits also illuminate more recent history, including the story of Black Mountain College, the interesting proliferation of religious conference centers in the area, and the community's most famous resident, the Reverend Billy Graham.

Lake Eden Arts Festival (LEAF)

377 Lake Eden Road
Black Mountain, NC 28711
828-686-8742
info@theLEAF.com
<http://www.theleaf.com/>

If you are visiting in May or October, consider joining the swarming mass of humanity that comes to camp, eat, and make music and merriment during the Lake Eden Arts Festival (LEAF), held on Camp Rockmont's 600 acres. The festival presents continuous performances on four stages over three days. More intimate workshops with musicians, storytellers, healers, visual artists, and poets are offered during the day. Vendors bring folk art, crafts, and all kinds of food for purchase on the grounds. LEAF emphasizes world folk music, with performers from African, Latin, Celtic, blues, Zydeco, bluegrass, French, Appalachian, and Russian traditions. Held during each festival, the Poetry Slam is a rigorous, high-energy competition among performance poets of all skill levels and experience, offering $1,000 in prizes to finalists.

Festival participants may camp, reserve a cabin, or stay off site. Swimming and canoeing are permitted in the camp's two lakes, and festival-goers may otherwise make use of the camp's climbing walls, tennis courts, hiking trails, and the daredevil zip line that extends over the lake. Families with children (but not pets) are welcome. Full-festival and one-day passes are available. Attendance is limited to 5,000.

MFA Program for Writers at Warren Wilson College
P.O. Box 9000
Asheville, NC 28815-9000
828-771-3715
mfa@warren-wilson.edu
<http://www.warren-wilson.edu/~mfa/>

Check for dates of morning lectures by faculty and evening readings that are open to the public when students and faculty are in residence at <http://www.warren-wilson.edu/~mfa/public_schedule.rtf>.

To find out more about the writers who serve as faculty in the Warren Wilson program, look for *The Story Behind the Story: 26 Stories by Contemporary Writers and How They Work*, edited by Peter Turchi (the director of the program) and Andrea Barrett (New York: W. W. Norton, 2004). This collection features short stories by Warren Wilson faculty members plus "the story behind the story"—an essay by each writer describing the inspiration and technical challenges behind the stories they've contributed.

Swannanoa Gathering
c/o Warren Wilson College
P.O. Box 9000
Asheville, NC 28815-9000
828-298-3434
gathering@warren-wilson.edu
<http://www.swangathering.org/>

Held every summer over a seven-week period, the Swannanoa Gathering is a series of public concerts and residential workshops in various folk arts, including songwriting, held on the campus of Warren Wilson College. Weekly themes have included Cherokee heritage, dulcimer playing, swing music and dance, Celtic music, old-time music and dance, guitar playing, and contemporary folk music. For current schedules, registration information, and other details, visit the website.

Swannanoa Public Library
101 West Charleston Street
Swannanoa, NC 28778
828-686-5516
<http://www.buncombecounty.org/governing/
depts/Library/locations_Swannanoa.htm>

The Folk Art Center's shop and gallery are managed by the Southern Highland Craft Guild.

Swannanoa Public Library has an active friends group that often sponsors musical events during the summer. The library also features a mural with dozens of storybook characters. To visit, turn right on US 70 from Patton Cove Road, proceed to the next traffic light, turn left, go across the bridge to a yield sign, and turn right (onto Old Highway 70). In less than 0.5 miles, turn left onto Grovemont Avenue. In another 0.3 miles, you'll come to Grovemont Square, a grass field with a rock wall. Go around the square to the right. The red brick library is adjacent to the playground.

Folk Art Center
Southern Highland Craft Guild
382 Blue Ridge Parkway
Asheville, NC 28805
828-298-7928
info@craftguild.org
<http://www.southernhighlandguild.org>

The Folk Art Center, built in 1980, is headquarters for the Southern Highland Craft Guild, an organization begun in 1930 that today represents more than 800 craftspeople living and working in the mountains of North Carolina, South Carolina, Alabama, Georgia, Kentucky, Maryland, Tennessee, Virginia, and West Virginia. The guild promotes indigenous crafts of the region and encourages the highest standards of design and workmanship among its members. The Folk Art Center showcases the best of these crafts through its store and through a year-round schedule of exhibits, demonstrations, celebrations, and workshops.

The center also hosts two annual events that incorporate storytelling. In September the Heritage Weekend and in November the Tellabration both provide opportunities for visitors to experience some of the most talented taletellers in the mountains. Check the website for specific dates and times.

From Swannanoa, take US 70 West, and you'll come to a well-marked access point for the Blue Ridge Parkway at Oteen. Take the Parkway north. In less than 0.5 miles, you'll reach the center at milepost 382.

Canton : Cold Mountain : Lake Logan : Balsam

Meet the living relatives of Charles Frazier's protagonist Inman in the novel *Cold Mountain*. Understand the legacy of western North Carolina's lumbering and paper manufacturing industries. Fish for trout in the same streams that former North Carolina poet laureate Fred Chappell frequented as a boy, and smell the balsam at the highest point on the Blue Ridge Parkway in the rugged landscape that inspired so many Cherokee myths.

Writers with a connection to this area: Fred Chappell, Donald Davis, Charles Frazier, Kaye Gibbons

■ CANTON

As you head into Haywood County on I-40 from east or west, the smell reaches you first; then you can see the white plumes rising from Canton's towering paper mill. At night the mill, running 24/7, is radiant with a pinkish-orange light, the continuous plumes of steam glowing. To some, this great belching artifice encircled by green mountains seems a menace. But when the former proprietor of a Cincinnati greeting card store, Peter Thomson, came to Canton in 1906 and launched the Champion Paper and Fiber Company here, the new plant promised steady work and the prospect of prosperity for many. Now the plant is owned by its workers, one of the few employee-run industrial operations in North Carolina.

Through four semiautobiographical novels, Canton native and former North Carolina poet laureate Fred Chappell has painted a vivid picture of this hardscrabble papermaking town, here called Tipton, and other more pastoral locations around Haywood County, where he was born in 1936.

In *I Am One of You Forever* (1985) we first meet Jess Kirkman, a ten-year-old boy who spends considerable time wondering

tour 2

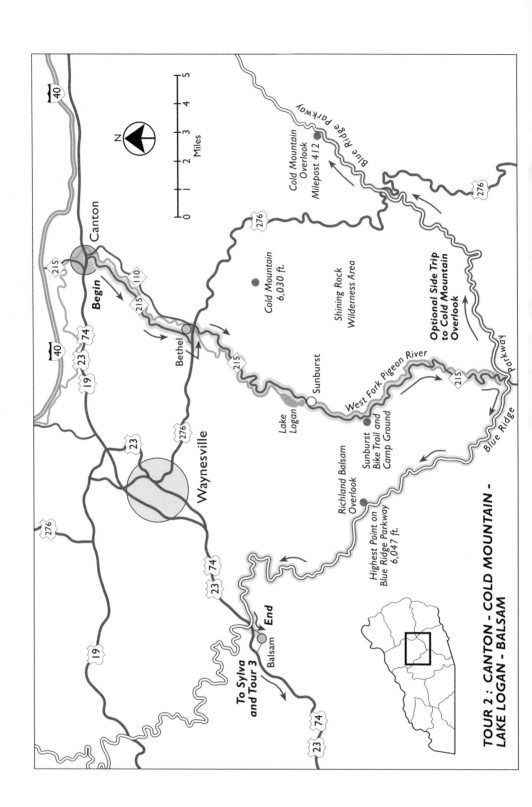

TOUR 2 : CANTON - COLD MOUNTAIN - LAKE LOGAN - BALSAM

From Mears Avenue, Canton, known in the fiction of Fred Chappell as the town of Tipton, and its famous paper mill.

at the comings and goings of his "quare" uncles and other rascally family members.

In *Brighten the Corner Where You Are* (1989), Chappell takes on rural education, covering a single day in 1946 in the life of Jess's father, Joe Robert Kirkman. The central character's opinions on evolution and his nonstandard teaching methods end up making the day described his last as a science teacher in fictional Tipton.

In *Farewell, I'm Bound to Leave You* (1996), Jess and his mother, Cora, spend hours recalling the tales of Jess's dying grandmother, while in *Look Back All the Green Valley* (1999), the adult Jess Kirkman returns once more to Tipton and Harwood (Haywood) County to see after his ailing mother. He vows to her that she will receive her final wish: to be buried beside her husband. However, a new gravesite for two must first be found. Jess hosts a community picnic and makes a plea to neighbors and old friends for a pair of donated plots. In the process, he also revisits in memory the life and death of his father, a furniture store owner by day but a madcap inventor, practical joker, and prognosticator of the future in his off hours. In this book, the author also reveals that the adult Jess Kirkman, who happens to be a poet and professor of English at the University of North Carolina at Greensboro, has written all his books under the pen name Fred Chappell, and the boundary between memoir and fiction gets fuzzier.

The following passage gives a flavor for this series and captures Chappell's wry humor. The year is 1940, and ten-year-old narrator Jess Kirkman describes an outing with Johnson Gibbs, an orphaned teenager hired to help with the Kirkmans' farm chores. Earlier in the chapter, Johnson confides in Jess that he has enlisted in the army and will be leaving soon. On this day, his eighteenth birthday, Johnson receives a fly rod from the Kirkmans. Right away, Jess and Johnson go fishing, presumably on the West Fork of the Pigeon River. Johnson pretends that he knows how to fly fish while Jess observes:

He got the fly caught in the sleeve of his blue cotton shirt and while he was working it free the line wrapped around the rod tip. Then the fly hooked into his shirt collar. Now he couldn't see it so he took off his shirt, setting the butt of the rod on a stone. When the hook came out of the cloth the rod nearly flipped into the stream and he grabbed at it with both hands. His shirt dropped in and floated down toward me. I lifted it dripping with my cane pole.

"Just spread it out on that bush," he said. "It'll dry in a jiffy."

"Looks like it might take you some time to get used to the new rig," I said and might have said more if I'd trusted his temper.

His expression was distant, his eyes glazed with obsession. "I don't believe this pool is just right for a fly rod."

How'd you know? You ain't got a hook in it yet. But I didn't speak aloud.

"I'll move on upstream and give this one to you. Ought to be a good baiting pool. Come on when you finish and catch up with me."

"Okay."...

I found Johnson half a mile upstream. He was lying on a big rock in the sunlight with just his underwear drawers on. His tan cotton pants were spread out beside him; they were soaking. He was lying so still he might have been dead.

"What happened to you?"

He sat up with a jerk. "I hooked a fish!" he shouted. Then he relaxed and spoke in a quieter tone. "I swear to God, Jess, he was as big as my leg. Swear to God. But I was standing in an unsteady place and I fell off in the water."

The west fork of the Pigeon River near Canton, where Fred Chappell's characters Jess Kirkman and Johnson Gibbs might have fished for trout.

"Did he get away?"

He nodded solemnly. "I'll get him. We'll come back again and I'll catch him next time for sure." He lay back again and closed his eyes.

"Where's your rod?"

"Right over yonder. Ain't it a dandy? Come over here and set a minute, I'll tell you something."

I went and sat. "What?" I said.

He opened his eyes and talked in confidential tones to the blue sky above. "I ain't never been fishing before. This is the first time. But I've thought a lot about it."

"You mean you ain't never been fly fishing."

"I never been fishing period. Where's a orphan boy going to go fishing?"

"I never thought."

"This is the best thing that ever happened. This is the best time I ever had."

I listened to the rush and gurgle of the stream; there were a thousand voices in it.

"There ain't nothing better than this," Johnson said. "From here on out it's all downhill." He sat up and hugged his knees. "I bet the best time is over for me after this."

—From *I Am One of You Forever*, by Fred Chappell (Baton Rouge: Louisiana State University Press, 1985), 23–25.

"Ole Fred," as this North Carolina writer likes to sign his letters, has inspired generations of younger writers at the university in Greensboro, where he was hired fresh out of the master's program at Duke University to assume the responsibilities of the late poet Randall Jarrell in 1965. Though he has lived in the Piedmont with his wife, Susan, for decades and written eight novels, Chappell is equally revered as the author of more than a dozen books of poetry. Winner of the prestigious Bollingen Prize and the Aiken Taylor Award in poetry, Chappell writes poems that are by turns highly formalist, infused with classical allusion, given to wicked satire, and sometimes plainspoken, full of images of the farms and people of Haywood County. Chappell easily ranks among North Carolina's most versatile and learned writers.

DIRECTIONS

Though Fred Chappell's novels refer to it as the Challenger Paper Mill, today the historic Champion Mill goes by the name of Blue Ridge Paper Products, Inc. It is possible to drive through the heart of company property and to witness the machinations of papermaking up close. The shortest route into Canton off I-40 is to take exit 31 onto NC 215 South (Champion Drive). Approximately 1.5 miles beyond the interstate, bear left onto Champion Drive. (Staying on NC 215 instead of bearing left onto Champion Drive will take you directly into downtown Canton.) This facility was the first to make bleached pulp from southern pine trees and the first to make paper from this pulp. Tours inside the plant are available by advance appointment.

Once through the industrial complex, Champion Drive becomes North Main Street. Turn right on Main, which will carry you into the heart of town. Note that Church Street (also US 19/23/74) is the main artery through Canton. The town is built on a series of steep hills, with dramatic views of the mill and the surrounding mountains.

The Canton Area Historical Museum provides a concrete glimpse of Canton's past and some of the social influences on native son Fred Chappell. It's located at 36 Park Street, which loops off Church Street and runs parallel to it across the Pigeon River. The museum is brick, set back from the street, next door to the county courthouse. In this small, charming repository, the community has contributed an eclectic array of artifacts and photos documenting small-town life in a twentieth-century mountain mill town. An old clothes press, parts of a moonshine still, war memorabilia, old photos of Canton at the turn of the twentieth century, a football poster for the 1948 "Paper Bowl" tournament, a textile exhibit, and a "shrine" to Canton's most distinguished literary product, Fred Chappell, are on the main floor.

Downstairs displays, maps, photos, and portraits document the Champion Paper Company's early years in the region. This portion of the museum also has photos of the Sunburst settlement, where from 1912 to 1926 loggers cleared virgin timber then dammed a creek to create Lake Logan, a corporate resort for Champion employees, described further in the Cold Mountain driving tour that follows. An enormous crosscut saw, a training yoke for the oxen that dragged the trees out of the forest, and samples of the "googaloo" currency issued by Champion to its workers for use in the company store are also on display.

The museum has an ample collection of brochures, maps, and other information on local walking, hiking, biking, golfing, horseback riding, fishing, skiing, gem mining, and rafting opportunities in Haywood County. For more information on Canton, see <http://www.cantonnc.com/>.

COLD MOUNTAIN DRIVING TOUR

By following the West Fork of the Pigeon River, you can take in views of Cold Mountain and Lake Logan and climb to the highest point on the Blue Ridge Parkway before heading down to Balsam on this slow meander of approximately forty miles.

To begin, follow NC 215 South (the Old River Road) out of Canton. Look to the right and you'll soon see the old Canton High School, Fred Chappell's alma mater. It now serves as the Canton Middle School. The West Fork of the Pigeon River runs alongside the highway here on your left and flows briskly back toward town. You might easily imagine Chappell's characters Jess Kirkman and Johnson Gibbs stealing away to a site along these banks to fish for trout. In May blackberries cascade in profusion along this roadside, and old plantings of weigela and rhododendron brighten the well-kept yards. Red-roofed barns and herds of goats along this stretch of road, lovely in all seasons, earn its designation as a "scenic byway" by the North Carolina Department of Transportation.

Continue on NC 215 as it winds through the countryside. Approximately five miles outside of Canton you will come into the Bethel community. Here you can see Cold Mountain ahead.

Asheville-born writer Charles Frazier explained in a journal he kept for salon.com in July and August of 1997 that he had long been fascinated by the impact of the Civil War on his ancestors in these parts. When his father told him of a man named Inman who was wounded in the war and decided to walk home rather than stay in the hospital, Frazier's imagination kicked into high gear. He set out on Inman's trail—a pursuit that lasted five years. When he had nearly finished the novel that would also become a highly acclaimed film in 2003, Frazier came to the Bethel area to look for W. P. Inman's unmarked grave. Here, among a scattering of unreadable stones, Frazier took in the spectacular view of Cold Mountain and the forks of the Pigeon River, a spot where the Cherokee long before had occupied a village they called Kanuga.

The Inman gravesite is believed to be near the corner of Old River Road (NC 215) and Sonoma Drive, in the cemetery adjoining Bethel United Methodist Church.

Continue on NC 215 until it forms a "T" with US 276. Turn left on 276, and look for the Bethel Grocery on your right. If you step into the grocery for a snack, chances are you'll run into a descendant of W. P. Inman. Controversy about Frazier's novel still flares up now and then in conversations among community members here. According to Kent Stewart, the former proprietor of a bookstore in nearby Waynesville, one of W. P. Inman's more vocal descendants is convinced that his forebear has been unduly maligned as a deserter in Frazier's book.

Local Civil War reenactors have complained the opposite, claiming that Inman was "four times worse" than presented, since the real soldier likely deserted his duties more than once, Stewart explained.

Everyone, Charles Frazier included, agrees that the author took wide liberties with the story for his own purposes. And in the same way that Asheville residents fell into a swirl of heated talk following the publication of Thomas Wolfe's first novel in 1929, when they recognized themselves and their town in the book, the Inmans of Haywood County are happy to offer their definitive opinions about Frazier's fiction.

Before leaving Bethel Grocery, face the gas pumps and look over the store roof. Cold Mountain is straight ahead. For photographs, however, another of Inman's distant cousins led us to this view of Cold Mountain:

Turn right out of the grocery and go to the stoplight where NC 110 crosses US 276. Cliffside Outfitters is on the far-right corner before you. Turn left and

A view of the mountains novelist Charles Frazier made famous, seen from the Bethel area of Haywood County.

follow 110 across the East Fork of the Pigeon River. Drive up the road "a ways" and turn right at Silver Bluff. Head up this road until you have an unobstructed view of Cold Mountain to the south rising before you to its steep peak of 6,030 feet. On cloudy days, however, the summit may be obscured.

Head back south on NC 110 to the stoplight at US 276. Proceed through the stoplight, since NC 215 now continues straight ahead. (Cliffside Outfitters is on your far left.) Here the cut through the valley will soon narrow as the West Fork of the Pigeon River continues to race beside the road. Striking views of Cold Mountain rising in the distance beyond fields that are fully planted in summer will continue for a mile or so.

Soon the daylight will be dimmed by so many overhanging trees and by

The cold, deep waters of Lake Logan, where paper magnate Reuben Robertson loved to sit, whittle, and tell tall tales in his hunting lodge.

the sheer rise and drop on either side of the road. In several winding miles, you will come to Lake Logan, a deep, cold, black lake that was built to replace the stands of virgin timber harvested by Champion Paper Company for the jaws of the Canton pulp mill in the early twentieth century. Here Champion CEO and occasional poet Reuben Robertson built himself a hunting lodge with a large dance floor, several rustic cabins, and another lodge across the lake called "Sit and Whittle" that is complete with a bar, card tables, and an enormously long and thick meeting table created by a single felled tree from the nearby forest. A big man, Robertson had furniture built to his own size in the popular Mission style of the era. Lamps with mica shades still create soft light for card games and reading.

Robertson entertained dozens of dignitaries in this remote resort. A picture of the pulp tycoon beside Richard Nixon and Billy Graham is prominent in the Canton Museum. According to one official at Lake Logan, the lodge was also the site of secret planning for the Apollo moon mission and a number of other sequestered gatherings of U.S. government officials as late as the Nixon era. Reuben Robertson died in 1973 at the age of ninety-three and by then had donated Champion lands to help create the Great Smoky Mountains National Park and the Shining Rock Wilderness area up ahead.

The 4,400 acres around the lake are protected today by a partnership of the Conservation Fund, the U.S. Forest Service, the State of North Carolina, the Boy Scouts, and the Episcopal Diocese of Western North Carolina. Lake Logan accommodations are available to groups for workshops and conferences. Tours for prospective conference-goers are available by appointment by calling Lake Logan Conference Center at 828-646-0095. Or visit their website: <http://www .lakelogan.org/>.

Continue a few miles farther south from Lake Logan along NC 215 to reach the Sunburst Campground. A rocky eight-mile bicycle loop also begins here. Sunburst was the name of the camp set up for the initial logging operation of Champion Paper in the area, also described in Donald Davis's novel, *Thirteen Miles from Suncrest* (1994). Historic photos of the effort show teams of burly men dwarfed by mammoth trees, their arms outstretched, demonstrating the daunting girth of a single fir. Carl Schenck, the chief forester of the Biltmore Estate until he was fired, came to Sunburst in 1909 to run the first forestry school in the country, which he had founded while still at Biltmore. Schenck taught his students reforestation techniques here.

Beyond Sunburst the road begins to climb steeply through a number of switchbacks. Watch for pullouts suitable for photographing the small waterfalls all along the way or for trout fishing in the rushing West Fork. As the road nears the Blue Ridge Parkway, dramatic views of the Shining Rock Wilderness are off to the left. When the road crests, it intersects the Parkway. Here the Parkway follows the steep ridge that divides Haywood and Transylvania Counties, and farther south, Haywood and Jackson Counties.

If you head north on the Parkway toward Mount Pisgah, you can get another angle on Inman's mountain at the Cold Mountain Overlook between mileposts 412 and 411. It's a dramatic stretch of road worth seeing. If, instead of turning onto the Parkway, you continue straight ahead on NC 215 South, you'll end up in Rosman, a town located near the headwaters of the French Broad River, considered in Tour 10.

But to continue on this tour, turn off of NC 215 to head south on the Blue Ridge Parkway.

At the Cowee Mountain Overlook beyond milepost 430, you can see the Cowee Mountain range far in the distance beyond the Tuckasegee Valley. The

Cowee Valley was important to the Cherokee and is mentioned both in Frazier's *Cold Mountain* and in naturalist William Bartram's classic volume *Travels through North and South Carolina, Georgia, East and West Florida . . .*, first published in 1791. (See Tours 3 and 5 for more on Bartram.)

At the Haywood/Jackson Overlook at milepost 431, look to the northwest to see where you've just been in Haywood County. If the day is clear, Lake Logan will be in the middle distance, a diamond-shaped mirror. Here you are riding the ridge of the Great Balsam Range and can especially appreciate the hard work of the Civilian Conservation Corps in constructing this miraculous mile-high road in the 1930s as part of FDR's New Deal. Toward Haywood County is the Shining Rock to the right, which has to catch the light just so to be seen from this distance. Turn and face the other direction and you are looking into Jackson County.

At the Richland Balsam Overlook just beyond milepost 431, the Parkway reaches the highest point along its entire 469 miles. Clear views to the east and west make it worth a long stop. Here the Parkway also comes near the Old Judaculla Fields, a grassy bald that was farmed by a giant, according to Cherokee myth.

Before leaving the Parkway to visit the town of Balsam below, you might want to read the selection offered here from *Cold Mountain*. In it Charles Frazier describes friendly times in Inman's youth when the Cherokee who hunted these lands and the white settlers who climbed the mountain for cooler air met up to play games, eat, and drink heartily:

> The two groups camped side by side for two weeks, the younger men playing the ball game most of the day, gambling heavily on the outcomes. It was a contest with no fixed time of play and few rules so that they just ran about slamming into each other and hacking with the rackets as if with clubs until one team reached a set number of points scored by striking the goal posts with the ball. They'd play most of the day and then spend half the night drinking and telling tales at fireside, eating great heaps of little speckled trout, fried crisp, bones and all.
>
> There in the highlands, clear weather held for much of the time. The air lacked its usual haze, and the view stretched on and on across rows of mountains, each paler than the last until the final ranks were indistinguishable from sky. It was as if all the world might be composed of nothing but valley and ridge. During a pause in the play, Swimmer had looked out at the landforms and said he believed Cold Mountain to be the chief mountain in the world. Inman asked how he knew that to be true, and

The highest point on the Blue Ridge Parkway is at Richland Balsam Overlook near the Cherokee's mythic Judaculla Fields.

Swimmer had swept his hand across the horizon to where Cold Mountain stood and said, Do you see a bigger'n?

Mornings on the high bald were crisp, with fog lying in the valleys so that the peaks rose from it disconnected like steep blue islands scattered across a pale sea. Inman would awake, still part drunk, and walk off down in a cove to fish with Swimmer for an hour or two before returning for the beginning of the game. They would sit by the rushing creek, stickbait and rockbait on their hooks. Swimmer would talk seamlessly in a low voice so that it merged with the sound of the water. He told tales of animals and how they came to be as they are. Possum with bare tail, squirrel with fuzzy tail. Buck with antlers. Painter with tooth and claw. Uktena with coil and fang. Tales that explained how the world came about and where it is heading. — From *Cold Mountain*, by Charles Frazier (New York: Vintage Books, 1997), 19.

When you've traveled twelve more miles down the Parkway, beyond the Pinnacle Ridge Tunnel, stop to appreciate the view from the Waynesville Overlook, 0.9 miles beyond milepost 440. Then exit the Parkway at Balsam Gap and descend to US 23/74. Sylva is twelve miles west; Waynesville is eight miles east; but if you have time, you'll want to have a look around the historic Balsam Mountain Inn, where North Carolina novelist Kaye Gibbons once came for a writing retreat and where songwriters from as far away as Nashville and Atlanta gather several times a year to trade songs, offer workshops, and perform.

■ LITERARY LANDSCAPE

Canton Branch Library
11 Pennsylvania Avenue
Canton, NC 28716
828-648-2924
<http://www.haywoodlibrary.org/liblocations.htm>
The Canton Public Library has a complete collection of Fred Chappell's books and also offers public Internet access. From Main Street on the block between Adams and Academy, turn straight uphill on Mears Avenue, which comes into Main right beside the "Churches of Canton" mural. Mears will dead-end into Pennsylvania Avenue. Turn left on Pennsylvania, and the library is down the street, on your right at the corner of Bailey.

Balsam Mountain Inn
68 Seven Springs Drive
Balsam, NC 28707
828-456-9498
800-224-9498 (toll free)
<http://www.balsaminn.com/>
At one time, the Balsam Depot was the highest train station east of the Rockies. Begun in 1905 and opened to guests in 1908, the Balsam Mountain Springs Hotel, as it was first called, served rail travelers seeking cool air and the curative powers of seven freshwater springs at this site. Merrily Teasley, a native of Greeneville, Tennessee, came upon the abandoned inn on a hike in 1990 and soon bought and restored the three-story Victorian to its former glory, securing its future by listing it on the National Register of Historic Places.

This inn is a place full of stories and, some visitors say, a few ghosts. Since Teasley's renovations, the inn is also a meeting place for singer/songwriters, who hold workshops here. Framed verse and local pottery, quilts, and other crafts are on display up and down the main halls of the first floor. The Balsam Inn library has 2,000 volumes, and for the past thirteen years guests have been keeping room diaries, so the narrative of the place continues. No televisions or phones are in the rooms. Breakfast is included in the room tariff. Daily dinner and Sunday lunch is also available to guests and by reservation on a space-available basis to others.

Turn right from the Parkway access road west toward Sylva on US 23/74. Watch for a left turn lane only 0.1 miles beyond the Parkway overpass. A small, green sign notes the village of Balsam at this left turn. Once on the Balsam road, turn right up a hill, cross the railroad tracks, and continue for one-third of a mile. The driveway to the Balsam Inn is across the tracks again and up a steep hill. Look for the large sign in the inn's steep yard.

Sylva : Dillsboro : Cullowhee : Highlands

More than once Hollywood has headed to these hills to shoot adventure films and capture the local color of the steep highlands where so many legends and tall tales still thrive. At the Mountain Heritage Museum you can learn about the Cherokee alphabet—the first written Native American language. Experience the dark wonder of the massive rhododendron thickets and the cold rushing streams that have long stirred local poets to create passionate portraits of the people and landscapes.

Writers with a connection to this area: Mary Adams, William Bartram, Sallie Bissell, Rick Boyer, Sean Bridgers, Sue Ellen Bridgers, Kathryn Stripling Byer, Gary Carden, Catherine Carter, Thomas Rain Crowe, Thomas Meyer, John Parris, Collin Wilcox Paxton, Walker Percy, Dannye Romine Powell, Ron Rash, Jonathan Williams

■ SYLVA

Sylva was named for a Danish wanderer who stopped here on his way to the Asheville area and ended up working in a local sawmill until his mysterious departure a few years later. William Sylva was so well liked that the townspeople named the post office in his honor in 1880. When the railroad came through in 1889, the town was incorporated and became the Jackson County seat. Today Sylva is a papermaking town that's home to a thriving community of fewer than 2,500 residents who proudly proclaim to tourists that they are "in the middle of the most." You'll find more than a half-dozen good restaurants within strolling distance of the courthouse, including Spring Street Café below the City Lights Bookstore. Lulu's Café on West Main is another favorite among the local literati, featuring Greek, Mexican, Indonesian, and Italian dishes along with southern fare.

Among Sylva's most distinguished writers was columnist

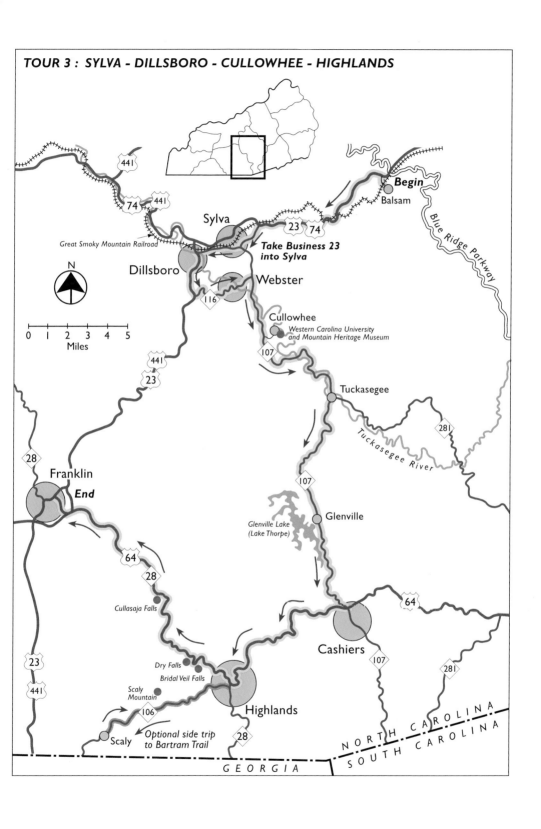

TOUR 3 : SYLVA - DILLSBORO - CULLOWHEE - HIGHLANDS

Begin
Balsam

Blue Ridge Parkway

441

74 441

Sylva

Great Smoky Mountain Railroad

Take Business 23 into Sylva

23 74

N

0 1 2 3 4 5
Miles

Dillsboro

Webster

116

Cullowhee
Western Carolina University
and Mountain Heritage Museum

441
23

107

Tuckasegee

281

Tuckasegee River

28

Franklin
End

107

64

28

Glenville Lake
(Lake Thorpe)

Glenville

Cullasaja Falls

64

Dry Falls
Bridal Veil Falls

Cashiers

107

281

Scaly
Mountain

106

Highlands

28

Scaly

Optional side trip
to Bartram Trail

23
441

NORTH CAROLINA
SOUTH CAROLINA

G E O R G I A

Sylva writer John Parris and his wife, Dorothy, helped to create the Mountain Heritage Center at Western Carolina University to preserve the cultural traditions Parris wrote about in his columns for the Asheville Citizen-Times *newspaper. Courtesy of Western Carolina University.*

John A. Parris Jr., whose works are featured throughout this trail and the next. Parris was born in Sylva in 1914 and began working for the *Jackson County Journal* at age thirteen. He later joined the United Press, posted first to Raleigh then to New York, London, and North Africa. After World War II, he joined the Associated Press as a diplomatic correspondent in London before being sent to New York to cover the United Nations. In 1947, he returned to western North Carolina to try his hand at creative writing. Parris published *The Cherokee Story* in 1950 and soon became director of public relations for the Cherokee Historical Association. He was best known, however, for his books on the mountain traditions of western North Carolina, which were compilations of the popular columns he wrote for the *Asheville Citizen-Times* newspaper under the title "Roaming the Mountains."

Over two decades Parris traveled to small communities across the mountains collecting legends and lore from old-timers. Though his writing often wavers between sentimental nostalgia and pure poetry, he was an important, if informal, oral historian for the region. His books are out of print and somewhat hard to find, but they are still a useful resource, offering first-hand accounts of traditional practices now in decline such as hog killing, beekeeping, and soap making.

Parris and his wife, Dorothy, an artist, lived in Sylva for nearly fifty years in a cabin built from chestnut logs hand-hewn by his great-grandfather. Over the years, Parris strongly advocated for the creation of a center to preserve the traditions and cultures of the mountains. He was the first recipient of the Mountain Heritage Award presented each year by Western Carolina University as part of its Mountain Heritage Day celebration—an outgrowth of the university's Mountain Heritage Center that Parris envisioned.

John Parris died in 1999. Today the John A. Parris Jr. and Dorothy Luxton Parris Distinguished Professorship in Appalachian Cultural Studies at Western Carolina University commemorates their contributions to the region.

Sylva is also home to Sue Ellen Bridgers, a writer whose novels for young adults have taken on issues such as mental illness, domestic abuse, mental retardation, and the hardships of migrant children. Bridgers has published seven novels to date. Her straightforward and honest style has won her a number of "best book" awards from the American Library Association, among other national distinctions. Bridgers's novel *Sara Will* managed to cross the boundary of young adult fiction to find equal popularity among adult readers. In it, Bridgers describes small-town life as might be experienced in Sylva with an understated sense of humor:

> Jonathan had come to Tyler Mills because it was a little town, a little school district. He was afraid of the competition of a bigger pond. Tyler Mills was a place to get ahead without doing much. A male high school teacher could work his way into the principal's office without doing anything besides being there and behaving himself. Waiting it out. He could wait until the man ahead of him retired or died. Meanwhile he taught civics and sociology to freshmen and sophomores, American history to juniors, and coached the girls' basketball team with more enthusiasm than ability.
>
> At twenty-five, he had begun to survey the local terrain, contemplating the availability of someone like Swanee Hope Burney, who one afternoon peered at him over the laxatives in Pearson's Drugstore, her feather duster held aloft like a bright red wing. She was wearing a white smock over her homemade dress. Swanee always wore the jacket Mr. Pearson provided, which she believed gave her a professional look.

She had smiled at Jonathan Calhoun, her cheeks flushed pink, and said, "Could I help you?" in such a sweetly suggestive voice that he was bound to buy something. A bottle of milk of magnesia sprang into his hand and from his fingers into hers, and then she was clanging the cash register, opening her palm for his money, dropping change through his trembling fingers so he had to gather it up off the counter, pennies spinning everywhere. She gave him the white bag heavy with antacid and a smile, such a smile that she felt her face exploding with it, blue eyes flashing, lips red and full, yellow hair flying around her burning face. She was like a display of fireworks, hot and crackling. —From *Sara Will*, by Sue Ellen Bridgers (New York: Harper & Row, 1985), 129–30.

Originally from Greenville, in the eastern part of North Carolina, Bridgers grew up on a tobacco farm, married her English professor at East Carolina, and finished her undergraduate degree at Western Carolina University after her youngest child entered elementary school. That same year, Bridgers published her first novel, *Home before Dark* (1976). In recent years, she has been involved in filmmaking with her son, Sean, an actor.

Sean Bridgers landed the role of the *"Charlotte Tribune"* reporter in the locally filmed *Nell*, starring Jody Foster. Soon after, Sean and his mother wrote the screenplay for *Paradise Falls*, an independent feature that was shot in the area and won the Hollywood Discovery Award in 1998. The movie also featured the music of North Carolina's Red Clay Ramblers, a band that includes writer Bland Simpson. Sean Bridgers's acting credits also include the movie *Sweet Home Alabama* and the HBO series *Deadwood*.

Sylva is also the homeplace of storyteller Gary Carden, who was featured in a 2004 documentary film produced for public television called *Mountain Talk*. Carden has written several plays, including one about the late nineteenth-century outlaw and bootlegger Major Lewis R. Redmond, who lived in the region. Carden was cocreator, with Highlands author Collin Wilcox Paxton, of *Papa's Angels: A Christmas Story* (1996), which was made into a CBS "Sunday night movie" in 2000. Carden also cowrote, with Nina Anderson, *Belled Buzzards, Hucksters & Grieving Specters: Appalachian Tales, Strange, True & Legendary* (1994).

In his tale "The Swinett," Carden describes a typical day in the Sylva Barbershop around 1945. Willard, Ardell, and Boogie, "three old guys that are sorta famous in Sylva for telling lies," are sitting around the shop when a stranger wearing a sport coat and tie comes in and introduces himself as Stanley. He tells the men that he is in the market to purchase some "rustic instruments" for his collection and figures this "quaint" town might be a good prospect. Then from the "liars' bench," Willard asks:

"In your collection of rustic instruments, do you have a swinett?" It got real quiet then. I could hear the razor scraping on somebody's jaw. Then Stanley said, "I beg your pardon?"

"A swinett," said Willard. Then he spelled it.

"I'm afraid I've never heard of a . . . swinett? Is it a wind or a percussion instrument?"

"If you mean, do you blow it or beat it, well, most swinett players squeeze 'em." He looked at Ardell. "Don't they usually squeeze 'em, Ardell?"

"OH YES!" yelled Ardell. "SQUEEZE 'EM! YES!"

Stanley got out a little notebook and a pen and started making notes. "Like an accordion, then?"

"No," said Willard. "More like a pair of pliers. Professional swinett players use pliers." Boogie nodded wisely. "That they do."

Stanley looked confused. "Could you give me some specific details? For example, is it shaped like a zither or a trumpet?"

"I've seen round 'ens," said Willard. "You ever seen a round swinett, Boogie?"

"I have. They brought one up to the Balm of Gilead Baptist church last year and played it at a revival. Never forget it."

"ME NEITHER," said Ardell. "MADE ME CRY."

"Played 'The Old Rugged Cross,'" said Boogie.

"But most of 'em are square or rectangle. About 20 feet by 40 feet." Stanley stopped writing. "See what you do is, you fill a swinett with pigs. Little pigs that go wee-wee, and big boars that go Oink, Oink. Forty pigs will give you a pretty good musical range. Then you bore holes around the top of the box. Pull their tails through the holes 'n anchor 'em down." Stanley stared at the Liars' Bench guys who all nodded solemn as owls.

"You try to arrange them pigs according to scale, like do, ray, me, fai, soo, you know."

"THE CHORDING IS THE HARD PART!" said Ardell. Boogie nodded. "Take about six men to play a swinett right, and they've got pliers in both hands."

"Hit is a wondrous thing when it is done right," said Willard.

Stanley put his pen up and closed his notebook. Then, he left. Nobody said anything for a while.

Then Ardell said, "SOME FOLKS CALL EM HOGOLAS!"

"He's gone, Ardell," said Willard. Ardell was surprised. "MUST HAVE JUST REMEMBERED SOMETHING HE HAD TO DO!"

"You guys are something else," said Wimpy. "Maybe you ought to go on the road. See if you could get on the Opry."

"Is it true?" I said. "A hymn sung by squealing pigs?"

Everybody stared at me. "Well, Harley, hit's true if you believe it," said Willard.

"Don't tell him that!" said Albert. He was under a steaming towel and sounded all muffled. "He already probably believes in snipes. When did he come back? Must have been when I was looking at that bloody hatchet that was used to dismember the 'Tampa Temptress.'"

"What's a snipe?"

Willard grinned. "Put down that gory magazine and I'll tell you."

Albert made little clucking noises under that towel. I think he was laughing.

—From *Mason Jars in the Flood and Other Stories*, by Gary Carden (Boone, N.C.: Parkway Publishers, 2000), 195–96.

Other writers besides long-time residents Gary Carden and Sue Ellen Bridgers have also used Sylva as fodder for fiction. In her fourth novel, *Legacy of Masks* (2005), Asheville-based writer Sallie Bissell has her protagonist Mary Crow come to Hartsville, North Carolina, in pursuit of a new job with the Pisgah County district attorney. In this passage, astute readers will recognize that Bissell's setting is strikingly similar to the Jackson County courthouse in Sylva. Bissell says she's blended aspects of Haywood, Jackson, and Swain Counties to create her fictional Pisgah County:

The Confederate soldier stood on the forty-sixth of the one hundred and five concrete steps that led from Main Street to the Pisgah County Courthouse. Rifle at his side, he'd kept a weather-beaten watch for any encroaching Yankees for as long as Mary Crow could remember. Passing him on her fourth grade Civics field trip, she'd found him impressively fierce. Six years later, as she'd rushed past to apply for her driver's license, she thought him quaintly embarrassing. Today, nearly twenty-five years after their first acquaintance, the old boy seemed comforting and familiar. Not much else about Pisgah County did.

"Hey Johnny Reb." She paused for a moment in the puddle of shade cast by the towering bronze figure. Already she was breathing heavily from her climb, and she still had fifty-nine steps to go. She'd forgotten how hot

Up the one hundred-plus steps to the Jackson County Courthouse in Sylva, as described by mystery novelist Sallie Bissell.

the early June sun could be in the Carolina mountains, and she'd foolishly worn her prosecutorial black suit. Deathwrap. Comfortable in the relentlessly air-conditioned courtroom of Atlanta, on these steps, Deathwrap felt like a portable sauna, buttoned in the front and zipped tight at the waist.

"Shoot," she hissed, leaning against the base of the statue. Already she'd torn her hose and sweated through her underwear. Pretty soon she'd have big damp circles under her arms. In her business it was never good to be visibly nervous; to be both nervous and sweating did not bode well at all.

Nonetheless, she had an appointment with D.A. George Turpin in four minutes, and she could not be late. Squaring her shoulders, she resumed her ascent to the courthouse. As her high heels clicked on the steps, she gave a rueful smile at the irony of her undertaking. When she was eighteen she'd wanted to leave Pisgah County forever. Today, at thirty-five, she couldn't wait to come back home. . . .

She finally reached the hundred and fifth step, and without pausing, strode in the vaulted lobby of the old courthouse. She passed a gaggle of secretaries clad in frothy print dresses, hurrying to begin the day's work. Suddenly she felt even more out of place in Deathwrap. Swathed in black among women clad in the colors of melting sherbet, she must look like the Grim Reaper, working her next victim. When she glanced over her shoulder and caught one of the secretaries casting a curious eye back at her, she knew without a doubt that she would be the gossip tidbit du jour. Did y'all see that girl dressed in black? Who was she? You just don't see clothes like that around here. She must be some fancy pants, over from

Raleigh. Don't kid yourself, honey. Didn't you see that hair? She was pure Cherokee.—From *Legacy of Masks*, by Sallie Bissell (New York: Bantam, 2005), 1–2.

Sallie Bissell has written four mystery novels featuring Mary Crow, the feisty criminal justice attorney from the Eastern Band of the Cherokee. *In the Forest of Harm* (2001) and *A Darker Justice* (2002) feature sites around Asheville. In *Call the Devil by His Oldest Name* (2004), Mary Crow follows the historic Cherokee Trail of Tears across Tennessee as she seeks to recover her kidnapped godchild.

In Sylva, you can follow in the footsteps of Mary Crow and hike the hundred-plus steps leading up to the Jackson County Courthouse, as do many local folks for exercise. This 1913 neoclassic revival building perches high above the revitalized town center of Sylva and is a great place to stop and let kids blow off a little steam. Have them count the steps as they climb and enjoy the eye-popping view at the top. Then come down carefully and stand in the mist of the fountain at the foot of the hill. Often claimed to be the most photographed courthouse in the state, you can also see it rising boldly above town if you're driving by on US 23/74.

■ DILLSBORO

Head out of Sylva on Business 23 and you'll be in Dillsboro before you can blink. Dillsboro is the town where St. Louis-librarian-turned-writer Horace Kephart arrived in 1904 by train from the Midwest and asked permission to camp on farmland about a mile out of town. Kephart had abandoned his family and the throb of St. Louis, which, at the time, was playing host to some 20 million visitors for the 1904 World's Fair celebrating the centennial of the Louisiana Purchase. Having half-heartedly attempted suicide back in St. Louis, Kephart was a troubled man now desperate for the peace and isolation of the deep woods. Arriving in Dillsboro he immediately began documenting, in a straightforward but lyrical style, what life was like among the mountain people he came to love and who came to love him. Comparisons of Horace Kephart to Thoreau are common because of his themes and his language:

This is the country that ordinary tourists shun. And well for such that they do, since whoso cares more for bodily comfort than for freedom and air and elbow-room should tarry by still waters and pleasant pastures. . . . When I went south into the mountains I was seeking a Back of Beyond.

Before the turn of the twentieth century, Horace Kephart studied in Florence, Italy, where he became an avid hiker in the Apennines and Alps. In 1904 he made his way to Dillsboro, where he sought refuge from modern life in the Smoky Mountains. Photo courtesy of Western Carolina University.

Horace Kephart   Florence, Italy
1886

This for more reasons than one. With an inborn taste for the wild and romantic, I yearned for a strange land and a people that had the charm of originality. Again, I had a passion for early American history; and in Far Appalachia, it seemed that I might realize the past in the present, seeing with my own eyes what life must have been to my pioneer ancestors of a century or two ago. Besides, I wanted to enjoy a free life in the open air, the thrill of exploring new ground, the joys of the chase, and the man's game of matching my woodcraft against the forces of nature, with no help from servants or hired guides.—From *Our Southern Highlanders: A Narrative of Adventure in the Southern Appalachians and a Study of Life Among the Mountaineers*, by Horace Kephart (Knoxville: University of Tennessee Press, 1976), 29–30.

Some 200 people live in Dillsboro today, but the village is alive with craft galleries, candy and ice cream stores, fancy and family restaurants, and a generally festive air that centers on the Great Smoky Mountain Railway and the Floyd McEachern Historical Railroad Museum. Everything is within walking distance. Self-guided float trips on the nearby Tuckasegee River are popular, and local raft rental agencies can help you plot your course downstream. Overnight accommodations are plentiful, including cottages, bed and breakfasts, elegant

A train departs on the route taken by Horace Kephart from Dillsboro to Bryson City.

inns, and guesthouses. Dillsboro's Jarrett House is one of North Carolina's oldest inns, where extravagant southern meals are available in the dining room.

You can ride the same rails that Horace Kephart took out of Dillsboro, heading deeper into the mountains. The Great Smoky Mountain Railway provides old steam and diesel trains that leave every morning for a scenic pull along the Tuckasegee River all the way to Bryson City—a distance of 32 miles round trip. The train passes by the preserved site of the spectacular train wreck in the movie *The Fugitive*, which starred Harrison Ford. Engine 1702 of this railway also appeared in a film by Sue Ellen and Sean Bridgers, *Paradise Falls*, and was in the screen version of Tennessee Williams's play *This Property Is Condemned*, starring Natalie Wood and Robert Redford.

Once in Bryson City you can extend your excursion through the Nantahala Gorge with a picnic lunch reserved in advance. Gourmet dinner trains, a mystery theater train, sunset travel to Whittier during the summer, and a fall leaf-viewing excursion are all part of the seasonal offerings of this enterprise, which is part of the American Heritage Railway System. Reservations are required. Ticket prices vary. See <http://www.gsmr.com> or call 800-872-4681 (toll free).

Western Carolina University's Mountain Heritage Center honors the life of storyteller Ray Hicks of Beech Mountain.

■ CULLOWHEE

Head south from Dillsboro on US 23/441 toward Franklin, and watch for NC 116 coming in on your left. Turn left on this scenic jog on 116 back toward the east, through the little town of Webster. Then, in several miles you'll come to NC 107. Turn right on 107 and head south toward Cullowhee. Watch for the signs to Cullowhee and Western Carolina University and exit accordingly. Cullowhee and Sylva are only about seven miles apart, so students at the university frequent the restaurants, shops, and music venues in both towns.

Western Carolina University has a respected English Department and, within it, a program in professional writing that includes coursework in screenwriting, technical writing, and writing for the professions, in addition to more traditional offerings in fiction, creative nonfiction, and poetry. Novelist and poet Ron Rash, whose work appears elsewhere in this trail, holds the John A. Parris Jr. and Dorothy Luxton Parris Distinguished Professorship in Appalachian Cultural Studies at Western Carolina. Rick Boyer, a suspense writer, directs the program in professional writing, and poets Catherine Carter and Mary Adams are also among the faculty members here.

Local writer Kathryn Stripling Byer, winner of the Lamont Poetry Prize from the Academy of American Poets, was appointed North Carolina's poet laureate in 2005. She often writes about the hardships of mountain life among earlier generations in western North Carolina. Byer was raised in southwest Georgia, graduated from Wesleyan College in Macon, Georgia, and then came to North Carolina to earn a Master of Fine Arts at the University of North Carolina at Greensboro. She studied there with Allen Tate, Fred Chappell, and Robert Watson before teaching for a time at Western Carolina University. Among her award-winning poetry collections are *Catching Light* (2002), *Black Shawl* (1998), *Wildwood Flower* (1992), and *The Girl in the Midst of the Harvest* (1986). She has been an important mentor to many emerging writers in the state and beyond.

This Byer poem speaks of the river that flows through Cullowhee south along NC 107.

TUCKASEGEE
Wherever I walk in this house
I hear water. Or time.
Which is water, the same

Tuckasegee that runs past my window.
What matter that some days I weary
of it like the songs I hum
over and over again in the kitchen
pretending I cannot hear water departing
though I so plainly hear it
if only from habit? A sequence

of bones rots beneath where I walk
on the trail that unwinds down the hill
to our yard where the leaves also rot.

Every morning I braid what is left
of my hair so that I may unbraid it to braid
it again. So we harvest our gardens

that winter will lay waste.
We mend seams that pull apart
slowly and scrub sweat from what
we have sewn. With the same hands
we knead bread and gather the crumbs

as they fall, put away
what we take out and take stock
of what we have left. It is all the same

work. It has always been
done, this undoing,
ongoing, no matter who
paces the rooms of the houses,
alongside the banks,
whether praising
or cursing whatever is living
or dying within them. Until

it runs out like the river,
our time is the music
the water makes, leaving
who's left of us listening.
—From *Black Shawl*, by Kathryn Stripling Byer
    (Baton Rouge: Louisiana State University Press, 1998), 50.

■ TUCKASEGEE

Continue south from Cullowhee on NC 107, following the Tuckasegee River until it forks in the little village of Tuckasegee, where you will bear right, continuing on 107. Poet and translator Thomas Rain Crowe lives here. In addition to working abroad over a number of years, Crowe was cofounder and director of the San Francisco International Poetry Festival, a founding editor of *Katuah Journal: A Bioregional Journal of the Southern Appalachians*, and founder of New Native Press. His recording label, Fern Hill Records, is devoted to recordings that combine the spoken word and music. In addition to his many far-flung interests, Crowe has been recently writing about his experiences in the North Carolina mountains. His creative nonfiction memoir, *Zoro's Field: My Life in the Appalachian Woods* (2005), began as a series of columns for the *Smoky Mountain News*.

In this poem, Crowe offers a familiar image from the region:

THE SAW-MILL SHACK
    —*for John Edwards Lane*
I have come to this land,
how many years.

Alone, and for many months,
I have built this saw-mill shack.
Stone stacked and mortared on stone,
logs laid and joyned in joints,
rough oak boards nailed to beams and rafters
with 9" spikes.
Eat lunch each day listening to
rushing stream running over rocks,
through rhododendron, off Doubletop Mountain.
Sound of grouse wings drumming in the woods—
With roof on, windows in,
and woodstove sitting in the hearth,
I stand outside gazing at what
these hands have done.
(An old chimney, still standing and covered in vines,
now a place to live.)
Tired from labor and a body
too old for work.
Lay another flat, smooth stone into the outyard wall.
   —John's Creek
     Jackson County, NC
     December 2001

—By Thomas Rain Crowe, from *Nantahala: A Review
of Writing and Photography in Appalachia* 2, no. 2
(Winter–Spring 2004), <http://www.nantahalareview
.org/issue2-2/featured/shack.htm>.

Farther south on 107, you'll come to the town of Glenville and Thorpe Reservoir, more recently named Glenville Lake, the highest lake east of the Mississippi, at an elevation of 3,500 feet. Built in 1940 by the Nantahala Power and Light Company, which was owned by the Aluminum Company of America (Alcoa), the reservoir was designed to support aluminum production for World War II, like several other lakes in the region, including Fontana (see Tour 5). In 1981, Duke Power licensed the facility. Here you will find pleasant camping along the shore, a cool swim, and, often, good fishing.

Continue south and you'll come to Cashiers (pronounced "CASH-ers"), where you'll pick up US 64 West toward Highlands and cross the line from Jackson into Macon County. The elite resort towns of Sapphire, High Hampton, and Lake Toxaway lie to the east on US 64 in Transylvania County. Likewise, Cashiers and Highlands have been developed in a country club style, with both modest and expensive resort homes, some in exclusive, gated communities.

■ HIGHLANDS

CALICO
This mountain laurel
is an apron

whose
delicacy

is no silly frill
pink and girlish

but whose hem
takes up May.
—From *At Dusk Iridescent*, by Thomas Meyer
(Winston-Salem: Jargon Society, 1999), 20.

With a few deft strokes, Highlands poet and translator Thomas Meyer paints a vivid picture of the dense foliage of this section of the North Carolina mountains in spring. Year-round, sunlight must work hard to find the forest bottom in these thickets of rhododendron and laurel along the roadside. Highlands claims to be the highest small town in North Carolina at an elevation of 4,118 feet. The resulting temperatures from such altitude and shade have drawn well-heeled seasonal residents for the better part of a century from places such as Atlanta and Charleston. Novelist Walker Percy, who spent his undergraduate years at the University of North Carolina at Chapel Hill, often traveled from his home in Covington, Louisiana, to write and relax in the cool air of Highlands during the summers from the mid-1970s and into the 1980s. Percy and his wife, Bunt, stayed here at an unpretentious brown cottage with a wide porch that overlooks Lake Sequoyah. It was there that Charlotte poet and journalist Dannye Romine Powell interviewed Percy for her book *Parting the Curtains: Interviews with Southern Writers* (1994). Percy's novel *The Second Coming* (1980) is set in a golfing community in North Carolina called Linwood, which some readers assumed to be the elite resort of Linville near Grandfather Mountain. Actually, the setting was largely based on Percy's golfing experiences in Highlands.

In this area, you're likely to hear the hard "Rs" of mountain folk right alongside the soft "ahh" pronunciation of the same consonant as it comes out of the mouths of those, like Walker Percy, who were born in points south. In Highlands the *Atlanta Journal-Constitution* is the daily newspaper of record, and the barbecue here is smoked and sauced with something red and sweet—no sharp vinegar (pronounced "vinegah" by the transplanted lowlanders).

For its size, Highlands has a remarkable number of upscale antique shops, galleries, and purveyors of pricey home furnishings, jewelry, and clothing. It hosts an annual chamber music festival, and wine tastings are a popular pastime.

Highlands's most notable homegrown writer is poet, publisher, illustrator, and iconoclast Jonathan Williams, who studied at Princeton and then came back south to study at the revolutionary Black Mountain College described in Tour 1. Though he was born in Asheville in 1929 (the same year Thomas Wolfe's *Look Homeward, Angel* was published), Williams has lived on his Skywinding Farm about ten miles south of Highlands for most of his life, with frequent jaunts to England for inspiration.

Williams has published more than fifty books of his own and has brought attention to many other avant-garde writers through his Jargon Press, founded in 1951. Jargon was first headquartered in Penland, North Carolina, and now has offices in Winston-Salem. Williams's own collections include *An Ear in Bartram's Tree* (1969), *Blues and Roots/Rue and Bluets* (1971), and *Elite/Elate Poems* (1979). He has been honored with Guggenheim and National Endowment for the Arts Fellowships and was recipient of the 1977 North Carolina Award in Fine Arts.

Williams's work is ever irreverent, full of wordplay. His poems are funny and at the same time manage to exhort readers to share in the author's outrage at America's lapses into mediocrity. As might be expected, a number of his poems turn a critical lens on the Highlands upper-class social milieu while celebrating the indigenous mountain culture:

THREE SAYINGS FROM HIGHLANDS, NORTH CAROLINA
But pretty though as
roses is
you can put up with
the thorns
   —Doris Talley, Housewife & Gardener

you live until you die—
if the limb don't fall
   —Butler Jenkins, Caretaker

your points is blue
and your timing's
a week off
   —*Sam Creswell, Auto Mechanic*

—From *Blues and Roots/Rue and Bluets: A Garland for
   the Southern Appalachians*, by Jonathan Williams
   (Durham, N.C.: Duke University Press, 1985).

Highlands is also home to Collin Wilcox Paxton, the writer and actress who played the tragic character Mayella Euell in the 1962 film version of Alabama novelist Harper Lee's *To Kill a Mockingbird*, starring Gregory Peck. Paxton was raised in Highlands, where in 1939 her parents and their neighbors founded the Highlands Community Theater, now known as the Highlands Playhouse. On this local stage she began her acting career in *Our Town*, by Thornton Wilder. She attended high school and college in Knoxville at the University of Tennessee and continued her theater studies in Chicago.

Collin Wilcox moved to New York and was accepted to the Actors Studio, where she studied with Lee Strasburg for eight years. Following appearances off and on Broadway, she eventually moved to Los Angeles, appearing in *The Sea Gull* under the direction of John Houseman. Playwright Tennessee Williams soon asked her to repeat her leading role as Isabel in *Period of Adjustment* at the Royal Court Theatre in London.

During her long career, the actress has appeared in films based on the books *Jaws 2*, *Catch 22*, North Carolina writer John Ehle's *Journey of August King*, and *Midnight in the Garden of Good and Evil*. Her first television role was in Eudora Welty's *Member of the Wedding*, produced for *Playhouse 90*. She returned to Highlands in the late 1970s and married Scott R. Paxton, with whom she founded the Highlands Studio for the Arts, now known as the Instant Theatre. She worked with Sylva storyteller Gary Carden to write *Papa's Angels: A Christmas Story* (1996), which was later made into a TV movie. As artistic director of the Instant Theatre, Paxton oversees free acting classes for children, teens, and adults and offers students an opportunity to perform on stage.

■ BARTRAM TRAIL

From 1773 to 1777 Philadelphia naturalist William Bartram traveled throughout the southeast studying the plants and indigenous peoples of the region. He documented his journeys in *Travels through North and South Carolina, Georgia,*

East and West Florida, which has been kept in print by various publishers over the decades. Most recently, Bartram's elegant eighteenth-century prose struck a chord with novelist Charles Frazier, whose *Cold Mountain* protagonist, Inman, reads from Bartram along his journey. Arguably Bartram's lyricism influenced Frazier as he gave voice to Inman. The formal prose of an earlier century shines through in this passage from Bartram:

> The day being remarkably warm and sultry, together with the labour and fatigue of ascending the mountains, made me very thirsty and in some degree sunk my spirits. Now past mid-day, I sought a cool shaded retreat, where was water for refreshment and grazing for my horse, my faithful slave and only companion. After proceeding a little farther, descending the other side of the mountain, I perceived at some distance before me, on my right hand, a level plain supporting a grand high forest and groves: the nearer I approached, my steps were the more accelerated from the flattering prospect opening to view. I now entered upon the verge of the dark forest, charming solitude! as I advanced through the animating shades, observed on the farther grassy verge of a shady grove: thither I directed my steps. On approaching these shades, between the stately columns of the superb forest trees, presented to view, rushing from rocky precipices under the shade of the pensile hills, the unparalleled cascade of Falling Creek, rolling and leaping off the rocks; the waters united below, spread a broad glittering sheet over a vast convex elevation of plain smooth rocks, and are immediately received by a spacious bason, where trembling in the center through hurry and agitation, they gently subside, encircling the painted still verge; from whence gliding swiftly, they soon form a delightful little river, which continuing to flow more moderately, is restrained for a moment, gently undulating in a little lake: they then pass rapidly to a high perpendicular steep of rocks, from whence these delightful waters are hurried down with irresistible rapidity. I here seated myself on the moss-clad rocks, under the shade of spreading trees and floriferous fragrant shrubs, in full view of the cascades. —From *Travels of William Bartram*, ed. Mark Van Doren (New York: Dover Publications, 1955), 277–78.

Today the North Carolina Bartram Trail Society maintains a hundred-mile memorial footpath to honor William Bartram. The trail actually begins in Georgia and crosses the North Carolina state line in Macon County near Rabun Bald, continuing along the ridge tops all the way to Cheoah Bald in Graham County. Along the way, it crosses the Appalachian Trail twice.

To get to the trail, head southwest on NC 106 out of Highlands toward Dillard, Georgia. Just three miles south of town, you may want to make a stop at Glen Falls, which can be reached from a dirt road marked by a U.S. Forest Service sign. The steep, one-mile hike down to a dramatic series of three sixty-foot cascades is a good spot to read from William Bartram before heading down the road to pick up the memorial trail.

To get to the Bartram Trail from Glen Falls, continue driving south on NC 106 and look for the Osage Overlook. If you cross the Georgia line, you've gone too far. Stop at the overlook to get a view of Scaly and Osage Mountains. Across the road is the Bartram Trail entrance. This long trail is divided and mapped in seven sections. The Bartram Trail Society strongly urges hikers to obtain the relevant section map, which is available from the U.S. Forest Service. The trail blazes are marked in yellow with a number of side trails marked in blue.

If you'd rather proceed north from Highlands to connect with Tour 4, you can still pick up the Bartram Trail in Franklin, where it ascends the Nantahala Mountains to the 5,385-foot Wayah Bald, the highest point on the trail. For more complete information on the trail, see <http://www.ncbartramtrail.org/> or e-mail info@ncbartramtrail.org.

■ CULLASAJA GORGE

To end this tour, head once more out of Highlands on US 64/NC 28 toward the Macon County seat of Franklin, eighteen miles away, where you can pick up Tour 4. Notice the well-kept second homes of Highland's summer residents that are tucked away on the hills and along the steep banks of the many-fingered Lake Sequoyah, so named for the Cherokee chief who invented the first written language among Native Americans. Soon the road enters the Nantahala Forest and begins its sharp descent alongside Cullasaja Gorge. This road is not for the faint-hearted: it is narrow, flanked on one side by a rock wall and on the other side by a sheer drop-off into the spectacular gorge.

Bridal Veil Falls comes first; you can easily see it from the road. Next comes Dry Falls, four miles out of Highlands. Park and walk to this seventy-five-foot falls. Bust Your Butt Falls, which is seven miles outside of Highlands, is the fourth falls along this route and quite popular with children. The most dramatic, Cullasaja Falls, is a 250-foot cascade that's nine miles from town. All along this road there are not as many pullouts as you might wish, but then building this narrow lip of a road was a feat in the first place, so proceed slowly and experience it all. To obtain a map of the many waterfalls in the area, visit: <http://www.highlandsinfo.com/maps/mapwaterfalls.htm>.

City Lights Bookstore

3 East Jackson Street
Sylva, NC 28779
828-586-9499
888-853-6298 (toll free)
more@citylightsnc.com
<http://www.citylightsnc.com/>

Opened in 1984 by local storyteller and writer Gary Carden, this homey bookstore is a good place to begin your visit in Sylva. It's right downtown, one block up the hill from Main Street at the corner of Spring and Jackson streets. "Our goal is to share the literature of the Appalachian region with the world and the world of good books with our community," proclaims the City Lights website. Joyce Moore purchased the shop in 1986 and moved it to its present location with great fanfare. According to North Carolina poet laureate Kathryn Stripling Byer, "City Lights is a beacon in this area. Joyce Moore and her staff are regional treasures."

The bookstore also houses Spring Street Editions, a small publishing concern that issued *Gatherings: Poems by 36 Western North Carolina Poets* in 2001 and Byer's 2003 chapbook, *Wake*. The bookstore hosts regular readings for children and adults and has a large selection of used books across all genres along with some CDs and gifts. Curiously, like half a dozen other bookstores in this part of the state, City Lights has a resident cat. Her name is Miss Kitty, and she generally stays close to the cash register waiting for a belly rub. Like the old-fashioned general store of yore, on one evening a week City Lights hosts a spirited card game at a long table set out in the North Carolina section toward the back of the shop.

Jackson County Public Library

755 West Main Street
Sylva, NC 28779
828-586-2016
<http://www.fontanalib.org/sylva/>

Right down the steps from the courthouse in Sylva is the Jackson County Library. The library hosts a regular story time for children on Thursdays and has an active friends organization that runs a used bookstore at 536 West Main Street (across from the *Sylva Herald* newspaper offices). Computers with Internet access are available in the library.

A cozy reading room in City Lights Bookstore of Sylva.

The Well House
65 Craft Circle
Dillsboro, NC 28725
828-586-8588

Since 1977, this German deli in Dillsboro has been making its own sauerkraut for amazing Reuben sandwiches on pumpernickel bread. Homemade soups and barbecue are also specialties on the menu here. Long a favorite of local novelist Sue Ellen Bridgers, the restaurant is perched high on the hill overlooking Dillsboro. The staff will pack you a picnic by request. If you're coming from Sylva on US 23/74, turn left on US 23/441 toward Franklin, cross the bridge over the Tuckasegee River, and take the first driveway into the Riverwood Shops.

Hunter Library
Western Carolina University
176 Central Drive
Cullowhee, NC 28723
828-227-7485
<http://www.wcu.edu/library/>

Western Carolina University's Hunter Library is home to the papers and photos of author and oral historian Horace Kephart. Novelist Sue Ellen Bridgers also donated her archives to Special Collections. Extensive materials on the Cherokee Indians, including more than 250 original issues of the *Cherokee Phoenix*, a national newspaper published by the Cherokee Nation from 1828 to 1834 using both English and the Cherokee syllabary, are also preserved here. These newspapers document the struggle of the Cherokee people to hold onto their land, reject assimilation, and organize themselves politically. The newspaper ceased publication shortly before the forced removal of the Cherokee people to Oklahoma on the Trail of Tears. Call for hours and rules regarding the use of these Special Collections.

Mountain Heritage Center

150 H. F. Robinson Building
Western Carolina University
Cullowhee, NC 28723
828-227-7129
<http://www.wcu.edu/mhc/>

With three major galleries, the Mountain Heritage Center on the WCU campus presents a changing array of permanent and traveling exhibits on site and several virtual exhibits available on the Internet. The center focuses on the Appalachian region—specifically on its music, crafts, environment, and local cultural practices. Demonstrations related to aspects of mountain culture such as preserving and canning vegetables, blacksmithing, pottery making, and mountain music and dance are a regular practice. The center also hosts slide show/lectures on environmental topics and a number of summer day camps for children. Regular weekend cultural arts programs for families are called "Arti-Facts." School groups visit the center regularly for special programs. Admission to exhibits is free. Visit the website for a complete calendar of events.

WCU Spring Literary Festival

c/o English Department
Western Carolina University
Cullowhee, NC 28723
828-227-7264
<http://www.litfestival.org>

In recent years, the WCU Visiting Writers' Series, the English Department, and several other campus organizations have put together a three-day literary festival with guest lectures, readings, panel discussions, workshops, and a banquet. Generally, all events are free and open to the public. Check the website for details.

Highlands Playhouse

362 Oak Street
Highlands, NC 28741
828-526-2695
<http://www.highlandsplayhouse.org>

With four productions a year drawn from popular theater, this group is still going strong after more than a half-century. Call for dates and performance times.

Instant Theatre Company

348 South 5th Street
Highlands, NC 28741
828-526-1687 (studio)
828-342-9197 (box office)
info@instanttheatre.org
<http://www.instanttheatre.org/>

This local troupe launched by Scott and Collin Wilcox Paxton in 1981 offers less traditional productions and an opportunity for local performers, writers, directors, and technicians to hone their craft and work with young people in the area.

Cyrano's Bookshop

390 Main Street
Highlands, NC 28741
828-526-5488
<http://www.cyranosbookshop.com/>

With a gallery on one side and a terrific coffee shop and music listening room on the other, this little bookstore is a cozy place to look for new titles, light reading material, and regional literature.

Franklin : Hayesville : Brasstown : Murphy : Texana

This region inspired the first novel ever written in North Carolina and gave birth to a national treasure—the John C. Campbell Folk School. Explore remote areas where refugees of the Civil War hid themselves and where moonshine was made with impunity. Stories abound, including that of a rare Appalachian enclave of African Americans that has endured for more than 150 years.

Writers with a connection to this area: John C. Campbell, Olive Dame Campbell, Jan Davidson, George Ellison, Charles Frazier, Peter Jenkins, Terry Kay, Silas McDowell, Barbara McRae, Janice Townley Moore, Charles F. Price, Margaret Siler, Nancy Simpson, Robert Strange, Shirley Uphouse

■ FRANKLIN

Franklin, the seat of Macon County, is an important crossroads. It is surrounded by dramatic mountains—the Cowees lie to the north and east, the Nantahala Mountains to the west. Due south along the Little Tennessee River is a passage to Atlanta—making Franklin a frequent first stop for Georgians seeking the cooler air of western North Carolina. Franklin's population nearly doubles in summer.

Nicknamed "Ruby City" and known for its gem shows and rock shops, Franklin also has the literary distinction of being home to Silas McDowell, a prolific writer, botanist, and apple grower in the nineteenth century. McDowell was the first in the region to propose the concept of thermal belts—a principle important to orchard owners. Thermal belts, he hypothesized, are zones on the mountainside where frost and freezes are less common than in the valleys and on the mountaintops.

According to Bryson City naturalist and columnist George

tour 4

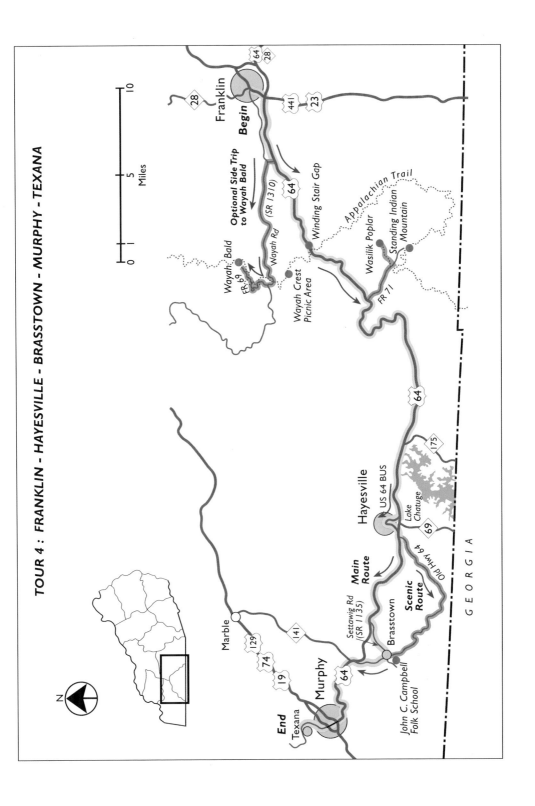

TOUR 4 : FRANKLIN - HAYESVILLE - BRASSTOWN - MURPHY - TEXANA

Ellison, Silas McDowell discovered or introduced at least fifteen new apple varieties during the 1850s and collected specimens for other botanists, including Asa Gray. McDowell published his writing in *Harper's*, the *North Carolina Planter*, the *Raleigh Observer*, and *Southern Cultivator*. He also served as the local clerk of court.

Silas McDowell was known in town as a keen student of history and a talented teller of local legends. He is credited as the source for much of the background material that served as the basis for North Carolina's first novel. *Eoneguski, or, The Cherokee Chief: A Tale of Past Wars* was written by U.S. senator Robert Strange and published in 1839 by Franck Taylor Publishers of Washington, D.C.

Before taking up writing, Robert Strange had served as district court judge in Waynesville and often traveled to Franklin, where he met and befriended Silas McDowell. He was elected to the U.S. Senate in 1836 and finished his historical novel after two years in Washington.

Strange earned an advance of $600 for the book, based loosely on local legends. It traces the life of John Welch, a half-French, half-Cherokee man from Franklin who is called upon to avenge the death of one of his Cherokee clansmen. The incident sets off a series of revenge killings until Eoneguski, a wise Cherokee chief and counselor, stops the killing and later uncovers his own kinship to Welch.

According to Franklin writer and publisher Barbara McRae of Teresita Press, Strange's novel "was an ambitious border romance in the [James Fenimore] Cooper tradition." She notes that its popularity was limited, however, in part because the book "presented unflattering portraits of some powerful western North Carolina families." Issued around the time of the Cherokee removal, the book also suffered because "people did not want to be troubled by Strange's humanistic presentation of the Cherokees" (see <http://www.teresita.com/html/eoneguski.html>).

Today, the entire text of the novel is available online as part of the UNC–Chapel Hill Library's Documenting the American South project. In this passage from the introduction to the novel, the narrator describes his first visit to Franklin, where he is soon taken on a tour of area waterfalls by the local clerk of court, undoubtedly Silas McDowell thinly disguised as "Mr. McDonald."

An hour's riding brought us where Mr. McDonald informed me our horses could no longer be useful; we accordingly tied them to a limb of a tree, and began, on foot, to encounter the very steep ascent formed by the mountains so closing in as to leave only a very narrow pass for the brawling stream. After laborious climbing for another hour, we reached the Falls, which, I confess, disappointed me, and I was even so impolite as to acknowledge it to my guide. But the wild and picturesque scenery through which I had passed would have repaid me for my fatigue, had I found nothing more. But the phrenologists say my organ of alimentiveness is a good deal developed, and proves that I have an especial relish for good eating and drinking; and I do not know that the aforesaid propensity of my nature has ever been more highly treated than on my present visit.

As we turned to descend—"We must take a salmon home with us for dinner," said Mr. McDonald.

"A salmon?" said I, in unfeigned surprise.

"Yes," replied my host, in his quiet way, "a salmon."

"You are jesting with me," said I.

"Indeed I am not," said Mr. McDonald, deliberately seating himself by the side of the stream we had regained, and pulling off his coat, shoes and stockings, and rolling up his pantaloons and shirt sleeves.

In a moment more he was in the water, turning over the large rocks, with as much earnestness as if he had expected to find a bag of gold beneath each of them. I looked on, puzzled what to think of my new acquaintance. At length he succeeded in slightly shaking a very large rock, which defied all his efforts to turn it over, when instantly there dashed from beneath it what, at first, appeared to me to be a perfect monster. Mr. McDonald immediately rushed in pursuit, and a more amusing spectacle I never witnessed for twelve or fifteen minutes. The water was splashed about in every direction, so as to leave not a dry garment upon the pursuer, as a large fish darted from one hiding place to another, with fruitless efforts to avail himself of it. Sometimes the hand of the extraordinary fisherman was fairly upon him, but the lubricity of his scales would save him, and afford him another chance for escape. At length, however, when nearly exhausted with his bootless exertions, Mr. McDonald succeeded in dexterously thrusting his hand into the gills of the fish, which now lashed the water into a perfect foam, and sent the spray in every direction, like a shower of rain. But the relentless foe held on, with tenacious grasp, and dragged him to the shore. My assistance now seemed necessary to prevent the captive from regaining his native element, so completely had the captor expended his strength in the double labor of turning over the rocks to dislodge the game and securing it afterwards.

As soon as Mr. McDonald had sufficiently recovered himself, we re-paired to our horses with our prize, which he fastened behind his saddle. We then proceeded to his house, where Mrs. McDonald prepared for us a most sumptuous dinner, of which the captive fish constituted an impor-tant part, and was, by far, the finest, both in looks and flavor, I had ever tasted.—From *Eoneguski, or, The Cherokee Chief: A Tale of Past Wars*, by Robert Strange (1839, see <http://docsouth.unc.edu/nc/strange1/strange1.html>).

A historical marker to Silas McDowell is located southeast of Franklin on US 64/NC 28, which bypasses downtown. The marker is at the intersection with Peaceful Cove Road (SR 1677).

Even in the 1830s, as described by novelist Robert Strange, the Nikwasi In-dian Mound in downtown Franklin was a popular attraction with visitors. The Nikwasi site is reportedly the largest and best-preserved mound in western North Carolina, and the only one that is publicly owned. Look for the Nikwasi Mound beside Business 441 (Main Street) in downtown Franklin. Because this region was home to the Cherokee people when the white settlers moved in, many tribal names and legends are still much a part of the local landscape. The Indian settlement at the site of present-day Franklin was originally named Nikwasi.

■ WAYAH BALD

Head west out of Franklin and drive toward Hayesville on US 64 to reach Wayah Bald. It's a bit of a drive to get there, but once you do, there's a paved walk to the summit that's wheelchair accessible. At the top, the bald has an observation tower built by the Civilian Conservation Corps in the 1930s, mark-ing the intersection of the Bartram Trail and the Appalachian Trail. Four states are visible from this tower on clear days. As local historian and writer Marga-ret Siler tells us, Wayah is the Cherokee name for wolf, and though the wolves disappeared with the coming of the white settlers, this bald is notable for its wildflowers and the white and pink azaleas that burst forth in May and June. (By contrast, Standing Indian Mountain—also on this tour—blooms in profu-sion with purple rhododendrons, says Siler.) Wayah Bald is reportedly a good site for bird watching. Warblers, grouse, scarlet tanagers, veeries, and ovenbirds have been spotted here. Archaeological evidence suggests that native peoples as far back as 300 B.C. have used Wayah. Wayah is also a setting in Charles Frazier's second novel, *Thirteen Moons* (2006).

On US 64, three miles out of Franklin, look for Old Murphy Road and the Wayah Bald sign. Turn right and drive 0.2 miles to Wayah Road (SR 1310). Turn left and continue for nine miles to Wayah Gap and Forest Road 69. (Wayah Crest Picnic Area is on the left.) Turn right onto FR 69 and drive 4.4 steep miles to the Wayah Bald parking area.

■ STANDING INDIAN MOUNTAIN

A little farther west of Franklin is the legendary Standing Indian Mountain. To get there, continue on US 64 to the Clay County line and look for Forest Road 71 (gravel) on the left. On this road, before you get to the Standing Indian campground, you might want to stop for the three-quarter-mile trail to the enormous Wasilik Poplar, a tree so large that foresters at the beginning of the twentieth century apparently did not cut it because they knew they couldn't carry the lumber out of its steep location.

Proceeding from this stop, you can reach the trailhead for Standing Indian by continuing on FR 71 six miles to Deep Gap. From the parking area, the top of Standing Indian Mountain is a moderate five-mile hike.

The story of Standing Indian Mountain is told by poet and oral historian Margaret Redding Siler, who came from Georgia to Macon County in 1900 to marry. She was especially curious about her husband's deep roots in the area, including his kinship to Jacob Siler, who first settled here in 1818. In the 1930s, she recorded oral histories from Civil War survivors and at least one former slave from Yancey County.

In her writing, Siler frequently reveals her unabashed horror at the historic mistreatment of the Cherokee people. She became a student of the Cherokee language under the tutelage of her father-in-law, Albert Siler. In her collection of stories and memories called *Cherokee Indian Lore and Smoky Mountain Stories*, first published in 1938, she offers a rudimentary vocabulary and pronunciation guide. She also preserves many early legends from both Cherokee and white pioneer families.

In "Why the Mountains Are Bald" Siler recounts the legend of Tau-keet-ta —a great monster that "swooped down from the clouds" and carried off one of the Cherokee children "in talons bigger than a man's hand." Indian braves "finally traced the monster to a hiding place or den on the steepest side of You-wah-chula-na-yeh, Standing Indian Mountain. The Indians could not trace the Tau-keet-ta's flight because of the forests on the mountain crests. With their crude stone axes, they cleared the timber from the tops to have a clear view of the terrible bird's movements," Siler writes. Eventually, with the help of the Great Spirit, a great storm arose and split the mountain in half, revealing the monster's den. The native people vowed that never again should any mountain-top be covered with timber that concealed the dens of the Tau-keet-ta. "It was through this legend that Standing Indian got its name," writes Siler. "Through the ages, the weather has worn away the arms of the figure, but a pillar of stone with a head still stands, giving the name, as the Cherokees would say it, Indian Standing, not Standing Indian" (*Cherokee Indian Lore and Smoky Mountain Stories*, by Margaret Siler [Franklin, N.C.: Teresita Press, 1980], 34–37).

■ CHUNKY GAL MOUNTAIN AND WINDING STAIR GAP

Continuing west on US 64 toward Hayesville you'll also cross Chunky Gal Mountain—so named in Cherokee legend and now a spot popular with rock hounds. At Winding Stair Gap (watch for the sign) there's an 8.8 mile hike to another summit, named Siler Bald after William Siler, brother of Jacob, the first Siler to come west to these mountains. This bald is 5,216 feet at the peak and offers views close to 360 degrees.

This territory appears frequently in the work of Nancy Simpson, author of the poetry collections *Across Water* (1983) and *Night Student* (1985). Simpson was for many years the director of the North Carolina Writers' Network West and is resident writer at the John C. Campbell Folk School. This poem describes a nighttime drive over Winding Stair Gap:

NIGHT STUDENT
It is the first shooting star my eyes have seen
breaking blackness above the university parking lot.
I am impressed with Jones,
The spectacular mark he made on my paper.
I have it beside me two hours from home.

Truth is up there over the steering wheel,
keeping up, 60 mph on Franklin By-Pass.
Socrates said so. I would like to ask
the Know-It-All what makes stars break.

I drive slow on Standing Indian Mountain
and count the times Jones asked in class,
Is it logically consistent? Ten.
On the radio, static reception,

Linda Ronstadt is singing about a broken lady
waiting to be mended.

I see my face in the rear view mirror,
not a wife anymore, not a mother,
a thirty-eight year old freshman
chewing leftover cheese crackers
that crumble on my fingers, star showers
into the floorboard.

What was it I saw up there, white against black,
like white hairs in brunette,
like the white line on the pavement?

What is it at two minutes past twelve,
this funnel cloud in me, this song of Forsythia
makes me stop my car at Shooting Creek
to search in space above trees
where headlights do not reach?

Star, one cut with your sword,
you have sliced the night open for me.
—From *Night Student*, by Nancy Simpson
    (Pittsford, N.Y.: State Street Press, 1985), 21.

■ LAKE CHATUGE

By now, you've come a distance of thirty-five miles from Franklin to reach
Hayesville, the county seat and the only incorporated township in Clay County,
one of the smallest counties in North Carolina. Just before you get to town,
you'll see Lake Chatuge on your left. In 1942 the Tennessee Valley Authority
created the lake, Clay County's most beautiful human-made resource. A quiet,
relatively undiscovered body of water, Chatuge has camping, cottages, and
boat rentals all around the shoreline that circles from North Carolina into Georgia and back. Georgia novelist Terry Kay set his eleventh book, *The Valley of
Light* (2003), here. Part of what makes the lake so striking is the view of Brasstown Bald, Georgia's highest peak, and the pale blue Tusquitee Mountains in
the distance. In Cherokee "Tusquitee" means the place "where the water dogs
laughed," a phrase that Charles F. Price used as the title for his fourth novel
about the region.

Price, who has probably written more about this area than any other novelist, was born in Clyde, North Carolina, and now lives in Yancey County, south of Burnsville. His father was a Methodist minister who was born to a farming family in Clay County. His mother attended Penland School in Mitchell County when it was an Episcopal mission for poor mountain children. The family traveled from town to town in the mountains as Price's father was appointed to different congregations. Price left the region to attend High Point College and the University of North Carolina at Chapel Hill. He worked for many years as a journalist, consultant, and Washington lobbyist before returning to his native region to write.

Price's first novel, *Hiwassee: A Novel of the Civil War* (1996), details the story of conflicts among families in the region before and after Emancipation. *Freedom's Altar* (1999), his second novel, earned him the Sir Walter Raleigh Award for the best work of fiction by a North Carolinian. In it Price continued the story begun in the first novel, loosely based on his father's family history during Reconstruction. His third novel, *The Cock's Spur* (2000), takes on yet another generation of the Price family, including a moonshiner-turned-government spy. In the novel Price also introduces the character of Hamby McFee, a mixed-blood misfit who turns up again in Price's fourth novel searching for a giant bear. In the scene excerpted here, Hamby McFee's nemesis, G. G. M. Weatherby, a greedy timber developer, is also in pursuit of the elusive great bear:

> In the stillness he heard it breathe. A hoarse chuffing like a locomotive laboring up a steep grade. He dared not even move. There was a round in the chamber of the Winchester but he would have to cock the hammer before he could shoot and as close as the bear was, it might well hear the snick of the hammer and bolt back into the forest. Weatherby sure as hell didn't want that. But neither did he want a scared bear blundering over him by accident in a blind fog.
>
> He considered his options. His heart might be throbbing from the thrill of his plight but he was as calm as he had ever been, and as he debated what to do, he could not help noting with pride how serene and confident he felt, how certain of his own mastery. Above the chuffing of the bear he heard its great weight shift in the rhododendron, heard the stalks pop and the leaves shiver. Another wave of its bitter smell passed over him. The moist air hung heavy; he could feel no breeze; if the bear were so close and had not yet caught his scent, he must be in its lee. Like all its kind the beast was nearsighted; the fog was thick as fleece; maybe it didn't even know he was there. If that was right, then he had the advantage.

He rested the tip of his thumb on the knurled spur of the hammer. That was when the bear came. Nothing had ever moved so fast. All he saw was a blur of cinnamon as huge as the side of a boxcar. That and the sweep of the mighty paw. He only had time to feel the round and empty hole in the middle of him that he had never felt before but that he nevertheless knew was the fear he had always denied, and then there was a shock; the Winchester sailed end-over-end; a blast of hot breath scorched him; and he was down. Stunned, he rolled off the rock and lay on his back in the wet bracken. Somewhere a bird sang.—From *Where the Water-Dogs Laughed: The Story of the Great Bear*, by Charles F. Price (Boone. N.C.: High Country Publishers, 2003), 82.

■ HAYESVILLE

Just beyond Lake Chatuge, take the business loop of US 64 to find downtown Hayesville, the county seat. With its beautiful valleys and relative isolation, Clay County offers rich material to the writers who live and visit here. Like a number of other Appalachian Mountain counties, Clay was formed during the Civil War when residents of the southeastern end of Cherokee County elected not to secede from the Union and formed their own county. Named in honor of Henry Clay of Kentucky, the name might just have easily been evoked by the distinctive veins of gummy red dirt running through the landscape here.

The county's political cussedness continues today, as evidenced in Hayesville, with its population of fewer than 300 residents. This tiny town manages to support not just one but two weekly newspapers—the *Smoky Mountain Sentinel* and *Clay County Progress*—which have long conducted a vigorous and ongoing partisan debate from their perches on opposite sides of the town square. The square itself is classic, with a gazebo for band concerts and a handsome tree-shaded lawn. The 1889 Clay County Courthouse, recently renovated, is on the National Register of Historic Places.

A historical marker on the square commemorates Fort Hembree, founded in 1837. The fort served as one of the key holding sites for the Cherokee people who were rounded up by General Winfield Scott for removal on what came to be known as the Trail of Tears. Today poet Janice Townley Moore lives with her family on the site of Fort Hembree. She was poetry editor of *Georgia Journal* for a dozen years and is professor of English and chair of the Humanities Division at Young Harris College, just across the state line in Georgia.

Living on the site of Fort Hembree,
we hear the moan of wind
circling our house.
We show guests the greenest spot
on the lawn where the Fort's sunken well
now yields a weeping cherry.
Our son finds stones in the garden,
declaring them arrowheads
and disks of granite
where he says Indians once ground corn.
Today he brings for my belief
two jagged triangles, says
This little Indian was just starting
to make arrowheads
and that's as good as he could carve.
These with a dozen tomahawk heads
smoothed by the creek
line our carport for all to admire.
We bruise our toes upon them in the dark.
—Used by permission of Janice Townley Moore

■ BRASSTOWN AND THE JOHN C. CAMPBELL FOLK SCHOOL

Brasstown, a little crossroads where craft stores line up their wares on the sidewalk, can be reached from Hayesville by heading west on US 64 toward Murphy. (Watch for signs to Brasstown and turn left at Settawig Road [SR 1135].) Or you can take a more scenic and leisurely route on Old Highway 64 West, which comes out of downtown Hayesville and crosses over the newer and larger US 64. On this ten-mile meander, Cherry and Shew Bird Mountains appear on the left, where the Devil's Post Office is tucked away. Poet Nancy Simpson explains that the Devil's Post Office was once the site where young people left love notes in the cautious days of formal courtship. Farther along, as the road comes close to the town of Brasstown, the creek by the same name runs briskly alongside the road on the left.

In recent years, Brasstown has received national attention as the home of the annual New Year's Eve "Possum Drop." Clay Logan is the proprietor of Clay's Corner, a local gas station and regular venue for live music and ice cream. Each

December, Logan catches a possum several weeks before the festivities and feeds the animal extravagantly. To ring in the New Year, he suspends the possum in its cage outside the store and lowers it slowly and harmlessly to the ground. A Possum Queen is also crowned during the celebration. The only requirement to enter the pageant is that all contestants must be male. (Note that Clay's Corner also specializes in possum-themed souvenirs.)

Brasstown is also the address for the John C. Campbell Folk School, located just across the creek in Cherokee County. (Turn across the creek at Clay's Corner and follow the signs.) Olive Dame Campbell and her friend Marguerite Butler founded the historic school in 1925.

Olive Dame Campbell, born in Massachusetts, was a writer and a student of folklore. She first came to southern Appalachia with her husband, John C. Campbell, a midwesterner who had studied education at Williams College and theology at Andover Theological Seminary. Before meeting Olive, John had been principal of a school in the mountains of northern Alabama, worked briefly in Wisconsin, and then returned to the Appalachians as principal of a school in Tennessee. He became dean and later president of Piedmont College in Demorest, Georgia. Through all these appointments, John C. Campbell developed a keen interest in the economic struggles of the Appalachian people.

Campbell's first wife, Grace, died in 1905, and two years later, he resigned from Piedmont College, married Olive Dame, and took a much-needed European vacation. Not long after, John and Olive Campbell moved to the southern highlands, where John had finally obtained financial support to conduct his long-hoped-for survey of the region. He aimed to focus on the social conditions of mountain life and the needs of the people. By 1913, John and Olive Campbell had established a base of operations in Asheville and had become friends of Warren Wilson and other denominational and secular "missionaries" who sought to ameliorate the poverty and lack of social services in the region.

With ongoing funding by the Russell Sage Foundation, the Campbells traveled all over Appalachia. For her part, Olive collected ballads and studied the handicrafts of the mountain people. Her song collection, begun in 1907 and written down from memory, was eventually reproduced in the book, *English Folk Songs from the Southern Appalachians* (1917), coauthored with Cecil J. Sharp. The story of Sharp's and Campbell's work together became the basis for the film *Songcatcher*, filmed near Asheville and released in 2000.

Meanwhile, John Campbell collected reams of data and had begun outlining a book that many observers were eager for him to publish, but Campbell demurred, preferring to continue his research over a number of years. In their travels, both Campbells came to the conclusion that although their living conditions needed improvement, mountain people possessed strong and valuable traditions that should be preserved. The Campbells believed that education—properly offered as an affirmation of local talent—could help deter young people from leaving the region for a better living elsewhere.

Murphy native Jan Davidson, current director of the John C. Campbell Folk School and a writer himself, explains: "John Campbell was in Washington, D.C., in May of 1919 when he got an urgent call to come to New York to see about the possibility of additional funding for his work. He and Olive ran all the way to Union Station and made the train, but John then suffered a heart attack from the exertion. By the time they reached New York, a doctor told the Campbells that there wasn't much time left."

John asked Olive to write a few things down. He told his wife that he looked forward to heaven where he would see the two infant daughters the couple had lost early in their marriage. He also said he planned to have a talk with Saint Paul about his theology.

John C. Campbell died that day in New York City at the age of fifty-one. Olive buried her husband in Medford, Massachusetts, and went straightaway to their small cottage in Nantucket, where she pulled together all of her husband's notes. "So the real author of *The Southern Highlander and His Homeland* was Olive Dame Campbell," says Jan Davidson.

"It is this book," Olive modestly writes in the preface, "completed from the notes and material which he left and from a knowledge of his general point of view and conclusions, that is now presented to the public. No one can be more conscious of its limitations and defects than the editor, whose office—great as was the happiness that attended it—was not always an easy one" (*The Southern Highlander and His Homeland* [1921; Lexington: University Press of Kentucky, 1969], xv).

And here the story of the John C. Campbell Folk School actually begins. After completing the book, Olive and a friend, Marguerite Butler, traveled to Denmark to study the folk school movement there. *Folkehøjskoles* were places where Danish farmers learned basic skills to help them thrive on the land and build a stronger rural spirit. Founded by Danish poet, hymn writer, and theologian N. F. S. Grundtvig, the folk school was an alternative to book-based academics; it was designed to foster civil discourse, neighborly debate, civic pride, and hands-on learning. The schools sought to encourage rural folk to stay on the land and maintain their agricultural identity rather than leave for the city or other European countries.

"Olive also wrote the only book in English on the folk school movement," Jan Davidson says. She and Marguerite Butler returned to the United States with

"I am just a common farmer, I sing behind the plough . . ." was Olive Dame Campbell's choice of a motto for the John C. Campbell Folk School.

a mission. They were determined to start a folk school in Appalachia. When Butler came to Brasstown and described their dream to Fred Scroggs, a local merchant, Scroggs talked up the idea to his neighbors, and some 200 citizens showed up to meet with Butler several weeks later. Scroggs himself donated seventy-five acres to start the school, and local residents pledged their labor to build the facilities. The John C. Campbell Folk School started in 1925 and was dedicated to the memory of Olive's late husband. Today, most of the school's buildings are on the National Register of Historic Places. Surrounded by cultivated fields and tree-shaded walking paths, the school's more than 300 acres and twenty-some buildings reflect a handsome aesthetic, filled with color, light, and creative energy.

As Jan Davidson once put it: "In the beginning this school was started by people from 'off'—that's what we call people who aren't from around here. People from 'off' came here to civilize the mountain people and . . . to run this school. Well now," Davidson said with a grin, "the school is run by me and mostly other people from here, and people from 'off' come *here* to get civilized."

Though its mission has changed somewhat over the years, the John C. Campbell Folk School still preserves and perpetuates traditional handicrafts, indigenous performing arts, and skills for living on the land. The school's weeklong and weekend classes are taught by practitioners. There are no grades, exams, or lectures. Students learn by doing while living in community. Blacksmithing, quilting, spinning, basket weaving, beading, broom making, jewelry, glassblowing, genealogy, book arts, dance, embroidery, cooking, clay, woodturning, and storytelling are among the residential workshops offered from January to September each year. Creative writing workshops also have an important place in the school's catalogue. Visitors are welcome on campus to observe classes, tour the museum and craft store, and attend evening performances. Dinner is available to daytime visitors by advance reservation.

Readings featuring faculty and students take place in the "Living Room" of the Folk School's administrative building every third Thursday night of the month, sponsored by the North Carolina Writers' Network West. They're well attended by students taking classes in other disciplines. Community music performances are held on Friday evenings, and a concert series takes place on Sundays. For more information visit <http://www.folkschool.org> or call 1-800-365-5724.

■ MURPHY

Continue west on US 64 to reach Murphy. Always cited as the westernmost town in North Carolina, probably because it rolls off the tongue well when paired alliteratively with Manteo to the east, Murphy is a sprawling town with chain stores and fast food eateries along its bypass. However, take the time to explore the main artery, called Valley River Avenue downtown. Murphy's old-fashioned town center has an ice cream shop, a classic drug store, antique shops, many ethnic restaurants, and an office supply store that sells handsome hardcover journals.

The Cherokee County Courthouse, on the corner of Peachtree and Central, was built in 1926 of blue marble. The Cherokee County Museum, next door, has an interesting collection of artifacts from the many settlements of native and European peoples in the county.

■ TEXANA

Up a steep hill, only a mile from downtown Murphy, is the historic African American community of Texana, named for Texana McClelland who settled here in the 1850s. Tennessee writer Peter Jenkins documented this tenacious settlement in his book *A Walk Across America*. A bestseller when it was reissued by Perennial Press in 2001, the book was first published in 1979. Jenkins lived

Texana is a historic African American settlement north of Murphy that was described in A Walk Across America, *by Peter Jenkins.*

for a time in this African American enclave in the Smoky Mountains—a rarity in a region where American Indians and European Americans predominate.

Today, Texana still has some 150 residents, and the centerpiece of the community is the Mount Zion Baptist Church, an impressive facility that sits on the site of the original First Baptist Church. First built as a log structure, the church was replaced in 1881 and again nearly one hundred years later. Up until the 1920s, the children of Texana attended school in this church. Finally, residents built a one-room schoolhouse that was the only African American school in Cherokee County until the Texana and Murphy schools were integrated in 1965. According to the North Carolina Language and Life Project at N.C. State University, "Each year at homecoming, community members gather at the church to read the biography of Texana and recount stories of early life in the community. Residents have always viewed Texana as a strong black community, and a few years ago community members began an oral history and quilt project in order to preserve stories of kinship and history in the community." (See <http://www.ncsu.edu/linguistics/code/Research%20Sites/texana.htm>.)

At the central crossroads in downtown Murphy where Valley River Avenue and Tennessee, Hiawassee, and Peachtree Streets all meet at a traffic light, turn onto Tennessee Street, heading away from the courthouse. You'll pass the Henn Theater with its bright orange "H" and go across two bridges. Look for a Texaco station and turn left on Texana Road, only 0.8 miles from the town center. This lane will carry you straight uphill and into historic Texana.

■ LITERARY LANDSCAPE

Books Unlimited

60 East Main Street
Franklin, NC 28734-3025
828-369-7942

A good place to hunt down Macon County history, Books Unlimited has both new and used volumes. With a nod toward both nineteenth-century poetry and twentieth-century science fiction, the bookstore's two resident cats are named Emily Dickinson and Yoda. The cats lounge around the two large store-fronts on Main Street that comprise the store. Books of regional interest here include a number of hard-to-find titles, such as *Cherokee Indian Lore and Smoky Mountain Stories*, by Margaret R. Siler, first published in 1938 and reissued by the author's heirs in 1993 and again in 2000.

Philips and Lloyd Book Shop

66 Church Street
Hayesville, NC 28904
828-389-1492

This Hayesville bookstore offers an impressive selection of works by mountain writers, an ample selection of mysteries and romance novels, and many handcrafted gifts, cards, antiques, crafts, and photos.

Moss Memorial Library

26 Anderson Street
Hayesville, NC 28904
828-389-8401

One block west of the Hayesville Square, around the corner on Anderson Street, is the Moss Memorial Library, where a long row of computers is available for online use by visitors. Here, books by North Carolina writers are specially designated by a blue band on the spines, just above the Dewey decimal number. This friendly library is also full of tropical plants and has a meeting room with old photos of town residents and a historical mural. Despite the county's modest size, the library system also has three branches and a bookmobile. With a backdrop of Standing Indian Mountain, the Friends of the Library Bookstore, just across the street from the Moss Library, helps support this flourishing library system with used book sales.

Clay County Historical and Arts Council

21 Davis Loop
Hayesville, NC 28904
828-389-6814

A roadside exhibit just outside town, where US 64 and Fort Hembree Road connect, provides a closer look at the historical site that is now privately owned. For more regional history, visit the Clay County Historical Arts Museum, located in the old county jail on Davis Loop (Business 64). This collection presents local artifacts and exhibits related to the significant influence of the Cherokee population before the removal.

Country Cottage

983 NC 69
Hayesville, NC 28904
828-389-8621

Before heading west from Hayesville toward Brasstown and the John C. Campbell Folk School, you might consider a meal at the Country Cottage Restaurant, just off US 64 at NC 69. Local poet Nancy Simpson says, "Country Cottage has been written up in *Southern Living* and in the Sunday supplement of the *Atlanta Journal and Constitution*. People come from far away to eat here and seem willing to wait if necessary." Country Cottage is a large complex—on one side the Cottage Deli offers sandwiches and a salad bar, and on the other side is the Cottage Bakery, where their famous breads and pies are made.

The Curiosity Shoppe

Shoppes of Murphy
46 Valley River Avenue
Murphy, NC 28906
828-835-7433

Recommended enthusiastically by Murphy writer Shirley Uphouse, the Curiosity Shoppe is dedicated to the support of local and regional writers in a number of ways. Every Saturday morning, the bookstore hosts a story hour for children. Visiting writers and musicians also come in to sign books and CDs, and, as possible, the store coordinates visits by writers to local schools. They help sponsor the annual Cherokee High School prose and poetry contest and the local middle school's "Battle of the Books." Owner Linda Ray says, "Our shelves boast every book we can find relating to local/regional history, and we carry every local author we can get our hands on." And, yes, the store had a resident cat on the day of our visit, but this Siamese was such a howler that Linda Ray admitted she might not let him continue to "mind" the store.

Robbinsville : Cherohala Skyway : Fontana : Almond : Nantahala Gorge

Meet Horace Kephart—the man who helped preserve the Great Smoky Mountains with his lyrical prose and his practical insights on mountain living, hunting, and camping. Learn his recipes for how to cook a possum or how to bake a whole wild turkey in clay. See some of the oldest trees in North Carolina and ride the most crooked road in the state. Follow the Snowbird Cherokee medicine trail to learn about the storied plants and people that have thrived here for more than two centuries.

Writers with a connection to this area: William Bartram, Olive Tilford Dargan, Gail Godwin, David Brendan Hopes, Horace Kephart, Marshall McClung, Robert Morgan, Duane Oliver, Ron Rash

To begin this tour from Murphy, head northeast on US 19/74/129 toward Andrews. You'll be traveling alongside the Valley River, where once there were many Cherokee settlements and where some native people still live today. The valley is remarkably flat, with high mountains rising on either side; only beyond Andrews does the road begin to climb. When you finally reach Topton, turn left on US 129 toward Robbinsville. Here the Snowbird Mountains form the boundary between Cherokee and Graham Counties; two thirds of the latter is national forest. Graham was the last county in the state to acquire a four-lane highway, and even now that highway only stretches part way into the county from the east near the site of writer Olive Tilford Dargan's long-gone home at Almond. Around 8,000 people live in this rugged county, which is bordered to the north by the Great Smoky Mountains National Park.

tour 5

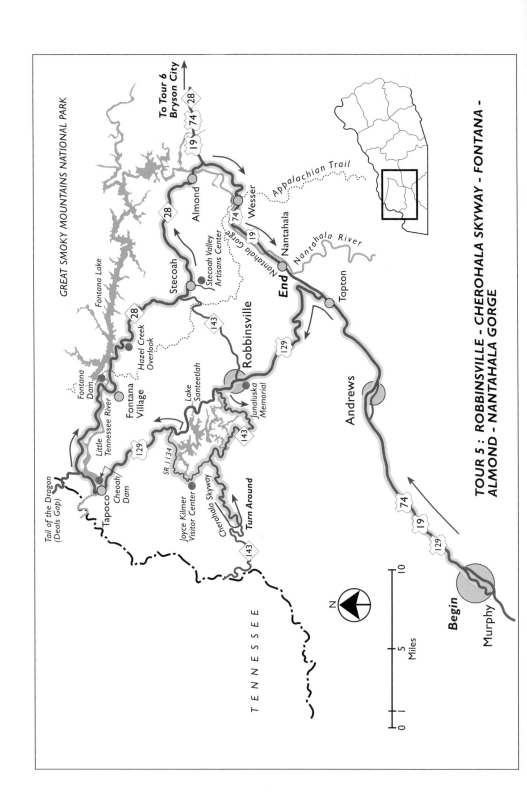

TOUR 5 : ROBBINSVILLE - CHEROHALA SKYWAY - FONTANA -
ALMOND - NANTAHALA GORGE

GREAT SMOKY MOUNTAINS NATIONAL PARK

To Tour 6
Bryson City

Almond

Wesser

Appalachian Trail

Nantahala

Nantahala River

Stecoah

Stecoah Valley
Artisans Center

End

Topton

Fontana Lake

Hazel Creek
Overlook

Robbinsville

Fontana Dam

Fontana Village

Little
Tennessee River

Lake
Santeetlah

Junaluska
Memorial

Andrews

Tail of the Dragon
(Deals Gap)

Tapoco

Cheoah
Dam

SR 1134

Joyce Kilmer Visitor Center

Cherohala Skyway

Turn Around

TENNESSEE

N

Begin

Murphy

0   1   5   10
        Miles

■ ROBBINSVILLE

Storytelling, rather than the written word, prevails in Robbinsville, the headquarters of the historic Snowbird Indians of the Cherokee tribe and their rich oral traditions. At the crossroads of US 129 and NC 143, Robbinsville is just below Lake Santeetlah, created on land purchased by the Aluminum Company of America (Alcoa) in 1910. Over a period of years, Alcoa built a number of hydroelectric dams in western North Carolina and eastern Tennessee to power its aluminum smelting facility in Alcoa, Tennessee. Santeetlah, completed in 1928 by damming the Cheoah River, is a smooth, jade wonder that juts into dozens of steep, fingered coves in the Nantahala National Forest. Driving around the lake is a slow endeavor but rewarding for the play of light among the trees and the surprising glimpses of deep water. The lake is a refuge for smallmouth and largemouth bass, walleye, crappie, sunfish, and trout. Boat rentals are available.

Inexpensive lodging in Robbinsville now includes a new, high-rise hotel and several older, more traditional motor lodges. And if you didn't bring a tent and camping gear, Robbinsville is a good overnight resting place from which to make forays into some of the most remote and pristine mountain landscape that North Carolina has to offer. (The 1994 movie *Nell*, starring Jodie Foster as a mountain waif who never had contact with civilization, was filmed here.)

■ JUNALUSKA MEMORIAL AND MUSEUM

Head north out of Robbinsville on Main Street (US 129), and in a half-mile on the left you will see signs to the hilltop gravesite of Junaluska, an important figure in Cherokee history.

Here in Graham County, the Cherokee people call themselves the Snowbirds after the nearby Snowbird Mountains. In Robbinsville the Snowbirds are the keepers of Junaluska's sacred grave and memorial site. Unlike some Snowbird people who were able to hide in this remote region during the Removal, Junaluska was captured and forced to make the trip to Oklahoma on the Trail of Tears with thousands of the Cherokee people. As many as 5,000 Native Americans died on this trek in the fall and winter of 1838–39, but Junaluska survived and walked back to the Cheoah Valley two years later. Nearby Tatum Gap is part of the Trail of Tears route, and native people sometimes walk the path to remember the hardships of their ancestors.

Before the Removal, Junaluska had first earned notice by refusing to band with other native peoples to defeat the white intruders. Then, in 1812, Junaluska

Stories of outstanding Snowbird Indians have been placed along the Medicine Trail at the Junaluska Memorial near Robbinsville.

fought alongside the army of Andrew Jackson to defeat the Creek people. He was credited with saving Andrew Jackson's life in the Battle of Horseshoe Bend. Later, when gold was discovered on Cherokee lands, the U.S. government declared all treaties invalid, and Jackson (by this time U.S. president) ordered the removal of the Cherokee to Oklahoma. Junaluska traveled to Washington, D.C., to make his case against the forced removal of his people and to remind President Jackson of the various treaties the government had signed. Jackson refused to see him.

Not until Junaluska returned from the Trail of Tears did the U.S. government fully acknowledge his status as a war hero with a "gift" of $100 and a land grant of more than 300 acres in what is now Robbinsville. Junaluska and his wife, Nicie, lived on this land for the rest of their lives and were buried at this site, which has long been part of the Snowbird Indian Council grounds.

A small pile of stones originally marked Junaluska's grave. The large stone memorial and plaque, dedicated in 1910 by the Winston-Salem chapter of the Daughters of the American Revolution (DAR), has been preserved by the Snowbird people. In addition to the DAR stone, the gravesite is now circled by seven impressive granite markers that represent the seven Cherokee clans and tell the life story of Junaluska. Each marker is inscribed in English and in the Cherokee syllabary—the written alphabet created for the Cherokee by Sequoyah (see Tours 6 and 15).

Just beyond the memorial, the caretakers have also created a Medicine Trail that winds back and forth down the wooded hill on a cleared path. Every few dozen yards, markers designate the medicine plants found there. Ginger, rattlesnake plantain, witch hazel, sassafras, arbutus, and buffalo nut are among the prolific specimens. Benches along the path are set near short stories written by local people, typed up, and sealed in plastic against the weather. These narratives are a tribute to the lives of people and families who are honored members of the Snowbird. Their names, like the medicine plants, are pure poetry—Soloman Bird, Armstrong Cornsilk, Lois Calonehuskie.

Storytelling in the Native American tradition involves an acute awareness of place—of recognizing signs in the natural world and remembering the stories of the ancestors as they relate to sacred sites. The Cherokee tell tales that involve very specific places. The Medicine Trail is a contemplative walk among the ancestors and heroes of this region and a powerful form of expression.

The Junaluska Museum, down the hill, has a collection of artifacts found in the area and dating back to 8,000 B.C. Exhibits of artwork, crafts, and old photos and a distinctive collection of books are also housed here. For more information, visit <http://www.junaluska.com/> or call the museum at 828-479-4727.

■ CHEROHALA SKYWAY

From the Junaluska site, continue north on US 129 and turn left on NC 143. Here the road winds beside a long finger of Lake Santeetlah and climbs toward the Cherohala Skyway, a breathtaking two-lane road that rides the crest of the mountains. It is one of only twenty roads in the United States designated as National Scenic Byways. You may want to stop for a visit to the Snowbird Mountain Lodge before or after your drive on the Cherohala Skyway. Take NC 143 to the left to approach the Skyway. (Note that you'll come back on the same road to continue on to Joyce Kilmer Memorial Forest to the right of this fork in the road.)

The name Cherohala is a hybrid of "Chero" from "Cherokee" and "hala" from "Nantahala." The road runs fifteen miles across the tops of unspoiled mountains in North Carolina and extends another twenty-one miles into Tennessee, ending at the town of Tellico Plains. The Skyway was the pipe dream of a Tennessee man in the late 1950s who organized an annual wagon train trip along this route from his home in Tellico Plains all the way to Murphy. The highly publicized journey stirred interest in the idea of building an automobile road, but it took an act of Congress, over thirty years, and $100 million to realize the vision.

Be aware that there are no amenities on the Skyway other than restrooms. There are no access roads either, only breathtaking views and occasional pullouts with hiking trails, descriptive exhibits, and historical information. Hardly any sign of civilization other than the road itself is visible from this route, which is especially popular with motorcyclists. Some estimates suggest, however, that only an average of ten cars per day make the trip. Travel with a full tank of gas, plenty of water, and some snacks. It takes about forty-five minutes to drive the full length of the North Carolina section of the Skyway in one direction.

■ HOOPER BALD AND BIG HUCKLEBERRY KNOB

All along the Cherohala Skyway you can stop at a series of pullouts — Santeetlah Gap, Hooper Cove, Shute Cove, and Wright Cove — before you reach the Huckleberry turnout, where a grim story once unfolded. According to *Graham Star* correspondent Marshall McClung:

> It was a bitter, cold day with snow and fog, December 11, 1899. Paul O'Neil and Andy Sherman from Mill Hall, Pennsylvania, employees of the Heiser Lumber Company, left the mouth of Sycamore Creek on the Tellico River in Tennessee bound for Robbinsville, North Carolina.
>
> On September 6, 1900, Forrest Denton, who was deer hunting with others, found their remains three-fourths of a mile from the present gravesite near a small stream, then unnamed, but since known as Dead Man's Run.
>
> The men had apparently missed the trail down Hooper Ridge between Hooper Bald and Horse Pen Gap. A jug containing moonshine whiskey was found near their bodies. The sheriff and coroner of Graham County were summoned and an inquest was held. The jury found that both men were frozen to death while lost and intoxicated. The jury directed that O'Neil's skeleton be given to Doctor Robert J. Orr in Robbinsville as a medical exhibit, while the remains of Sherman, badly mangled by wild animals, were buried in an unmarked grave on Big Huckleberry Knob.
>
> A copper plate telling the story was erected by Robert B. Barker, a retired attorney from Andrews, North Carolina, who made it a point to mark

The stone outcropping with mysterious writing on Hooper Bald along the Cherohala Skyway.

many graves in western North Carolina and erect monuments that tell their story. A metal cross was added many years later by a group also from Andrews that visits the area every year.

In early 1988, *The Heartland* series became interested in the story and sent a film crew to Big Huckleberry Knob to film a short story entitled "Dead Man's Run." It was shown on national television in February, 1988 on CBS and was carried locally by WBIR television station from Knoxville, Tennessee.—From "The Story of Dead Man's Run," by Marshall McClung, *Graham Star*, October 24, 1991, <http://main.nc.us/graham/mcclung/Dead%20Man's%20Run.html>.

At Hooper Bald, the next turnout, at 5,290 feet, there's a mysterious bit of writing on a rock. Park here for an easy quarter-mile hike on a gravel trail that leads to the bald. Once you're on the bald, follow the grass footpath and look to your right for a stone outcropping low to the ground at the edge of an overlook. This soft rock, now sadly defaced by dozens of tourists, is purported to have words on it that date back to the era of Spanish exploration.

The mystery writing is at the bottom right edge of the rock and reads "PRE-DARMS CASADA, SEP. 1615." Officials at the McClung Museum at the University of Tennessee in Knoxville have suggested that the inscription is perhaps a Spanish stakeholder's claim on Hooper Bald. Then again, it might be very early graffiti. No one really knows.

If you are a bird enthusiast, this trail is also a good spot to look for migratory birds. On the day we visited, a red-breasted grosbeak made an appearance, and we also came upon some unnerving evidence on the trail that might have been from a very large feline. In May, the wildflowers are spectacular.

At the next pullout, called Santeetlah, you have reached the highest point on the Cherohala Skyway and a nice spot for a picnic. You are about halfway to the Tennessee state line. Drive on or turn back. For our next stop on this tour we return to the beginning of the Cherohala Skyway.

■ JOYCE KILMER MEMORIAL FOREST

Where the Cherohala Skyway intersects with NC 143, the entrance to the Snowbird Lodge is on your right, and State Road 1127 to Joyce Kilmer Memorial Forest is more or less straight ahead. Here the road descends into 3,800 acres of deep virgin hardwood—the last remnant of virgin forest in the state. If you've come from a sunny day above on the Cherohala Skyway, the dark understory will make you think you forgot to remove your sunglasses. This dense North Carolina forest was designated in 1936 to preserve a piece of rare wilderness while honoring the writer who gave us "Trees," the evergreen poem that so many baby boomers were forced to memorize and recite in elementary school ("I think that I shall never see / A poem as lovely as a tree"). Of course Joyce Kilmer was also known as a journalist killed in action during World War I. According to Kilmer's son, Kenton, he wrote "Trees" in 1913 while living in New Jersey.

After driving downhill for approximately 2.5 miles, you'll cross Rattler Ford and come to a crossroads. Straight ahead is a sign noting the Maple Springs Observation Point, a 4.5 mile dead-end road that at its end provides an impressive view of the forest when the weather is not foggy. The Joyce Kilmer Memorial

A plaque commemorates poet Joyce Kilmer, author of "Trees,"
in the North Carolina forest named for him.

Trail, a two-mile loop, is to your left. There's ample parking at the trailhead. You'll see a reproduction of Kilmer's poem in bronze and an image of the poet in his World War I battle hat at the trailhead. There's a map of the trail under the small shelter. Follow the loop trail to the right or left—either way you will cross Little Santeetlah Creek on a footbridge and ascend into the extraordinary old-growth forest.

At the trail's midpoint, there's another bronze plaque with a brief biography of Kilmer. Connecting to the first loop is another three-quarter-mile upper loop where you can stand among poplars that are more than a hundred feet tall and fifteen to twenty feet in circumference. To return to the parking lot, take the lower loop back. There are benches along the way for reading David Brendan Hopes's piece on the forest excerpted here. Hopes is a creative writing professor at the University of North Carolina at Asheville:

> Rob and I make a pilgrimage to Joyce Kilmer Memorial Forest, at the western tip of North Carolina. We drive through mountains darkened with storm and scurrying cloud, dazzled with zigzags of light. We've gone there because it is one of the few stands of mountain vegetation not bulldozed by glaciers, a forest ecosystem continuous beyond anything else above the tropics. The old woman in the parking lot, she with the anemone in

her buttonhole, the guardian, ancient dryad, tells us that we will find the largest hemlock in the world. What we do surely find is a land perhaps too alive, too redolent with the breath of trees. The air is so moist as to be visible. The lungs pull at their own corners, trying to get bigger. It is like finding yourself sealed in a terrarium.

It is the richest forest I have ever seen: life upon life, root under root, ply over ply, golden toadstools gnawed by black and gold beetles, snow colored anemone backed by trunks of lustrous, absolute black, the red of broken hemlock, the silver of mist, silver flashes of braided creeks in the understory, orange and pale of fungus, rust-backed toads, gigantic millipedes of elegant dust-rose and pewter, blood-red wake-robin, over all, of course, green, green, and green. Dazzling green. Electric green. Moss green. Shadowy viridian. Emerald. Jade. Mist green. Sea green. Hemlock silver-green. Gold-green of the tulip-poplars diffusing down from two hundred feet above our heads.

It is almost incredible that I notice another color amid those colors, but I do, and whisper to Rob, "Behind you."

A Blackburnian warbler harvests the path's edge at our feet. Rob stands, a latter-day Moses, awestruck by the Burning Bird. The warbler, not similarly impressed, takes its sweet time. We grow impatient, and brush past the gleaning bird, he yields the path just enough for the seams of our jeans to pass him by.

Rob says, "I didn't know birds were so different." Such a comment would sound ignorant if I didn't know what he meant. He goes—or at least went, until he met me—in the wildwood to get away from things, to close his eyes into the mist of nothing in particular to rest. I go to the wildwood to enter the storm of the particular, to name the names of things, to be about my proper business.—From *A Sense of the Morning*, by David Brendan Hopes (Minneapolis: Milkweed Editions, 1999), 223–24.

To continue on the driving tour, return to the crossroads and continue straight ahead through the Horse Cove Campground. This gravel route (State Road 1134) will take you back to US 129. (You may also opt to go back to Robbinsville by retracing the route back up to the entrance of Cherohala Skyway and taking NC 143 back toward town.) However, to get to 129 on the gravel road, you'll drive slowly through beautiful woodlands around the north end of Lake Santeetlah. When you reach US 129 you may turn north to visit the village of Tapoco or turn south to return to Robbinsville by following alongside the western shore of Lake Santeetlah.

If you do go north, US 129 just beyond Tapoco Lodge takes a sharp turn northeast beside the Cheoah Dam and continues alongside the Cheoah Lake (also an Alcoa project). Approximately one-eighth of a mile from Tapoco Lodge, NC 28 goes east toward Fontana, while US 129 turns due north. Known as the "Tail of the Dragon" or Deals Gap, this stretch of US 129 goes to Maryville, Tennessee, with 318 curves in only 11 miles. Like the Cherohala Skyway, it is wildly popular with motorcyclists and drivers of small sports cars who seem to enjoy pushing their luck on the relentless curves.

■ FONTANA

If the Dragon's Tail is not tempting, continue on NC 28 alongside Cheoah Lake to Fontana, the site of North Carolina's largest TVA project. Fontana Dam backs up the various creeks that flow into a low-lying basin stretching for nearly thirty miles. The resulting lake is nearly 12,000 acres. In 1942 the United States needed more electricity to power factories engaged in the building of war materiel. The Fontana Dam project, still controversial to this day among some local families, was launched by the TVA and completed in two years. Old homesteads were flooded, and some 2,000 people had to relocate to higher ground.

You can visit the Fontana Dam from May to November. There's a visitor center, and tours of the electric plant are also conducted daily. The Appalachian Trail actually crosses the dam, the highest such structure east of the Rocky Mountains. You can also drive across the dam. Since 9/11, however, security here is tight. You can't stop your car on the dam to take photos. Views from the opposite side, however, are worthy of a photo.

Access to Fontana Lake is relatively limited, with only four public boat ramps located along the southern shoreline. (The northern shoreline is in the Great Smoky Mountains National Park and is virtually inaccessible except by boat.) Historic Fontana Village is the largest resort area on the lake, with an inn, cabins, shops, and private cottages. A marina, stables, hiking and biking trails, a pool, a waterslide, and a campground are nearby. Fontana Village is located south of the dam, just off NC 28. For more information, visit <http://www.fontanavillage.com>.

■ HAZEL CREEK OVERLOOK

HORACE KEPHART
Outside the tent on the Little Fork
of the Sugar Fork of Hazel Creek

a man is writing. His table boards
on upended kegs, he drafts meticulously clear
paragraphs and weights the finished pages
with a shotgun shell. Squirrels rippling
in the trees above do not distract him.
The jug by a white pine is stopped with a cob.

Each sentence he scratches with economy
is payment on a vast unpayable obligation:
to his parents for the years of college, for
the special courses at Cornell, for his tenure
cataloguing Petrarch in Florence, for the girl,
his Laura, married in Ithaca and taken
west, for the librarian's post in St. Louis,
for the study of Finnish, for the unwritten
history of western exploration that
excused long camping holidays and nights
away from home and expensive rare editions,
for the weeks of drinking and sulk.

Lean as a mountaineer himself, galluses
swing at his sides, he scribbles to the young
his intensity of woodcraft, weapons survival,
and of the hillmen his archaic friends and landlords,
makers of spirits. Even now one's loose
hog crashes through the brush into his camp
and knocks a tentline from its stob so
the canvas home sags at one corner on
his narrow cot, and breaks the clothesline.
As he jumps to shout and whack it back
into the undergrowth the unfinished sheet
from an early chapter of *Our Southern Highlanders*
peels off the desk and luffs like a wounded
dove out through the scrub and leaves to the creek.
—From *At the Edge of the Orchard Country*, by Robert Morgan
   (Middletown, Conn.: Wesleyan University Press, 1987), 3.

Images of whole mountain communities underwater because of various
TVA projects in the region have inspired a number of poets, including Robert
Morgan, who pays homage here to Horace Kephart, the librarian from St. Louis

Fontana Reservoir as seen from the Hazel Creek Overlook, near the area where Horace Kephart lived for three years long before the dam and lake were built by the TVA.

who first brought national attention to the rugged terrain and people around Hazel Creek. Thanks to Fontana Lake, Hazel Creek is even more inaccessible today than it was when Kephart came in 1904 to study the region.

Horace Sowers Kephart was born in Pennsylvania and studied at several universities to become a librarian and scholar of history. He worked at Yale University before moving to St. Louis, where he collected material on the American frontier for the library.

As a young man, Kephart had worked in Florence, Italy, and habitually hiked in the Alps and Apennines. His love of the mountains was stirred again as he began taking trips to the Ozarks from St. Louis. He eventually decided his true calling was to live in the highlands, not in the city. Abandoning his wife and children, Kephart moved to the Smokies and earned a living writing. He managed to inspire the trust of the mountaineers he met and often went hunting with them for wild game and sometimes a jug of moonshine from one of the local distillers.

Kephart first published *Our Southern Highlanders* in 1913. The book was wildly popular across the nation. Even Kephart's wary subjects loved the stories and the mountain characters he captured on paper; Kephart gained notoriety and earned the fondness of local people around Bryson City, where he ultimately settled.

In 1922, Kephart added three more chapters for a new edition of his book. Thereafter, the book was reprinted eight times. Novelist Wilma Dykeman remembered that her father would read Kephart aloud to the family on their trips to the Smokies when she was a child.

In 1967, *Our Southern Highlanders* finally went out of print, but the University of Tennessee Press brought it back a decade later. It continues to be popular. In 2001, North Carolina–born singer/songwriter Daniel Gore, along with a group of talented musicians, created a series of songs based on Kephart's writing called "Ways That Are Dark," which he recorded on the Elephant Rock label (<http://www.elephantrock.com>).

While researching *Our Southern Highlanders*, Kephart lived for three years on the Little Fork of Sugar Fork near Hazel Creek and fell in love with the landscape:

> For a long time my chief interest was not in human neighbors, but in the mountains themselves—in that mysterious beckoning hinterland which rose right back of my chimney and spread outward, almost to three cardinal points of the compass, mile after mile, hour after hour of lusty climbing—an Eden still unpeopled and unspoiled. . . .
>
> The Carolina mountains have a character all their own. Rising abruptly from a low base, and then rounding more gradually upward for 2,000 to 5,000 feet above their valleys, their apparent height is more impressive than that of many a loftier summit in the West which forms only a protuberance on an elevated plateau. Nearly all of them are clad to their tops in dense forest and thick undergrowth. Here and there is a grassy "bald"; a natural meadow curiously perched on the very top of a mountain. There are no bare rocky summits rising above timberline, few jutting crags, no ribs and vertebrae of the earth exposed. Seldom does one see even a naked ledge of rock. The very cliffs sheathed with trees and shrubs, so that one treading their edges has no fear of falling into an abyss. . . .

And yet these very mountains of Carolina are among the ancients of earth. They were old, very old, before the Alps and the Andes, the Rockies and the Himalayas were molded into their primal shapes. Upon them in after ages, were born the first hardwoods of America—perhaps those of Europe, too—and upon them to-day the last great hardwood forests of our country stand in primeval majesty, mutely awaiting their imminent doom.—From *Our Southern Highlanders: A Narrative of Adventure in the Southern Appalachians and a Study of Life Among the Mountaineers*, by Horace Kephart (Knoxville: University of Tennessee Press, 1976), 50–53.

In addition to this now-classic volume, Kephart also wrote a delightful cookbook, entitled *Camp Cookery: Outdoor Secrets from 1910*, reissued in 2001 in a pocket edition from Applewood Books of Bedford, Massachusetts. In it, Kephart covered a range of methods for cooking all manner of game. Among the delicacies are baked deer head, squirrels—fried, broiled, stewed, and barbecued —and beaver or porcupine cooked in clay, not unlike a Cornish game hen. Kephart also offers practical advice: how to skin an eel, how to preserve birds in warm weather, how to light a match in stiff wind, and what provisions and utensils to pack without burdening yourself on an overland journey.

He also offers many useful warnings: "To call our possum an opossum, outside of a scientific treatise, is an affectation. Possum is his name wherever he is known and hunted, this country over. He is not good until you have freezing weather; nor is he to be served without sweet potatoes, except in desperate extremity" (71). Kephart offers a recipe for "possum hot," cooked in a Dutch oven. He concludes: "It is said that possum is not hard to digest even when eaten cold, but the general verdict seems to be that none is ever left over to get cold" (72).

Today, unless you travel by boat from the southern shore of Fontana Reservoir—as descendants of the Hazel Creek community do in an annual pilgrimage to their family gravesites—the best place to view the general area where Horace Kephart lived in the woods is from NC 28 south of Fontana Village. The Hazel Creek Overlook is set high above Fontana Reservoir, a Coke-bottle-green body of water that contrasts dramatically with its red clay shoreline when the water level is low. Look to your left for the turnout to the overlook as you're headed from the dam south toward Stecoah.

A touching hand-carved sign erected in honor of the early Hazel Creek residents tells the story of this community settled by white people before 1830. As the sign explains, in this watershed alone, some 201 million board feet of lumber were produced at the turn of the twentieth century, with significant damage to the environment. Copper was discovered here in 1883 and was briefly profitable. More than a half-century later, the area became part of the Great Smoky Mountains National Park, partly due to Kephart's vigorous efforts.

In 1989, scholar and Hazel Creek descendant Duane Oliver wrote a study entitled *Hazel Creek, From Then Until Now*. The booklet is a typewritten and perfect-bound monograph that can be found at the Nantahala Outdoor Center in Bryson City. It offers a native's view of a region that, Oliver argues, Horace Kephart tended to over-romanticize. Based on oral histories passed down through generations and collected by the author, the book is an entertaining document full of anecdotes and vivid details of life in this craggy country at the turn of the twentieth century:

> Eagles as they still do, lived on the creek. One day in the 1890s, an eagle dropped a piglet into the yard of Orville Welch who was living on Echoah Branch on Eagle Creek. He kept this strange gift from the heavens, not knowing where the eagle had gotten it, and it grew into a fine hog.
>
> In addition to the wild animals, there was wild turkey, grouse and pheasant, and the streams were full of fish. The largest and tastiest fish in the creek were the native speckled trout. When Taylor and Crate started their logging operation on Hazel Creek in 1892 its speckled trout were wiped out below the splash dams due to the logs tumbling down the creek which killed the fish and ruined their breeding nests on the bottom of the creek. Above the splash dams the fish were plentiful, for in 1898 Granville Calhoun and his brother-in-law, Judd Hall, caught 476 in four-and-a-half hours. — From *Hazel Creek, From Then Until Now*, by Duane Oliver (self-published, 1989), 31.

■ ALMOND

Continuing east on NC 28, past the Tsali Recreation Area, near the widest part of Fontana Lake, you'll cross from Graham into Swain County to come upon Almond, located just before the intersection of NC 28 and US 19/74. Like the settlement at Hazel Creek, most of the original village of Almond—the site of the mountain home of playwright, social activist, and fiction writer Olive Tilford Dargan—is now under the waters of Fontana Lake.

From My Highest Hill: Carolina Mountain Folks (1941) is a collection of short stories written by the Radcliffe-educated Olive Tilford Dargan, a Kentuckian who came in 1906 from New York City with her husband to live in a log cabin near Almond. Dargan had earned the funds to buy her mountain land from two successful books of plays, written in verse. The Dargans stayed in North

Carolina for six years, though Olive got little writing done during that time, living in such close quarters with her ailing husband. For a time she traveled alone to England where she wrote another collection of verse drama and a book of poems. She returned to the United States in 1914; her husband mysteriously died at sea the next year; and by spring of 1916, Dargan was back in her beloved cabin alone.

By 1919 she found herself writing narratives about the three tenant families that lived on her land. She published several of these pieces as short stories that were then collected in a 1925 book titled *Highland Annals*. Praise for her work earned Dargan an honorary doctorate from the University of North Carolina, though the book, published by Charles Scribner's Sons, did not sell well.

Part of Dargan's goal in the writing had been to refute what she felt were unfair stereotypes of mountain women as presented by Horace Kephart and by the much more patronizing prose of a local-color writer, Mary Noailles Murfree. As Anna Shannon Elfenbein explains in her introduction to the 1998 edition of Olive Dargan's collection, "While Dargan was writing the stories that later became *From My Highest Hill*, busloads of tourists who had absorbed such ideas were invading Almond and nearby Bryson City each summer to gawk at the mountaineers as curiosities at best and subhuman species at worst" (xix).

Ultimately Dargan lost her cabin to fire in 1923 and retreated to West Asheville to spend her winters, though she would revisit her land in the Smokies every summer for the rest of her life. In the late 1930s, Dargan decided to re-issue her story collection with a new title, *From My Highest Hill*, hoping the publication might coincide with the dedication of the Great Smoky Mountains National Park. Dargan also hoped to refute the hayseed image of mountaineers presented in yet another book that had come out in 1935. Muriel Earley Sheppard's *Cabins in the Laurel*, published by the University of North Carolina Press with striking photographs by New Bern's Bayard Wootten, had offended many local people. (See Tour 11.) For her new book, Dargan set about reworking and improving many of the stories from *Highland Annals* and invited Wootten to photograph her neighbors in Swain County. It would be the last book Wootten ever illustrated.

From My Highest Hill, published by J. P. Lippincott in 1941, was not a commercial success. Still, historians say it stands today as one of the most accurate representations of the folk dialect of the period in existence, made more poignant by the fact that the old site of the little town of Almond is now deep under the waters of Lake Fontana. The book was reissued by the University of Tennessee Press in 1998 and is finally being rediscovered for its powerful images of a challenging life in these hills.

"If ever I have a home of my own, it will be in these mountains," Dargan wrote on her first visit to the Smokies as a college student ("Olive Tilford Dargan," by Virginia Terrell Lathrop, *North Carolina Libraries* 18 [Spring 1960]: 69). She made good on her dream and lived in Almond most of the period from 1906 to 1923, helping to document the local folkways through her fiction. In this passage she describes a berry-picking adventure:

I stood on the doorstep balancing destiny. Below me lay the Post Office, unvisited for a week. But half a mile above me were the still crests of content. Should I go up or down?

Serena, happening by with designs of her own, saved me the wrench of decision. "If you want any strawberries this year," she said, "you'd better get 'em before the Mossy Creek folks have rumpaged over Old Cloud field. They slip up from the north side an' don't leave a berry fer manners. I'm goin' right now. I always go once. I can stay until night if I want to, 'cause sister Vallie is at my house to-day. I'm like it says in that song, 'Free A Little Bird.' I called Jay to come with me, but he goes a little deer in springtime."

I provided buckets and cups, as expected, and we started. The high ridge field where the berries had rambled had its name from an Indian, Old Cloud. He had lived there behind the cloud that, it was said, always lay on the ridge before so many peaks had been stripped of their pine and poplar and balsam that held the clouds entangled and the sky so close. After the land had passed to the settlers it had taken forty years of reckless and monotonous tillage to reduce the rich soil to half-wild pasture enjoying the freedom of exhaustion.

I had been under roof for three days, and the spring air produced the usual inebriation. Several times I left Serena far behind, but she always caught up, and we reached the top together. Here, panting, I dropped to a bed of cinquefoil, while Serena stood unheated and smiling.

"Did you ever run, Serena?"

"I always take the gait I can keep," she answered, her glance already searching the ground for berries. "It's all sage-bresh here, but the other side 'o that gully is red with 'em. We've got ahead of Mossy Creek this time."

I was looking at the world which the lifted horizon had given me. North by east the Great Smokies drew their lilac-blue veil over a wilderness of laurel. I could see the oblong swell of Clingman, and felt again the onslaught of a day when my body had been wrapped in the odor of its firs and heathery mosses. South lay the Nantahalas, source of clear waters. West—but what were names before that pageant of peaks that rose in every form, curved swaying, rounded, a loaf, a spear, shadowed and un-shadowed, their splotches of green, gold, and hemlock black, flowing into blue where distance balked the eye and imagination stepped the crests alone. It seemed easier to follow than to stay behind with feet clinging to earth. Affinity lay with the sky.

Serena was steadily picking berries.

"But, Serena," I called, "just see!"

"I come here once a year," she said, standing up, "an' I never take my look till I've filled my bucket." And she was on her knees again.

—From "Serena and Wild Strawberries," in *From My Highest Hill: Carolina Mountain Folks*, by Olive Tilford Dargan (Knoxville: University of Tennessee Press, 1998), 53–55.

Today wild strawberries are not so easy to find around here, nor is the time to pick them. Perhaps nowhere else on this trail are the consequences of such "progress" more visible. Almond is now little more than a modern post office set back from the new four-lane highway—the first such wide road to reach into Graham County from Swain. The broad slice through these steep hills that it took to build the highway has been planted with nonnative grasses for erosion control. The proprietors of the campground on the shores of Fontana say it is still possible to hike back toward the remnants of the original Almond, but the site of Olive Tilford Dargan's beloved hilltop cabin is underwater. Still, her stories offer the authentic voices of the spirits that yet live here.

■ NANTAHALA GORGE

This tour ends with a quick jaunt down to the Nantahala Gorge. Turn south from Almond on US 19/74 and you'll soon come to Wesser, a town that's all about whitewater rafting. The Nantahala River runs alongside the road here. Water levels are controlled by the dam keepers at Nantahala Lake to the south. In the late afternoons and at night, this river is little more than a trickle, but come morning, when the dam is opened up, the rushing water becomes a favorite venue for families and church groups who bump along in rubber rafts and kayaks clotting up the river.

The Nantahala Outdoor Center, an employee-owned enterprise begun in 1972 by Payson Kennedy, has grown to include float trips all over the region—on the Ocoee, Pigeon, French Broad, Nolichucky, and notably, the Chattooga—the rapid river that forms part of the border of Georgia and South Carolina, made famous by the movie based on James Dickey's novel *Deliverance*. Kennedy and his river guides assisted in the production, with Dickey himself taking a small role in the controversial 1972 film that starred Jon Voight and Burt Reynolds.

Western Carolina University professor Ron Rash set his novel *Saints at the River* (2004) along the fictional Tamassee River, but he admits that he also had the white water and dangerous drops of the Chattooga in mind. Rash told the audience at the 2004 North Carolina Writers Conference, held in Cullowhee, that he hoped his book neither sentimentalizes nor demonizes mountain people, but instead presents a "much more sympathetic and complex view" than Dickey's novel managed.

Whether you opt to take your own white water ride here on the Nantahala or not, the stretch of highway between Wesser and Topton delivers striking scenery alongside the river, though it can back up with heavy rafting traffic.

Two other literary connections also inform this route: William Bartram, the eighteenth-century naturalist whose work influenced and is quoted in Charles Frazier's novel *Cold Mountain*, traveled near here and met the famous Cherokee chieftain Atakullakulla in May of 1776, just two months before the fireworks started in Bartram's hometown of Philadelphia with the Declaration of Independence. A state historical marker noting Bartram's meeting with the Cherokee chief is located on the line between Swain and Macon County at the Patton's Run overlook. Bartram's Trail (described in detail in Tour 3) crosses the river again at the Nantahala Outdoor Center's rafting "put-in" and climbs to Cheoah Bald, part of the Appalachian Trail, on the border of Swain and Macon County. From there, the "Western Extension" of the Bartram Trail continues along the crest of the Snowbird Mountains toward Tennessee.

A bit farther south on US 19/74, past Topton and four miles before you reach Andrews, is Granny Squirrel Gap—the small community that Asheville native Gail Godwin portrays in her novel, *A Southern Family*, excerpted in Tour 6.

■ LITERARY LANDSCAPE

Fading Voices Festival
c/o Junaluska Museum
P.O. Box 1209
Robbinsville, NC 28771
828-479-4727

Like their relatives up the road on the Cherokee reservation lands known as the Qualla Boundary, the Snowbirds maintain their native ways through storytelling in the Cherokee language, handcrafts, and an annual Memorial

Day festival called "Fading Voices." Nonnative people are welcome to attend these festivities. The Snowbird people also frequently host gospel singings in late summer.

Graham County Ramp Festival
Graham County Rescue Squad Building
Moose Branch Road
Robbinsville, NC 28771
<http://www.grahamcountytravel.com/activities.html>
If you are visiting in April, Robbinsville is headquarters for North Carolina's premier ramp festival, celebrated for more than thirty years. The ramp is a distinctively pungent variety of wild onion that grows at higher elevations as far north as Canada. The Graham County Ramp Festival celebrates the annual harvest in spring and offers hearty, inexpensive meals that generally include other, more familiar dishes—trout, chicken, baked beans, cornbread, potato salad. Proceeds benefit the Graham County Rescue Squad.

Graham County Public Library
80 Knight Street
Robbinsville, North Carolina 28771
828-479-8796
<http://main.nc.us/graham/library.html>
Next to the Community Services Building in downtown Robbinsville, this friendly library also serves students from the Graham Center of the Tri-County Community College. Story hour for children is on Thursday mornings, and a large conference room is available for community events. It is one of the four libraries in the Nantahala Regional Library System that serves Cherokee, Graham, and Clay Counties.

Bryson City : Cherokee :
Great Smoky Mountains National Park

Visit the grave of Horace Kephart. Travel to the heart of Cherokee country and appreciate the oral traditions of this legendary region where whole towns are buried under the waters of
Fontana Lake and where the customs and culture of the native
people are celebrated in an unparalleled interactive museum
full of mystery and magic.

*Writers with a connection to this area: Michael Chitwood,
John Ehle, George Ellison, Deborah Kinsland Foerst, Charles
Frazier, Hanay Geiogamah, Gail Godwin, Kermit Hunter,
Horace Kephart, Sequoyah*

■ BRYSON CITY

A river runs through it, and so does the railroad. Built on
the level shore of the Tuckasegee River and surrounded by hills
and lush green mountains, Bryson City is home to both mountain natives and others who have moved here to launch tour-
ist-driven businesses or to retire in an easygoing small town.
On the Friday we visited, the local barber, dressed in his white
jacket with big pockets, came in at noon for the flounder special at the family restaurant across the street from the Smoky
Mountain Community Theater. The barber took his place at
a table of other seniors. The young owner of the restaurant,
dressed in a farmer's cap and sleeveless T-shirt with a pack of
cigarettes bulging in his breast pocket, stopped by the table to
check iced tea levels.

"Why is there a sign on the door that the place'll be closed
tomorrow?" the barber asked.

"Because I'm taking the day off to ride my bike," answered
the owner as he leaned over to dole out refills.

Such is the unforced pace of Bryson City, the town where

tour 6

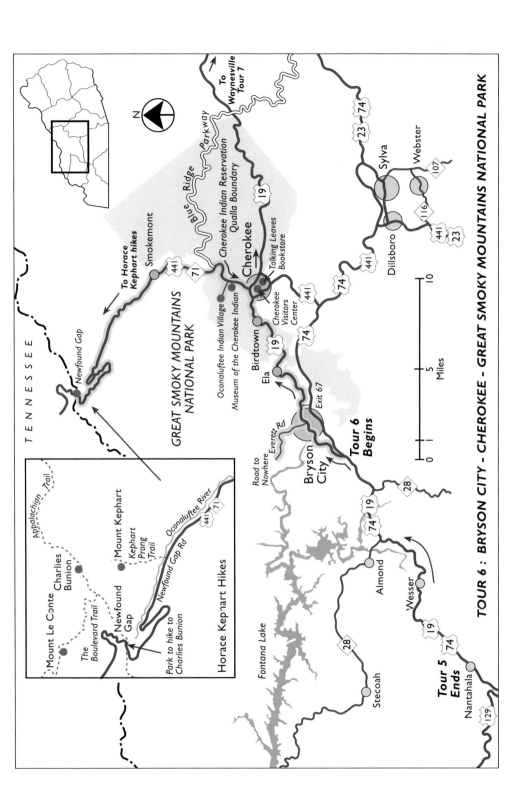

TOUR 6 : BRYSON CITY - CHEROKEE - GREAT SMOKY MOUNTAINS NATIONAL PARK

writer Horace Kephart spent the last years of his life in a boardinghouse. Today three railroad tracks run parallel to the river that meanders through the west side of town. Tourist business is good, due in part to the presence of the Great Smoky Mountains Railway. Hunting and fishing also continue in these parts as they did in Kephart's day. An outdoor gear store advertises "Guns and Ammo, Flys and Knives." And just above Main Street in the Bryson City Cemetery, on a steep hill with a full view of town to the south and the Smokies to the north, is the final resting place of Horace Kephart.

Local writer and naturalist George Ellison has helped keep Kephart's legend alive. Ellison's regular columns in the *Smoky Mountain News* often feature stories of Kephart and his hiking companion, the Japanese photographer George Masa. Ellison has collected these essays in *Mountain Passages: Natural and Cultural History of Western North Carolina and the Great Smoky Mountains* (2005). He also wrote the introduction to the 1976 edition of Kephart's *Our Southern Highlanders*, in which he elaborates on Kephart's local legacy:

> His most important writing during the 1920s was done on behalf of the movement that eventually culminated in the establishment of the Great Smoky Mountains National Park. Kephart's role in the movement was considerable. He wrote articles for periodicals and newspapers advocating the establishment of a park in the Smokies, carefully explaining time and again why the area should be preserved. Many of his pieces were accompanied by the excellent photographs of his Japanese friend George Masa, who spent as much time in the Smokies with Kephart as he did in his Asheville studio. Together they caught the spirit of the high mountains and watersheds in words and pictures. Kephart did not live to see the park become an actuality, but he died knowing it was assured. — From *Our Southern Highlanders: A Narrative of Adventure in the Southern Appalachians and a Study of Life Among the Mountaineers*, by Horace Kephart (Knoxville: University of Tennessee Press, 1976), xliii–xliv.

Kephart and another writer from Georgia, Fiswoods Tarleton, were killed in April of 1931 in a taxi they had hired to drive them to a local bootlegger. The taxi driver, who likely shared in the moonshine that Kephart had just purchased, lost control of the vehicle on a curve heading back into Bryson City. Kephart's family, including two sons, a grandson, and his estranged wife, whom he had left long ago in St. Louis, came to North Carolina for the funeral. According to reports in the *Asheville Citizen-Times*, hundreds of mourners stood outside the packed auditorium at the high school where services were held, so beloved was Kephart in the region. Of his commitment to the environment, Kephart was quoted in his obituary in the *Asheville Citizen-Times* on April 3, 1931: "I owe my life to these mountains, and I want them preserved that others may profit by them as I have."

To visit Kephart's grave, look for the intersection of Main Street and Veterans Boulevard in Bryson City. Here Main Street becomes School Road and climbs uphill to the cemetery that overlooks downtown. Follow School Road a short way uphill until it curves to the left. Continue straight ahead on Arlington, looking for the cemetery sign on your right at Hillside Road. Turn right onto Hillside and drive just past the school, where you'll see a small dirt lane on the left beside the graveyard. Park here next to the stone wall. You may notice a triangle-shaped stone set in the wall near a giant oak tree. This triangle points toward the Kephart grave about forty yards away. Appropriately, the Kephart marker is an irregular boulder, uncut, with only a bronze plaque mounted on it. The day we visited, the squirrels had left nutshells on his gravestone just as they had the day Chapel Hill poet Michael Chitwood paid his respects.

LOOKING FOR HORACE KEPHART'S GRAVE, BRYSON CITY, NC
I don't think he's up here
in the oak-filtered light
and grease fumes from the Hardee's
down on Spring Street.
He's slipped off again
into the blue haze over Deep Creek.
There's no one here to name that knob
off to the left
or to say what creek is flashing
its silver change
behind the Jackson Savings Bank.
There's just the squirrel
working a pine cone on a Quiett's stone
and the roots
tipping the carved markers with their slow crawl.
—From *Whet*, by Michael Chitwood
   (Athens: Ohio Review Books, 1995), 7.

Boy scouts honor Horace Kephart after his burial in Bryson City in 1931. Note the wooden marker. This picture was identified by the Asheville Photo Service as a George Masa photo in the Asheville Times, *November 16, 1931. Courtesy of the North Carolina Collection of the Pack Memorial Library, Asheville, North Carolina.*

■ THE ROAD TO NOWHERE

A controversy still simmers in Bryson City surrounding the creation of Fontana Reservoir and the lost communities now under its waters. When the U.S. government displaced some 1,300 families in 1943 by flooding the valley and creeks that stretch from near here back to Fontana Dam, they promised to build a road around the lake so that descendants might still visit the nearly thirty family graveyards on the north side of the waters, on property that is now part of Great Smoky Mountains National Park. By the end of 1969, only six miles of

Horace Kephart's grave today, a bronze plate set on a rugged rock outcropping.

the promised road, including a bridge and a 1,200-foot tunnel, had been completed, though plans called for an additional twenty-six miles of pavement to reach back toward the site of the historic settlements. Nothing more has been done since then.

"The Road to Nowhere," known today as Lakeview Drive, is worth the trip for the views of Fontana Reservoir and the undeveloped woodlands that flank it. Hikers often park at the dead end and follow one of three trails that lead several miles beyond the tunnel deep into the national forest.

DIRECTIONS

State Road 1364 is named Everett Road in downtown Bryson City and crosses Main Street near the Swain County Courthouse. Everett is also the street that crosses the railroad tracks right where the Great Smoky Mountain Railroad station is located. From Main, follow Everett across the river, across the tracks, and out of town. The road climbs uphill and soon turns into Fontana Road. In a few miles you'll leave human habitation behind as marked by the "Road to Nowhere" sign. After six miles the road is blocked at the tunnel, where a parking area is provided for hikers.

One day, thought Julia, as she passed through Cherokee on U.S. 19, I'm going to have to think about the Indians. I wonder how many Americans say that to themselves: One day I am going to have to think about the Indians. But it will have to wait until I get through thinking about the South.

Like all the other children she knew, she had been taken to the Cherokee Indian Reservation and the Oconaluftee Indian Village, where the descendants of the tribe that once owned much of Tennessee, the Carolinas, Georgia and Alabama dressed in feathers and moccasins and acted busy practicing their crafts for the descendants of the whites who had driven their own ancestors out. In college, she'd had a boyfriend who'd acted in Unto These Hills. She had visited him backstage and watched him and the other college actors smearing red Pan-Cake makeup all over their white bodies for the evening performance. But she had managed never to think much about what any of it meant." —From *A Southern Family*, by Gail Godwin (New York: Avon Books, 1988), 368–69.

In *A Southern Family*, North Carolina–born novelist Gail Godwin captures the superficiality of the tourist experience of Cherokee, North Carolina, from earlier decades. These days a different opportunity is in store as you depart Bryson City and head northeast on US 19 through the villages of Ela, Whittier, and Birdtown. On this route travelers enter the Cherokee Indian Reservation, also known as the Qualla Boundary. The Eastern Band of the Cherokee has its headquarters here, and in recent years significant resources and effort have been applied to improve the local presentations about the Cherokee people and their history, trumping the stereotypical representations of "Indians" still visible in old neon motel signs. As leases have expired on longstanding gift shops owned by nonnative people, authentic Indian crafts have begun to replace cheaply made, inauthentic bow-and-arrow sets, headdresses, and tomahawks.

The success of tribal-owned gambling casinos in town has also demonstrably raised the standard of living among the Cherokee people through a revenue-sharing plan with each member of the tribe — good news for those challenged by the whims of a federal government that has broken so many treaties over time.

Cherokee writer Deborah Kinsland Foerst lives on the Qualla Boundary and teaches at Cherokee Middle School, where she helped students launch a school newspaper called *Tsa la gi Hi go hi* ("Cherokee Reader"). The following poem is a pantoum, a poetic form that originated in France but is based on a form from Malaya. Appropriately, the style has the effect of a chant:

LIGHTS IN THE SMOKIES
Granny Myrt says the lights protect,
but only special people can see the lights
because the lights are really flames from fires
set in our mountains by medicine men.

But only special people can see the lights
shimmering at Straight Fork, Bigwitch, the Kituwah mound
set in our mountains by medicine men.
Something had to be done after the Removal.

Shimmering at Straight Fork, Bigwitch, the Kituwah mound.
People are still greedy.
Something had to be done after the Removal
to keep and protect what little we had left.

People are still greedy.
Strong medicine had to be used
to keep and protect what little we had left.
They doctored our mountains.

Strong medicine had to be used
because the lights are really flames from fires.
They doctored our mountains.
Granny Myrt says the lights protect.
—From *Lights in the Mountain: Stories, Essays and Poems by
   Writers Living in and Inspired by the Southern Appalachian
   Mountains*, ed. Nancy Simpson and Shirley Uphouse
   (Hayesville, N.C.: Winding Path Publishing, 2003), 16.

Literature by Cherokee writers is growing with successive generations, an important source beyond the body of work created by Anglo authors *about* the Cherokee. In 1936 Horace Kephart's wife adapted and published a slim volume of her husband's writing after his death, entitled *The Cherokees of the Smoky Mountains: A Little Band That Has Stood against the White Tide for Three Hundred Years*. The booklet is still in print in an edition published by the Great Smoky Mountains National Park and is locally available.

Another local rendering of Cherokee history is offered through an art form indigenous to North Carolina—the outdoor drama. Since 1950, more than 5 million people have seen *Unto These Hills*, which Gail Godwin mentions in the passage quoted above. The drama was written by Kermit Hunter, a white man from West Virginia who came to North Carolina after World War II to work for two years as the North Carolina Symphony Society's first business manager. Hunter then enrolled as a graduate student in the Department of Dramatic Art at the University of North Carolina at Chapel Hill, where the Carolina Play-makers produced three of his first plays. In 1948, when the Cherokee Historical Association sought writers to create a drama about the history of the Cherokee people, Hunter won the commission. *Unto These Hills* turned into his master's thesis at Carolina. Hunter stayed on at UNC to teach English while completing his Ph.D. During the long career that followed, Hunter taught at Hollins College, served as dean of the Meadows School of Arts at Southern Methodist University in Dallas, Texas, and, just before retiring, was senior lecturer at the University of Texas at Arlington. He wrote both fiction and dramas over the course of his career.

Today Hunter's original play has been transformed "from history-book tales of what happened to the Cherokee, to vivid insights into what it means to be Cherokee," say the tribal producers of the new version of the play. In 2006, the new script, score, choreography, set design, and costuming were transformed under the guidance of Kiowa playwright and director Hanay Geiogamah. The new show debuted with a cast that included dozens of actors from the Eastern Band of the Cherokee, with the aim of "conveying a more culturally authentic, historically accurate and Cherokee-centered experience." For information on performances, call 866-554-4557 or visit <http://www.cherokee-nc.com/unto_these_main.php>.

Two other nonnative accounts of the Cherokee story bear mentioning. John Ehle's 1988 novel, *The Trail of Tears*, based on the historical record, is a powerful account of that tragedy. More recently, Charles Frazier's second novel, *Thirteen Moons* (2006), also sheds light on Cherokee history in the region. Inspired by his experiences while researching the novel, Frazier has funded a project to help perpetuate the Cherokee language—spoken and written—especially among young people on the Qualla Boundary. The project will translate and publish works of literature in the Cherokee language, beginning with *Thirteen Moons*.

Heading north from Cherokee on US 441, beyond the shimmering neon of the 1950s-style motels and souvenir shops, you will shortly come to the entrance to the Great Smoky Mountains National Park. Here the road is divided by a grassy median. Commercial development ends. There are hikes and choice campgrounds and historic exhibits throughout the park—the stuff from which vacation memories are made.

The literary traveler will surely want to take the hike that Horace Kephart made often with his dear friend, photographer George Masa. Kephart and Masa actually named the first peak on this hike—Charlies Bunion. And from there, you can see the two peaks that were named later for Kephart and Masa, both of whom worked hard to see that the Great Smoky Mountains National Park became a reality in 1942.

From the park's south entrance, travel US 441 North nineteen miles to the Newfound Gap parking area. From there, directions for this hike are best given by Bryson City naturalist and writer George Ellison:

> Getting to Charlies Bunion is pretty much a cinch. Head north on the AT from the Newfound Gap parking lot, follow the trail signs, and before long—say, 2 to 4 hours, depending on whether you're a backcountry saunterer or a full-steam-ahead hiker—you're there. Leave early enough on a day that promises to be fair, pack trail snacks and a lunch, binoculars, the field guides of your choice, and you've got the makings of a nice day-hike. But remember: (1) it's always cooler this time of the year in the high country than you ever think it'll be; and (2) a squall will blow up if you don't carry rain gear. (Pack a poncho and it won't rain, guaranteed.)—From "How Mountain Names Came to Be," by George Ellison, *Smoky Mountain News*, October 10, 2001, <http://www.smokymountainnews.com/issues/ 10_01/10_10 01/back_then.shtml>.

In the same article, Ellison also recommends the four-mile hike over Mount Kephart and down Masa Knob, which is accessible from the Boulevard Trail, a spur that's about a hundred yards off the Appalachian Trail. He tells of how Charlies Bunion came to be so named, according to local legend:

> The curious place name resulted in 1929 when Smokemont native Charlie Conner was hiking with Kephart, Masa, and others along the high divide. When they paused for a rest on the rocks, Conner took his boots and

George Masa's photo of Horace Kephart resting on Mount Kephart, the peak that was named for him in 1928 before the Great Smoky Mountains National Park was officially created. Masa and Kephart helped to map trails for the U.S. Park Service in the area. From the Mitzi Tessier Photograph Collection, courtesy of Daniels Publications, a part of the North Carolina Collection of the Pack Memorial Library, Asheville, North Carolina.

Thomas Road was the first road built in the Smokies. George Masa took this photograph near Beech Flats, approximately six miles above Smokemont. Horace Kephart is seated in the Falcon-Knight automobile as the men paused along the rough ride to Newfound Gap. Courtesy of the North Carolina Collection of the Pack Memorial Library, Asheville, North Carolina.

socks off, exposing a bunion or two that rivaled the surrounding stones. Eying Conner's feet, Kephart remarked, "Charlie, I'm going to get this place put on a government map for you." This happened. (There are also several versions of this story, all true.)

The views from Charlies Bunion are special. To the west are Jump-Off and Mt. Kephart. To the northwest is Mt. Le Conte. To the north are deep gorges along the headwaters of Porters Creek. Off to the northeast is Greenbrier Pinnacle, while off to the east lies the jagged knife-edged region known as the Sawteeth Range. On a clear day you can almost see forever.—From "How Mountain Names Came to Be," by George Ellison.

■ **LITERARY LANDSCAPE**

Marianna Black Library
33 Fryemont Street
Bryson City, North Carolina 28713
828-488-3030
<http://www.fontanalib.org/brysoncity/index.htm>

Carved from a single California redwood by Peter Wolf Toth, this sculpture of Sequoyah stands outside the Museum of the Cherokee Indian on US 441 in Cherokee.

One block off Main Street in Bryson City on a slight rise overlooking town and the railroad tracks on the opposite side of the Tuckasegee River, this handsome little library is decorated with plantings of herbs and perennials. Computers are available for Internet access.

Museum of the Cherokee Indian
589 Tsali Boulevard
Cherokee, NC 28719
828-497-3481
<http://cherokeemuseum.org/>

Outside this museum an enormous sculpture of the head of Sequoyah is carved from a single giant sequoia tree. Sequoyah, also known as George Guess, was the Cherokee's first true man of letters. He single-handedly devised the Cherokee syllabary using some eighty-six characters that represent the sounds of the Cherokee language, thus transforming the Cherokee people very quickly into writers and readers. Reportedly, it took speakers of the language only two

Street sign in English and Cherokee syllabary near the Talking Leaves Bookstore in Cherokee.

weeks to master the letters. Some scholars have argued that the Cherokee might have had a written language before Sequoyah, but they do not question his important role in bringing widespread literacy to the Cherokee people.

Inside the museum, artifact marries technology to create an interactive journey across 12,000 years of history, creating a powerful experience for adults and children through exhibits, holograms, special computer-generated effects, audio, and photos. The museum bookstore also offers a large collection of relevant materials related to local history and literature. Open daily except Thanksgiving, Christmas Day, and New Year's Day. Admission fee.

Talking Leaves Bookstore

30 Nickeh Drive
Cherokee, NC 28719
828-497-6044

On US 19E between the Kentucky Fried Chicken and Grandma's Pancake and Steak, this bookstore offers an extensive collection of books published by and about Native Americans. The store also offers gifts, music, and native crafts. "Talking Leaves" was the name Sequoyah gave to his syllabary. Though he valued the notion of writing for his people, the term actually refers to the Cherokee attitude toward written documents; namely, that the words of white men dried up and blew away like leaves when the writings no longer suited their wishes, reflecting the Cherokee experience with the multitude of broken land treaties that eventually reduced the Cherokee from 140,000 square miles of land in the region to the current Qualla Boundary, which is approximately one hundred square miles. Note that most of the road signs here and elsewhere in the Qualla Boundary give street names in both English and the Cherokee syllabary.

Waynesville : Hot Springs : Marshall : Mars Hill

Visit arts-rich Waynesville, where many writers have been inspired over the years. Head into the "Kingdom of Madison," one of North Carolina's most rugged counties, where towns bear poetic names such as Trust and Luck, Sodom Laurel and Hot Springs. Learn about the songcatchers who first recorded the music of these steep hills and remote valleys.

Writers with a connection to this area: Sheila Kay Adams, Rob Amberg, Olive Dame Campbell, Donald Davis, Pamela Duncan, Keith Flynn, O. Henry, Michael McFee, Caroline Miller, Jim Wayne Miller, Della Hazel Moore, Dellie Chandler Norton, Ron Rash, Christian Reid, Cecil Sharp, Betty Smith, Elizabeth Daniels Squire, Manly Wade Wellman

Leaving Cherokee and the Qualla Boundary and heading east into Haywood County on US 19, you'll come through Soco Gap with its claim to "the most photographed view in the mountains." Continue on through Maggie Valley with its many tourist enterprises hawking molasses, honey, and boiled peanuts. Motels, restaurants, and an unusual number of riding stables run a dotted line through the valley. US 276 South will take you to Waynesville, where this tour begins.

■ WAYNESVILLE

Waynesville and the surrounding area have been depicted in the works of popular children's storyteller Donald Davis, who spent his early years on land that has remained in his family since 1781. Plott's Creek, as he calls it, is vividly described in his story collection, *See Rock City* (1996). Davis attended Davidson College and Duke Divinity School and spent twenty years as a Methodist minister before turning to storytelling and creative writing. He now lives on Ocracoke Island on North Carolina's Outer Banks and gives some 300 performances a year, mostly

tour 7

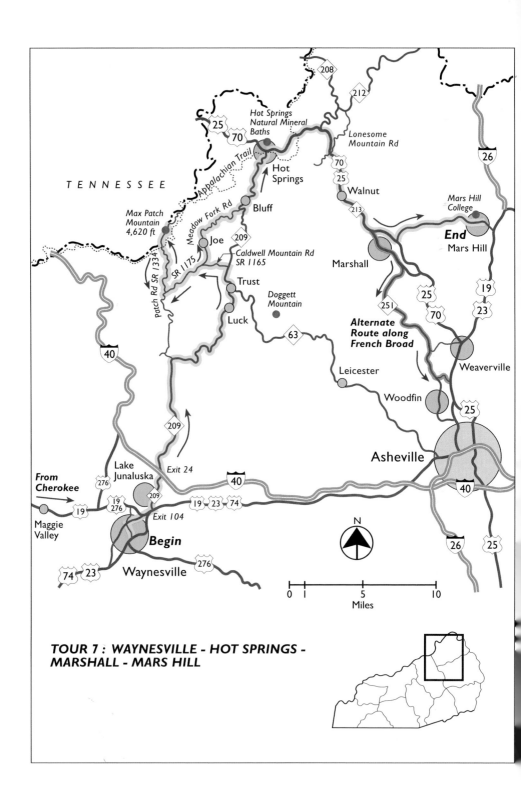

208

212

Hot Springs
Natural Mineral
Baths

25

70

Lonesome
Mountain Rd

26

TENNESSEE

Appalachian Trail

Hot
Springs

70
25

Walnut

Mars Hill
College

Max Patch
Mountain
4,620 ft

Meadow Fork Rd

Bluff

213

End
Mars Hill

patch Rd SR 1334

SR 1175

Joe

209

Caldwell Mountain Rd
SR 1165

Marshall

Trust

Doggett
Mountain

19

Luck

251

25

70

23

**Alternate
Route along
French Broad**

63

40

Leicester

Weaverville

Woodfin

25

**From
Cherokee**

Lake
Junaluska

Exit 24

276

19
276

209

Asheville

N

Begin

40

Maggie
Valley

Exit 104

19 – 23 – 74

40

74   23

Waynesville

276

26   25

0   1   5   10
Miles

**TOUR 7 : WAYNESVILLE – HOT SPRINGS –
MARSHALL – MARS HILL**

in schools and at storytelling festivals across the country. He has published more than a half-dozen story collections, several instructional books for would-be writers and storytellers, a raft of audio recordings, and a novel, *Thirteen Miles from Suncrest* (1994). The fictional territory for Davis's work—"Nantahala County" and the town of "Sulphur Springs"—bears strong resemblance to Haywood County and Waynesville.

The narrator of Davis's novel, Medford Henry McGee, receives a journal for his tenth birthday. In it he records an account of his life from 1910 to 1913. McGee lives on a farm with his family thirteen miles from the town of Suncrest near a massive logging operation. Davis is writing what he knows; this novel is likely based on the early experiences of his parents on the outskirts of Waynesville and the historic logging camp called Sunburst, described in Tour 2. In a compelling, naive style, Davis imagines the details of daily mountain life at the beginning of the twentieth century:

Sunday, March 20, 1910

Father says this is the hardest month of the winter. It is not because it is cold because it is not. It is hard as far as food goes. We are completely out of apples now. The pork in the smokehouse is down to just some fatback. We have some potatoes, which are kept in the bedroom so that they will not freeze and we have plenty of cornmeal so we know that we will not starve. But we do not have any cabbages left or carrots and the turnips are just froze into the ground. We can not even get a little mess of turnip greens right now but they will come out pretty soon.

We did have a little dry spell a week ago and Father burned off the garden to kill the weed seeds and then hitched up the mules to plow with. The mules are U. S. Grant and Robert E. Lee. Father named them that because he says that they are both real strong but that it is all but impossible to get them to cooperate and to pull together. Anyway he finally did get the garden plowed and harrowed.

He always plants peas on Saint Patrick's Day which was on last Thursday. But he planted a patch of turnips yesterday because it was in the dark of the moon. He says that things that grow under the ground grow better if you plant them in the dark of the moon and things that grow on top of the ground do better in the light of the moon. I like turnip greens better than turnips so I wish he had just waited and planted them when the moon gets light again.

What I wanted to know is what is best to do when Saint Patrick's Day comes in the dark of the moon like it just did. Should you still plant the

peas then or wait until the moon changes its phase? We always plant potatoes on Good Friday because Father says that you plant potatoes when
Jesus was in the grave. What if it is the light of the moon then? Maybe
it doesn't work out that way though since Easter slides around on the
calendar according to the moon anyway. I don't understand planting
by the moon.

If we can make it on cornbread and beans around here until about the
first of May we will start to have some turnip greens to go with them. It
just about hurts my jaws to even think about that but I am riting about
it because I know that the time is coming just like it does ever year. I hope
the peas come up.—From *Thirteen Miles from Suncrest*, by Donald Davis
(Little Rock, Ark.: August House, 1994), 27–28.

Waynesville was also home for many years to Georgia-born writer Caroline
Miller. In 1934 her novel *Lamb in His Bosom* won the Pulitzer Prize in fiction as
well as France's Prix Femina. The book became an immediate bestseller and has
remained in print over the years. Caroline Miller's celebrity quickly dimmed,
however, when Margaret Mitchell won the Pulitzer for *Gone with the Wind* only
three years later in 1937, becoming Georgia's second-ever fiction winner. Meanwhile, the fanfare that had surrounded Miller's meteoric success destroyed her
marriage to her high-school English teacher, who had also been her writing
coach.

Miller soon married Clyde Ray Jr., a florist and antique dealer in Waynesville.
She left Georgia to live in the North Carolina mountains and continue her writing. Her second novel, *Lebanon*, was published in 1944, but—unbeknownst to
the author until after publication—it had been drastically edited. The publishers claimed that World War II paper shortages necessitated the draconian cuts
to the text. Discouraged but undaunted, Miller finished other manuscripts in
her lifetime, but none made it into print.

After her second husband passed away, Miller spent her last years in a small
house in the hills near Waynesville and was buried in Green Hill Cemetery. In
the afterword to the 1993 edition of *Lamb in His Bosom*, published only a year
after Miller's death, historian and feminist critic Elizabeth Fox-Genovese credits Miller for writing what might well be the best representation of the lives of
southern whites who did not hold slaves during the antebellum period.

Coming into town on US 276, it is quickly apparent that Waynesville today is
not the sleepy crossroads of Caroline Miller's era or Donald Davis's youth. Now
with some 55,000 residents, Waynesville regularly celebrates its Appalachian

heritage through street dances, summer arts and craft shows, and an apple harvest festival in October.

Waynesville citizens also delight in bringing outstanding performers from far afield. As home to Folkmoot USA, an international dance festival held each year in mid-July, Waynesville's summertime population swells with visitors who come to see performances by dance and music groups from around the world. The Atlanta Ballet generally comes to town in late September for an annual performance at Haywood Community College. (For more information on local festivals and concerts, contact the Haywood County Arts Council, 828-452-0593 or see <http://www.haywoodarts.org/>.)

■ THE "KINGDOM OF MADISON"

MADISON COUNTY: JUNE 1999
Where North Carolina locks
like a final puzzle piece
into eastern Tennessee,
old songs of salvation rise
through static on Sunday night
in this mountain county where
my name echoes on gravestones
dimmed by time like the evening
a kinsman held fire, let it lick
his palm like a pet before
he raised that hand so that we might
see providence as his tongue
forged a new language bellowed
in a pentecostal blaze.
That is all I remember:
an unburned hand, those strange words,
what came before or after
on that long ago Sunday
dark as beyond headlights
as I practice smaller acts
of faith on hill crests, blind curves,
and though my life lies elsewhere
some whisper inside urges
another destination,

as if that unburned hand were
raised in welcome, still might lead
me to another state marked
by no human boundary,
where my inarticulate
heart might finally find voice
in words cured by fire, water.
—From *Raising the Dead*, by Ron Rash
    (Oak Ridge, Tenn.: Iris Press, 2002), 55.

To experience the blind curves and jagged hills of Madison County that Ron Rash describes, head northeast from Waynesville on us 19/23/74 back toward Asheville. Take exit 104 onto nc 209, which rolls north toward Hot Springs. This scenic route will soon cross I-40 at exit 24 and then travel through Haywood County's pastoral hills, where wide stretches of cultivated fields spread out on either side of the road. The cut through the countryside eventually narrows, flanked by forest, and begins to climb toward the lofty Madison County line. Coming along Cove Creek, the road makes a sharp dogleg to the right at Cove. Keep climbing.

Madison is made of mountains that were, and still are, challenging to traverse. Fortunately Manly Wade Wellman, one of North Carolina's most prolific writers across many genres, spent summers here and set about in his later years to write an interpretive history entitled *The Kingdom of Madison: A Southern Mountain Fastness and Its People* (1973).

Wellman was born in Angola, Africa, the son of a medical missionary. He worked a number of blue-collar jobs around the United States before becoming a journalist. After beating out William Faulkner for the Ellery Queen Short Fiction Prize in 1946, he moved to North Carolina and eventually landed in Chapel Hill, where he taught aspiring writers through the University of North Carolina's Evening College. As a naturally inquisitive journalist, Wellman absorbed volumes of historical detail from his adopted state. So skillful was he at exploring the "what if?" of his historical investigations that a new genre of historical mystery known as "speculative fiction" was considered by some to be his unique invention.

Wellman had published eighty books by the time he turned eighty. He tackled wild tales of science fiction, the very particular history of several North Carolina counties, and a number of mysteries and legends that had been passed down through generations. He also wrote several children's books. Fellow mystery writer Elizabeth Daniels Squire, who lived in neighboring Bun-

The pastoral journey from Waynesville into the "Kingdom of Madison."

combe County, wrote of Wellman: "And what kind of person is this man of many words who is probably North Carolina's most-published author? A man of strong opinions, raging interests, old fashioned courtliness, loyal friendship and quick readiness for a fistfight with anyone he believes has unfairly insulted him or anyone he loves" (Elizabeth Daniels Squire, *The Liz Reader*, ed. C. B. Squire [Johnson City, Tenn.: Silver Dagger Mysteries, 2002], 78).

Wellman fit in well in Madison County, and he loved its ancient geology. He also favored the dark and violent "bloody Madison" stories that are still told here, and tales of the frequent clashes between the hardscrabble settlers and those outsiders who came to "improve" their lot before and after the Civil War. With his mastery of classic literature and mythology, Wellman brought a broad

The Kingdom of Madison *author Manly Wade Wellman and his wife, Frances, photographed by mystery writer Elizabeth Daniels Squire. Courtesy of the North Carolina Collection of the Pack Memorial Library, Asheville, North Carolina.*

context to his commentary on the county, and he offers his own truth with hearty amusement at the fickle ways of humans. Here he introduces Madison:

> It is shaped somewhat like a fist, with its jagged knuckles against the lofty ridge of the Smoky Mountains along the Tennessee border, and it lies pent, but not cramped, among great heights, shaggy with trees. Its people are apt to answer the stranger, "I'm from Madison County," because most of them get their mail along the rural route, not in town. Their few towns and settlements are so small among the soaring crests and deep-plunging hollows, where roads wriggle their way like snakes. You can't get into Madison County save through a gap, sometimes a daunting gap, with a name like Sams or Devil's Fork Gap, Betsy's or Lick Log, or Fox Cabin Gap, Kate Gap or the gap called Windy.
> The French Broad River rips powerfully through the county's middle, fighting its way from between high cliffs upstream in the direction of Asheville at the southeast, then out again, beyond Hot Springs into Tennessee at the northwest. It is an old, old river among old, old mountains, and it has wallowed itself a canyon for a bed. Its chief tributaries are the

Laurel and the Ivy, also deeply driven into the rock. Some of the creeks are named Spillcorn and Sprinkle and Shut-in, Bull and Bear and Turkey and Doe; are named Paw Paw, White Oak, Brush Meadow, Big Pine, Little Pine; are named Puncheon Fork and Crooked Branch, Wolf Laurel and Little Laurel and Shelton Laurel. The mountains they wash are not the highest of the Appalachians, but they are high and steep enough. The tallest is Sandy Mush, just sixty feet less than a mile above the level of the distant sea. And there are Sugarloaf Knob, Max Patch, Bluff and Walnut and Hurricane, Bald and Little Bald, Big Butt, Hebo and Sodom. . . .

The rocks that make up these mountains, say geologists, in their scientifically guarded fashion, are among the oldest in the world. The Appalachians hereabouts have no date. They came before dates. . . .

Towering heights rose here in Earth's new formed crust, hurled upward like billows into gigantic peaks and combs and crests that solidified and stayed, while stormy winds of the ages swept around them. An arm of the ocean came washing there, and its creatures teemed and died and left their deposits of lime. As the waters gave back again, volcanoes belched their lavas upon the older rocks. The heights crumpled violently into new shapes, as though in the great fashioning hand of Creation itself. The mountains stood high and naked in the world's crass youth.—From *The Kingdom of Madison: A Southern Mountain Fastness and Its People*, by Manly Wade Wellman (Alexander, N.C.: Land of the Sky Books, 2001), 15–16, 23–24.

■ TRUST AND LUCK

Continuing on NC 209, at the top of Hebo Mountain, you'll cross the line into Madison County. Sandymush Bald and Little Sandymush Bald are to the south and southeast. Here you are near the southernmost tip of Madison County, bordered on the west by Haywood and on the south by Buncombe County. To the north is Tennessee. The Pisgah National Forest Boundary is on your right, as is spirited Spring Creek, which passes under NC 209 to the other side of the road just before you are in Luck.

Though Luck is hardly a busy point of commerce today, it's still on the North Carolina map and offers the much-photographed Pink J. Plemmons Groceries and Feed Store. The rusting gas pumps and the rushing sound of nearby Spring Creek—loud as a cloudburst on dry pavement—invite imagination and nostalgia. Ron Rash might well have been writing about the Plemmons Store in this poem:

COKE BOX

To get there, follow a road
rarely traveled anymore,
the blacktop pocked with pot holes,
scrub oak gnawing the shoulders,
left like a dry riverbed
after the four-lane was built.
Pull over where gas pumps stand
like old diving gear, globe-faced,
barnacled with rust. Barngray
arthritic planks raise a room
thick-shadowed, felt before seen:
floorboards slick with linseed oil,
breeze of ceiling fan, the store's
slow emergence like something
brought up from deep water,
and when all's surfaced it's there,
the lidded long metal trough
you open like a coffin
before plunging half an arm
in ice shards thick as gravel,
grabbling for glass, the dark
sugared water you will raise
to lips, swallow, that you might
imagine forty years back,
a man cancer-caught, AWOL
from his death bed, from women
who thought they'd hidden the truck
keys well enough. Close your eyes,
taste what he tasted, a cold
sweet longing slaked, imagine
his hand closing the coke box,
and know this is why you've come.
—From *Raising the Dead*, by Ron Rash, 54.

Rash, a Boiling Springs native whose poem "Madison County: June 1999" be-gins this section of the tour, heard many stories of Madison from his relatives, who have lived in the area since the mid-1700s. As a child, Rash spent time just over Doggett Mountain in nearby Leicester, where his grandfather, who

In Luck on NC 209, Madison County.

never learned to read, pretended to read Dr. Seuss's *Cat in the Hat* to his beloved grandson, making up a story to go with the pictures as he went along. Rash was always amazed how the story and words would change each time he sat with his grandfather, which, very early in life, convinced him of the magical power of writing.

From Luck, the road goes on to Trust, now marked only by an abandoned general store where NC 63 begins to wind over Doggett Gap to Leicester—pronounced variously as "Lester" and "LEE-sester." Now a bedroom community of Asheville, Leicester was the birthplace of poet, essayist, novelist, and scholar Jim Wayne Miller. Miller's dedication to the region kept him traveling across these mountains delivering lectures, giving readings, and helping to develop programs in the field of Appalachian studies for high school and college students.

Miller was the oldest of six children raised on a Leicester farm with both sets of grandparents nearby. His father was the service manager at the Firestone Tire Company in Asheville. Miller attended Berea College in Kentucky, studied in Germany, where he became fluent in the language, and developed a lifelong interest in German literature. Miller earned a Ph.D. in German language and American literature from Vanderbilt University. He joined the faculty at Western Kentucky University in 1963 and taught for several summers at the University of Tennessee and Appalachian State in Boone. Miller published countless essays, several translations of German works, eight poetry collections, and two novels. He received the Thomas Wolfe Literary Award for his poetry collection, *The Mountains Have Come Closer*, in 1980. In 1986, he was named poet laureate of Kentucky. Miller was a passionate teacher and a loyal student of Appalachia. His poem "Names" speaks to the vivid names of people and places in Madison County and specifically references Trust:

NAMES
Preachers and professors came into the mountains
brought Bibles, volumes of calf-bound classics,

stately Latin and Greek hexameters,
memories stacked to the rafters with chapter and verse.

Often they were the namers. Creaking west
through mountain gaps and passes, they scattered old-world

names over the new—the kings and prophets,
gods and goddesses of Greece, Rome, and the Holy Land.

Names set like marble monuments in wilderness
made muddy roads and new grounds numinous.

History, like a river out of banks,
set temples alongside shake-roofed barns.

So Mars Hill, where a Roman war god
had his temple, appeared a Baptist town

in North Carolina. The heathen goddess, Juno,
lives locally over a county line in Buncombe.

Though no blind Greek poet, Homer Hawkins,
who farmed for shares, had a thousand stories.

The Brier's grandfather, Hezekiah, fell tipsy
at a baptizing, into the pool, but clambered

out, unregenerate still, though like his namesake,
the Judean king, he detested idolatry.

Nobody was named Jesus in the mountains,
but Marys and Marthas, Matthews, Marks, Lukes

and Johns filled church and schoolroom benches.
Plato taught the Brick Church Sunday School

while Jupiter and Socrates lived as slaves,
graves unmarked in Brick Church Cemetery.

Hebrew kings ruled sixty-acre farms.
Isaiahs in overalls prophecied dry weather.

Vergil ran the mill and cleared newground.
Horace rived shakes and bottomed rocking chairs.

Other names grew up, rooted in local life
and wry reflection on it: Sandy Mush.

Hogeye, Rabbitham, Bearwallow, grittily
concrete, though close to abstract as Luck and Trust.

Then came those names, concessions to overwhelming
obviousness of numbers: Meadowstown, Surrett Cove.

And those taken from the Cherokee:
Cullowhee, Oconaluftee, Nantahala.

But if the lofty and the grand were humbled
in the homemade frames and faces of sang diggers,

farmers and squirrel hunters, the homely and low
discovered their own dignity and beauty

on Sugar Creek, at Snow Hill Gap, in Piney Grove.

—From *The Brier Poems*, by Jim Wayne Miller
    (Frankfort, Ky.: Gnomon Press, 1997), 122–24.

"The Old Home Place"—a landmark on Caldwell Mountain Road.

■ MAX PATCH

From the intersection of NC 209 with NC 63 continue on 209 beyond Trust and look for Caldwell Mountain Road (SR 1165), coming up soon on your left. Take Caldwell Mountain. You'll pass by a remarkable mural called "The Old Home Place," painted on a silo. When you reach the "T" at Meadow Fork Road (SR 1175), turn left. You'll then come to another crossroads. Turn right onto Patch Road (SR 1334) and follow the signs to Max Patch.

On the clear day in May that we drove along Meadow Fork Road, a cloud of yellow and black swallowtail butterflies was floating beside the road, individually landing on occasion for a sip of freshly puddled rainwater. A story called "It's a Sign" in local writer Sheila Kay Adams's first collection tells of a similar natural occurrence in this vicinity.

We had wandered through the mountains and gradually worked our way back down to the branch, where we had laid down on our stomachs and watched the minners dart back and forth through the shafts of sunlight that sifted down through the leaves of the buckeye trees. We dipped our fingers into the water and the minners came right up; and if we stayed real still, they would nibble our fingertips. If we moved our hands the slightest bit, they would streak off in all directions, only to return when the water became still again.

Suddenly out of nowhere, came the sound of a strong breeze—but the air was perfectly still. Granny looked up and about that time a big yellow and black butterfly landed on the bank beside her, and then another, and another. They swooped down out of the sky and covered the banks of the stream, the trunks of the trees, and me and Granny. They settled on our arms, our hair, our faces. I will never forget the way Granny looked with her hair and face and shoulders all covered with butterflies opening and closing their wings. Granny's skin looked to be a moving, living mass of yellow! And through the living yellow I could see Granny's shining blue eyes. I got so excited that I jumped up and started trying to catch them, and Granny spoke sharply to me for one of the first times in my life.

"Git down an' be still, girl!"

I was so startled and hurt by Granny's tone of voice that I did as I was told immediately. The butterflies soon settled back on me, and I looked at those on my arm. I could see their tiny bright eyes, their curled velvet tongues; even more, I thought I could see their "life's-blood" running through their paper-thin wings.

And then, in a fluid and beautiful motion, they lifted as one and spiraled into the blue September sky and were gone. Granny reached out and took me in her arms and held me fiercely for a minute.

"It's a sign, Sealy, it's a sign of some kind. God sent them butterflies just for us. I'm sure it's a sign."

—From *Come Go Home with Me*, by Sheila Kay Adams (Chapel Hill: University of North Carolina Press, 1995), 2–3.

Sheila Kay Adams was born and raised in Sodom, a small village not far from the Tennessee line. Adams is a former public school teacher who turned to storytelling and ballad singing as a way to share her rich Madison County heritage. She graduated from Mars Hill College in 1974 and has won many awards for her performances at folk festivals. Her first novel, *My Old True Love*, was published by Algonquin Books of Chapel Hill in 2004.

"It's a sign" when butterflies gather to drink from a rain puddle in Madison County.

Continue on the Patch road, following the signs to Max Patch. From the top of Max Patch Mountain on a clear day, you can see Mount Mitchell (Yancey County) and Roan Mountain (Mitchell County) in the far distance, but this high grassy knob of some 350 acres also overlooks the closer Smokies and the Black Mountains. The Appalachian Trail traverses the summit at 4,500 feet.

Park in the designated lot and hike about a quarter-mile to the summit. In late spring, if you take the looping path to the left, you may have a chance for some good bird watching and wildflower identification along the way (and the climb is not as steep). As the trail reaches the grassy bald, you'll see bluebird houses every thirty yards or so, which are vigorously visited in the springtime.

Max Patch is a great place to picnic, fly a kite, and read from Sheila Kay Adams's story collection or from Asheville native Michael McFee's fine poetry collection, *Sad Girl Sitting on a Running Board* (1991). McFee studied at Cornell University with North Carolina poet and novelist Robert Morgan. Today he teaches creative writing at the University of North Carolina at Chapel Hill.

In his long, narrative poem "Grace," McFee describes the events of the summer of 1945 at the Grace Lumber Mill, where young Molly comes to visit her

Along the trail to the Max Patch summit.

older sister, Lois, who is keeping the books at her father-in-law's lumber operation, waiting for the return of her husband from World War II. At age fourteen, Molly spends her days exploring the countryside in Haywood County on Salem, a five-gaited Morgan horse.

GRACE (EXCERPT)

Max Patch is a four-mile ride. By the time
they arrive, its spring-pool is a miracle,
a draft of heaven on the tongue. Their climb
across the bald is mild, a soft ramble
through buttercups and uncut grass. Several
false summits swell; Molly and Salem know
not to pause, to press on to that table
of slate, the Altar Rock, where the view flows
unhindered in every direction, in blue rows

of mountains and valleys that never stop,
everything slowly refined into sky

Traveling back in time on the road to Max Patch.

at the horizon, as if God had dropped
that Rock during creation at the eye
of this Appalachian puddle, then fired
it fast, fixing these geologic waves
for Molly to sit at their focus. Why
was Max Patch bald, were there really huge caves
inside, was this a ritual rock where Cherokee braves

sacrificed virgins? Molly could rehearse
all the legends, and often did, looking
for Indian hieroglyphics, a deep curse
or blessing carved into the Altar Rock,
a verbal arrowhead, a clue, a shock

from the inscrutable past. But not today.
She lets the animals loose, a winded flock,
then sits crosslegged at the heart of the great
warm stone, facing west, to eat lunch and meditate . . .
—From *Sad Girl Sitting on a Running Board*, by Michael McFee
    (Frankfort, Ky.: Gnomon Press, 1991), 66–67.

■ HOT SPRINGS

From Max Patch, retrace your route on Patch Road, looking for Little Creek Road, which will come in shortly on your left. Look for a sign indicating the direction to Hot Springs. Follow Little Creek Road, which merges with Long Branch Road and dead-ends at Meadow Fork at a place called Joe. Turn left on Meadow Fork, heading generally northeast, back to NC 209. At 209 turn left and follow alongside Spring Creek through Bluff. You'll pass the Rocky Bluff gorge and campground on your right before coming into the town of Hot Springs. The Appalachian Trail has come along in the deep woods beside you from Max Patch and now emerges, proceeding right through town on 209, crossing the French Broad River by bridge before turning back to an unpaved trail.

Before you get as far as the main part of town and the river, however, watch for a state historical marker on your right, placed in front of a large Victorian house with a terraced yard. As mentioned in Tour 4, *English Folk Songs from the Southern Appalachians* (1917), coauthored by Olive Dame Campbell (who founded the John C. Campbell Folk School) and Cecil J. Sharp, was significantly shaped by the musical talents of Madison County residents at the beginning of the twentieth century. As the historical marker notes, Sharp and his research assistant, Maud Karpeles, met the Campbells in Asheville and then traveled all over Madison County collecting songs passed down from memory over the centuries by European settlers here. The film *Songcatcher* (2000) was partly based on Sharp's travels and Campbell's previous song collecting. (Writer and balladeer Sheila Kay Adams from nearby Sodom was a technical adviser and singing coach on the film.)

The two-story Victorian house belonged to Jane Gentry, who hosted Sharp and Karpeles when they visited in 1916. Today the house (and Gentry's piano) belongs to Elmer Hall, a former minister and natural foods restaurateur who is now a gourmet chef and innkeeper. Hall runs Sunnybank Inn—a by-invitation-only bed and breakfast that caters to through-hikers, musicians, and other returning guests who appreciate the vegetarian fare and low-tech accommodations. Hall also sponsors an annual retreat for wild mushroom hunters.

Collection of old license plates near Joe in Madison County.

For more on local musical traditions, see *Jane Hicks Gentry: A Singer among Singers* (1998), written by Hot Springs ballad singer, storyteller, and recording artist Betty N. Smith. The book earned the Willie Parker Peace History Book Award given by the North Carolina Society of Historians. A graduate of the University of North Carolina at Greensboro, Smith performs across the South, teaching about the musical history and heritage of the region. In 1999 the Appalachian Writers Association honored Smith for her cultural preservation work. Her one-woman show, *Mountain Riddle*, was produced by the Southern Appalachian Repertory Theatre in Mars Hill.

In addition to hosting songcatchers, Hot Springs has long been a stopping place for weary travelers and those seeking rest and respite in the mountains.

In the early 1800s, a road between Asheville and the Tennessee line was begun. This "turnpike" crossed the French Broad at Warm Springs (today's Hot Springs) and climbed toward the Tennessee line at Paint Rock. As the road was improved, additional accommodations for travelers sprang up, including a popular tavern in Warm Springs and another establishment owned by the family of future North Carolina governor Zebulon Vance several miles to the southeast. Travelers who suffered the rocky, cliffside trails — including the famous Methodist preacher Francis Asbury, who wrote at length of his miserable journeys through these mountains — were especially appreciative of the opportunity for a warm soak in the hot waters that still bubble up naturally on the banks of the French Broad.

When it was finally completed, the Asheville Turnpike ran from Greeneville, Tennessee, to Greenville, South Carolina (and ultimately on to Charleston). It was the favored route of "drovers" — farmers who drove their pigs and sheep to market, often in enormous herds. Businesses prospered in Warm Springs thanks to these passing travelers, and as word of the natural hot springs spread a brisk tourist business also began. What had been a modest tavern near the springs in 1831 became James Patton's Warm Springs Hotel in 1837. The building burned in 1840 and was rebuilt as a brick hotel with 350 guest rooms and a dining room that could seat somewhere between 500 and 600 guests. It was then known as Patton's White House.

Manly Wade Wellman explains that in 1862, James Henry Rumbough, who owned an overland carriage business, bought Patton's White House and soon left his wife behind to guard the property against looters while he fought in the Civil War. Rumbough came home a decorated Confederate colonel with plenty of money in his pocket and resumed running the hotel quite profitably.

In 1875, writer Frances Christine Fisher Tiernan of Salisbury, North Carolina, visited the French Broad Valley and wrote her travelogue as a novel under the gender-ambiguous pen name of Christian Reid. *The Land of the Sky: Adventures in Mountain By-Ways* sold well nationwide and has remained in print for more than a century. The purple prose Reid heaped on Warm Springs only increased business, and the "Land of the Sky" became a permanent moniker attached to Asheville and environs. Reid wrote of her first trek to Warm Springs:

The air is like crystal, and a glory of sunlight streams on the river with its masses of rock, and the mountains that overshadow it. In the five miles that lie between our place of lodging and the banks of Laurel, the picturesque loveliness changes and deepens constantly. The river grows more

and more tumultuous, and its waves wear caps of foam like the breakers of the ocean, as they plunge in stormy rapids over its hidden rocks.
—From *The Land of the Sky: Adventures in Mountain By-Ways*, by Christian Reid (Alexander, N.C.: Land of the Sky Books, 2001), 44–45.

Alas, the author's touring party had to cross the swirling river, which had risen precipitously from constant spring rains, and the drama of their crossing is extravagantly rendered. But the reward, as it turns out, is worth the risk:

It is not possible to imagine a stronger sense of contrast than that of which we are conscious on coming to this gay watering place out of the wild gorge through which we have passed, and after the rough life of which we have had a glimpse. We feel as if we had entered by magic into another world. Here is a large hotel, with all the appliances of civilization; well-dressed people in every direction on the piazzas and lawn; stir, movement, and all that air of do-nothing gayety which pervades such places.
—From *The Land of the Sky*, by Christian Reid, 48.

By the time the railroad made it to Warm Springs in 1882, the virtues of the town and its curative waters had been written about in dozens of journals and magazines. However, Charles Dudley Warner, a popular Massachusetts-born essayist of the era and a close friend of Mark Twain, did not find the hotel particularly elegant in 1884. He nevertheless enjoyed the hot baths, according to Wellman.

Later that year, the Warm Springs Hotel burned to the ground, and Colonel Rumbough was forced to sell his property to a group of investors from New York who not only rebuilt the hotel but also changed the town's name to *Hot* Springs as a marketing ploy. Now called the Mountain Park Hotel, the new resort had 200 guest rooms that were lit by gas and heated with steam, some with open fireplaces. The new structure housed a dining room that could seat 300, a ballroom, and more than a thousand feet of verandahs, some with glass sun parlors. As local writer Della Hazel Moore tells us, resident physicians were always available to assist ailing guests, and an orchestra played in the ballroom every night for those inclined to party. In addition to sixteen marble-lined pools in a new bathhouse, the owners added a hundred-foot-long swimming pool. They also developed Hot Springs's first golf course, called Wana Luna, named after a legendary Cherokee couple—Wana and Luna—who supposedly jumped to their deaths at nearby Lover's Leap.

The Mountain Park Hotel in Hot Springs, where O. Henry (William Sydney Porter) brought his second wife for their honeymoon in 1907. The hotel burned to the ground in 1920. Print donated by Father Graves, used courtesy of the North Carolina Collection of the Pack Memorial Library, Asheville, North Carolina.

Short story writer O. Henry (William Sydney Porter) brought his second wife, Sara Lindsay Coleman, to the Mountain Park Hotel for their honeymoon. (Porter, who was born in Greensboro, spent time in the mountains around Asheville and is buried in the Riverside Cemetery in Asheville. See Tours 8 and 9.)

No matter how popular the facility, however, the cost of such extravagant amenities in this remote spot soon forced its New York investors to put the Mountain Park Hotel up for sale. E. W. Grove Sr., who would eventually develop the Grove Park Inn and the Grove Arcade in Asheville, considered purchasing the property, but Colonel Rumbough rushed to buy it back and ran it until 1913, when he sold it for $100,000. Once again seriously damaged, this time by a disastrous flood in 1916, the hotel and grounds were then leased to the U.S. government for the internment of German soldiers, including the German Imperial Band, during World War I.

Finally, in 1920, according to newspaper reports, it took only an hour and a half for the Mountain Park Hotel to burn to the ground.

Della Hazel Moore's history of Hot Springs outlines major historical events and notable stories from its famous and infamous families. In this excerpt, she describes a writer in residence in the early 1900s whom Manly Wade Wellman also mentions in *The Kingdom of Madison*. Wellman had a bit less sympathy than Moore about Sally Weir, whom he characterized as being "condescendingly preoccupied with the dwellers in mountain coves, who may not have had her own educational and cultural advantages" (133).

Two other interesting people who lived at Hot Springs for a while were Mrs. Royce and her daughter, Sally Royce Weir. They had a unique house built on the mountain opposite the warm springs, overlooking the French Broad River. The house was designed by one of the women. The architecture of the house was peculiar. Men did the heavy work, but much of the building of the house was performed by the women. A door that was thought to be a china cabinet was an enclosed secret stairway.

The ladies spent a lot of time having wells dug, trying to find hot water. It was very dangerous for a stranger to walk on their property, as one never knew if one would fall into a well. They named their place, "The Tempest." Mrs. Weir was an author. She recorded some of the old legends that were published by the press of S. B. Newman of Knoxville Tennessee in 1906. — From *Hot Springs of North Carolina*, by Della Hazel Moore (Johnson City, Tenn.: Overmountain Press, 1992), 56.

Today with a population of some 650 residents, Hot Springs is a welcome taste of civilization for through-hikers on the Appalachian Trail and a good place to begin a day's worth of hiking for those who want to follow the AT across the river bridge and up to Lover's Leap for a dizzying view of the town and river valley below. Rafting enthusiasts also gather here before and after they ride the French Broad, as do travelers seeking a dip in the comforting geothermal waters.

Hot Springs has several restaurants, a pub, and shops that sell antiques, crafts, outdoor gear, fishing supplies, gifts, and ice cream. Bluff Mountain Outfitters offers public Internet access and carries local literature, including Della Hazel Moore's book. See <http://www.bluffmountain.com>.

Because of the hot springs, quite a number of massage therapists have moved here. Accommodations around Hot Springs include half a dozen bed and breakfasts, a number of rental cottages and cabins, a couple of motels, and three retreat centers.

Not far from Hot Springs is the community of Sodom Laurel, documented by award-winning photographer Rob Amberg. *Sodom Laurel Album* (2002) is Amberg's oral history and photography project that captures two decades of community life in the area. Amberg reckons with the coming of Interstate 26 and the inevitable changes to formerly isolated communities that such a major traffic artery brings. He focuses much of the book on his relationship with the late Dellie Chandler Norton, writer Sheila Kay Adams's great-aunt and a distinguished storyteller and ballad singer who received a North Carolina Folk Heritage Award in 1990. The book also includes a CD of performances by Norton and other local musicians.

As you follow US 25/70 out of Hot Springs toward Marshall, you'll pass by Lonesome Mountain Road, which leads up to the Sodom Laurel community, and you'll pass by the community of Walnut, which figures in Pamela Duncan's *Moon Women* (2001). Duncan set her first novel in Madison County, though she was born in Asheville and grew up in Black Mountain, Swannanoa, and Shelby. It's the story of three generations of mountain women, inspired by stories from Duncan's maternal grandmother.

"Now I go up to Madison County a couple of times a year with my Uncle JoJo," Duncan explains on her website:

> We stop at the little white Methodist church in Walnut to put flowers on my grandmother's grave, and afterward I wander through the graveyard feeling a little lost and a little found at the same time. I'm not a native of Madison County, but because of my grandmother's stories, that graveyard is like a library, so many of the names familiar, so much behind each name, whole volumes waiting there in silence. From the graveyard, JoJo and I usually drive the corkscrew curves down to Barnard, across the French Broad River, and up on Slatey Knob to visit our cousins. We're always welcomed with open arms in spite of long absence, and that's when I feel a little bit like maybe I do belong.—From <http://www .pameladuncan.com/work3.htm>.

■ MARSHALL

Marshall has been called the town that's a mile long and a street wide, because it is perched along the narrow shore of the French Broad, where the bank rises steeply. Here the Madison County Courthouse, a number of other government agencies, and a few commercial ventures make a quiet go of it. Blanahassett Island, sitting in the middle of the river, just across the bridge from downtown, is headquarters for the Madison County School System.

Marshall is home to poet and songwriter Keith Flynn, who is also the founding editor of the *Asheville Poetry Review*, a biannual journal of poems, interviews, translations, essays, historical perspectives, and book reviews. Under Flynn's guidance, the journal has published North Carolina and international writers and has achieved a wide distribution. Flynn is the author of *The Talking Drum* (1991), *The Book of Monsters* (1994), and *The Lost Sea* (2000).

■ MARS HILL

To visit nearby Mars Hill, come back up the hill from downtown Marshall to the 25/70 Bypass and take NC 213 into this little college town that sits above the new stretch of Interstate 26 connecting Asheville with Erwin, Tennessee.

Mars Hill College is the oldest educational institution in western North Carolina. It was established as a boarding school in 1856 under the name of French Broad Baptist Academy and did not become a junior college until 1921. It was approved as a four-year institution by the Baptist Convention in 1960 and awarded its first four-year degrees in 1964. Today the English Department offers a concentration in professional writing. The Renfro Library continues to enhance its special collections on local art, history, and literature, including the Bascom Lamar Lunsford Folk Music Collection, the Southern Appalachian Photographic Archives, and the Gertrude M. Ruskin Collection of Cherokee Indian artifacts and materials. For more information, see <http://www.mhc.edu/>.

■ FRENCH BROAD CORRIDOR

If you'd like to get a long, close view of the French Broad River, consider driving an alternate route south from Main Street in Marshall on NC 251 all the way into Woodfin, on the northern outskirts of Asheville. Here the road follows the river closely on the right and is flanked by sheer cliffs along the left. As you come nearer to Asheville, several parks including the Walnut Island River Park and Ledges Whitewater River Park offer picnic tables, hiking and biking paths, and tubing put-ins. NC 251 eventually becomes Riverside Drive in Asheville, which is discussed in Tour 8.

Along this stretch the French Broad is flowing north, back toward Marshall. The river is wide and, by turns, shallow and quite deep. Exercise caution if you decide to get wet. If you keep to the riverbank, be sure you've brought along a copy of *The French Broad*, Wilma Dykeman's history of the river, first published in 1955 as part of Holt Rinehart's Rivers of America Series.

Dykeman's landmark book drew instant attention nationwide and continues to sell well in the region. Carl Sandburg blurbed the first edition with high praise. More than forty years after its initial publication, the book was honored by the Library of Congress. Using oral history techniques and extensive historical research, Dykeman—whose regional novels are also still popular—writes about every area touched by the river, from its headwaters in Transylvania County near South Carolina to its meanderings in Buncombe and Madison County and across the Tennessee line.

■ LITERARY LANDSCAPE

Wall Street Book Exchange
181 North Wall Street
Waynesville, NC 28786
828-456-5000

This jam-packed Waynesville shop has more than 30,000 used books for perusal and purchase, including a good selection of regional literature and some obscure titles. Be sure to save plenty of time if you're an inveterate browser. Just one block east of Main, Waynesville's Wall Street is a charming lane that runs behind and below the shops of Main Street and is accessible by two different walkways that run between Main and Wall. If parking on Main is a challenge, Wall Street is a good alternative.

Osondu Booksellers
184 North Main Street
Waynesville, NC 28786
828-456-8062
<http://www.osondubooksellers.com/>

Waynesville's first bookstore opened in 1870 near this site and was incorporated as Waynesville Book Company in 1907. Today Osondu is the place in Waynesville to find local literature, a strong selection of regional fiction and poetry, and maps.

Haywood County Public Library
678 South Haywood Street
Waynesville, NC 28786
828-452-5169
<http://www.haywoodlibrary.org/>

This library hosts an ambitious schedule of programs for children and adults. The Haywood Writers Group meets monthly in the library auditorium.

For more than a dozen years, local scholars have led "Let's Talk About It" programs organized by the North Carolina Humanities Council to consider a literary or historical topic in depth. The Friends of the Library also hosts a Great Books discussion series each year. Public access computer terminals are available in this handsome stone facility near the center of town.

Hot Springs Resort & Spa

315 Bridge Street
Hot Springs, NC 28743
828-622-7676
800-462-0933 (toll free)
info@nchotsprings.com
<http://nchotsprings.com/>

Though only a few remnants of the Mountain Park Hotel's marble pools remain, the natural springs still run hot. The unpretentious Hot Springs Resort and Spa, built on the site of the hundred-acre Mountain Park Hotel, allows visitors to imagine the former glory of this turn-of-the-twentieth-century tourist mecca. You can soak here in one of the open cabanas that house individual hot tubs spread out among the trees along the shore of the French Broad River. The resort offers bodywork massages, has a conference center for groups, and is continuing to develop a range of overnight accommodations, including jacuzzi suites, cabins, and campsites. The Madison County Arts Council's annual fundraiser, known as the Bluff Mountain Festival, is also held every year on the grounds of the Hot Springs Resort and Spa. See <http://www.madison countyarts.com/>.

Penland & Sons

50 South Main Street
Marshall, NC 28753
828-649-2811

This old-fashioned dry goods store sells books and more in Marshall. Former Madison County Arts Council director Anne Rawson recommends it for jeans and flannel shirts, quilts and produce, canned goods, books, and equipment. In the heart of downtown Marshall next to Chapels A and B of the local funeral home, the store has remained in the Penland family for generations and is the authentic article. Boxes of old-fashioned stick candy and bags of sugared orange slices sit near recently crafted local pottery, church fans, and crisp ladies handkerchiefs. A glass case holds pork-pie hats that were fashionable for men in the 1940s.

Fresh produce is nearly always available at Penland & Sons Dry Goods in downtown Marshall.

Clearly the store still caters to the particular clothing needs of its local clientele. In addition to the excellent collection of books that all have some connection to Madison County—including Wellman's *The Kingdom of Madison*—Penland & Sons displays historic photos of Marshall in the wake of floods, receiving visiting dignitaries, and enjoying various family and church gatherings. A full collection of booklets on local genealogy and cemetery locations is also on sale.

From the produce baskets set on the sidewalk outside the store we bought the local mountain favorite in season—greasy beans—and some fresh okra. Mrs. Penland weighs the produce inside. You can weigh yourself, too, for a penny on the old scale just inside the door.

Madison County Public Library

1335 North Main Street
Marshall, NC 28753
828-649-3741
<http://madisoncountylibrary.org/>

On a high hill above downtown Marshall, Madison County's very contemporary main library is full of light and provides striking views of the surrounding mountains. Public Internet access is available here along with extensive programming for children and adults, including arts and native crafts demonstrations, a book club, and a special Madison County genealogy collection. There are also branch libraries in Hot Springs and Mars Hill.

Southern Appalachian Repertory Theatre

44 College Street
Mars Hill, NC 28754
828-689-1239 (tickets)
828-689-1384 (office)
sart@mhc.edu
<http://www.sartheatre.com>

Comedy, drama, and music—both standards and world premieres of works about Appalachian culture and heritage—have been a part of the schedule of the Southern Appalachian Repertory Theatre (SART) since 1975. Established in collaboration with Mars Hill College, SART also sponsors ScriptWorks, an annual playwrights' conference and script competition begun in 1982. Every year some one hundred full-length, unpublished and never-produced plays and musicals compete for the chance to be mounted in SART's home, the historic Owen Theatre on the Mars Hill campus, in the season following the competition.

Mars Hill College Bookstore

15 South Main Street
Mars Hill, NC 28754
828-689-1248

Though this shop primarily caters to students and carries textbooks associated with the Mars Hill curriculum, it does stock titles by local writers, including Betty Smith and Sheila Kay Adams, and carries recordings by local musicians.

Literary Speakers Series

c/o Madison County Arts Council
828-649-1301
<http://www.madisoncountyarts.com>

This annual program of the Madison County Arts Council is run by a committee that usually includes local writers. The events are held at different times throughout the year and move from site to site. Readings have been held in barns, inns, school auditoriums, coffee shops, and the public library. Writers give readings and answer questions from the audience. Often the events will combine literature with music or some other art form, such as a quilt show. Writers who participate in the series are also invited to speak at one of Madison County's six schools when they come to town. Consult the arts council for a schedule.

Weaverville and North Asheville

From short story master O. Henry to contemporary mystery writers Sallie Bissell and Liz Squire, this neck of the woods has been a source of respite, recreation, and inspiration to literati for more than a century. F. Scott Fitzgerald wrestled with writer's block at Asheville's Grove Park Inn while his wife Zelda fought mental illness at Highland Hospital. Learn about the unhappy day that Fitzgerald encountered Thomas Wolfe's mother; visit Wolfe's grave in Riverside Cemetery; and observe the rarest of mountain flowers in the Asheville Botanical Gardens.

Writers with a connection to this area: Sallie Bissell, Tony Buttitta, Richard Chess, Jonathan Daniels, Wilma Dykeman, John Ehle, F. Scott Fitzgerald, Zelda Fitzgerald, Charles Frazier, Gail Godwin, Tommy Hays, O. Henry, David Brendan Hopes, Horace Kephart, Sidney Lanier, Valerie Ann Leff, Sharyn McCrumb, Joan Medlicott, Robert Morgan, Peggy B. Parris, Carl Sandburg, James Seay, Janet Beeler Shaw, Nina Simone, Elizabeth Daniels Squire, Thomas Wolfe, Charlotte Young

Once a rural mill town, Weaverville is now a bedroom community to Asheville. In the early 1900s, William Sydney Porter, better known as O. Henry, lived here briefly and based the short story "Let Me Feel Your Pulse" on his experiences in Asheville and Weaverville. The story is one of only two he ever wrote about his native North Carolina.

O. Henry's narrator is a hypochondriac whose search for a cure to his enigmatic illness eventually brings him to Pineville (in reality Asheville, where O. Henry spent time near the end of his life). From Pineville he goes out into the country near Weaverville for the cure:

I heard of a country doctor who lived in the mountains nearby. I went to see him and told him the whole story.

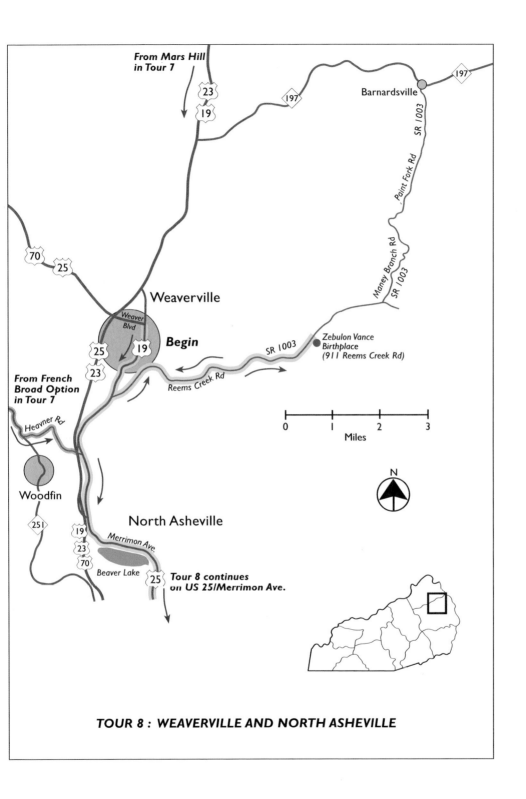

From Mars Hill
in Tour 7

23
19

197

197

Barnardsville

SR 1003

Paint Fork Rd

Maney Branch Rd

SR 1003

70
25

Weaverville

Weaver
Blvd

Begin

25

19

23

From French
Broad Option
in Tour 7

Heavner Rd

Woodfin

251

19

23

70

North Asheville

Merrimon Ave.

Beaver Lake

25

SR 1003

Reems Creek Rd

Zebulon Vance
Birthplace
(911 Reems Creek Rd)

0   1   2   3

Miles

N

Tour 8 continues
on US 25/Merrimon Ave.

TOUR 8 : WEAVERVILLE AND NORTH ASHEVILLE

Ornate timepiece in downtown Weaverville.

He was a gray-bearded man with clear, blue, wrinkled eyes, in a home-made suit of gray jeans.

In order to save time I diagnosed my case, touched my nose with my right forefinger, struck myself below the knee to make my foot kick, sounded my chest, stuck out my tongue, and asked him the price of cemetery lots in Pineville.

He lit his pipe and looked at me for about three minutes. "Brother," he said, after a while, "you are in a mighty bad way. There's a chance for you to pull through, but it's a mighty slim one."

"What can it be?" I asked eagerly. "I have taken arsenic and gold, phosphorus, exercise, *nux vomica*, hydrotherapeutic baths, rest, excitement, codeine, and aromatic spirits of ammonia. Is there anything left in the pharmacopoeia?"

"Somewhere in these mountains," said the doctor, "there's a plant growing—a flowering plant that'll cure you, and it's about the only thing that will. It's of a kind that's as old as the world; but of late it's powerful scarce and hard to find. You and I will have to hunt it up. I'm not engaged in active practice now: I'm getting along in years; but I'll take your case. You'll have to come every day in the afternoon and help me hunt for this plant till we find it. The city doctors may know a lot about new scientific things, but they don't know much about the cures that nature carries around in her saddlebags."

So every day the old doctor and I hunted the cure-all plant among the mountains and valleys of the Blue Ridge. Together we toiled up steep heights so slippery with fallen autumn leaves that we had to catch every sapling and branch within our reach to save us from falling. We waded through gorges and chasms, breast-deep with laurel and ferns; we followed the banks of mountain streams for miles; we wound our way like Indians through brakes of pine—road side, hill side, river side, mountain side we explored in our search for the miraculous plant. As the old doctor said, it must have grown scarce and hard to find. But we followed our quest. Day by day we plumbed the valleys, scaled the heights, and tramped the plateaus in search of the miraculous plant. Mountain-bred, he never seemed to tire. I often reached home too fatigued to do anything except fall into bed and sleep until morning. This we kept up for a month.

One evening after I had returned from a six-mile tramp with the old doctor, Amaryllis and I took a little walk under the trees near the road. We looked at the mountains drawing their royal-purple robes around them for their night's repose.

"I'm glad you're well again," she said. "When you first came you frightened me. I thought you were really ill."

"Well again!" I almost shrieked. "Do you know that I have only one chance in a thousand to live?"

Amaryllis looked at me in surprise. "Why," said she, "you are as strong as one of the plough-mules, you sleep ten or twelve hours every night, and you are eating us out of house and home. What more do you want?"

"I tell you," said I, "that unless we find the magic—that is, the plant we are looking for—in time, nothing can save me. The doctor tells me so."

"What doctor?"

"Doctor Tatum—the old doctor who lives halfway up Black Oak Mountain. Do you know him?"

"I have known him since I was able to talk. And is that where you go every day—is it he who takes you on these long walks and climbs that have brought back your health and strength? God bless the old doctor."
—From "Let Me Feel Your Pulse," in *Sixes and Sevens*, by O. Henry (1911),
    <http://www.readbookonline.net/readOnLine/1922/>.

Weaverville, and more specifically the Reems Creek area, was also home to Elizabeth Daniels Squire, a versatile journalist and mystery writer who revealed in her later years that she had struggled with dyslexia all her life and yet had managed to make a highly successful career in letters. (In a similar vein, Squire's popular character Peaches Dann, an absent-minded detective, struggles with her memory but nevertheless manages to solve many crimes in Squire's seven books about her.) Squire won the coveted Agatha Award for short fiction and served as chairwoman for the southeastern chapter of the Mystery Writers of America. She also spoke at many conferences, both for mystery writers and for those struggling with memory and reading challenges. In this excerpt she describes the role that books played in helping her overcome her reading challenges and ultimately in determining her career path:

The books that set me on the path toward becoming a writer were riproaring page turners. I had trouble learning to read. I had to go to summer school in the first grade. Had there been ability reading groups in second grade, I would have been in the lowest.

But as I grew older, my aunt Ann Bridgers, who was a playwright, gave me books that were so exciting that I had to read them whether I could or not: *Tom Sawyer, Treasure Island, A Tale of Two Cities, Moby Dick, The Three Musketeers, Twenty Thousand Leagues Under the Sea* and *Les Miserables*, as well as short stories by Edgar Allan Poe and Arthur Conan Doyle. These were original and unabridged. Most were complete with long Victorian words.

But nobody stood over me and insisted that I read every word. Nobody told me I wasn't trying if I read a word backwards. I slipped over long words. They were musical mystery. Gradually, as I kept coming across the same word, I learned it from context. If I read something backwards, context kept me on track.

I began to see how a writer could keep the magic going. Because the bones show in a page-turner, even a great one. To any would-be writer, I recommend this whole school of books, modern or ancient, from the works of Homer to the novels of Stephen King. . . .

By the time I was 15 years old, I had made up my mind to write some kind of adventure. My father, Jonathan Daniels, wrote editorials that made some people mad and others chuckle. He wrote books about contemporary history. He said writing was a great career and adventure was okay. I was pleased at my choice, and happily oblivious to the difficulties. (Like getting published.)

Then my aunt introduced me to Eudora Welty—first to her writing, then in person. I was inspired. The wonderful gentle Southern comic touch in her writing really got me. I wanted to write stories that would make people smile with recognition at how things are. Even later, when I wrote my first mystery, *Kill the Messenger*, I wished I could write like she did. I still do.—From *The Liz Reader: A Collection of Shorter Works by Elizabeth Daniels Squire (1926–2001)*, ed. C. B. Squire (Johnson City, Tenn.: Overmountain Press, 2002), 5–6.

Liz Squire's husband, C. B. "Chick" Squire, tells a story very characteristic of this writer/activist. When Squire visited the North Carolina governor's Western Residence—an impressive mansion on Sunset Mountain overlooking Asheville—she was horrified to find nothing on the bookshelves there but Reader's Digest Condensed Books. "Liz immediately went to then-Governor Jim Hunt's administrator for the residence and said it was a crime with so many fine North Carolina authors to have only abridged books on the shelves," Chick explains. When the governor's assistant asked Squire what she wanted to do about it, "Liz contacted writers all across the state and their publishers, asking them to donate books, and once all was said and done, about 200 writers came to a party at the mansion to celebrate the big new library collection."

Liz Squire began her career as a journalist in Connecticut before returning to her native North Carolina in 1979. Her first book, *Kill the Messenger* (1990), was loosely based on her father, Jonathan Daniels, who served as publisher of the *Raleigh News and Observer* and was press secretary to President Truman. (Her grandfather, Josephus Daniels, had founded the newspaper and was secretary of the Navy under Woodrow Wilson.)

Squire died in 2001. She is buried in the Maney Branch Cemetery in northeastern Buncombe County.

Sallie Bissell is another mystery writer who lives in the area and draws heavily on local legend and the landscape for her inspiration. Though she was born and lived for many years in Tennessee, Bissell's work is largely set in North Carolina. She has conflated certain aspects of Jackson, Haywood, and Swain Counties in her novels *Legacy of Masks* (2005) and *In the Forest of Harm* (2001). Bissell says, "The laurel hell mentioned in *In the Forest of Harm* is located in Moore County, Tennessee, though a similar but smaller hell is visible from the Craggy Gardens Visitors Center on the Blue Ridge Parkway just above Weaverville." (A laurel hell—a useful setting for a thriller—is a thicket of rhododendron that tends to grow on steep banks and is practically impenetrable. Horace Kephart tells us in his *Book of Camping and Woodcraft* (1906) that mountaineers also used terms such as "laurel slicks," "woolly heads," "lettuce beds," and "yaller patches" to describe them.)

Bissell's second novel, *A Darker Justice* (2002), mentions a number of sites in and around the Asheville area. As Bissell explained in an interview: "A building on the old Highland Hospital grounds—where Zelda Fitzgerald lost her life—is the model for Sergeant Robert Wurth's paramilitary academy. Many of my pages have been worked out mentally while walking through Riverside Cemetery, where Thomas Wolfe is buried. Place is hugely important to me both as a writer and a reader." An excerpt of Bissell's work can be found in Tour 3.

Another popular writer, Joan Medlicott, makes her home in nearby Barnardsville. After several careers, Medlicott began writing a self-help book for women when she was fifty-eight, but her first real success came at age sixty-four, when she turned to fiction. Medlicott's first novel, *The Ladies of Covington Send Their Love* (2000), details the lives of three older women who move from a Pennsylvania boardinghouse to live together in a rambling farmhouse in a village called Covington, which is based on the Mars Hill area. As of this writing, Medlicott had finished five books in the Covington series and another novel about a different group of characters set in South Carolina and the Caribbean. The Covington series has struck a chord with "women of a certain age" by taking on issues of aging, illness, loss, and recovery.

Medlicott's books are a virtual scavenger hunt of local sites. Her characters attend plays at Mars Hill College and regularly visit the Sunnyside Café (828-658-2660) and the Athens Restaurant (828-645-8458), both on Main Street in Weaverville. At the Athens, Medlicott's characters are usually served by Polly, an actual waitress who gave Medlicott permission to use her name. There's also mention of the Weaverville Milling Company (828-645-4700)—an upscale restaurant on the route to the Zebulon Vance Birthplace. In *The Spirit of Covington* (2003), Medlicott's character Amelia buys daylilies from Consider the Lilies, a business in Barnardsville. "People around here love it," says Medlicott of her use of actual names in the novels.

Administered by the Department of Archives and History of the North Carolina Department of Cultural Resources, the Zebulon Vance Birthplace, just outside Weaverville, is open weekdays with no admission charge at 911 Reems Creek Road, 828-645-6706. Zebulon Vance, who turns up in a number of historical novels about North Carolina, grew up on this 800-acre homestead, where his father provided overnight accommodations for travelers along the Buncombe Turnpike. Zeb's early adventures in the immediate region are skillfully detailed by Manly Wade Wellman in *The Kingdom of Madison*. As a young boy, the enterprising Vance befriended the owner of the Warm Springs Hotel in neighboring Madison County and, according to Wellman, "gathered wildflowers to peddle to the hotel guests. Noticing that little girls sold their bouquets more readily than he, he donned a pinafore and profited accordingly" (57).

Later, when Vance was back from Washington College, where he had been sent at the age of thirteen, he worked as a desk clerk at the hotel and became involved in local politics. At fourteen, he campaigned vigorously on behalf of the Whig Party. His passion for politics led him to be elected governor of North Carolina, to distinguish himself during the Civil War, and to serve three terms and part of a fourth representing the state in the U.S. Senate. Though the Vances were unusually prosperous, their homestead offers a glimpse of both the ingenuity of the early settlers and the hardships they faced living on the land. Zeb Vance's Civil War years are rendered in carefully researched historical fiction in *Ghost Riders* (2003) by Sharyn McCrumb, who is profiled in Tour 16.

DIRECTIONS

Head south on Main Street out of Weaverville and look for Reems Creek Road on your left and watch for signs to the Vance Birthplace. Take Reems Creek to the intersection of State Road 1103 and turn left. The Vance Birthplace will be on your right. For an interesting side trip, Reems Creek Road (SR 2109) continues east and becomes Ox Creek Road, a scenic drive that winds its way for five miles up to the Blue Ridge Parkway. North on the Parkway is Craggy Gardens (mentioned by Sallie Bissell) and the Wayside Museum at milepost 365; to the south is the Folk Art Center at milepost 382, described in Tour 1.

■ NORTH ASHEVILLE

Business 19/23 coming out of Weaverville eventually merges with US 25 to become Merrimon Avenue on the northern outskirts of Asheville. This road runs beside the last stretch of Beaverdam Creek before it flows into the French Broad River. The dammed portion of the creek forms the sixty-seven-acre Beaver Lake, which will be on your right. This area was home for many years to Wilma Dykeman—novelist, environmental writer and activist, and regional historian. She writes:

> The French Broad is a river and a watershed and a way of life where day-before-yesterday and day-after-tomorrow exist in an odd and fascinating harmony. . . . I should like to think that by some unmerited but longed-for magic I have spoken for a few of the anonymous dead along its banks and up its mountains. For the Negro baby drowned in the river when its

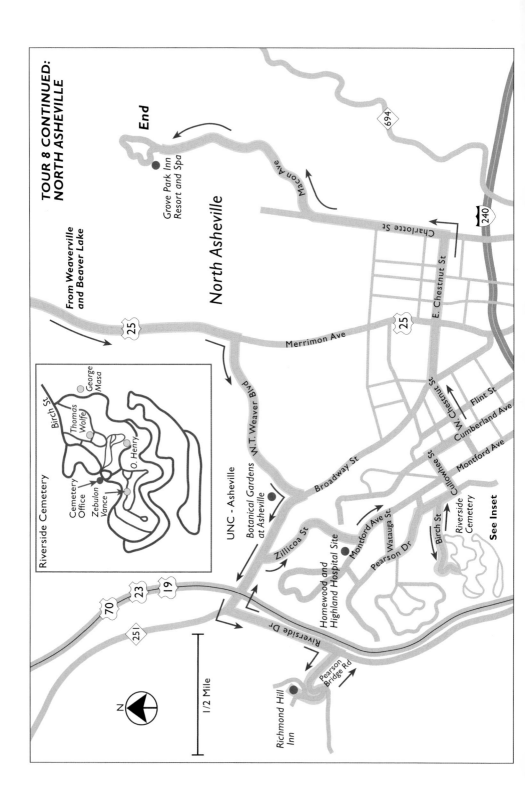

TOUR 8 CONTINUED:
NORTH ASHEVILLE

End

Grove Park Inn
Resort and Spa

From Weaverville
and Beaver Lake

North Asheville

Riverside Cemetery

Birch St

George
Masa

Thomas Wolfe

Cemetery
Office

Zebulon
Vance

O. Henry

UNC - Asheville

Botanical Gardens
at Asheville

W. T. Weaver Blvd

Merrimon Ave

Broadway St

Zillicoa St

Homewood and
Highland Hospital Site

Montford Ave St.

Pearson Dr

Watauga St.

Birch St

Riverside
Cemetery

See Inset

Richmond Hill
Inn

Riverside Dr

Pearson
Bridge Rd

Flint St

Cumberland Ave

Montford Ave

W. Chestnut St

W. Chestnut St

E. Chestnut St

Charlotte St

Macon Ave

1/2 Mile

N

25

70

23

19

251

25

694

240

mother tried to swim from slavery and bring it into freedom. For the sheriff who was shot in the back from a laurel-thicket ambush as he picked his way along a fog-blanketed early-morning trail. For the minister in a windowless log church who made foot washing a symbolic ceremony of humbleness and brotherhood. For the old taletellers around the country stores and the urbane newcomers who seek but have not found as yet. For these and for the river itself, mountains, lowlands, woods, gullies, springs and ponds and brooks I should like to speak, to quicken understanding.
—From *The French Broad*, by Wilma Dykeman (Newport, Tenn.: Wakestone Books, 1992), 25.

It is the novelist's eye for the particular detail that makes *The French Broad* such an engaging history. Dykeman writes of the native peoples and their relationship to the river, the coming of white settlers, the river's role in the Civil War, the growth of agriculture and industry in the region, and characters—such as Thomas Wolfe and F. Scott Fitzgerald—who brought a certain glamour to the idea of tourism. *The French Broad* holds up remarkably well, even with its sometimes heavy-handed 1950s optimism. Dykeman was even then an environmental champion, and she was a gifted storyteller, making this history essential reading on your literary tour.

Today, the Lakeview Park neighborhood still bears some markings of the area that Dykeman particularly loved. "There has been much living on Beaverdam," Dykeman writes. "It is one of the oldest settled outskirts of Asheville, meaning one of the oldest cleared too, and evidence still runs red and thick with every rain" (345).

The lake is a good stopping point to get your bearings in Asheville. A trail runs around the lake and connects with the adjoining Beaver Lake Bird Sanctuary. Find a bench and read from Dykeman, for whom the proposed Wilma Dykeman RiverWay and Urban Corridor Plan has been named. This ambitious, multiyear plan calls for mixed-use development, including low-impact businesses, artist studios, and housing, along with a variety of recreational opportunities on the banks of the French Broad through and beyond Asheville, all the way to the North Carolina Arboretum.

From here, continue on Merrimon Avenue toward downtown Asheville and look for Weaver Boulevard coming in on your right. Turn right and soon you'll come to the main entrance for the University of North Carolina at Asheville—a place where literary activity thrives.

Known for its strong liberal-arts emphasis in undergraduate education, UNC-A includes within its popular continuing education offerings the Great

Future novelist and naturalist Wilma Dykeman (still in her teens) stands to the right and in front of the towering Thomas Wolfe. Both were guests at a cabin in Oteen (outside Asheville) in the summer of 1937. The photo was probably taken by Frank Clodfelter. Courtesy of the Thomas Wolfe Collection of the Pack Memorial Library, Asheville, North Carolina.

Smokies Writing Program. Directed by novelist Tommy Hays, this program offers ongoing, off-campus workshops in prose and poetry geared to both novices and seasoned writers. Hays, a native of South Carolina and graduate of the MFA program at Warren Wilson College, is the author of three novels, *Sam's Crossing* (1992), *In the Family Way* (1999), and *The Pleasure Was Mine* (2005). Valerie Ann Leff is cofounder and codirector of the program. She has lived in Asheville since 1996 and published her first novel here, *Better Homes and Husbands* (2004). "I'm sort of the corollary to Thomas Wolfe," Leff once told a book reviewer. "He moved to New York and wrote about Asheville. I moved to Asheville and wrote about New York. Fortunately, my book is shorter."

UNC-Asheville's Literature and Language Department offers an undergraduate concentration in creative writing led by Richard Chess, who also heads the university's Center for Jewish Studies. Chess is the author of three volumes of poetry, *Tekiah* (1994), *Chair in the Desert* (2000), and *Third Temple* (2007). His creative writing colleagues include David Brendan Hopes (see Tour 5) and emerita writing teacher Peggy B. Parris, for whom a visiting writer series has been named. Parris's first novel, *Waltzing in the Attic* (1990), was translated into German in 1992 and became a bestseller in Germany. Her second novel, *His Arms Are Full of Broken Things* (1996), is an imagined autobiography of the Victorian poet Charlotte Mew.

UNC-Asheville has an aggressive program of oral history collection, and the D. H. Ramsey Library is home to these archives along with an important collection of artifacts from historical figures of the region, including Reuben Robertson of Champion Paper Company, whose personal papers reveal that he also tried his hand at poetry (see Tour 2).

The collection also holds the papers of Charlotte Young, longtime teacher and principal in the local public schools and friend of playwright and short-story writer Olive Tilford Dargan. Young was born in Candler, graduated from Western Carolina University, contributed articles to the *Asheville Citizen-Times*, and was among the founders of the North Carolina Poetry Society. She was an aficionada of mountain ballads and music, served in the Federal Writers' Project during the 1930s, and published her first volume of poetry at 74 and her sixth at the age of 106.

Adjacent to the UNC-A campus, the Botanical Gardens at Asheville showcase the extraordinary biodiversity of the region, which has often found its way into local literature. In particular these gardens provide one of only two spots in town where you can see the rare *Shortia galicifolia*, or Oconee Bell, first discovered by the French botanist André Michaux, who climbed Grandfather Mountain in 1794 and wrongly declared it the highest peak in North America. The plant was then "lost" for nearly a century until "rediscovered" by Asa Gray, one of the first American scientists to promote Charles Darwin's theories of evolution. This unusual flower, related to the galax, has been the subject of poems, songs, and volumes of scholarly citations by historians and botanists. As Robert Morgan's poem attests here, the plant was once found in profusion in Transylvania County. According to staff at the gardens, the specimens here came from one such patch that was dug up before the flooding that created Sapphire Lakes.

LOST FLOWER

Old Asa Gray from Harvard looked high
in the mountains for the shortia
that Michaux had discovered and plucked
on the Blue Ridge and dried for his collection
back in France almost a century before.

No botanist had seen its bloom, nor
knew where to climb for the dazzling beds
the Frenchman had extolled in his journal.
Professor Gray named it *shortia galacifolia* for
a friend and sent assistants every summer
to the highland to explore the summits
for the herb that had no relative except
one cherished breed in China,
a sacred mountain flower.
But when they found the shortia abloom
in oriental profusion all over the south
flank of Transylvania County late in the last
century, it gloried slopes lower
than expected, haunting just above the coves
at the edge of South Carolina and in the shade
of heavy woods, curd-white and shy in the
trash of the forest floor, smaller than its
Chinese twin, and called by neighbors
the Oconee Bell for where it rang quiet
on the lower elevations, no higher
than the best-fed springs.
—From *Groundwork*, by Robert Morgan
  (Frankfort, Ky.: Gnomon Press, 1979), 12.

On the half-mile loop that circles through the gardens you can find the Oconee Bell approximately halfway around the trail alongside the shelter that is located between the Hayes Cabin (an original from Madison County) and the Sunshine Garden gazebo, where many weddings are held. Trail maps are available in the Botany Center.

The Oconee Bell generally blooms in late February or early March. The Botanical Gardens are open from sunrise to sunset year-round. In warm weather, the rocky creeks that flow through the property are popular for wading and shoreline picnics.

Another literary site worth seeing nearby is Richmond Hill, where Georgia poet Sidney Lanier camped in 1881, trying to overcome a chronic illness by taking in the mountain air. Eight years after Lanier's departure, the hill became the site of former ambassador and congressman Richard Pearson's family mansion, now the Richmond Hill Inn.

In 1890, with their new house completed, the Pearsons invited the entire

The Lost Flower: rare Oconee Bells at the Botanical Gardens at Asheville.

town of Asheville to a July Fourth celebration here, and nearly a third of them —reportedly some 5,000 citizens—showed up. According to family legend, Pearson hired 1,000 men to build a mile of road in one hour on the western shore of the French Broad in anticipation of the party guests. Today the Pearson mansion is one of Asheville's most elegant inns and dining spots.

Built in the Queen Anne style, the house was a modern marvel of its time with running water, a baggage elevator, a communications system, and ten fireplaces. Saved from demolition in 1981 by the Preservation Society of Asheville and Buncombe County, the house was moved 600 feet to accommodate the construction of the Western North Carolina Baptist Retirement Home. It was eventually renovated for $3 million by its present owners, who also added Gabrielle's Restaurant, so called in honor of Richard Pearson's wife. The rooms on the third floor are named after writers John Ehle, Gail Godwin, Wilma Dykeman, F. Scott Fitzgerald, and Carl Sandburg. For more information see <http:// www.richmondhillinn.com> or call toll-free, 800-545-9238.

The Sidney Lanier Garden, a reflective spot just behind the inn, has a monument to the poet, commemorating his stay on Richmond Hill in the last months of his life. Lanier suffered from tuberculosis, which he contracted in a Union prisoner of war camp at Point Lookout in Maryland during the Civil War. Like

Richmond Hill Inn, on the site where poet Sidney Lanier camped in 1881 in an effort to recover from a chronic lung ailment. A garden on the grounds is named for him.

Charles Frazier's character Inman in *Cold Mountain*, Lanier made his way home to Georgia on foot when he was finally released from prison.

Known as Georgia's poet of the marshes, Lanier was advised by his doctor to move to a higher elevation. As William Hayes Ward explains in the memorial introduction to *Poems of Sidney Lanier*:

> His medical adviser pronounced tent-life in a pure, high climate to be the last hope. . . . But how short was his day, and how slender his opportunity! From the time he was of age he waged a constant, courageous, hopeless fight against adverse circumstance for room to live and write. Much very dear, and sweet, and most sympathetic helpfulness he met in the city of his adoption, and from friends elsewhere, but he could not command the time and leisure which might have lengthened his life and given him opportunity to write the music and the verse with which his soul was teeming. Yet short as was his literary life, and hindered though it were, its fruit will fill a large space in the garnering of the poetic art of our country.—From *Poems of Sidney Lanier, Edited by His Wife* (New York: Charles Scribner's Sons, 1894), xxix, xli, <http://docsouth.unc.edu/southlit/lanier1/lanier.html>.

From the Botanical Gardens, turn right on Weaver Boulevard and take an immediate right on Broadway, which will pass under 19/23 and end at Riverside Drive. Turn left on Riverside and watch for Pearson Bridge Road, which will come in on your right. Pearson Bridge crosses the French Broad River. Turn right on Richmond Hill Drive and watch for the driveway to the Richmond Hill Inn on the right.

■ HOMEWOOD AND HIGHLAND HOSPITAL

From here, the literary tourist may be interested in visiting nearby Highland Hospital, a psychiatric institution whose most famous patient was Zelda Fitzgerald, wife of the novelist F. Scott Fitzgerald and an accomplished writer in her own right.

Leaving Richmond Hill, return to Riverside Drive at the bottom of the hill and turn left. Soon you'll come again to Broadway. Turn right, passing under the 19/23 overpass and then turn on Zillicoa, the first street on your right. Head up the hill on this winding street, being careful to stay on Zillicoa.

Though all but one building from the original hospital is gone, Homewood, the residence of Zelda's psychiatrist, Dr. Robert Carroll, stills stands at 19 Zillicoa Street. An old stone stairway in the embankment along Zillicoa also provides evidence of the original Highland complex.

Zelda Sayre Fitzgerald, born in Montgomery, Alabama, in 1900, suffered from a mental illness that did not surface full-blown until she was thirty. Married a month after the publication of Scott Fitzgerald's novel *This Side of Paradise*, in 1920, the Fitzgeralds lived a glamorous life, moving from New York to Paris to the Riviera. By the time her husband's most famous novel, *The Great Gatsby*, came out in 1925, Zelda had also begun publishing her own writing, and the literary competition apparently began to tax the marriage. Perhaps to divert the contest, Zelda took up ballet in her late twenties. She still continued to publish stories and essays, though sometimes under her husband's byline, which earned a higher fee, thus helping to underwrite the couple's spendthrift lifestyle.

Zelda's effort at a professional ballet career in France was physically and emotionally punishing. She suffered her first breakdown in 1930. She was diagnosed as schizophrenic in a clinic in Switzerland, though over the next several years she would continue writing, publish a play, and even take up painting. Zelda's 1932 novel, *Save Me the Waltz*—now available in *The Collected Writings of Zelda Fitzgerald* (1991)—did not sell well, and later that year she entered another psychiatric hospital, this time in Baltimore.

Homewood was the residence of Zelda Fitzgerald's psychiatrist, Robert Carroll, who was among the founders of Highland Hospital. Tryon musical prodigy Eunice Wayman (later known as Nina Simone) and composer Béla Bartók performed on the same piano on different occasions here.

In 1934, she suffered yet another breakdown and was moved from Baltimore to a hospital in New York, where she soon managed to secure an exhibition of her paintings at a prestigious gallery. In the same year, Scott Fitzgerald's *Tender Is the Night* was published to mixed reviews. By now, Fitzgerald's alcoholism was a serious threat to his health. While Zelda spent the summer of 1935 back in another Baltimore hospital, Scott retreated to the Grove Park Inn in Asheville complaining of a lung ailment.

In 1936, for financial reasons, he moved Zelda to Highland Hospital, where she received a regimen of vigorous exercise and electroshock treatments. Scott

A fire at the Central Building of Highland Hospital on the night of March 11, 1948, claimed the life of Zelda Fitzgerald and eight other female patients. Photo by Ewart M. Ball, editor, Farmers Federation News, *Asheville. Courtesy of the North Carolina Collection of the Pack Memorial Library, Asheville, North Carolina.*

moved in once more to the Grove Park Inn from July to December of 1936 to be near his wife. He then took off for California to work as a screenwriter. Scott Fitzgerald died of a heart attack in 1940 in the apartment of his girlfriend, Sheilah Graham, a Hollywood gossip columnist. Zelda was living with her mother in Alabama at the time of Scott's death but would continue to be institutionalized at Highland Hospital off and on for the rest of her life.

Highland's central facility, located just three buildings to the east of the Homewood mansion, burned to the ground in March of 1948. Zelda Fitzgerald reportedly died of smoke inhalation in the fire, which was caused by faulty wiring. A single slipper found underneath the body identified her remains.

Homewood was built by Robert Carroll, who came from Duke University to Asheville in 1904 to help launch Highland Hospital on this dramatic hilltop. Used today for weddings and business events, Carroll's manor home was built in 1927 in a style that the Homewood proprietors suggest was meant to echo Duke University's Gothic buildings (though they were actually under construction during the same period). When Carroll married his second wife, a concert pianist, he added a turret and a 1,500-square-foot piano room paneled in cherry. According to Homewood's current staff, the Carrolls once hosted both the Fitzgeralds and the Vanderbilts of Biltmore House for a private concert by the Hungarian composer and pianist Béla Bartók in the enormous piano room.

Later, Tryon-native and musical prodigy Nina Simone (then known by her given name, Eunice Wayman) took piano lessons here before her admission to the Juilliard School. Simone described the sessions in her autobiography, *I Put a Spell on You* (New York: Pantheon, 1991). "I had lessons with Mrs. Carrol [*sic*] twice a week and practised every day, practised hard. I got up at four in the morning, before anyone else, and played until eight. In all I averaged five hours a day at the piano the whole time I was in High School" (33). Simone eventually became a celebrated jazz singer and pianist who spent her later years as an expatriate in France. More of her story is provided in Tour 12.

■ RIVERSIDE CEMETERY

Two minutes away from Homewood is the historic cemetery where Thomas Wolfe, O. Henry, and several other notable figures on this trail are buried. To visit the Riverside Cemetery, continue on Zillicoa Street until it dead-ends, then turn left onto Montford Avenue. Follow Montford 0.1 miles to Watauga Street and turn right, then turn left in 0.2 miles onto Danville Place, which merges with and becomes Pearson Drive. Soon thereafter watch for Birch Street on your right. The cemetery is at 53 Birch Street. (See inset on p. 156.)

Since Riverside Cemetery's establishment in 1885, many local and state leaders have been laid to rest on these historic grounds among the sturdy oaks and rolling lawns. (You can pick up a more detailed map of the Riverside Cemetery listing all of the notable gravesites at the Asheville Visitors' Center downtown.)

George Masa, the Japanese photographer who worked closely with Horace Kephart, is buried here. His stone is a simple granite slab with his name and dates carved on the top.

O. Henry's grave is also marked by a simple granite slab with the name "William Sydney Porter" carved on top. Though he was born in Greensboro, where he was raised by his aunt and worked in his uncle's drugstore, William Sydney Porter left North Carolina for Texas at the age of nineteen. He held a variety of jobs, was married, and eventually fled the country. Porter had been accused of embezzlement at an Austin bank where he worked as a teller. To escape prosecution, he went first to New Orleans and then Honduras. He later returned to

Horace Kephart's hiking companion, photographer George Masa, came to Asheville in 1915 and is buried in Riverside Cemetery. This photo, on Shining Rock, was made in 1931 by Juanita Wilson. Original photo from Ambler family scrapbooks. Courtesy of the North Carolina Collection of the Pack Memorial Library, Asheville, North Carolina.

the United States to see after his ailing wife. After she died, Porter, whose guilt in the bank case remains uncertain, was finally convicted and served time in an Ohio prison. While incarcerated, he worked for the prison pharmacist and wrote a number of formulaic stories that were published under various pseudonyms. In 1902, released for good behavior, Porter moved to New York and permanently assumed the nom de plume of O. Henry. In 1907 he married the sweetheart of his youth, Sara Lindsay Coleman, of Weaverville, and the couple honeymooned in nearby Hot Springs. O. Henry died soon after, in 1910, and was buried here, not far from the grave of Zebulon Vance.

The grave of Thomas Wolfe is inscribed with quotations from *Look Home-ward, Angel* and *The Web and the Rock*. Newspaper editor Jonathan Daniels (father of Elizabeth Daniels Squire, also considered on this tour) was a pallbearer at Wolfe's funeral and described the event in his 1941 essay collection:

> The coffin was heavy. There was a steep terrace up to the lot in the cemetery, and we cut the turf on it with our shoes. I remembered while we moved toward the long hole in the yellow clay that O. Henry was buried

The simple grave of William Sydney Porter (O. Henry), who wrote a number of his clever short stories while serving time in an Ohio prison for embezzlement.

somewhere in the same cemetery and that he had looked at the mountains around us without getting an idea into his head. But Tom had been a mountain man who could see city streets as well as people in cities and in the mountains also. Perhaps he was home in both. It was a magnificent day. In the late afternoon sun there was mist on the mountains, or perhaps it was smoke from the noisy trains, which run down in the valley of the French Broad. Their whistles had been forever in Tom's head. —From *Tar Heels: A Portrait of North Carolina*, by Jonathan Daniels (New York: Dodd, Mead, 1941), 233–34.

■ GROVE PARK INN

This tour concludes with a visit to Sunset Mountain and Asheville's historic resort, the Grove Park Inn. Turn right on Birch Street, and when you reach Pearson Drive, turn right. Turn left on Cullowhee and then right on Montford Avenue. Very soon you'll turn left on Chestnut and follow it across Cumberland, Flint, Broadway, and Merrimon until you reach Charlotte Street. Turn left (north) onto Charlotte Street and watch for Macon Avenue on your right. Take Macon 0.8 miles. The Grove Park Inn will be on your left at 290 Macon Avenue.

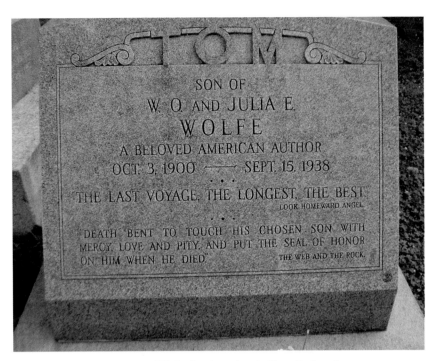

He did come home: Thomas Wolfe's final resting place in Riverside Cemetery.

The Grove Park Inn was built by E. W. Grove, a St. Louis businessman who invented Grove's Tasteless Chill Tonic, designed to cure malaria. Grove made a fortune at the beginning of the twentieth century on his patent medicines, which later included nose drops and a laxative. He bought this property on the side of Sunset Mountain after being inspired by the rough-hewn wood and stone lodges in Yellowstone Park. His son-in-law designed the building, which was miraculously completed in one year. William Jennings Bryan was on hand to make a speech for the opening in 1913. Since then, more than a half-dozen U.S. presidents, many celebrities, and writers Will Rogers, Margaret Mitchell, Alex Haley, Charles Kuralt, George Plimpton, Charles Frazier, Pat Conroy, and Jan Karon, among others, have stayed here. Photographs of guest luminaries are located in the Simmons Wing, which was added in 1984. The Vanderbilt Wing, the newest, was completed four years later.

Every year, the Grove Park marks F. Scott Fitzgerald's birthday, September 24, with performances of jazz from the 1920s and special tours of the rooms that Fitzgerald occupied for his two extended stays in 1935 and 1936. Rooms 441 and 443 are still furnished with period pieces from Fitzgerald's time. The rooms are in the Main Inn, accessible by a small, ninety-one-year-old elevator that was

Thomas Wolfe's funeral was held at the First Presbyterian Church at 40 Church Street in downtown Asheville (two blocks southeast of Pack Square). Among the pallbearers were Wolfe's University of North Carolina classmate playwright Paul Green; his drama professor, Frederick Koch; and Raleigh newspaper editor Jonathan Daniels. The honorary pallbearers lining the walkway included legendary Scribner's editor Maxwell Perkins and playwright Clifford Odets. Photo by John E. Jones. Courtesy of the Thomas Wolfe Collection of the Pack Memorial Library, Asheville, North Carolina.

built into the massive stone shaft that serves as a chimney for one of the inn's enormous fireplaces.

Fitzgerald's inability to control his drinking—he sometimes consumed thirty-five beers a day, which he actually considered a reprieve from his usual intake of several bottles of gin—did not make him a favorite guest of the Grove Park, which initially prohibited alcohol. During the summer of 1935, the off-and-on drama of his affair with a young married woman also put him at odds with the management. (Eventually the young woman was, like Zelda, committed to a mental hospital.) Then, in 1936, when Fitzgerald reportedly fired a revolver in his room in a lame suicide threat, the hotel required him to have a nurse present at all times for the rest of his stay that year.

On yet another occasion, according to Tony Buttitta in his 1987 memoir

The Lost Summer, Fitzgerald fled the Grove Park and sought refuge in "My Old Kentucky Home," the boardinghouse run by Thomas Wolfe's mother. After a thorough tour of the Wolfe house, Buttitta, Fitzgerald, and the lugubrious Mrs. Wolfe—who had been talking nonstop through the entire visit—suddenly fell silent. Buttitta writes:

> We were back at the screen door. I opened it and we stepped out on the porch. She followed and asked if we would take the room. I turned to Fitzgerald, who was leaning against a porch post to steady himself. He wasn't doing a good job; she noticed his shaky movements and sharply grimaced. Her lips shut tight; she pursed them nervously, and then tilted her head proudly.
> "I never take drunks—not if I know it."
> Mrs. Wolfe opened the screen, walked inside, and slammed it behind her. Then I took Fitzgerald by the arm and he slowly followed me down the steps. A hangdog look was on his face. About ten paces away he freed himself and staggered off. He stopped, pursed his lips as she had done, and pointed a shaky finger at the old house.
> "Poor Tom! Poor bastard! She's a worse peasant than my mother!"
> —From *The Lost Summer: A Personal Memoir of F. Scott Fitzgerald*, by
> Tony Buttitta (London, U.K.: Robson Books, 1987), 68–69.

Rebuffed by Thomas Wolfe's mother, Fitzgerald took off for Lake Lure to avoid running into his mistress's husband, who was visiting at the Grove Park Inn. The husband had finally come to see about his wife and her ailing sister. Both had been living at the inn for quite some time, purportedly to improve the sister's health.

Despite these various adventures in and around Asheville, Fitzgerald only mentions the city twice in his work, once in passing in the short story "The Ice Palace" and again in *The Great Gatsby*, when we first meet Jordan Baker: "I knew now why her face was familiar—its pleasing contemptuous expression had looked out at me from many rotogravure pictures of the sporting life at Asheville and Hot Springs and Palm Beach. I had heard some story of her too, a critical, unpleasant story, but what it was I had forgotten long ago" (75th anniversary edition [New York: Charles Scribner's Sons, 2000], 31). For her part, Zelda never wrote of her time in Asheville other than in letters to Scott from Highland Hospital.

Tony Buttitta's memoir—originally published in the United States by Viking in 1974 as *After the Good Gay Times*—is the primary account of the summer of

1935 and Fitzgerald's foibles at the Grove Park Inn. Buttitta was an aspiring novelist who had come to the mountains with his wife to launch a bookstore in the lower arcade of the George Vanderbilt Hotel. He met Fitzgerald by chance one night when the famous author, who had been partying in the ballroom above, came downstairs looking for a bathroom. Fitzgerald tapped on the bookshop window. Buttitta was working on his novel after hours.

Curiously, Buttitta logged the many encounters with Fitzgerald that would follow from that summer evening in the flyleaves of some sixty books in his Asheville bookstore. The friendship that developed was by turns intimate and strained.

Buttitta was then a recent graduate of the University of North Carolina at Chapel Hill. He and his classmate, Milton "Ab" Abernethy, had been the founding editors of a successful student literary magazine called *Contempo*. In creating the magazine, the students had struck up correspondences with an enormous list of prominent authors of the day, including Conrad Aiken, Sherwood Anderson, Kay Boyle, Erskine Caldwell, e. e. cummings, Hilda Doolittle (H. D.), T. S. Eliot, William Faulkner, Langston Hughes, H. L. Mencken, Eugene O'Neill, Ezra Pound, Upton Sinclair, Gertrude Stein and Alice B. Toklas, Wallace Stevens, and William Carlos Williams — many of whom had also contributed their work to the magazine. (These letters and literary submissions are part of the North Carolina Collection at UNC-Chapel Hill.)

Abernethy and Buttitta also launched the Intimate Bookshop in Chapel Hill in 1931, a low-budget enterprise that catered to students by selling remaindered books at bargain prices and by "renting" for pennies the review copies of books they received as the editors of *Contempo*. As it turned out, the Chapel Hill bookstore would continue operation through several owners until it was purchased in the mid-1960s by Wallace Kuralt, brother of journalist Charles Kuralt. By contrast, Buttitta's version of the Intimate Bookshop in Asheville only lasted briefly.

The Fitzgerald that comes through Buttitta's memoir is unpredictable, moody, desperate, and lost. Buttitta writes:

> That summer in Asheville everything had crashed about him. He was
> a physical, emotional, and financial bankrupt. He smoked and drank
> steadily, but ate very little; he took pills to sleep a few hours, and he could
> scarcely write what he thought was a decent line. He was a stranger in
> Asheville and suffered from loneliness in spite of his saying that a writer
> must have solitude to practice his craft. His visits to our bookshop kept
> him from feeling completely out of touch with the world of books and

writers, and I think they cheered him during some of his loneliest times. When he talked to me I often had the impression that he was not speaking of himself, but of someone else, and that I served him not only as a companion but also as a sounding board for his ideas.—From *The Lost Summer*, by Tony Buttitta, xii.

Buttitta visited Fitzgerald several times that summer in his rooms at the Grove Park Inn—sometimes for friendly conversations, once for a formal interview, and at least once to bring Fitzgerald a bottle of gin.

In 1997, on his book tour for *Cold Mountain*, novelist Charles Frazier stayed in Room 360 at the Grove Park Inn. (The door of Frazier's room, like that of Fitzgerald's, is now marked with his name on a gold plaque.) In a daily journal Frazier kept for *salon.com* during the tour he wrote:

I was born here and spent a great deal of time here growing up. My father remembers as a teenager seeing Thomas Wolfe walking around town, towering over everyone, a celebrity. I stay in the old section of the Grove Park Inn, and the place looks like 1920. Monumental stonework and fireplaces big enough to parallel park Lincoln Town Cars in. Upstairs there are high ceilings, arts and crafts furnishings, Roycroft lights. Fitzgerald, his writing career in a shambles and his wife in a nearby mental hospital, spent two miserable drunken summers holed up on the fourth floor in the '30s. I walk past his room. No visible ghosts or bad karma leaking from under the door.

Back in my room, I sit at the window. The hotel has a sweeping view of the mountains to the west. Cold Mountain is out there, 40 miles away, but hidden in the haze.—From "Cold Mountain Diary," by Charles Frazier, *salon.com*, August 21, 1997, <http://www.salon.com/aug97/colddiary970821.html>.

Upstairs in the hall beside Fitzgerald's fourth-floor rooms, visitors can see what Frazier and Fitzgerald saw coming and going during their stays—the third floor Palm Court—an open atrium furnished with leather and wicker, period lamps with mica shades, painted details on the walls with an Art Deco/Egyptian flavor, and potted palms. Though Frazier didn't witness any spirits, some professional ghost hunters have claimed to see strange lights and experience odd energy fields here. One guest of the hotel fell to her death in the Palm Court atrium in the 1920s. Known as "the Pink Lady," she is reported to haunt the hallways.

The Palm Court at the Grove Park Inn, as seen from the floor where F. Scott Fitzgerald kept a room and was a troublesome guest in the 1930s.

Though this deluxe resort has various dress codes for the seasons and many exclusive events, it is usually possible to park and simply stroll through the Great Hall in casual clothes and have a drink on the sunset patio. The poem "Mountains by Moonlight," written by James Seay, a professor of creative writing at the University of North Carolina at Chapel Hill, begs to be read in one of the rocking chairs here.

MOUNTAINS BY MOONLIGHT
The postcard artist Harry Martin
could have gone to Mars
and not found a better full moon
for his Mountains by Moonlight.
It looks like a photograph
that's been hand-tinted and stars added.
When they were young
our grandparents sent it home
wishing everyone was there in the space
for writing messages.

Old postcard of the Grove Park Inn. Lake County Discovery Museum, Curt Teich Postcard Archives.

The matte finish softens the moonlight
to where it's almost melancholy.
We don't know whether to lie down
and embrace our aloneness together on Earth
or fly to the moon.
It's pure nature,
not a Model T or AAA sign in sight,
but we know that outside the frame
the technology's in place for flight,
organ transplants, just about anything
you could imagine.
We know that beyond the mountains by moonlight
there is an architecture
our grandparents had to leave finally
in the same way they left these mountains.
We know that when we draw arrows,
as they did, to hotel windows
it's both to separate ourselves
from the sheer sameness of things *my room
was here* and yet redouble the evidence
we were part of that sameness

my room was there.
Once for a magazine article
I located Scott Fitzgerald's room
at the Grove Park Inn in Asheville
by standing in the parking lot
and counting up to the window
that he had x'd on a postcard.
From the terrace he could see
the lights of Highland Hospital
where Zelda thought she was talking
to Christ and William the Conqueror and Mary Stuart.
Not even the mountains by moonlight
could put him to sleep,
so he took Luminal and Amytal
and a young married woman from Memphis.
Two years later he was in Hollywood.
We don't know if it was silliness
or loneliness that prompted the postcard
he sent to himself at the Garden of Allah
where he had rooms.
When they came home they brought us honey
in small jars shaped like bears,
assembly-line tom-toms with rubber heads,
cities we could shake into blizzards.
They asked if we got the cards.
Next year it would be palm trees
and a crescent moon.
We couldn't imagine them under those moons
with anything other than hearts
lifting to the broadened horizon.
We couldn't imagine them as having ever
doubted the light as they found it.
—From *Open Field, Understory: New and Selected Poems*,
 by James Seay (Baton Rouge: Louisiana State University
 Press, 1997), 80–81.

For more information on the Grove Park Inn, visit <http://www.grovepark inn.com> or call 800-438-5800.

Bess Tilson Sprinkle Memorial Library

41 North Main Street

Weaverville, NC 28787

828-645-3592

One of eleven branches in the Buncombe County system, the Weaverville library also houses the Town Museum in its basement. It has a strong collection of books for young adults and many volumes on local history. Computer terminals with Internet access in English and Spanish are available.

Log Cabin Motor Court

330 Weaverville Highway (25 South)

Asheville, NC 28804

828-645-6546

800-295-3392 (toll free)

<http://www.cabinlodging.com/>

If you're a movie buff, you may want to have a look at this old-style motel established in 1929 just south of Weaverville on Business 19/23 (Main Street). These rustic cabins were built over the decade of the 1930s and still provide tourist accommodations, now with wireless Internet access. They were also used in the filming of *Thunder Road*, a 1950s cult classic about moonshining and fast driving, written by and starring Robert Mitchum. In the office lobby, there are photographs of the movie stars on location. If you ask, the current proprietors may also lead you to cabins nineteen and twenty up the hill, where a number of scenes were shot. The manager told us that the early diaries and guest registers from the original owners might soon come back to the motel for display.

Writers at Home Reading Series

c/o Great Smokies Writing Program

University of North Carolina at Asheville

828-232-5122

<http://www.unca.edu/gswp/>

In addition to their creative writing classes for adults held all over Asheville each semester, UNC-Asheville's Great Smokies Writing Program sponsors regular readings by local and regional writers, including students in the program. The Writers at Home Reading Series is free and open to the public. It meets on the third Sunday of the month during spring and fall semesters. The readings are held at Malaprop's Bookstore/Café, described in Tour 9.

Accent on Books

854 Merrimon Avenue

Asheville, NC 28804

828-252-6255

800-482-7964 (toll free)

With a focus on metaphysics, psychology, religion, and children's books, this shop comes highly recommended by Joan Medlicott. "They always have a supply of my work," she says, "and they are very helpful to order anything. Just great people to work with." The store works frequently with local churches, therapists, and other spiritual organizations in identifying materials for conferences and other educational events. Accent on Books also carries a large selection of commercial greeting cards and cards by local artists. The shop is located near the Fresh Market on Merrimon Avenue, approximately one mile southeast from Beaver Lake toward downtown Asheville.

Reader's Corner

31 Montford Avenue

Asheville, NC 28801

828-285-8805

rcorner@bellsouth.net

This bookstore offers new and used compact disks in addition to its impressive stock of more than 20,000 used, rare, or out-of-print volumes. Most are hardback, and the selection includes local and regional literature, outdoor guides, archaeology, anthropology, and books on southern Appalachia. This store is a good place to check for first editions of Thomas Wolfe, rare autographed volumes by local authors, and such out-of-print books as the works of John Parris. The bookstore also serves as the local sponsor for the Prison Book Project of Asheville, a volunteer group that sends books to indigent inmates in North Carolina, South Carolina, Kentucky, Tennessee, Georgia, Alabama, Florida, and Mississippi. Here you can also meet Crumpet, yet another of western North Carolina's bookstore cats, who weighs twenty-two pounds. On the day we visited, Crumpet was serving as a formidable paperweight for a stack of neighborhood newsletters beside the cash register.

1900 Inn on Montford

296 Montford Avenue

Asheville, NC 28801

828-254-9569

800-254-9569

<http://www.innonmontford.com/>

As at the Richmond Hill Inn, the rooms in this bed and breakfast honor writers who have lived or passed through Asheville—Thomas Wolfe, F. Scott Fitzgerald, Edith Wharton, O. Henry, and Zelda Fitzgerald (for whom the entire 1,000-square-foot third floor is named). "Zelda's Retreat" is actually a suite of five rooms. The inn also has cozy fireplaces and whirlpools in the rooms and claims to have the largest Norway maple in North Carolina in the yard. Monday, Thursday, and Saturday are live music nights.

Downtown and South Asheville

Take to the streets that Wolfe and Fitzgerald haunted on Asheville's urban walking tour. See the world's largest residence, which novelist Henry James declared a "gorgeous practical joke" and novelist Edith Wharton called "a divine landscape." Visit the Asheville bookstore that appears in a recent romance novel.

Writers with a connection to this area: Emöke B'Racz, Tony Buttitta, Olive Tilford Dargan, Jude Deveraux, Wilma Dykeman, F. Scott Fitzgerald, Gail Godwin, O. Henry, Henry James, Michael McFee, Arthur Newton Pack, John Parris, Peggy B. Parris, Edith Wharton, Thomas Wolfe

Maxwell Perkins, Thomas Wolfe's celebrated editor at Charles Scribner's Sons, once wrote that a visit to Asheville was essential to understanding Thomas Wolfe's writing. Perkins was quite taken with the dramatic mountains surrounding this town and the challenge of arrival by train in the early twentieth century. Today, Asheville—known as Altamont in Wolfe's *Look Homeward, Angel*—is an easier destination. In the past two decades, the city has drawn artists, new immigrants, and retirees like a magnet. Among its 70,000-plus residents is tremendous diversity, and the city's vital arts and literary scene continues to bloom.

A good way to get acquainted with the downtown area, the 1.7-mile Asheville Urban Trail takes about two hours on foot. Thirty stations tell the story of Asheville's history and culture through sculptures, plaques, and monuments. (See <http://www.justasheville.com/urban.html> to print out a map of the trail in advance of your trip.)

Initiated by the City of Asheville, this ambitious public art project has been designed by volunteers and built with generous donations from organizations and individuals. Visitors following the urban trail gain perspective on the various in-

tour 9

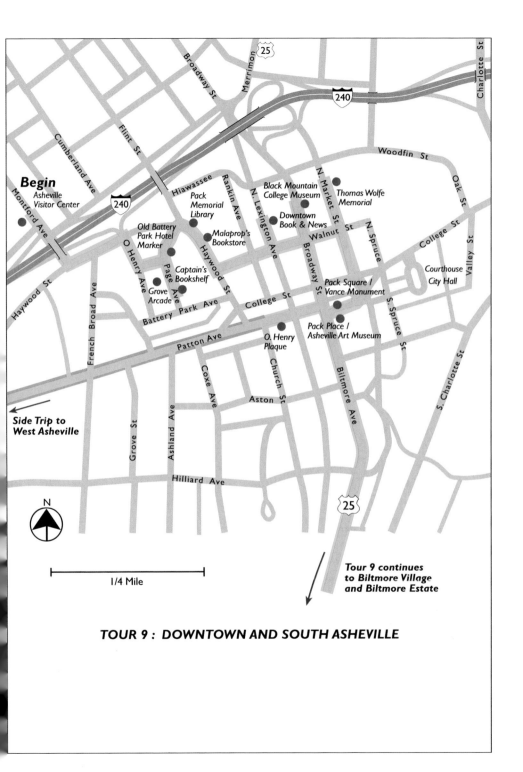

Begin
Asheville
Visitor Center

Montford Ave

Cumberland Ave

Flint St

Haywood St

French Broad Ave

Broadway St

Merrimon

25

240

Woodfin St

Oak St

Charlotte St

Hiawassee

Pack
Memorial
Library

Rankin Ave

N. Lexington Ave

Black Mountain
College Museum

N. Market St

Thomas Wolfe
Memorial

College St

Valley St

Old Battery
Park Hotel
Marker

O. Henry Ave

Malaprop's
Bookstore

Haywood St

Downtown
Book & News

Walnut St

N. Spruce St

Courthouse
City Hall

Captain's
Bookshelf

Page Ave

Grove
Arcade

Battery Park Ave

College St

Broadway St

Pack Square /
Vance Monument

S. Spruce St

Patton Ave

O. Henry
Plaque

Pack Place /
Asheville Art Museum

Church St

Coxe Ave

Aston St

Biltmore Ave

S. Charlotte St

Grove St

Ashland Ave

Hilliard Ave

25

**Side Trip to
West Asheville**

N

**Tour 9 continues
to Biltmore Village
and Biltmore Estate**

1/4 Mile

TOUR 9 : DOWNTOWN AND SOUTH ASHEVILLE

fluences that have shaped Asheville over the years. Pink granite icons are embedded in the sidewalks to indicate the era in the city's history that is represented through each piece of art—a feather for the Gilded Age; a horseshoe representing the frontier period; an angel for "The Times of Thomas Wolfe"; the courthouse for "An Era of Civic Pride"; and an eagle representing "The Age of Diversity." Children will enjoy sleuthing their way along the trail to find each new station and the icons that accompany them, and adults will appreciate the clever ways in which local artists have represented Asheville's milestones.

The walk also offers a good look at downtown Asheville's remarkable architecture—from the Art Deco of the S & W and Kresge buildings to the Beaux Arts design of City Hall to the contemporary work of I. M. Pei on Pack Square.

The trail begins in front of the Asheville Art Museum on Pack Square, where bricks commemorate the donors who have made this project possible. The Asheville Art Museum is now housed in the building that was once the Pack Memorial Library. The trail then crosses Patton Avenue to the actual town square, where a monument to Zebulon Vance was erected at the beginning of the twentieth century. At station two, beneath the Vance obelisk, a life-sized bronze piglet and wild turkey commemorate the drover's trail that ran right through the square on its way from east Tennessee to Charleston, South Carolina, as described in Tour 7.

Pack Square also has a literary connection. This crossroads where Broadway becomes Biltmore Avenue and is intersected by Patton Avenue was named for Asheville philanthropist George Willis Pack, a man who made his fortune in the timber industry and who, like Champion Paper's Reuben Robertson, then became interested in forest conservation. Pack encouraged his son, Charles Lathrop Pack, to join the conservation movement. Charles eventually became president of the American Forestry Association and founded the American Nature Association. The elder Pack donated the land for Pack Square to Buncombe County in 1900; his only requirement was that it remain in the public trust forever.

Pack's grandson, Arthur Newton Pack, was a writer who served as editor and publisher of *Nature Magazine*. He tells the story of Pack Square slightly differently:

My grandfather had moved from the north to Asheville, North Carolina, when the Civil War was still a too recent memory for many, and "damn-yankees" were widely hated. In due course he had made many friends and eventually been asked to become sole trustee for the public square which was duly named in his honor—"Pack Square." Indeed he held title

Historic "cigar store Indian" at Pack Square, described in Michael McFee's poem "Pocket Watch."

to it during the remainder of his life and passed on the trusteeship to my father. —From *We Called It Ghost Ranch*, by Arthur M. Pack (Abiquiu, N.M.: Ghost Ranch Conference Center, 1965), 28.

At one time, Pack Square was also the site of western North Carolina's first opera house. Here, too, W. O. Wolfe, Thomas Wolfe's father, established the monument shop where he imported stone angels and other figures to be sold as grave markers. While the square is no longer the same as in Wolfe's era, you can still find some of the details mentioned in Asheville native Michael McFee's poem below. The cigar store Indian, for example, is now tucked behind glass in the corner bar next to the Bistro 1896 restaurant. Finkelstein's Pawn Shop, with its bold red awning, is also just down the block on Broadway.

Thomas Wolfe's father, W. O. Wolfe, stands front and center before his monument shop at 22 Pack Square sometime around 1890. Thomas Wolfe's uncle, William Harrison Westall, stands beside the doorway and his maternal grandfather, Thomas Casey Westall, is upstairs on the balcony. Courtesy of the Thomas Wolfe Collection of the Pack Memorial Library, Asheville, North Carolina.

POCKET WATCH (EXCERPT)
We walked by the ghost of Wolfe's stone shop,
by the library with the wooden Indian
whose headdress I stroked on our weekly visits,
by the jaundiced adult book store

into Finkelstein's Pawn Shop on Pack Square,
its walls loud with stereos and guitars.
Mom and I stood at the splintered counter
and studied the trays of hocked pocket watches

and finally asked if we could see the Elgin.
"A good little watch," said the mustached man
as he unscrewed the back casing to show us
that perfect Swiss movement, those 17 jewels.
—From *Sad Girl Sitting on a Running Board*, by Michael McFee
   (Frankfort, Ky.: Gnomon Press, 1991), 35.

Continuing on the Urban Trail, Station Four also has a literary connection. It honors O. Henry's story "Gift of the Magi." The descriptive plaque, set into the sidewalk, is flanked by bronze representations of the famous hair combs and watch fob that the husband and wife in O. Henry's story bought with great sacrifice as Christmas gifts for each other. Ironically, the wife sold her long, beautiful hair and the husband pawned his watch—each to afford the gift for the other. The placement of Asheville's bronze representation of the story—in front of a substantial ATM—has its own irony: O. Henry worked as a bank teller in his early years and was convicted of embezzlement, for which he served time in prison. He would, no doubt, be amused by the location of this tribute.

The next literary marker comes at Station Eleven, where a bronze guest book lists the names of some of the famous people who stayed at the Battery Park Hotel, including F. Scott Fitzgerald and big band leader Glenn Miller, who played swing in the ballroom here. Today the hotel is a retirement home.

Station Thirteen, near the Wolfe House, presents a bronze replica of Thomas Wolfe's enormous size-thirteen shoes.

DIRECTIONS

The best place to start any tour of downtown Asheville is the Visitor Center, at 36 Montford Avenue (exit 4c off I-240). Pick up a city map here, and be sure to get a map for the Urban Trail, then head to Pack Square at the intersection

On Asheville's Urban Trail: detail of combs set in the sidewalk to commemorate O. Henry's story "The Gift of the Magi." Asheville Area Arts Council, Urban Trail Station #4.

of Patton Avenue and Broadway/Biltmore Avenue. There's a private parking deck down the hill on Biltmore Avenue beyond Pack Place, or you may want to use one of Asheville's three public parking decks—the Civic Center Deck, the Rankin Avenue Deck, or the Wall Street Deck.

A visitor could spend days exploring different sections of Asheville, but for the literary tourist, a few more streets stand out and must be noted here as an addendum to the walking tour. You may choose to integrate these sites as you take the Urban Trail or visit them separately.

■ THOMAS WOLFE MEMORIAL

52 North Market Street
Asheville, NC 28801
828-253-8304
<http://www.ah.dcr.state.nc.us/sections/hs/wolfe/wolfe.htm>

Thomas Wolfe continues to be a controversial figure in American letters, dividing readers into roughly two camps—those who love his lyrical, baroque style and those who cannot manage to wade through it. But like a handful of other writers from his era—Hemingway and Fitzgerald among them—Wolfe's personal story, both tragic and triumphant, still captures the imagination of most readers. Probably more words have been written *about* Wolfe than he wrote himself in his short life. It all started when Asheville was scandalized by his first novel.

In *The French Broad*, Wilma Dykeman gives us her unfettered take on Asheville's reaction to the 1929 publication of *Look Homeward, Angel*:

> Here, now, was a novel dealing with the places and people Tom Wolfe had known. "Why it is Asheville," they cried. "It is we. It is me!" And they searched one another's faces. This was a sense of bankruptcy deeper than even the failure of the banks they were soon to experience. Distilled through the consciousness of a boy who soaked up, spongelike, every detail of the life in which he was growing up, laid open on the pages of a book, were their lives and not only the wonder of life and beauties of seasons and landscapes, but the snickering secrets too, the shadowy corners and evil appetites. He had said this was "a story of the buried life," but what many wanted buried was life itself. . . .
>
> With the usual perverseness of humanity, the people of Asheville did not seem shocked at much of the deceit and folly and wickedness and waste that Wolfe found—they were shocked only that he exposed it. They did not look into their civic and social life and wonder how they could cure it of cancerous growths so other adolescents growing up would not be exposed to the same cynicisms and falsehoods. They said, instead, "The book's unspeakable. People don't write about such things. It isn't nice." And others said, "Look at what he wrote about his own family. Why they're ruined."
>
> The Wolfes were not so easily ruined. On the contrary, they were made immortal. —From *The French Broad*, by Wilma Dykeman (Newport, Tenn.: Wakestone Books, 1992), 222–23.

The Wolfe House, built in 1883, was recently renovated for $4.2 million after an arsonist's fire in 1998 had done significant damage. In 1906 Julia Wolfe bought the boarding house for $6,500 when her son Tom was six. Today it can still evoke the spirits of those who lived here.

Of course the "Old Kentucky Home," referred to as "Dixieland" in Wolfe's first novel, probably never looked so handsome as it does today. Until the most recent renovations, the structure had been deteriorating for nearly a century. Wolfe himself did not paint a pretty picture of it. In the novel he called it big, cheaply constructed, and painted a dirty yellow.

A year after Thomas Wolfe died at the age of thirty-eight from tubercular meningitis, the bank auctioned the house to pay back taxes and the defaulted mortgage. Undeterred, Julia Wolfe stayed in the house and bought it

The porch of the Thomas Wolfe Memorial in Asheville, where Julia Wolfe told F. Scott Fitzgerald that she did not rent to "drunks."

back within three years with the proceeds from Tom's estate. When she died in 1945, at the age of eighty-five, the rambling structure was left to her surviving children. In 1948, a fledgling nonprofit called the Thomas Wolfe Memorial Association purchased the house from the family and operated it as a museum until the City of Asheville took it over in 1958. In 1973, the house was designated a National Historic Landmark. It became a State Historic Site in 1976, administered by the North Carolina Department of Cultural Resources.

Now visitors can once again tour the house and the extraordinary new museum adjacent to it. Annually, on May 16—the date preceding the day in 1916 when Thomas Wolfe left for college at the University of North Carolina at Chapel Hill—the Wolfe Memorial recreates the scene by having "boarders" in period costumes lead the tours. Peggy Parris, an emeritus professor at the University of North Carolina–Asheville, described the event in a short story. Her narrator is Fulton Fanning, a retired CPA:

This Saturday, my interest in historical places draws me out into the sunny afternoon. I decide to visit Thomas Wolfe's home, the boarding house his mother ran, which he called Dixieland in his first novel. I had seen in the *Citizen-Times* that a group of amateur actors were recreating "A Weekend in May, 1916" costumed in the period, pretending to be boarders in the house and such, chatting with visitors as you go through.

Tall trees spread full and green, shading the huge white house. For about 10 minutes, I share the swing on the side porch with a solemn, long-haired young man in an unseasonable black overcoat and gold wire rim glasses, gripping a copy of *Look Homeward, Angel*. We glide back and forth in a leisurely arc, waiting our turn to be part of a tour group. Half a dozen other young men and women in jeans and T-shirts lean against the clapboard wall or sit on the porch railing, waiting, too. Their conversations are hushed, as if we're gathered at a holy shrine. I remember then, how I was drawn to Wolfe's tortured Eugene Gant when I was in college and assigned to read *Look Homeward*, how I felt "O Lost, and by the wind grieved, ghost, come back again" when my mother died at about the same time. That moment, rocking gently in the Wolfe's porch swing, I'm shocked at the intensity of my longing for her. I fumble out my handkerchief to cover the sudden and embarrassing tears. Never in the 35 years since her death have I missed my mother so keenly.

Just then, the screen door opens, and a woman in a long, dark skirt and starched shirtwaist steps out. Her auburn hair is piled up in a loose knot on her head, a pendant watch pinned on her bosom. She reminds me of a sepia photograph in the family album of young Agnes Mary Fulton, when she was teaching in a one-room country school years before she met my father. I stand up and follow the little group into the Wolfe house and back to 1916.—From "In the Land of Sky," by P. B. Parris, *North Carolina Literary Review* 2, no. 1 (1994): 158, 161–62.

Asheville native Michael McFee offers this reminiscence of the reopening of the Wolfe house written especially for this guidebook:

When I was growing up in the mountains, from the mid-1950s through the early 1970s, Asheville wasn't such a groovy little city, Thomas Wolfe's name wasn't so ubiquitous, and his mother's boardinghouse wasn't yet an official historic site. "The Old Kentucky Home" was just 48 Spruce Street, where Tom's brother Fred offered occasional tours of the twenty-nine rooms. He didn't seem to like the house or his family very much: when my mother and I first visited, in 1968, I remember he pointed out, unapprovingly, where his famous younger sibling crept along the roof to sneak into a female guest's room.

A few years later, after I read *Look Homeward, Angel* (at sixteen: just the right age, just the right place), I went back solo, and the ramshackle place was much more interesting: it had become Wolfe's "Dixieland," and its drafty high-ceilinged rooms—some dim, some sunny—seemed haunted with ghosts of stories, the place itself a rambling gossipy character.

I headed off to college in 1972 to study design, but soon transferred to Wolfe's alma mater and decided to become a writer myself. When a dozen-story hotel opened right across Spruce Street from his house in the mid-1970s, I heard that copies of *Look Homeward, Angel* had been placed in each bedside table drawer, beside the Gideon's Bibles. Who could resist such a detail? I put it into a poem called "Asheville," which was ironic, allusive, and dreadful.

Graduate school, marriage, work, child, and parents' deaths—it was decades before I got back to what had become the Thomas Wolfe Memorial. In fact, it was almost too late, after the devastating arson of 1998: I didn't visit again until the fall of 2002, when a huge blue tarp still covered the partially collapsed roof, the north side of the rambling house was all plastic and tarpaper and 2 × 4 braces, and smoke damage haunted the windows. Four years into its restoration, the sun did not shine bright on "My Old Kentucky Home," and it didn't look like it ever would again.

Memorial Day weekend, 2004. I stand where I rattled the chain-link construction fence only twenty months earlier, but can barely believe what rises before me: the Thomas Wolfe Memorial, gloriously intact, painstakingly and sympathetically resurrected. In fact, the old boardinghouse seems much closer to its 1916 state than when I visited it as a teen: the slate roof, the exterior yellow paint, the interior plaster, the furnishings— everything looks just like it did the year Tom left for college at Chapel Hill.

But, appropriately for the nature of this particular place, it's not overdone, a lifeless museum of early twentieth-century Americana. As I stroll through the house—around Julia's kitchen, up the creaky central stairs, past the bed where W. O. unwillingly spent his last days—it's easy to imagine that the family or boarders just stepped out and might be back shortly.

Which is to say: The place feels exactly right. Like home, again.

■ GROVE ARCADE

One Page Avenue
Asheville, NC 28801
828-252-7799
info@grovearcade.com
<http://www.grovearcade.com/

This 269,000-square-foot architectural wonder takes up a whole city block, flanked by Page Avenue on one side and O. Henry Avenue on the other. Opened inauspiciously in 1929, the Grove Arcade has had a checkered history, for a time housing federal bureaucrats. After languishing for many years, it was reopened in 2002 through the work of a public/private partnership between the City of Asheville and a historic preservation organization. In his memoir, *The Lost Summer*, Tony Buttitta gives his impressions of the Grove Arcade on the day F. Scott Fitzgerald came to call at the offices of the North Carolina Symphony, where Buttitta occasionally worked in 1935:

> I was typing a publicity release when he walked in the bare office on the ground floor of the Arcade. A book was under his arm; I recognized it by the cover drawing—Ben Hecht's *Afternoons in Chicago*. He waited outside while I finished, pacing the wide, deserted corridors that echoed with every step he took. He was surprised to see only a half-dozen tenants in the building; most of the shops and offices were vacant or hadn't been completed for occupancy. The Arcade was a white elephant, and it was typical of the time; the symphony had been donated space there as a cultural organization to help give the impression that prosperity was just around the corner.
>
> The massive edifice squatted on a bulldozed hill. I made a point of telling Fitzgerald that Wolfe had lamented that the hill had lost its graceful contours in the name of progress. The Arcade was one of the two Boom structures—the other being the Grove Park Inn—which were built as memorials by E. W. Grove, the patent medicine Chill Tonic King. It had been started on a grander scale than Old Gant in Hendersonville; con-

The Grove Arcade, where Fitzgerald often visited his friend Tony Buttitta, now houses upscale shops and residences.

struction had been halted at the fourth floor, making it the worst local calamity of the Crash, except for a couple of sensational suicides. —From *The Lost Summer: A Personal Memoir of F. Scott Fitzgerald*, by Tony Buttitta (London, U.K.: Robson Books, 1987), 27–28.

The Arcade is now a bustling marketplace with dozens of upscale specialty shops offering fresh produce, coffee and wines, home furnishings, crafts, antiques, and fine art.

■ WEST ASHEVILLE

If you turn right on Montford Avenue from the Visitor Center parking lot, and then right onto Haywood Street, you cross Patton, which changes briefly to Clingman Avenue, then crosses the French Broad River and becomes Haywood Road. Here you'll find the sturdy neighborhoods of West Asheville, where modest homes are being renovated and businesses—coffee bars, pubs, retro furniture shops, a natural foods store, and more—are springing up to cater to Asheville's twenty-somethings. West Asheville also offers more ethnic restaurants per block than just about anywhere else in town.

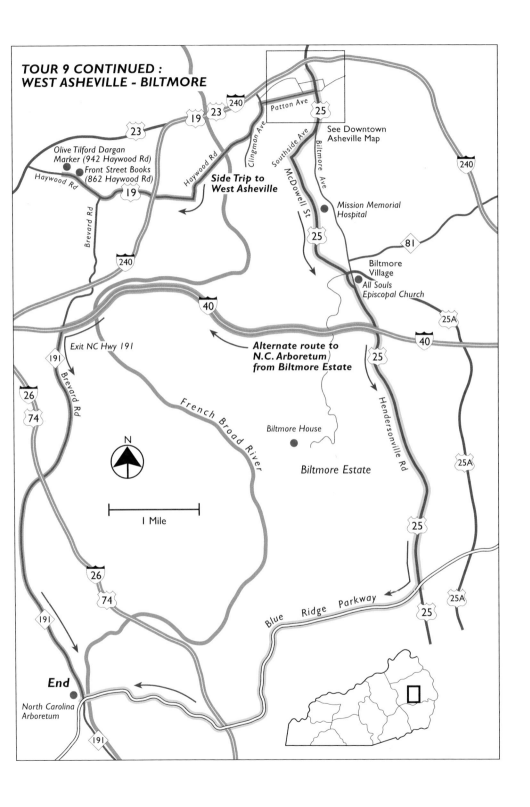

**TOUR 9 CONTINUED :
WEST ASHEVILLE - BILTMORE**

240

19 23

240

23

Patton Ave

Clingman Ave

25

See Downtown
Asheville Map

240

Olive Tilford Dargan
Marker (942 Haywood Rd)
Front Street Books
(862 Haywood Rd)

Haywood Rd

Haywood Rd

Southside Ave

Biltmore Ave

19

**Side Trip to
West Asheville**

McDowell St

Mission Memorial
Hospital

Brevard Rd

240

25

81

Biltmore
Village
All Souls
Episcopal Church

40

Exit NC Hwy 191

**Alternate route to
N.C. Arboretum
from Biltmore Estate**

40

25A

191

Brevard Rd

26

74

French Broad River

Biltmore House

Biltmore Estate

Hendersonville Rd

25

25A

N

1 Mile

26

74

Blue Ridge Parkway

25

25A

191

End

North Carolina
Arboretum

191

Activist writer Olive Tilford Dargan outside her home, known as Bluebonnet Lodge, at 58 Balsam Road in West Asheville, circa 1930. At one time the house belonged to Rutherford Platt Hayes, son of President Rutherford B. Hayes. Courtesy of the North Carolina Collection of the Pack Memorial Library, Asheville, North Carolina.

In 1924, novelist and playwright Olive Tilford Dargan bought a cabin in West Asheville just off Haywood Road. She spent her winters here, returning to the Smokies in warmer weather. Unfortunately, all that's left to see is a historical marker near the West Asheville branch library at 942 Haywood Road.

Though Dargan made important contributions to our understanding of mountain folkways in the early twentieth century through her story collection, *From My Highest Hill* (considered in Tour 5), she was also known in her time as a passionate advocate for the rights of textile workers—an interest she developed while living in West Asheville.

Moved by the violent strike at Gastonia's Loray Mill in 1929, Dargan wrote a novel about the political awakening of a female textile worker, Ishma Waycaster, who joins with union organizers to plan a strike.

To avoid being typed by her gender or her past publishing credits, Dargan adopted the pseudonym Fielding Burke and sent off her "proletariat novel," *Call*

Home the Heart, to New York. Longmans, Green and Company published it in 1932 to positive reviews, and the book sold well. Dargan would go on to write two more novels about the struggles of blue-collar workers using the pen name of Fielding Burke. She also completed three poetry collections, all of which are out of print. Her third, *The Spotted Hawk*, published by John F. Blair of Winston-Salem in 1958, won North Carolina's Roanoke Chowan Prize. Olive Tilford Dargan died in Asheville in 1968 at the age of ninety-nine.

■ BILTMORE HOUSE

1 Approach Road
Asheville, NC 28803
828-225-1333
800-624-1575 (toll free)
<http://www.biltmore.com>

Asheville's most visited attraction, Biltmore House, is the largest private residence in the United States. This 175,000-square-foot, French-style chateau has more than 250 rooms, including 34 bedrooms and 43 bathrooms. It was originally surrounded by 125,000 acres, most of which were later donated to the Pisgah National Forest. Now the estate covers a mere 8,000 acres.

The library's 24,000 volumes reflect the tastes of the house's original occupant, George Vanderbilt. His family still owns the property, to which they have added a winery, luxury hotel, and historic horse barn. According to Eileen M. Heenan, the Biltmore's associate archivist and librarian, George Vanderbilt was fluent in French, German, Spanish, and Italian and could read Latin, Greek, Hebrew, and Sanskrit. His interests ranged over art and architecture, travel and topography, philosophy and religion, and nineteenth-century British and American literature. The novelists Henry James and Edith Wharton were among his friends.

Allison Ensor, an English professor at the University of Tennessee in Knoxville, has researched and written about the separate visits of James and Wharton to Biltmore House in 1905. The two couldn't have had more disparate reactions to the mansion, the scholar tells us in "'Wasted Monstrosity' or 'Divine Landscape': Henry James and Edith Wharton Visit Asheville's Biltmore House" (Tennessee Philological Association meeting, Columbia, Tenn., Feb. 26, 2004).

Henry James had published in the previous year what would be his last novel, *The Golden Bowl*. He came south in February of 1905 to escape the harsh northern winter but found Biltmore under a blanket of snow. James, then in his sixties and ailing from gout, vehemently complained in a letter to his good friend, Edith Wharton, about his first night at Biltmore House. He said one of his front teeth "came out last night in bed with the chattering of my jaws" (*Letters/Henry James*, ed. Leon Edel [Cambridge, Mass.: Harvard University Press, 1984], 4:345).

He also called the chateau a "strange colossal, heartbreaking house," then went on to declare it "so gigantic and elaborate a monument to all that *isn't* socially possible here" (4:346–47). The aristocratic James, only recently returned to his native America after years of living in Europe, had ridden the train to Asheville through the stark Appalachian winter, horrified by the hardship and poverty he'd seen along the way.

Going on about Biltmore House, he told Wharton, "It's in effect like a gorgeous practical joke—but at one's own expense, after all, if one has to live in solitude in these league-long marble halls and sit in alternate Gothic and Palladian cathedrals, as it were—where now only the temperature stalks about—with the 'regrets' sighing along the wind of those who have declined" (4:346–47).

Allison Ensor reports that James endured Biltmore approximately ten days and then headed on to Florida and ultimately California, where he was finally warmer and happier ("'Wasted Monstrosity,'" 7–8).

Edith Wharton and her husband Teddy also arrived at Biltmore in winter, though it was the end of 1905. They were to spend the Christmas holidays with the Vanderbilts. Wharton had just published *The House of Mirth* and, perhaps with some spirit of malice, brought the Vanderbilts an autographed copy as a holiday gift. In the book, Wharton had unflatteringly drawn upon her childhood acquaintances in New York City with Mrs. William Astor and Cornelius Vanderbilt (George's father) to send up the materialistic world of the super-rich. Already Wharton had published a criticism of Victorian excess: *The Decoration of Houses* (1897), written in partnership with architect Ogden Codman Jr. So how would she view the home her dear friend Henry James had called "a gorgeous practical joke"?

Wharton wrote to her friend, Sara Norton:

The journey here was frightfully fatiguing, but this divine landscape, 'under a roof of blue Ionian weather,' makes up for all the hardship and prolongs for me the sweet illusion of autumn. . . . Yesterday we had a big Xmas fete for the 350 people on the estate—a tree 30 feet high, Punch & Judy, conjurer, presents & 'refreshments.'. . . In this matchless weather the walks thro' the park are a joy I should like to share with you—great sheets of fruited ivy pouring over terrace walls, yellow stars still shining

Old postcard of the Biltmore House, circa 1935. Lake County Discovery Museum, Curt Teich Postcard Archives.

on the branches of the nudiflora, jasmine, & masses of juniper, heath, honeysuckle, rhododendron & laurel making an evergreen covert so different from our denuded New England lanes.—From *The Letters of Edith Wharton*, ed. R. W. B. Lewis and Nancy Lewis (New York: Scribner, 1988), 100.

Ensor found no evidence to suggest that James or Wharton ever returned to Biltmore after 1905. Henry James did, however, write a play and two travelogues and began *The Ivory Tower* before his death in 1916. This incomplete novel, published posthumously, confronted the darker aspects of the excess wealth that James had witnessed in his American travels during the Gilded Age, including his Biltmore excursion. For her part, Edith Wharton would continue writing and become the first woman to win the Pulitzer Prize—for the novel *The Age of Innocence*, in 1921.

In more recent years, Biltmore House has been the site of several films based on novels, including *Being There*, by Jerzy Kosinsky; *The Last of the Mohicans*, by James Fenimore Cooper; and *Forrest Gump*, by Winston Groom.

With the opening of the inn on Biltmore Estate, the visits by Henry James and Edith Wharton have now been duly commemorated. Henry James would probably be a bit happier today if only he could stay in the 1,200-square-foot suite named for him on the fifth floor. The Wharton Suite—of the same size and with the same amenities—is on the sixth floor.

All Souls Episcopal Church in Biltmore Village, where Gail Godwin's mother regularly attended services.

Gail Godwin at a book signing for A Southern Family *held in her hometown of Asheville in September 1987. Photo by Daniel W. Millspaugh. Courtesy of the North Carolina Collection of the Pack Memorial Library, Asheville, North Carolina.*

DIRECTIONS

The most scenic route to Biltmore House from downtown Asheville begins at Pack Square where Broadway becomes Biltmore Avenue (US 25) as it crosses Patton Avenue. Follow Biltmore Avenue down the hill beside Pack Place, past McCormick Field (ballpark for the Asheville Tourists minor league baseball team), past St. Joseph's and Mission Hospitals and into Biltmore Village. The entrance to the Biltmore Estate is on your right.

Across from the entrance to the Biltmore Estate are the shops, galleries, and restaurants of Biltmore Village and, most notably, All Souls Episcopal Church, which figures prominently in Asheville writer Gail Godwin's story, "Mother and Daughter Ghosts: A Memoir," in *Evenings at Five: A Novel and Five Stories* (2004).

Both of Gail Godwin's parents were from North Carolina. When they divorced, Godwin lived with her mother and grandmother in Asheville and attended Catholic school. She went to Peace College in Raleigh for two years and then finished a degree in journalism at the University of North Carolina at Chapel Hill. She landed her first reporting job at the *Miami Herald*, but eventually decided she wanted to write fiction. (Godwin's mother had been a reporter for the *Asheville Citizen-Times* and wrote romance novels on the side.) Godwin completed her Ph.D. at the University of Iowa and has since written ten novels, several story collections, and libretti for two operas. She has lived many years in upstate New York. She still returns to Asheville often.

■ NORTH CAROLINA ARBORETUM

100 Frederick Law Olmsted Way
Asheville, NC 28806
828-665-2492
<http://www.ncarboretum.org>

Located in the Bent Creek Experimental Forest of the Pisgah National Forest, the North Carolina Arboretum is open daily, weather permitting, except Christmas Day. The 426-acre grounds, established in 1985 and affiliated with North Carolina's public university system, has some sixty-five acres of cultivated gardens and ten miles of hiking and biking trails through the forest. The attractive Visitor Education Center, surrounded by pools and manmade waterfalls and sculpture, is the site of adult education programs, plant and quilt shows, exhibits, meetings, and demonstrations. The various formal gardens have perennial collections augmented by seasonal annuals—some in large terra cotta pots. There is a gift store and café, and guided tours of this horticultural wonder are available to small groups. Among the special botanical collections here is the Bonsai Display, one of only two such collections in the southeast, and a Heritage Garden, featuring plants that are used in traditional mountain crafts. The Greenhouse and Production Facility on the grounds are used to enhance the plantings in the arboretum's formal gardens. This institution was the vision of Frederick Law Olmsted, best known as the designer of New York City's Central Park who was also landscaper for the Biltmore Estate.

Here, you can also find the Oconee Bell, or *Shortia galicifolia*, as described in Tour 8. These rare plants are located in the Native Azalea Repository at one of the lowest levels on the grounds, across a wooden bridge over Bent Creek. To get there, ask for a map from the Visitor Center and head toward the amphitheater. Facing downhill, the trail to Bent Creek is on the left side of the amphitheater. Follow the trail downhill, cross the Garden Trail, and continue beside a rock wall. When the trail comes to a "T," turn left and look for the Native Azalea Repository. Take the bridge across the creek and walk a few yards. The plants, mixed in a patch of galax, are marked with a small nameplate. Like the lenten rose, they tend to bloom early—in late February or early March.

It is a testament to the power of story that this preglacial flower, which may have once circled the globe, has now made its way into a contemporary song written by old-style country music artist Gillian Welch and her partner David Rawlings. They have also adopted the name "Acony" for their record label.

DIRECTIONS

You can take the Blue Ridge Parkway to milepost 393 or, from the Biltmore Estate, get on I-40 West at US 25 and follow it to the exit for NC 191/Brevard Road and head south toward Brevard. Signs to the arboretum will be on your right, two miles after you cross I-26.

■ LITERARY LANDSCAPE

Black Mountain College Museum & Arts Center

56 Broadway Street
Asheville, NC 28801
828-350-8484
bmcmac@bellsouth.net
<http://www.blackmountaincollege.org/

This combination gallery and museum opened in 2003 to commemorate the legacy of Black Mountain College, an innovative school that ran from 1933 to 1956 in nearby Black Mountain. (For a more complete description of the college, see Tour 1.) Though the museum's hours are fairly limited, the site regularly hosts exhibits of art, photographs, papers, and other materials from the distinguished students and faculty of the college. The center also produces special symposia and publications related to the history and legacy of Black Mountain College. Call for hours and scheduled events.

Downtown Books & News

67 North Lexington Avenue
Asheville, NC 28801
828-253-8654

Asheville's premiere newsstand offers a wide range of literary journals and other hard-to-find publications. Downtown Books & News also sells used paperbacks. A panoply of art galleries, restaurants, and antique shops surrounds the store's three adjoining storefronts on Lexington Avenue. Open every day.

Arts2People

P.O. Box 1093
Asheville, NC 28802
828-582-0431
<http://www.arts2people.org/>

This nonprofit group hosts the Lexington Avenue Arts and Fun Festival in September and has been involved in a public mural project for the neighborhood and a spoken word poetry program offered at the Swannanoa Valley Youth Development Center. The poetry curriculum combines classical poetry and hip-hop performances as a means to encourage incarcerated youth to write about their experiences.

Malaprop's Bookstore / Café

55 Haywood Street
Asheville, NC 28801
828-254-6734
800-441-9829 (toll free)
info@malaprops.com
<http://www.malaprops.com>

There's nothing like a bookstore owned by a writer. Emöke B'Racz, a poet born in Hungary to a prominent family, is a dedicated reader and writer who has built a bookstore that caters to regional writers and challenges every reader to stretch and try the work of new authors across all genres. The bookshop has also evolved over more than two decades into a music venue, a café, a card and gift shop, an Internet portal, and a popular gathering spot where the feeling of community is palpable.

"Perhaps that's why Malaprop's was selected as best independent bookstore in the country in 2000," says local novelist Peggy Parris. "Author readings and signings, open mic evenings, and other literary events are scheduled here all the time. The bookstore staff is exceptionally knowledgeable and helpful."

Malaprop's has a life in fiction as well. Romance writer Jude Deveraux, who has more than 30 million books in print, has written a novel set in North Carolina called *Wild Orchids* (2003). In it, the main character phones Malaprop's to place an order for books.

Pack Memorial Library

67 Haywood Street
Asheville, NC 28801
828-250-4700
<http://www.buncombecounty.org/governing/
depts/Library/locations_Pack.htm>

Just a few doors up Haywood Street from Malaprop's, toward the Asheville Civic Center, you'll find the city's main library, with its extraordinary collection of old postcards and photographs. The North Carolina Collection here also features local history, genealogy resources, and a Thomas Wolfe collection. At one time Wolfe's books were banned from the city, but the story goes that F. Scott Fitzgerald—who had the same Scribner's editor, Maxwell Perkins, as Wolfe—marched in with new copies of Wolfe and insisted the library take them as a gift and put them back on the shelves in the mid-1930s.

Captain's Bookshelf

31 Page Avenue
Asheville, NC 28801
828-253-6631
captsbooks@aol.com
<http://www.captainsbookshelf.com/>

Up the block from the Grove Arcade and across Page Street is another fine Asheville bookshop. The Captain's Bookshelf deals in rare, antique, first edition, and used books, with a strong selection of regional literature and history. The shop also regularly hosts art shows by local and out-of-town artists.

Writers' Workshop of Asheville

387 Beaucatcher Road
Asheville, NC 28805
828-254-8111
info@twwoa.org
<http://www.twwoa.org/>

Begun in 1985, this nonprofit enterprise, run by Karen Ackerson, sponsors regular writing classes and workshops across genres and is now housed in a bed and breakfast where writers can also retreat to work. Over the years, the workshop has brought a long list of distinguished writers to Asheville for readings and conferences. A manuscript critiquing service and annual contests in poetry, fiction, memoir, and creative nonfiction are also part of the workshop's regular programming.

Asheville Poetry Review
c/o Keith Flynn, managing editor
P.O. Box 7086
Asheville, NC 28802
<http://www.ashevillereview.com/>
Robert Bly, Lawrence Ferlinghetti, Joy Harjo, Gary Snyder, Sherman Alexie,
Eavan Boland, Yevgeny Yevtushenko, and Fred Chappell are among the writers
whose work has appeared in this biannual journal of poetry, reviews, essays,
and interviews, whose scope reaches far beyond the region.

Poetry Alive!
70 Woodfin Place
Suite ww4c
Asheville, NC 28801
828-255-2636
800-476-8172 (toll free)
poetry@poetryalive.com
<http://www.poetryalive.com/>
Presenting verse as theater since 1985, Poetry Alive! is a high-energy professional touring company that performs year-round for schoolchildren, library
groups, and festivals across the United States and beyond. The actors travel in
pairs and present poetry from memory—classic to contemporary. They also
conduct in-school residencies and provide workshops for teachers. The organization has published its teaching methodology in a series of educational books
and sells recorded performances on CDs and audiotapes.

Front Street Books
862 Haywood Road
Asheville, NC 28806
828-236-5940
<http://www.frontstreetbooks.com>
This independent publishing house specializes in books for children and
young adults. They have a strong commitment to new writers; half their authors are previously unpublished.

Barnes & Noble
83 South Tunnel Road
Asheville, NC 28805
828-296-9330

This busy place is Ruth Bell Graham's favorite bookstore in Asheville, where writers' groups, readings, book clubs, and informal gatherings around a variety of literary topics occur often. Call for the current schedule of events.

Brevard : Rosman : Green River : Zirconia : Flat Rock : Hendersonville

Learn about the ill-fated *Mountain Lily* and the highest steamboat line in America—a much-recorded story of political folly. See the amazing white squirrels of Brevard. Visit the headwaters of the storied French Broad—one of the oldest rivers on the planet. Stop by Carl Sandburg's former home, where the furnishings are just as the poet left them more than four decades ago. See the angel made famous in Thomas Wolfe's first novel.

Writers with a connection to this area: Mart Baldwin, Michael Chitwood, Wilma Dykeman, F. Scott Fitzgerald, DuBose Heyward, Robert Morgan, John Parris, Ann B. Ross, Carl Sandburg, Paula Steichen

From the North Carolina Arboretum at the end of Tour 9, it's a pleasant ride toward Brevard on NC 191 South to NC 280 and on into Brevard. The French Broad makes a dramatic U-turn at the arboretum and the Bent Creek River Park, where local folks like to fish, picnic, and ride the challenging mountain bike trails. The river is close to the road for a short distance south and then curves away on your left as the road continues south. The literary tourist may be interested to know that when you come to where NC 191 and NC 280 split at Mills River you are in the vicinity of Horse Shoe, where timbers from the ill-fated steamboat the *Mountain Lily* were supposedly salvaged to build either the old Horse Shoe Baptist or perhaps French Broad First Baptist, the oldest church in the area. However, both of the old frame churches have been replaced by new brick structures, so, as Gertrude Stein said, "there's no *there* there."

That said, if you follow 191 south a short distance from Mills River, you'll come to a bridge over the French Broad. (You will

tour 10

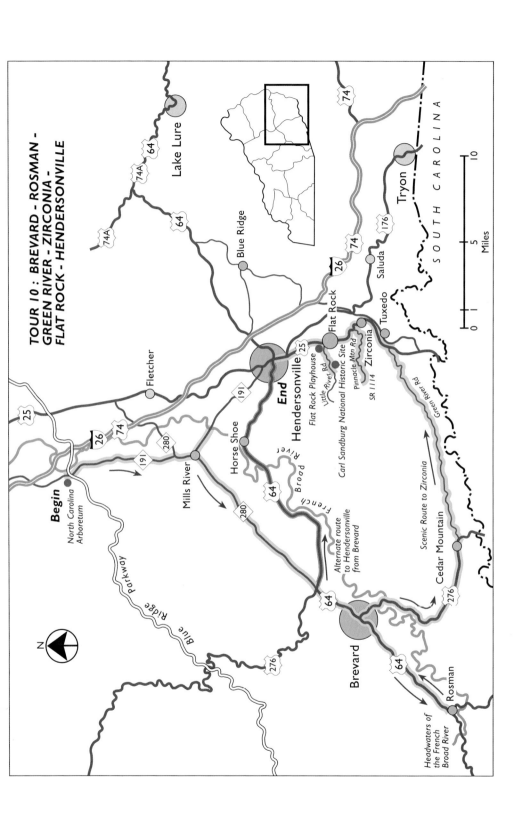

TOUR 10 : BREVARD - ROSMAN - GREEN RIVER - ZIRCONIA - FLAT ROCK - HENDERSONVILLE

N

Lake Lure

74A

74A

64

64

Blue Ridge

Fletcher

25

74

26

280

191

Mills River

Horse Shoe

191

End

Hendersonville

25

Flat Rock Playhouse

Little River Rd

Flat Rock

Carl Sandburg National Historic Site

Pinnacle Mtn Rd

SR 1114

Zirconia

Tuxedo

74

26

74

Saluda

176

Tryon

S O U T H   C A R O L I N A

Begin

North Carolina Arboretum

Blue Ridge Parkway

Broad River

French Broad River

64

Alternate route to Hendersonville from Brevard

280

276

64

Brevard

64

Rosman

Headwaters of the French Broad River

276

Cedar Mountain

Green River Rd

Scenic Route to Zirconia

0   1   5   10
Miles

Near Horse Shoe Bend, where the steam-driven Mountain Lily *ran aground on a sandbar in the French Broad River around 1880. Courtesy of the North Carolina Collection of the Pack Memorial Library, Asheville, North Carolina.*

return to NC 280 to reach Brevard.) Try to imagine a steamship laboring up these shallow waters as you read these accounts of the *Mountain Lily* debacle. John Parris begins the story:

> Chances are the folks who conceived the "Mountain Lily" would have run her one day right down to New Orleans if the government had really taken an interest in making the French Broad a steamboatin' river.
>
> Hendersonville and Brevard could well have become the highest inland seaports in America.
>
> The saga of the "Mountain Lily" began back in the 1870s when Congressman Robert Vance of Buncombe, egged on by his constituents, astounded his colleagues from the big river country by introducing a bill in Congress requesting a $50,000 appropriation to make the French Broad navigable.
>
> Most of the Congressmen had never heard of the French Broad, but it sounded like a big river and, since they apparently didn't want to admit their ignorance, the bill went through without a murmur.

Folks said later that Bob Vance could have got a million dollars just as easily, and some wondered why he didn't, since the French Broad is a long, tough river that today would take billions to put into shape as a steamboatin' river.

With $50,000 at their disposal, U.S. Army engineers swarmed into the Carolina mountains and went to work on the French Broad.

Strangely enough, they confined their work along the headwaters of the river, building jetties and deepening the channel between the mouth of Ochlawaha Creek and Brevard, a distance of 17 miles.

No sooner was the work completed when Col. S. V. Pickens of Hendersonville organized the French Broad Steamboat Line to handle the river traffic.

Colonel Pickens was president of the company and he set out to build his own steamboats right here in the mountains where few folks had ever heard of a steamboat, much less seen one. — From "Steamboat on the French Broad — Horseshoe," in *Mountain Bred*, by John Parris (Asheville, N.C.: Citizen-Times Publishing Company, 1967), 262–64.

And from here, poet Robert Morgan picks up the story:

REAL AND ETHEREAL
Called the 'highest steamboat line
in America' they operated *The Mountain
Lily* on the French Broad back in
the 80's. The only navigable
stretch, from Fletcher to Brevard,
rose in the spring too
sassy to negotiate, and by
midsummer thinned so shallow the hull
scraped on rocky bottom.
The muddy cartway on the hills
was more reliable.
Not even jetties built
to deepen and narrow the channel
proved a remedy.
There's a picture someone made
of the sidewheeler stranded on mud
near the bend at Arden,
swaybacked and listing, stack

tilted like a gun.
Not so much a floating palace
as a tenement or bunkhouse
on a barge. They
salvaged the motor
and dismantled the rest for lumber—
Some of the planks in Horse Shoe Church
once steamed through the gap
into the stadium of mountains
with the Sunday bell warning of departure.
—From *Groundwork*, by Robert Morgan
    (Frankfort, Ky.: Gnomon Press, 1979), 13.

■ BREVARD

A popular summer destination for music aficionados and a retirement haven for people from across the nation, Brevard is a quaint village. Besides its daily calendar of summer musical performances, Brevard is also known as home to a flourishing population of white squirrels. Celebrated annually in a May street festival that includes a writing contest, Brevard's white squirrel population is born of an amazing tale.

The story goes that a Mr. Black of Madison, Florida, discovered a pair of white squirrels playing one day in his pecan grove. He learned that the squirrels had escaped from an overturned carnival truck. Black caught the white squirrels and gave them to a friend, H. H. Mull, of Brevard, who in turn gave them to his daughter to keep as pets. Young Miss Mull hoped to breed the squirrels, but captivity seemed to discourage them.

In 1951, one of the squirrels escaped, so the Mulls mulled it over and decided to let the other one loose. Soon Brevard residents began spotting white squirrels all over town. In 1986, the Brevard City Council unanimously passed an ordinance protecting the white squirrels. Today the animals—which are not albinos—are generally easy to spot on the campus of Brevard College. They are quite accustomed to curious people with cameras.

On a book tour of Appalachian colleges and universities, Chapel Hill writer Michael Chitwood was introduced to Brevard's white squirrels and later devised his own story of their genesis, published for the first time here.

Brevard's white squirrels are accustomed to posing for photos in exchange for treats.

WHITE SQUIRRELS OF BREVARD

She was Esmeralda the Fortune-Teller. Her wooden wagon rocked through the mountains. Her skirts were shot with silver thread. Had no man and no need of one. Her blood was old country. You could hear her rumbling wheels for miles. What she said would begin a path to what would be. Even now. Just ask around. But, this was back when the moon's prophets still walked the land. People knew an ax under the bed would cut pain. Warts wore off after a good talking to. She conjured them white with a hand of High John the Conqueror. One pair, male and female. There's a glimpse of them yet. Nothing, nothing, in this world is ordinary.
—Used by permission of Michael Chitwood

From Brevard, you may want to take a side trip to Rosman on US 64 West to have a look at the headwaters of the French Broad River, or you may skip this side trip and leave Brevard via US 276, where the tour takes a remote route along the Green River Corridor toward Zirconia, the hometown of poet and novelist Robert Morgan, just south of Flat Rock and Hendersonville. If traveling on an unpaved road to see the Green River does not seem appealing, take US 64 East directly into Hendersonville/Flat Rock to complete this tour.

■ ROSMAN

This tiny town of some 500 residents is home to two surprising assets, the Pisgah Astronomical Research Institute, where a collection of optical and radio telescopes is available for use by scientists and students. It is also manufacturing headquarters for the Peter Vitalie Company—an international enterprise that employs local craftsmen to create elegant, hand-carved pool tables that sell for six figures. For the literary tourist, however, the most notable aspect of Rosman is its proximity to the headwaters of the French Broad River. On the far side of town, at the intersection of US 64, US 178, and NC 215, you are only a few miles from the source of the river, one of the three oldest on the planet. The other two are the Nile in Egypt and the New River, also in North Carolina. Such ancient geography is worthy of contemplation and a few more words from the river's most eloquent champion, the novelist and environmental writer Wilma Dykeman:

> Which is the time to know the river? April along the French Broad is a swirl of sudden water beneath the bending buds of spicewood bushes, a burst of spring and a breath of sweetness between the snows of winter and the summer's sun. August is a film of dust on purple asters along the country roads of the lower river, and a green stillness of heavy shade splattered with sunlight beside the upper river. October is a flame, a Renaissance of richness of red and amber, the ripeness of harvest in husk and bin. It is the golden span between the dry rattle of September's end and November's beginning.
>
> In this mountain country, November is the month for classic beauty. Lines are clear and simple. Colors are subdued earth shades. Only those who know well and deeply these hills and rivers and their valley can find them beautiful in this starkness, as a doctor may find a skeleton beautiful in its precision of bone and joint without the camouflage of flesh. November strips the trees and leaves their branches in etched design against the sky, strips the hills and reveals their contours—every winding path and rocky ridge and scooped-out gully—and finally reveals the river. No longer laced overhead with green limbs or half hidden under banks of bush and fern, the streams and springs and rivulets, as well as the river they feed, emerge in each sharp twist, each lazy pool, and become dark liquid lines threading the mountains and valleys. It is a fit time to trace the river's course. It is a fit time to meet the country and its people.—From *The French Broad*, by Wilma Dykeman (Newport, Tenn.: Wakestone Books, 1992), 6–7.

From this point up the river through Transylvania County, there are at least eight public and private river access points suitable for fishing or paddling by canoe, kayak, or inner tube. You can pick up an excellent river map at Headwaters Outfitters, the local rafting shop on US 64, beyond Rosman and just past the intersection with NC 215. Call 828-877-3106 or visit <http://www.head watersoutfitters.com/>.

The recommended map details the river by sections and was produced by River Link, a regional nonprofit that advocates for the economic and environmental revitalization of the French Broad River, including the Wilma Dykeman RiverWay Plan. See <http://www.riverlink.org>.

From here, return to Brevard on US 64 East.

■ GREEN RIVER CORRIDOR

To reach Flat Rock and Hendersonville on a scenic and rugged route, take US 276 South from downtown Brevard. If you were to continue south as far as the South Carolina state line, you would enter Caesar's Head State Park—a historic favorite with tourists for more than a century. Remaining on the North Carolina side, however, you'll find several pottery and art studios along this route. The now-narrow French Broad River also snakes wildly alongside 276, having come north from its headwaters near Rosman, slowly building toward its wider incarnation in Asheville and beyond. Before reaching South Carolina, we'll take a turn to visit the pristine Green River, an icon in the work of poet and novelist Robert Morgan, whose down-to-earth, accessible poetry and stories are a valuable companion for any first-time visitor to the Blue Ridge.

Watch for Cascade Lake Road beside Grammy's Restaurant, approximately seven miles out of Brevard near the village of Cedar Mountain. Turn left onto Cascade Lake Road, go about 50 yards, and then turn right onto Reasonover Road. After four miles, bear right onto Green River Road, where the pavement ends.

This beautiful, deep-wooded, narrow drive meanders alongside the Green River Preserve—a 3,400-acre, family-owned wildlife refuge that is also home to an environmental summer camp for youth. Drive slowly and watch for potholes and wildlife over the next four miles. Then the road will turn to pavement again. Follow the paved road another ten miles alongside the Green River and the several landscape nurseries that share its banks, which Robert Morgan speaks to in this fine poem:

ATOMIC AGE

In yards and medians on interstates,
on grounds of factories and hospitals
in Atlanta, Charleston, Memphis, Nashville,
see patches of Green River soil. For each
boxwood and sparkling pine, every dogwood
and maple from a nursery here, goes with
its ball of mountain dirt to the new bed.
Every rhododendron must keep its roots
in Blue Ridge loam. And while the loam
is scattered in clots of gunpowder black
all over the South, the topsoil in these
mountain coves gets thinner, pocked as sponges,
fissioned to the suburbs, cities, greasy
savings of centuries of leaf rot, forest mold
nursed by summit fogs and isolation,
sold to decorate the cities of the plain.
—From *Topsoil Road*, by Robert Morgan (Baton Rouge:
    Louisiana State University Press, 2000), 17.

Staying on Green River Road, you'll end up in the sleepy resort town of Tuxedo, at Business 25. Now you are near the homeplace of the versatile Morgan, whom some have called the poet laureate of Appalachia.

■ ZIRCONIA

To see Robert Morgan's hometown, take Business 25 North (not the major highway) out of Tuxedo and follow it into Zirconia. Raised on land inhabited by his Welsh ancestors in this remote area, Morgan remembers writing his first story one day in sixth grade while the rest of his class visited the Biltmore House. He writes on his website,

I did not have the three dollars for the trip, and rather than let me sit idle all day my teacher, Dean Ward, suggested I write a story describing how a man lost in the Canadian Rockies, without gun or knife, makes his way back to civilization. All day I sat in the classroom by myself working at the details of my character's escape from the wilderness. I was so absorbed in my story I was surprised to find the other students had returned that afternoon.—From <http://people.cornell.edu/pages/rrm4/bio/index.htm>

A promising student who started out in engineering and applied mathematics at North Carolina State University in Raleigh, Morgan also took a course with poet Guy Owen. "He encouraged me to write stories and poems about the place and people where I had grown up," Morgan explains. "One day he brought one of my stories to class, an account of visiting a great-grandmother in an old house in the mountains, and announced he had wept when he read the story. This was better praise than I had gotten in math classes, and I was hooked on writing."

Morgan soon transferred to the University of North Carolina at Chapel Hill, where he earned an English degree and worked with the irascible Jessie Rehder. He then earned a Master's of Fine Art in creative writing from the University of North Carolina at Greensboro and studied with Fred Chappell. The editors of *Lillabulero* magazine, William Matthews and Russell Banks, published his first collection, *Zirconia Poems*, in 1969.

Morgan began teaching at Cornell University in 1971 and has since published more than a half-dozen collections of poetry, several story collections, and a number of novels, notably *Gap Creek* (1999), which was a selection of the Oprah Book Club, creating instant national recognition of Morgan's talent. In recent years Robert Morgan has spent time in North Carolina as a writer-in-residence at several universities across the state.

Zirconia, once a mining town on the railroad line, is now a quiet community of longtime residents and a few newcomers. Drive through town, and just up the hill from the post office on Business 25 heading toward Flat Rock you'll come to a sharp curve. Watch for Pinnacle Mountain Road on the left. Robert Morgan writes about this road in his first story collection, *The Blue Valleys* (1989). For the literary tourist, a stop at Lucky Butler's Skytop Orchards, only one mile up Pinnacle Mountain Road, may serve as a good spot to read a bit from Robert Morgan while enjoying the view of the Green River Valley. At the beginning of your ascent, before you get to the orchard, you can also take a long view north if it is clear, though we suspect the north-facing view Morgan describes in his excerpt is about nine miles farther up this winding washboard road:

When she and Doug were dating they used to drive in his daddy's pickup up on Pinnacle and park. On a clear night the lights of Hendersonville seemed close, almost at their feet if they stood on the big rock on the north side. And sometimes when there was a high cloud cover they could see the flow of Asheville further on down the French Broad valley. Those were the times she remembered most from their courtship. If it was summer and they had worked in the fields, she had the glow of sunburn on her showered skin. In the cool night air her body sent out a kind of light, and she found an optimism hard to maintain at home with her sisters quarreling in their room and the floor gritty with dirt from the year and field. They could see from the mountaintop the lights of the new GE plant out near Flat Rock, its parking lot like a landing pad or lit runway. And there was the instrument factory over near Fletcher, and lights all up and down the valleys, along the roads, where in her parents' time there was no electricity, only oil lamps and handpumps at wells, and milkcans in the springhouse. —From "The Lost State of Franklin," in *The Blue Valleys: A Collection of Stories*, by Robert Morgan (New York: Simon & Schuster, 1989), 101.

■ FLAT ROCK

Returning to the bottom of Pinnacle Mountain Road, turn left to continue on Business 25—at this point designated as an official North Carolina Scenic Byway. In just a few miles you'll be in historic Flat Rock, with its stately homes and mature white pines that flank pristine yards and grassy horse pastures.

Once called the "Little Charleston of the Mountains," Flat Rock has hosted affluent white tourists from South Carolina's low-country plantations and from Europe ever since the Victorian era. As early as the 1730s, African Americans also traveled through East Flat Rock with the Cherokee, both as slaves and as free people. Writer Christian Reid, author of *The Land of the Sky*, traversed these parts with her friends on the way to Caesar's Head, just across the South Carolina State Line.

In recognition of its long and distinguished history, the entire Flat Rock district has been placed on the National Register of Historic Places.

Just before you get into town proper, watch for the long, elevated lawn of the Woodfield Inn on your left. It is the oldest inn in North Carolina, where there's a room named for its former neighbor Carl Sandburg and a smaller room called "Poet's Corner." The specialties of the Woodfield dining room these days are mainly fish and chicken, though earlier proprietors undoubtedly brought local wild game to the table. While the inn definitely shows its age in places, the accommodations have been recommended by a number of patrons of the Flat Rock Playhouse, according to Dale Bartlett, development director. For more information on the Woodfield Inn, call 800-533-6016 (toll free) or visit <http://www.woodfieldinn.com/>.

In his essay "Rockin' Chairs and Lemon Juleps," journalist John Parris tells us that the Woodfield

Dating back to 1852, Flat Rock's Woodfield Inn was known for lemon juleps and the Flat Rock rocking chair, according to John Parris.

... was once the rocking chair capital of the south and the only place in the mountains where a man could mix himself a julep with home-grown lemons. . . .

A few of the visitors who stop here now are told about the lemon trees and the lemons that come to ripening in July but few of them attempt to mix a lemon-julep.

Yet they sit on the overhanging gallery of the old hostelry and rock of an evening in rocking chairs which are poor copies of Squire Farmer's famous Flat Rock rocker.

The rocking chairs are lined up along the gallery like dragoons and they number into the twenties.

And of all of them there is only one—just one, mind you—of the original Flat Rock rockers turned out by Squire Farmer.

The guest who happens to occupy this rocker, even though ignorant in the lore of rockers, can't help but recognizing immediately that it is different from all the others.

This one—the Flat Rock rocker—doesn't creep.

It's made of walnut and walnut rockers just don't creep. There is a quality in walnut that causes it to cling to the floor. It will stay in place no matter how vigorous the rocking.

—From *Mountain Bred*, by John Parris, 281–82.

■ OLD FLAT ROCK POST OFFICE

Older than the Woodfield Inn and just a bit farther up the road on the right, across from Little River Road, is Flat Rock's original post office building, circa 1847, now home of the Book Exchange—a card shop and bookstore. At one time the U.S. Postal Service threatened to close their Flat Rock office, but the townspeople rose up to save it. Today, a new post office sits just across the road, while the old structure has been protected by its placement on the National Register of Historic Places. Just a few doors down from here, locals say, Carl Sandburg used to come with his guitar of an evening and perform for passersby. And the story goes that in 1945, the first letter—actually an invoice—that Carl Sandburg received at Connemara, his nearby home, was addressed to "Mr. Sanborn, c/o Connie Mary, Flat Rock, N.C." The post office knew exactly where to deliver it.

■ FLAT ROCK PLAYHOUSE

At the corner of Little River Road and Old Highway 25, diagonally across the street from the old post office, is Flat Rock Playhouse, considered by many critics to be one of the ten best seasonal theaters in the country. For more than fifty years, Flat Rock's resident company, the Vagabond Players, has performed in the region. Though the Vagabonds were organized by Robroy Farquhar in 1937, the troupe did not actually come to North Carolina until 1940, when they first performed in an old grist mill at nearby Highland Lake. After several seasons in different locations, the Vagabonds finally bought eight acres in Flat Rock —land that actually includes *the* flat rock, an old Indian landmark now noted by a state historical marker on the grounds. The Vagabonds literally pitched a tent for their shows until the playhouse was constructed. In 1961, the North

The Old Post Office Building in Flat Rock is on the National Register of Historic Places.

Carolina General Assembly declared the Flat Rock Playhouse the State Theater of North Carolina.

Today, from the middle of May to the middle of October, the playhouse presents a nine-show professional series, a summer and fall college apprentice and intern program, and a two-show season and cabaret series by the Theatre for Young People in residence here. They provide year-round classes and workshops for K–12 students and sponsor an annual playwriting contest for middle school and high school students. The top student play and the runners-up are then produced in reader's theater format at the playhouse.

Historically, the Flat Rock Playhouse has premiered or produced a number of works by or about North Carolina writers, including Paul Green, O. Henry, Thomas Wolfe, and many others. When he was able, Carl Sandburg would come down the hill from his home and play guitar and sing for audiences before shows. In 1962, the theater staged the first production of *The World of Carl Sandburg*, created by Norman Corwin and based on the author's many publications and letters. Sandburg—only five years from his death—loved the production, which eventually went to Broadway and starred Bette Davis and Leif Erickson.

Tours of the playhouse are available by calling ahead at 828-693-0731; for more information visit <http://www.flatrockplayhouse.org>.

■ CARL SANDBURG HOUSE

From Flat Rock Playhouse, take Little River Road a short distance and turn left into the visitor's lot for the Carl Sandburg House, which is managed by the National Park Service. It's a short walk beside the reflecting pond and up the hill to Connemara, the Irish name given to this house by the textile tycoon who sold the property to the Sandburgs. Originally built in 1838 for Christopher Memminger, secretary of the Confederate treasury during the Civil War, the eleven buildings and 264 acres are still home to the descendants of Mrs. Sandburg's nationally famous, prize-winning goat herd. Lillian Steichen Sandburg had begun raising goats when the Sandburgs lived in Michigan. This endeavor was one of the main reasons the Sandburgs decided to move to North Carolina and leave behind the harsh winters of the far north. Here Mrs. Sandburg made delicious Neufchatels, wheels of brie with anise or caraway seeds to flavor them, and buttermilk, butter, and yogurt from goat's milk. She soon signed a contract with a dairy in Hendersonville to sell the milk that was beyond her family's needs.

Carl Sandburg—poet, biographer, minstrel, and popular speaker—had already published several volumes of poetry, a number of children's books, and his Pulitzer Prize–winning multivolume biography of Abraham Lincoln before he came to Connemara. Yet when he moved to Flat Rock at the age of sixty-seven, he still had twenty-two more years of important writing ahead of him.

Both Sandburg and his wife flourished here, and two of the Sandburgs' daughters also lived full-time at Connemara. Daughter Margaret suffered from nocturnal epilepsy and needed supervision, while Janet, who was hit by a car as a child, had suffered some brain damage and was given to severe headaches. The Sandburgs' third daughter, Helga—a writer and her father's sometime literary assistant—also lived on the farm with her two children for a time.

Helga's daughter, Paula Steichen, vividly remembered many exotic days

Pictured among his wife's prizewinning goats, Carl Sandburg takes time from writing to be with his grandchildren, Paula and John Carl, at the Connemara barn. This photo is similar to an image published in Think *magazine in 1957 by Sandburg's brother-in-law, Edward Steichen. Courtesy of the North Carolina Collection of the Pack Memorial Library, Asheville, North Carolina.*

with her brother, John Carl, in the company of their grandfather, whom they called "Buppong." Sandburg would invent stories and play with the children, sailing their little boats in the small concrete pool that had once been a working fountain in front of the house. Paula Steichen's 1968 memoir, *My Connemara*, gives a vivid flavor of life on the farm:

> Gramma always declared that she bought Connemara because of the winding driveway banked with one-hundred-foot pine trees and an ivy-covered stone wall. For Helga, the decision was made when she sighted the sloping fields and spreading oak limbs under which the goats could

graze and rest content in the summer sun. For my grandfather the matter was decided when he stepped onto the front porch and looked past pillars to the distant dusky-blue hills. He put his hand on the porch railing and declared that Connemara would be the new home. He then chose two small loftlike rooms with western exposure for his own. Here in the years to come he would work undisturbed, often retiring to his bed just as the farmers in the family were rising below, putting coffee on the stove and calling the dogs to go with them to the early milking. Sometimes the writer would call or wave from his high windows as one struck out into the dark morning—the moon low and mellowed, giving one hint of the dawn to come. He would enjoy this waking of farm life as he was turning to sleep. "You look like you know where you are going," he would call out. "If you get lost, I bet you'll follow the stars."...

I grew to like the smell of cigar smoke through the rooms where Buppong worked. From under the table I could watch my grandfather's feet, toes resting inward as he typed or read, and hear the sound of his work—the rustling of papers, the swift, penciled shorthand, the click of the typewriter. Around the room were thick lead pencils in cigar boxes and orange juice cans which John Carl and I had covered with Christmas wrapping paper and presented to our grandfather at yuletides. There were also stacks of paper of every weight and grade—although the cheaper newsprint was by far the most popular with Buppong and his grandchildren. As I played with my stuffed animals or painted under the table, I felt that every house in the world was filled with typewriters and books and orange crates full of letters, and inhabited by a man whose toes turned inward, clad in their ancient shoes.—From *My Connemara*, by Paula Steichen (New York: Eastern National, 2002), 7–10, 87.

Carl Sandburg died in July of 1967 in the downstairs bedroom of Connemara with his wife beside him. The next year, Congress authorized the Carl Sandburg Home National Historic Site, making it the first national park to honor a poet. When Lillian Steichen Sandburg gave the property to the National Park Service, her only request was that the government caretakers leave the house as it was—as if the family had stepped out for a walk.

To this day, Connemara is filled with the Sandburgs' memorabilia and books—Carl's slippers by the chair in his sleeping quarters, a guitar propped against the piano in the living room, Lillian's notes and photos of the goat herd, and piles of magazines from the 1960s on the floor beside the staircase. Guided

The Sandburgs' kitchen as they left it.

tours of the house are conducted daily, and a bookshop in the basement of the house offers an excellent selection of volumes by and about the Sandburgs and recordings of the poet singing and reading his work. There is a small admission fee. For more information call 828-693-4178 or visit <http://www.nps.gov/carl>.

A Forest Service guide at Connemara recommended this poem, supposedly based on a print of a Japanese landscape, though the ranger observed that it was most likely inspired by the view from the many windows across the front of the house. As Sandburg so often did in his notes to his children and grandchildren and in his children's books, he has made up whimsical names for the valley and river he describes:

OLD HOKUSAI PRINT

In a house he remembers in the Howlong valley
not far from bends of the Shooshoo river
where each of the leaves of fall is a pigeon foot of gold on the blue:
there is a house of a thousand windows
and in every window the same woman
and she too remembers better than she forgets:
she too has one wish for every window:
  and the mountains forty miles away
  rise and fade, come and go,
  in lights and mist there and not there,
  beckoning as mountains seen on a Monday,
  phantoms traveled far away on a Tuesday,
  scrawls in a dim blot on Wednesday,
  gone into grey shawls on Friday,
  lost and found in half lavenders often,
  back again one day saying they were not gone,
  not gone at all, being merely unseen,
the white snow on the blue peaks no dream snow,
no dream at all the sawtooth line of purple garments.
Can a skyline share itself like drums in the heart?
—From *Honey and Salt*, by Carl Sandburg
  (New York: Harcourt, Brace, 1991), 69.

To reach Hendersonville, return to Business 25 and turn left. It runs directly into Main Street downtown.

■ HENDERSONVILLE

Witness the number of apple orchards in the vicinity, and you know that Hendersonville's climate is not quite as harsh as some other areas on this tour. This busy town of more than 10,000 residents has drawn a number of writers over the years, including F. Scott Fitzgerald, who spent a troubled November here writing three essays that rival William Styron's *Darkness Visible* for the bleak account of the depression he was suffering. In the fall of 1935, after Fitzgerald's dissolute summer at the Grove Park Inn (see Tour 8), he traveled to Baltimore to spend time with his wife, Zelda, who was hospitalized there. In November, he fled the cold weather in Maryland and headed south again, this time to Hendersonville, where he took a room at the new Skyland Hotel, a building that is still standing at 538 North Main Street.

Practically penniless and prompted by his agent's pleas for something to sell, he cranked out three confessional essays—"The Crack-Up," "Pasting It Together," and "Handle with Care." These three pieces were a no-holds-barred account of Fitzgerald's own desperation and depression. "In a real dark night of the soul it is always three o'clock in the morning, day after day," Fitzgerald wrote. Full of such one-line zingers, the essays were published as a series in the February, March, and April 1936 issues of *Esquire* magazine. That April, Zelda Fitzgerald was first admitted to Highland Hospital in Asheville.

Fitzgerald's colleagues—including Scribner's editor Maxwell Perkins, novelist John Dos Passos, and Ernest Hemingway—condemned the pieces as indulgent and embarrassing. Edmund Wilson posthumously collected the Hendersonville essays in *The Crack-Up* (1945).

Today you can step into the Skyland Hotel's lobby and see it as it was in Fitzgerald's era. While you're there, you may also want to visit the second floor to see what's on exhibit at the Art Center.

Hendersonville was also the summer home of South Carolina writer DuBose Heyward, author of the novel *Porgy* (1925), which he and George Gershwin transformed into the grand folk opera, *Porgy and Bess*. Heyward invited Gershwin to spend time with him in Charleston, where Gershwin immersed himself in Gullah culture as he prepared to write the music. Another low country novel, Heyward's *Mamba's Daughters* (1929), which became a Broadway musical featuring Ethel Waters, is still in print from the University of South Carolina Press. Heyward's *Peter Ashley* (1932) was reissued by the History Press of Charleston in 2004. Heyward also wrote the screenplays for Eugene O'Neill's *Emperor Jones*, starring Paul Robeson, and Pearl S. Buck's *The Good Earth*. His only novel that focused on life in the mountains, *Angel* (1926), is out of print.

Heyward reportedly lived off Old Kanuga Road in a residence called "Dawn Hill," on Price Road. He died in nearby Tryon. James M. Hutchisson, a professor at the Citadel, chronicles the life of this conservative, white businessman turned progressive advocate for racial equity in *DuBose Heyward: A Charleston Gentleman and the World of Porgy and Bess* (2000).

Among the writers who are working in Hendersonville today is Ann B. Ross, who once taught literature at the University of North Carolina at Asheville. Ross has now become a local celebrity as the creator of the *Miss Julia* series of comedic novels published by HarperCollins. The series details the life of a spunky, old-school southern widow lady living on her inheritance in a town much like Hendersonville.

Local mystery writer Mart Baldwin is the author of *Kill the Benefactor* (1995), *Over the Edge* (2001), and *A Diary to Die For* (2002). Though he has a Ph.D. in chemistry from the University of North Carolina at Chapel Hill, was a Fulbright scholar in Germany, and worked at Alabama's Redstone Arsenal for a number of years, Baldwin has now happily retired to the writing life.

■ WOLFE ANGEL

The final stop on Trail One takes us to the famous Wolfe Angel, a marble statue from Italy that was sold by Thomas Wolfe's father to the Johnson family of Hendersonville. This sculpture was the inspiration for the title of Wolfe's first novel. John Parris tells the story best:

> The fading red of a summer twilight touched the marble angel and spun just a whisper of a halo about its head.
>
> Back in the hills, the time-lost hills of a stonecutter's son, the first frost had come and with it a breath of autumn-come-Saturday and the prelude to the blaze that is October.
>
> Between the marble angel and the turn of the season there is a thing that brings to mind the young giant of the mountains whose words of prose and poetry will live as long as man can read.
>
> Each in its way was a part of him and each was a part of his tune.
>
> For him they represented the fable and mystery of time, and he wove them into his writings and made of them something to be recalled and remembered.
>
> He made of autumn and October in the hills a tapestry as vivid and colorful as nature's own brilliant-hued canvas.
>
> And he took a marble angel and gave it a halo and sent men on a 20-year search for it.
>
> They found it long after he was dead.
>
> They found it here in Oakdale cemetery.
>
> In all the world there probably is none as famous as this one.
>
> For it is the angel that Tom Wolfe was referring to in his memorable *Look Homeward, Angel*. . . .
>
> It was substantiated that not one but several angels stood on the porch of Wolfe's father's marble shop in Asheville over a 25-year period.
>
> But the angel here is the only one that answered the description given by Tom Wolfe in his writings, first in "An Angel On the Porch," which was his first short story. It appeared in Scribner's and later was incorporated as a chapter in *Look Homeward, Angel*.
>
> As described in his story:

"It had come from Carrara, in Italy, and it held a stone lily delicately in one hand. The other hand was lifted in benediction. It was poised delicately upon one phthisic foot."

In another place he referred to the lily as the "stip" which technically the flower is, while the other angels that stood on the porch of his father's shop carried either wreathes or unidentified flowers.

Until 1949 there had been a dispute about the identity of the angel.

There were some who insisted that Tom's "angel" rested in Asheville's Riverside Cemetery. Others said it was in a cemetery in Waynesville or Haywood County, while others still insisted that the real "angel" was in a cemetery in Whittier.

Mrs. Wolfe herself said it was not in Asheville. She said she believed it was here in Hendersonville.

So it was the search narrowed and came to an end in Oakdale cemetery where the marble angel marks the grave of Mrs. Margaret Bates Johnson.

Several years ago Mrs. Sadie Smathers Patton, the Hendersonville historian, was visiting Oakdale and discovered that the angel needed repairing.

Mrs. Patton discovered that a piece from the raised hand had broken off. This fragment lay nearby. She had it replaced. She also discovered that the entire angel was loose on the base. She had it reset.

Some who had searched for years thought the angel might even have been shipped out of the country.

For in one of Tom's stories he mentioned that it had been bought by Queen Elizabeth. But his mother cleared that up quickly. She said Tom had just changed things around in the story.

Actually the angel here was purchased from Tom's father in 1906 by the Johnson family. That would have made Tom six years old at the time.

Tom wrote that the angels his father bought at great cost and had sent from Italy were the joy of his heart.

As a boy they impressed him, one in particular—the one he made famous.

Just as he wrote that the stonecutter of *Look Homeward, Angel* had been impressed as a boy and wanting more than anything in the world to carve delicately with a chisel.

"He wanted to carve an angel's head," Tom wrote. "But he never found it. He never learned to carve an angel's head. The dove, the lamb, the smooth joined marble hands of death, and letters fair and fine—but not the angel."

The Wolfe angel in Hendersonville.

Tom Wolfe made of the angel remembered as a boy on the porch of his father's shop a sort of symbol.

It was something that had to do with time and the turning of the seasons.

The angel and October signified both sorrow and delight.

The angel was a "haunting sorrow for the buried men" which he felt in the golden warmth of October when there was "an exultancy for all the men who were returning" to the hills of home.

Soon it will be October. Tom Wolfe's month.

For back in the hills the first frost has come.

And here in Oakdale cemetery the fading red of twilight touches the marble angel and spins just a whisper of a halo about its head.

And the marble angel and the turn of the season nod to one another.

In the trees the wind whispers lines out of a book and they are lines that sound like the ones created by the young giant of the mountains — Tom Wolfe. — From "Of an Angel and a Giant of a Man — Hendersonville," in *Mountain Bred*, by John Parris, 315–17.

From Main Street downtown, head north to Seventh Avenue (US 64 East). Turn left and follow 64 for less than a mile. The Oakdale Cemetery is on both sides of the road on a knoll. The Wolfe angel is located on the left and is protected by a wrought iron fence. Look for the state historical marker as a guide.

■ LITERARY LANDSCAPE

Highland Books

480 North Broad Street

Brevard, NC 28712

828-884-2424

highlandbook@citcom.net

Tim and Peggy Hansen have run Highland Books for some three decades and provide "full, friendly and very knowledgeable service. And they are great for hosting readings by local authors," says local writer Ken Chamlee. Highland Books's regional collection is extensive. We even found a poetry collection by the late Jim Wayne Miller, whose works are getting harder to find.

Transylvania County Library

212 South Gaston Street

Brevard, NC 28712

828-884-3151

<http://www.transylvania.lib.nc.us>

The Brevard Library began in a little green cottage downtown that is long gone. Later the library took up residence in the old post office building. Today it has an impressive new home of 35,000 square feet where you will find a local history room, a substantial book and video collection, twenty-four computer stations, and ample community meeting space. A bookmobile traverses the county, supplementing the array of programs for children and young adults offered here.

The Book Exchange

2680 Highway 225

Flat Rock, NC 28731

828-693-8311

Across from the Flat Rock Post Office, this shop offers new and used books, greeting cards, and gifts. You will find volumes on the history of Flat Rock by local historians Louise Bailey, Sadie Patton, and Galen Reuther. Part of the proceeds from sales of books go toward local charities. Closed Sundays.

Mountain Lore Bookstore & Gift
408 North Main Street
Hendersonville, NC 28792
828-693-5096

This bookstore is local novelist Ann Ross's favorite: "The owner, Rick McKee, not only stocks the latest in fiction and nonfiction, but he also features an excellent selection of books of regional interest, as well as children's books. Mountain Lore is well worth a stop on anybody's literary trail," she says.

Henderson County Library
301 North Washington Street
Hendersonville, NC 28739
828-697-4725
<http://www.henderson.lib.nc.us/>

Just two blocks west of Main Street, between Third and Fourth Avenues, this lively library hosts regular events such as a foreign-film series, a roster of regional speakers, and a travel club, and has created a growing collection of materials on North Carolina genealogy and history. The Baker-Barber Collection documents the history and culture of western North Carolina from 1884 to the mid-1990s in extraordinary photographs. The library also has a permanent display of ware from the Pisgah Forest Pottery. The busts of several local authors, created by sculptor James Spratt, are in the North Carolina Room.

trail two

The Northern Mountains and Foothills : Voice

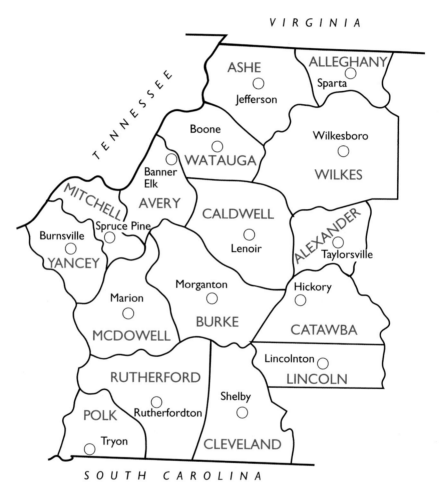

COUNTIES AND PRINCIPAL TOWNS OF
TRAIL TWO

A few years ago an ice storm splintered a large stand of pine trees on my grandmother Ledbetter's farm. When the broken timber was logged and removed, our whole family was shocked by how close the mountains were behind the ridge where the trees had stood. We all walked out the road past the barn to have a closer look, almost as if we had never seen them before. "These very mountains of Carolina," Kephart writes in *Our Southern Highlanders*, "are among the ancients of the earth. They were old, very old, before the Alps and the Andes, the Rockies and the Himalayas were molded into their primal shapes." Young's Mountain, Rumbling Bald, Chimney Rock, Shumont, World's Edge, White Oak: my family has apparently always lived in their shadow. They preserved in their hollows and laurel hells the words that tell us better than any others who we are. Words and blood are the double helix that connects us to our past.

As a member of the transitional generation, however, I am losing those words and the connection they make. And by losing language, I am losing the small comfort of shared history. I compensate, in the stories I write, by taking people up mountains to look, as Horace Kephart did, for the answers to their questions, to look down from a high place and see what they can see.

—From "The Quare Gene," in *Somehow Form a Family: Stories That Are Partly True*, by Tony Earley (Chapel Hill, N.C.: Algonquin Books of Chapel Hill, 2001), 80–81; originally published in the *New Yorker*, September 28, 1998.

The literature of the northern mountains and foothills of North Carolina's Blue Ridge includes the voices of longtime residents and observant newcomers. Between them, the tensions of insider and outsider are writ large. Several visitors who took up residence in these parts, notably Muriel Earley Sheppard, Margaret Morley, and Kathleen Moore Morehouse, documented mountain culture from a position of profound curiosity that was sometimes tinged with a tone of amused voyeurism—a perspective that was not always well received by local readers. The outsider's perspective is, however, a significant part of the literature here, along with the authentic local voices of Bandana poet Hilda Downer, Rutherford County novelist Tony Earley, and North Carolina's one-time poet laureate, James Larkin Pearson, of Moravian Falls, among many others. The cadence and twang of mountain speech in their writing is as musical as the tunes played here for generations on fiddle and banjo.

This region of North Carolina is also a place where tall tales of the mysterious and grotesque are still manufactured in abundance, just as moonshine once was. From the storytelling tradition among the Hicks family of Beech Mountain to contemporary mystery writers Sharyn McCrumb (whose family comes from Mitchell County), Rutherford County's Kay Hooper, Polk County transplant and cat fanatic Lilian Braun, and Boone novelist Scott Nicholson, these authors have produced dozens of cliff-hangers (and high sales figures) that have brought national attention to the region.

In years past, the mythology of these mountains also primed the imaginations of internationally acclaimed writers who set novels here, including grand master of mystery writing Phyllis A. Whitney, French novelist Jules Verne, and British-born Frances Hodgson Burnett, author of *Little Lord Fauntleroy* and *The Secret Garden*.

The literary tourist may also be interested to learn that playwright and actor William Gillette—whose stage characterizations of Sherlock Holmes were adopted by actor Basil Rathbone for film—lived for a time in Tryon, also the hometown of world-renowned songwriter and stylist Nina Simone. Social commentators W. J. Cash and Thomas Dixon—political polar opposites—are buried across the lane from each other in their hometown of Shelby in Cleveland County along this trail. And one of the nation's most popular and prolific novelists—Anne Tyler—spent her childhood at the foot of Celo Mountain, not too far from CBS journalist Charles Kuralt's favorite vacation spot: Grandfather Mountain. As in Trail One, we run into several literary giants along this journey—F. Scott Fitzgerald, Ernest Hemingway, Thomas Wolfe *and* Tom Wolfe, Marjorie Kinnan Rawlings, Margaret Mitchell, North Carolina's own John Ehle, and the prolific poet of place, Robert Morgan.

Burnsville : Micaville : Celo : Mount Mitchell

Eat famous country ham in one of journalist Jonathan Daniels's favorite Tar Heel restaurants. See the landscape that surrounded novelist Anne Tyler as a child. Hike among the exotic foliage and gemstones of the highest mountains east of the Mississippi.

Writers with a connection to this area: Jonathan Daniels, Abigail DeWitt, Louisa Duls, Wilma Dykeman, Tom Higgins, Everette M. Kivette, William G. Lord, Robert Morgan, Margaret Morley, Charles F. Price, Muriel Earley Sheppard, Timothy Silver, Anne Tyler, Thomas Wolfe, Perry Deane Young

When Thomas Wolfe came home to Asheville in 1937, he made a visit to the Grove Park Inn, where his friend F. Scott Fitzgerald was staying. According to Wilma Dykeman's account, the two literary lions exchanged pleasantries before Fitzgerald finally blurted out his writerly frustrations with the local scene:

> "This is a sterile town, Tom. Why do you come here for characters?" And Wolfe replied, "What are you talking about, Scott? I've just come from Burnsville over in Yancey County. I've been talking with my mother's uncle, John Westall over there. He's ninety-five, he was at Chickamauga, and he told me about it. My God, it was wonderful. I'm going to write it all down verbatim. There's your character, Scott, back in Yancey County. What did you expect to find up here at the Grove Park Inn? They're the same people you see at expensive hotels everywhere. But you go out in these mountains here—sterile, Scott? Don't you believe it." —From *The French Broad*, by Wilma Dykeman, (Newport, Tenn.: Wakestone Books, 1992), 225.

Yancey County is bordered by Buncombe and McDowell Counties to the south, Tennessee to the north, and the Toe River

tour 11

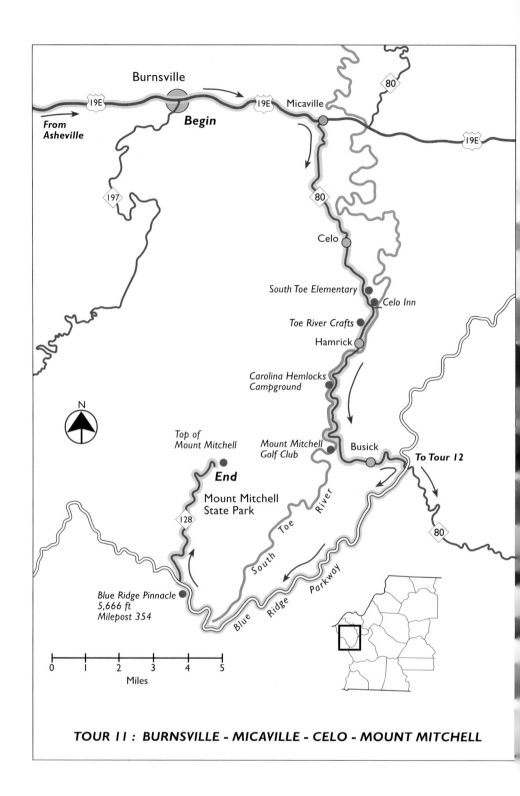

Burnsville

19E

From
Asheville

19E   Micaville

80

197

80

Celo

South Toe Elementary

Celo Inn

Toe River Crafts

Hamrick

Carolina Hemlocks
Campground

N

Top of
Mount Mitchell

Mount Mitchell
Golf Club   Busick

End   To Tour 12

Mount Mitchell
State Park

128   80

South   Toe   River

Blue Ridge Pinnacle
5,666 ft
Milepost 354

Blue   Ridge   Parkway

0   1   2   3   4   5

Miles

TOUR 11 : BURNSVILLE - MICAVILLE - CELO - MOUNT MITCHELL

Begin

and Mitchell County to the east. Here Thomas Wolfe found inspiration among his mountain kin. Today there are still plenty of tales for the literary traveler to discover, though the roads generally offer much easier access than in Wolfe's day. If you're coming from Asheville, head north on US 19/23 (the future I-26) toward Johnson City, Tennessee. In about sixteen miles, shortly after the exit to Mars Hill, look for the exit to Burnsville/Spruce Pine. Turn right onto US 19E.

This road winds a bit, but after several miles, it heads due east, climbing to the county line at Windy Gap, where the weather in winter can change in an instant as you cross from Madison County into Yancey. Coming down from Windy Gap, the road levels and straightens again, and then undulates gently through a dramatic valley toward the county seat of Burnsville. Here cattle, burley tobacco, corn, and apples still dominate the landscape.

Yancey County, formed in 1833, was once larger than it is today. Neighboring Mitchell County was pieced together in 1861 from a part of Yancey and several other counties when the residents on the eastern side of the Toe River opted not to secede from the Union during the Civil War. To this day, Democrats are purportedly the majority in Yancey County, while Republicans dominate Mitchell County.

According to historian Timothy Silver, at the time of its creation, Yancey County was home to an enormous ginseng "factory," where residents processed some 86,000 pounds of the medicinal root. "In 1840," he writes, "Yancey County [also] had thirty-two distilleries that annually turned out 5,790 gallons of whiskey, cider, and brandy" (*Mount Mitchell and the Black Mountains*, by Timothy Silver [Chapel Hill: University of North Carolina Press, 2003], 69).

As late as 1935, when oral historian Muriel Earley Sheppard published *Cabins in the Laurel*, her controversial outsider's account of the region, "the trading in blockade [homemade liquor] is neither flagrant nor defiant, but goes on steadily even though the court is generally strict with offenders brought under its jurisdiction." Local residents, says Sheppard, were "proud of their product as good housewives are proud of the flavor of their butter." Sheppard offers her own review of the 1930s home brew:

> The quality of Toe River corn whiskey is good, although sometimes the distiller puts in too much lye to hurry up his mash or works off a run in an oil drum and taints it. None of it is aged very long, but some of the higher alcohols and impurities can be eliminated by putting a charred oak stick in a half-gallon fruit jar of the liquor. Charred peaches will serve the same purpose. Good straight-run corn is the most popular, and apple and black-

berry brandy are the choicest and hardest to get. Third run sugar liquor is the meanest. — From *Cabins in the Laurel*, by Muriel Earley Sheppard, (Chapel Hill: University of North Carolina Press, 1991), 175.

To this day, both Mitchell and Yancey County are "dry" — meaning that state-sanctioned sales of alcohol have yet to be approved by voters here. It is debatable whether this situation is the result of the abundance of teetotaling church-goers or an ongoing cultural resistance to the government tax on alcohol. It's probably a bit of both.

Along your route to Burnsville, you are not far from the Lost Cove. Burnsville writer and illustrator Everett M. Kivette writes about this remote Yancey County village without electricity or mail service that was also known over decades for its homemade brandy and prolific ginseng production. His compendium of freelance articles, entitled *Epitaph for Lost Cove & A Very Special Mountain: An Appalachian Town with a Yankee Accent* (2000), is available for sale or loan at the Yancey Public Library. Kivette's articles — many of which were originally published in *The State* (now *Our State* magazine) and the *New York Times* — chronicle the changes brought by the steady march of development in the latter half of the twentieth century.

Kivette is among the many outsiders who came to Yancey County and made their mark in helping to organize the vibrant arts community that thrives here today. In addition to his freelance journalism, Kivette helped sustain a nationally recognized fine arts program begun here in 1946 by painters Edward Shorter and Frank Herring. Initially called the Burnsville Painting Classes, this summer school for adults was held at the Nu Wray Inn in Burnsville and later at a nearby fifty-two-acre camp called SeeCelo. Under Kivette's direction, the program was renamed Painting in the Mountains in 1966 and continued for three decades, providing instruction for a number of accomplished painters whose work can still be found in galleries across the Southeast.

Burnsville can also lay claim to novelist Charles F. Price, who settled near here in recent years. His work, mostly set in far western North Carolina, is discussed in Tour 4. Burnsville is also the birthplace of Tom Higgins, longtime sportswriter for the *Charlotte Observer* and the official biographer of NASCAR legend Junior Johnson.

■ BURNSVILLE

The speed limit drops precipitously as you come into Burnsville. Town Square is one block north of US 19E. Turn left at the traffic light at the top of the

Legend has it that both Mark Twain and Elvis dined here.

hill in the heart of town where signs direct you to the square. Here is the statue of Captain Otway Burns of Beaufort, a hero in the War of 1812 against England and the person for whom the town is named. On the square you'll also find the historic Nu Wray Inn, established in 1833, the same year as Yancey County. Mark Twain reportedly stayed here, as did Elvis Presley. Though the inn still accommodates overnight guests, it is best known for its country breakfasts, Sunday brunch buffet, and ample dinners, served nowadays on Thursday, Friday, and Saturday evenings. The menu has hardly changed since Raleigh journalist Jonathan Daniels offered his wry commentary on the feasts in his 1941 book *Tar Heels*:

> Everything is on the table in the Nu-Wray Hotel at Burnsville. Nobody waits to give an order. They bring it in, three or four kinds of meat, all the vegetables of the whole mountain countryside. There are dishes of homemade jellies and preserves. The country ham is excellent. The stout tables do not groan but the stuffed guest rising sometimes does. It is country plenty, country cooked and country served, but in proof that the persisting homesickness for country eating is not entirely based on legend, I think that even Thomas L. Clingman, whose name is on the biggest mountain in the Great Smoky Mountain National Park, would approve of the biscuits and the other hot breads, as well. . . .
>
> In North Carolina, even in 1875, when most other politicians were occupied entirely with the bitter ending of Reconstruction, he had real zeal left

over for the denunciation of "something called biscuits which was in fact rather warm dough with much grease in it."

"Within ten years," [Clingman] said, "as many people have died prematurely in this State from bad cookery as were slain in the war."—From *Tar Heels: A Portrait of North Carolina*, by Jonathan Daniels (New York: Dodd, Mead, 1941), 248–49.

Daniels goes on in his essay, called "Frying Pan and Jug," to inventory the many delicacies and various beverages offered up by Tar Heel cooks across the state and to dismiss Clingman's snobbery about the state's native dishes. He then returns to his inventory of the bountiful table at the Nu Wray: "The quantity is apt to be amazing to the visitor from the north, but the quality will generally help him get away with the quantity. It may amaze a visitor also, how many little rolls, light as feathers but fattening as cream, he can consume. 'Butter them while they're hot,' says his hostess. Such cooking may kill. And in a mortal world it is by no means a bad way to die" (263).

For more information on the Nu Wray Inn, call 800-368-9729 or visit <http://www.nuwrayinn.com>.

After sufficiently exploring Burnsville with its galleries, gift shops, and old-fashioned hardware store, take East Main Street from the town square, which will put you back out on US 19E. Turn left and continue east. It is a little over three miles to Micaville and the junction of NC 80 South.

■ MICAVILLE

So named for the prolific presence of mica, or isinglass, in the region, downtown Micaville is comprised today of a post office, an antique trading post, and the Micaville Grill, which proclaims itself by means of a hand-printed sign to have been "Voted the Best Grill in Micaville," not mentioning that it is the *only* grill here.

Not much has changed over the years. In her lyrical 1913 travelogue, Tryon writer Margaret Morley described Micaville as "a village that consists of a post office and very little else" (316):

It lies in the most important mica region of the mountains, where the rocks sparkle, the roads glitter, and nearly everyone is engaged one way or another in working in mica. You see women and girls sitting under sheds cutting plates of mica into regular shapes, and piles of mica waste glinting by the roadside, or flashing near the mouths of the mines on the hillsides.

Yet there is nothing here to suggest the hardships of a mining country, for the mines are for the most part near or at the surface, and the workers are the mountain people themselves. — From *The Carolina Mountains*, by Margaret W. Morley (Alexander, N.C.: Land of the Sky Books, 2002), 325.

Timothy Silver also writes about the mica bonanza of the late nineteenth and early twentieth centuries in this region. His book *Mount Mitchell and the Black Mountains* is part historical narrative and part outdoor journal. Silver notes that Thomas Clingman, the aforementioned biscuit hater, was also a shrewd businessman who had recently retired from the U.S. Senate in the 1870s when, Silver writes, "he convinced a group of New York mica merchants to bankroll a prospecting expedition in western North Carolina. Clingman knew that the best mica deposits would likely be found in Mitchell and Yancey counties." Indeed, the expedition "unearthed large sheets of 'rum-colored' muscovite or sheet mica, some of the finest specimens anywhere in the world" (199). The discovery created an economic boom for several decades. Hikers in the area still find evidence of the digging frenzy. (On Tour 16, in neighboring Mitchell County, you can collect your own mica specimens and pan for other gems and minerals.) For now, head south on NC 80.

■ CELO

The little community of Celo, some six miles south of Micaville, has an important literary connection. Watch for the sign to the South Toe Elementary School on the left as you enter Celo. Pulitzer Prize–winning novelist Anne Tyler briefly attended grade school here. (Drive up into the schoolyard to take in the extraordinary view of Celo Knob from the front of the old brick school.)

In 1948, when Tyler was in grade school, her family moved to the Celo Community, a land trust and utopian village founded by Arthur E. Morgan in 1937. Morgan had served as president of Antioch College, was the first chairman of the TVA, and at the time was reportedly the world's leading flood-control engineer. When a wealthy textile magnate asked him to suggest a good investment, Morgan convinced the man to purchase 1,200 acres in this area. Morgan himself settled in Celo and set about creating an "intentional community" of citizens with common values and social concerns that were generally in alignment with the Friends Service Committee — the Quakers — who were among the first Celo residents.

Anne Tyler's parents, Floyd and Phyllis Tyler, both Quakers, were drawn to Celo after having lived in several such intentional communities in the Midwest

Childhood home of novelist Anne Tyler in Celo.

and South. They built a house alongside the Toe River on land that was, and still is, held in a common trust by the community. The house—not visible from the road—stands today. Its current occupants still remember finding a pencil in one of the closets when they first moved in. On it was the name "Anne." When the present residents met Tyler and her father in 2005, Anne was curious to know if they'd also found the ring that she buried in the yard as a child. They had not.

The house, paneled entirely in chestnut, is surrounded by enormous trees and mature plantings of ivy, rhododendron, and japonica. Here the Tyler family practiced organic farming, raised livestock, and participated in community activities. Anne took art, carpentry, and cooking lessons and was reportedly writing stories as early as age seven. She attended a one-room school until South

Toe Elementary opened in 1952. Always the precocious student, Tyler was often asked to take over the class when her teacher had to go check on his cows.

In 1953 the Tyler family left Celo for Raleigh, where Anne would graduate from Broughton High School at the age of sixteen. She then studied with the legendary Duke English professor William Blackburn and the young novelist and poet Reynolds Price. She completed her bachelor's degree at Duke University in only three years. She published *If Morning Ever Comes* in 1964—the second novel she ever wrote but the first to be published. Tyler's second and third published novels—*The Tin Can Tree* (1965) and *A Slipping Down Life* (1970)—also take place in North Carolina. *The Clock Winder* (1972), her fourth novel, considers the story of a young woman making a transition from living in North Carolina to Baltimore, where Tyler's subsequent novels are set. Tyler has published seventeen novels and two children's books to date, including *The Accidental Tourist* (1985), which won the National Book Critics Circle Award in 1986 and was made into a film two years later. *Breathing Lessons* (1988) won the Pulitzer Prize.

Today Celo is headquarters for Cabin Fever University, a continuing education program run by the community that taps local folks who share their skills and talents with each other during the long mountain winters. It operates with only one dollar in tuition fees per student, which provides an annual catalog of some one hundred courses, including classes on literature and writing.

The curious name "Celo" has several tales attached to it. One story suggests that the word comes from the same root as celestial, meaning heavenly. Another, according to local historian Louisa Duls, is that the community was named for a dead body found on Celo Knob alongside a rifle. Duls says that the name "C. E. Low" was carved on the gunstock.

According to writer Tim Silver, when Elisha Mitchell first explored the region in 1835, Celo Knob was known as Young's Knob, named for Thomas Young's family, who lived at the base of the mountain. Playwright Perry Deane Young is one of Thomas Young's descendants. Even though distinguished historian William Powell suggests in *The North Carolina Gazetteer* (1976) that the name goes farther back and comes from the Cherokee word *selu*, meaning corn, Perry Deane Young disagrees. "That doesn't make sense to me; especially since the Cherokees never lived here and were long gone, even as hunters, by 1905 when the name first appeared on USGS maps," he says. "My theory is some mapmaker with a classics education was drawing on the Latin word for sky—I think it's *cielo*, that's what it is in Spanish." Multiple stories on a single topic are common in these mountains. The mystery must suffice.

Continue down NC 80 beyond the Celo Inn on the left, and you'll soon come to Toe River Crafts on the right. This community craft cooperative is generally open on weekends from late spring through the fall and is worth a visit to examine the handiwork of local artists and craftspersons.

Along this route you'll also pass several nursery and floral suppliers advertising galax, a distinctive plant native to the area. Wilma Dykeman explains:

> There are some who say that the galax grows nowhere else in the world except in the Southern Appalachians. The story goes that a doctor's wife in North Carolina first shipped it out of the state and received two dollars for every hundred leaves. Its beautiful shape, glossy texture and excellent keeping qualities made it popular in the cities. Foresters were among the first to encourage galax picking. Since galax and forest fire cannot inhabit the same area, foresters saw this industry as one sure way to combat fires with galax pickers as volunteer rangers quick to spot flames and present to help stamp them out before they spread. Since the leaves were, and are, pulled just above the roots, there is no threat to new leaves, just as large and healthy, that will come forth next year. Prices for galax have ranged, over thirty years, from forty to ninety cents per thousand leaves. Picked in the winter, between November and March, in large gunnysacks, sorted by the fire at night and tied in neat bouquets of twenty-five leaves, galax is perhaps the most unusual greenery.—From *The French Broad*, by Wilma Dykeman (Newport, Tenn.: Wakestone Books, 1992), 254–55.

Galax is so named because its tiny flowers appear as a galaxy of white, star-like blooms ascending on a single, narrow stalk. Florists favor galax for casket saddles and other arrangements that need to endure heat or cold for an extended period. The toothy green leaves of galax are heart-shaped and leathery. The scent of galax—an earthy perfume that is barely more pleasant than a passing skunk—is common in the woods here.

Though you could find galax in the dark woods all along this route, save your curiosity. Ahead is a most spectacular trail where galax is abundant.

Continuing on NC 80 South, you'll drive alongside the South Toe River on your left and probably catch a glimpse of folks trying their luck at snagging a trout along this handsome stretch of the valley. Then you'll cross the South Toe—"the merriest of trout brooks," writes Margaret Morley. Soon you'll be in the village of Hamrick, where Sally's Kitchen serves the only fresh pizza for miles. Two former cooks from the Park Service Restaurant high atop Mount Mitchell operate this tiny neighborhood café.

In another 0.3 miles, look for Carolina Hemlocks, a campground built by the Civilian Conservation Corps during the Depression. Here the Toe flows slow and deep around a bend, creating one of the best swimming holes in Yancey County. Local folks and visitors alike favor it for a cool dip on a warm day.

The road will soon wind and climb toward the Blue Ridge Parkway, passing the Mount Mitchell Golf Club and the Black Mountain Recreation Area, where the Mount Mitchell Trail and the Lost Cove Ridge Trail begin. When you reach the Blue Ridge Parkway, continue under the overpass and ascend to the Parkway on your right via the loop road. Turn left on the Parkway and you'll be heading south toward the highest peak in the eastern United States, Mount Mitchell.

■ BLUE RIDGE PINNACLE

In another ten scenic miles through the Twin Tunnels and Rough Ridge Tunnel, watch for milepost 354 and slow down. Before you come to milepost 355 you'll see a metal swing gate and dirt road (once a logging trail) on your left. If you feel like hiking, park on the grass beside the Parkway without blocking the gate. There may be other cars here, which is also a clue to help you locate the spot. Walk around the gate, and in a few yards down the logging road, you'll see a worn path that cuts sharply up the bank to your right. This thirty-minute hike to Blue Ridge Pinnacle is short but steep. It passes through three or four microclimates before reaching the rocky summit at 5,666 feet. As William G. Lord explains in his landmark *Blue Ridge Parkway Guide* (New York: Eastern Acorn Press, 1982), here "the parkway leaves the Blue Ridge and passes along a short connecting ridge to the Black Mountains. Surpassed only by Grandfather Mountain, 5,938 feet, the Pinnacle is the second highest in the entire Blue Ridge from Pennsylvania to Georgia. It marks the southern limit of the Parkway's location along the drainage divide between the Atlantic Slope and the Gulf of Mexico."

The trail begins gently through a shady, fern-covered stretch and then traverses a narrow sunny path through brambles of milkweed and blackberry before ascending sharply on a narrow, spruce-scented corridor. Step carefully through this tricky tangle of roots and rocks. Here the Asheville watershed is to your right, on the far side of a barbed wire boundary that runs beside you for a time up the mountain. In the fall, listen overhead for the buzzing warble of the cedar waxwings that migrate across these mountains and feed on red sumac berries until they are nearly too heavy to fly. Along this part of the ascent you

Old postcard showing the view from the summit of Blue Ridge Pinnacle near mile marker 354 on the Blue Ridge Parkway. The view has changed very little in this direction since 1935. Lake County Discovery Museum, Curt Teich Postcard Archives.

will also find the shiny green coins of galax, which, if it's early June, might even be in bloom. Study them closely. You'll need to catch your breath anyway. Pick a rock, sit, and read this Robert Morgan poem.

GALACKER: THE GALAX GATHERER
Along in late November after at least
one hard freeze, old man Revis took his sacks
along the creekbank and hindledges of
the cove to find a last autumn in the beds
and couches of the woods between the wagon
trace and the crest of the divide from its
north exposure. And there plucked on hands and
knees among the winter trash the cover
of this creeping herb, its evergreen
cut from jade and plated bronze, lacquered,
and wired deep in the mould. Each leaf had been
polished and dusted, teeth filed on the edges.
You rarely notice the milky blossoms
because undergrowth, only the black

The toothy leaves of galax.

leaves in winter sparkling. Those blessed by
coldest wind spitshine the floor maroon,
always clear of snow except where the roots
of an oak mop on the seepage and scrub
the water table bare. His thick hands
cropped and stuffed the mirror greens in bags,
but not with pressure as for cowbedding.
That night by the fire he'd tie the best in
booklets for shipping north, and rest, waiting
for his pay till after New Year's, two bits
per thousand.

         In the gloomy latter days
of a depression year I root on the
woods floor for the oiled metals, knees
in mud, hands rotten with cold, careful as
a numismatist foraging the flanks
of the hollow, not for the clabber
of the shaded blossoms nor pale salad

growth, but to forward out in sewn wreaths
and pamphlets of commemoration,
the pages of this local archaic herb.
—From *Groundwork*, by Robert Morgan
  (Frankfort, Ky.: Gnomon Press, 1979), 14.

Next you'll work your way through a laurel hell, scrambling both up and down by turns over a rocky shelf through fragrant firs. Eventually, after the last hard pull upward, you'll arrive at a dramatic tree whose spreading limbs nearly graze the ground. Stop here for a photo and prepare for the final few yards up a hill less demanding than the one you've just climbed. Near the summit, the understory will suddenly yield to a stairstep of rocks that are flanked by wild blueberry bushes. Keep climbing carefully.

Blue Ridge Pinnacle is unforgettable, no matter what season. On a clear day you can see the Seven Sisters toward the west and Mount Mitchell nearest by where NC 128 winds its way up the slope toward the summit's fire and radio towers. Due east you may be able to see Lake James near Morganton, a shiny mirror below Table Rock and Hawksbill (described in Tour 15). But if it's cloudy below, you may only see the highest peaks, rising like islands in a blue-gray sea. Or if the weather is really thick, then Mount Mitchell may come and go from view like a phantom. Here is a good place to write in your journal, take a few pictures, or nap, if the wind is not too ragged. This view of Mount Mitchell is actually better than the view *from* Mount Mitchell, some say. Contemplate with poet Robert Morgan the fate of the man for whom the mountain is named:

THE BODY OF ELISHA MITCHELL
The body of Elisha Mitchell
when it lay in the clear pool
beneath a waterfall below
his named and measured peak, white as
marble in the laurel gloom, was
stirred by shock ripples from the falls
and turned by eddies like a compass
needle pointing to the summit.
The icy spring water had kept
the body perfect for two weeks
as the searchers crisscrossed the Blacks,
Big Tom Wilson the bear hunter

and the Reverend Mitchell Junior
hacking into thickets to look
at every twig for sign of tracks.
They came to a cliff edge and saw
the body fifty feet below
staring past them at the peak
he'd measured highest in the east,
his eyes wide and blue and clear
as the eye of his barometer
used to get elevation. The
snowy body was unbruised by
rock or tree in the plunge, untouched
by fish or animal, though prick
marks would hint a rattler strike
may have sent him reeling down
the slope and over, falling numb,
the venom perfect for embalming,
the body white as a breathless statue.
—From *Sigodlin*, by Robert Morgan (Middletown,
   Conn.: Wesleyan University Press, 1990), 52.

By now you'll probably be ready to pick your way down from the Pinnacle slowly, the same way you came up. Back at your vehicle, drive on south just a mile to reach the entrance to Mount Mitchell State Park at NC 128. It's nearly five miles to the summit from here. After the Pinnacle hike, you might be in the mood for an excellent bowl of soup or chili or at least a cup of hot chocolate at the Mount Mitchell Restaurant on the way up. At the end of the road you can park and walk to the peak where Elisha Mitchell is buried, a spot that the nineteenth-century writer Charles Dudley Warner once called "the most majestic, most lonesome grave on earth." These days, Mitchell's grave can actually be quite crowded. Tim Silver describes another, more solitary spot nearby:

July

Mount Mitchell

   It is the season of fog and tourists. A few minutes before noon, thick clouds blow in from the southeast, shrouding the Blacks in a translucent haze and obliterating the view from the summit. The sightseers have come anyway.... Today the tourists spill onto the pavement, donning sweatshirts and half-joking, half-complaining about the July cold and damp-ness. Within minutes they begin the short walk to the crest of the East's highest mountain and Elisha Mitchell's grave.

I dutifully pull on a sweater and take my place amid the throng. But as the group moves toward the summit, I veer down a side path in search of another, older visitor attraction. These days it is mostly a geologic curios-ity, a giant slab of granite—some fifteen yards long and perhaps twenty feet wide—that overhangs an old trail several hundred feet below the mountaintop. In the 1850s it was a well-known landmark. Travelers called it the Cave, the Shelving Rock, or the Sleeping Rock, and it provided natu-ral shelter for those who stayed overnight in the high mountains. A light rain begins as I step beneath the cliff.—From *Mount Mitchell and the Black Mountains*, by Timothy Silver, 121.

Margaret Morley wrote of the same spot that Silver describes, but in the flowery prose of an earlier century:

The cave near the top of the mountain is formed by an overhanging ledge, and here it is customary, for those wishing to watch the sunrise from the summit, to spend the night. And it is worth the effort, even if one only sees the mountains emerge from the clouds for a moment to be again swallowed up by them, for it is seldom that the visitor gets more than a glimpse of the whole world at one time, from Mitchell's cloud-capped peak. It was in this cave on top of Mount Mitchell that one once arrived in a pouring rain, after a perilous climb up the eastern slope, to find, as sole trace of former visitors, a little can partly full of condensed milk, which saved, not one's own life, but that of a young squirrel rescued on the way up, and who became the hero of many pleasant subsequent adventures.—From *The Carolina Mountains*, by Margaret W. Morley, 312.

Though it is no longer in print, we can assume that Morley's 1904 volume, *Little Mitchell, the Story of a Mountain Squirrel* would give us the rest of *that* story.

From Mount Mitchell, you may easily return to Asheville by continuing south on the Blue Ridge Parkway, having made a good day's loop. Or you may retrace your tracks to the intersection of the Parkway with NC 80 to begin Tour 12.

Carolina Mountains Literary Festival

P.O. Box 355
Burnsville, NC 28714
cmlitfest@gmail.com
<http://cmlitfest.com/>

In 2006, a group of local citizens and business owners collaborated on an inaugural gathering that featured thirty-five writers in readings, workshops, panels, and book signings held in various sites around Burnsville. The festival's success has prompted organizers to make it an annual event.

Parkway Playhouse

202 Green Mountain Drive
Burnsville, NC 28714
828-682-4285
info@parkwayplayhouse.com
<http://www.parkwayplayhouse.com>

Burnsville's Parkway Playhouse has a bright red facade and an open-air amphitheater on the side. It is North Carolina's oldest continuously operating summer theater, celebrating fifty years of productions in 2006. It was launched as a summer venue for theater and drama students from the University of North Carolina at Greensboro. It was later administered for a time by the University of Miami and finally began operating independently in the 1990s, under the direction of the late William Dryer, a Celo resident and much-beloved supporter of the arts in the region. The theater now produces at least five shows per summer and also serves as home to the Burnsville Little Theater.

Celo Inn

45 Seven Mile Ridge Road
Burnsville, NC 28714
828-675-5132
<http://www.celoinn.com>

At the corner of NC 80 and Seven Mile Ridge Road, this rustic bed and breakfast, built from native hemlock, oak, and pine, opened in 1983. Here Celo's present-day novelist-in-residence, Abigail DeWitt, occasionally teaches writing workshops for her local and long-distance students. DeWitt grew up in Chapel Hill, attended Carolina Friends School in Durham and the Arthur Morgan

School in Celo, and studied at Harvard and the Iowa Writers' Workshop before returning to Yancey County. Her novel *Lili* (2002) is set in France. Like Anne Tyler, DeWitt also has a Duke connection: she is a frequent faculty member at the annual Duke Writers' Workshop, held in summer near Hendersonville.

Arthur Morgan School

60 AMS Circle

Burnsville, NC 28714

828-675-4262

<http://www.arthurmorganschool.org>

Celo's Arthur Morgan School, also near the Celo Inn, is a small, private school for grades seven through nine, while Camp Celo is a farm-home camp for boys and girls begun in 1948. The Rural Southern Voice for Peace (RSVP) and its journal, *Voices*, is also published here.

Old Fort : Chimney Rock : Lake Lure : Tryon

Visit Thomas Wolfe's "other angel"—the one his father lost in a poker game. See North Carolina's only geyser. Travel back in time to some of the state's most visited tourist attractions in the nineteenth and twentieth centuries, and meet the writers who wrote about them. Learn about the North Carolina resident who invented the trademark mannerisms and stage props for Sherlock Holmes. Walk along F. Scott Fitzgerald's daily route to buy ice cream.

Writers with a connection to this area: Margaret Culkin Banning, Freddy Bradburn, Lilian Jackson Braun, Frances Hodgson Burnett, Wilma Dykeman, Tony Earley, John Ehle, Payne Erskine, F. Scott Fitzgerald, William Gillette, Ernest Hemingway, Sidney Lanier, William G. Lord, Bascom Lamar Lunsford, Robert Morgan, Margaret Morley, Peggy Payne, Donald Culross Peattie, Elia Wilkinson Peattie, Nina Simone, Bob Terrell, Jules Verne, Phyllis A. Whitney

This tour begins at the junction of NC 80 and the Blue Ridge Parkway. Hikers and cyclists use the parking area on the south side of the Parkway, leaving their vehicles behind to journey by other means. In winter, cross-country skiers also park here to ski on the Parkway, which makes a very fine cross-country track when it is closed to traffic because the right of way is wide and mogul-free. And there's always a good chance that the snowfall on this stretch will be substantial because of the high elevation—more than 3,300 feet. Of course, as you wind your way south down NC 80 toward Marion from here— advisedly in first or second gear—you may wonder how skiers dare *drive* to the top in snow.

The descent begins as a slow and twisting proposition. The starting point, called Buck Creek Gap, is so named for the stream that begins here and flows down the mountain past Singecat Ridge—"a name that suggests someone's cat got bar-

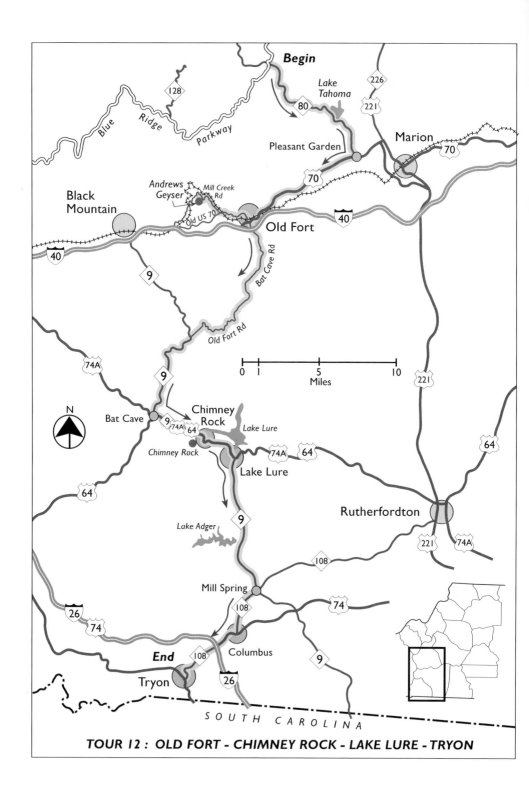

TOUR 12 : OLD FORT - CHIMNEY ROCK - LAKE LURE - TRYON

bered by a fire," William G. Lord writes in his *Blue Ridge Parkway Guide* (New York: Eastern Acorn Press, 1982). Beyond a series of ear-popping hairpin turns, Buck Creek will soon be rushing alongside the road, crossing back and forth under the pavement to Lake Tahoma and ultimately flowing into the Catawba River.

On the way down this 11.5-mile stretch, you'll pass several notable attractions. Just take it slow, stay on your side of the road, and tap the brakes.

At 3.5 miles you'll come to Buck Creek Trout (828-724-9612), a commercial farming operation where you can fish for live rainbow trout in the shady pond and pay for your catch by the pound. This fee-fishing business is also a wholesale supplier for many area restaurants. Poles and corn nuggets for bait are supplied, and the proprietor will clean your catch for an additional fee if you wish. (North Carolina State University's Extension Service provides a complete list of trout fee-fishing farms in western North Carolina, at <http://www.ces.ncsu.edu/copubs/ag/aqua/trout/033/>.)

Down the road another 0.2 miles, you'll see the entrance to Buck Creek Bowls (828-724-9048) on your right. Owner and artist Darrell Rhudy spends his winters in Raleigh and his summers here turning out extraordinary platters, bowls, urns, plates, and vases from wood native to North Carolina. His regular customers often bring him burls of ash, oak, maple, pecan, apple, dogwood, walnut, boxwood, and even osage orange. Rhudy turns them by hand on a wood lathe and finishes them with four coats of lacquer. Spalted wood—old burls infected by a fungus—creates spectacular variations in color and grain. Rhudy learned his craft at the John C. Campbell Folk School (see Tour 4), where he now teaches on occasion. His son Paul's work can also be found in the area.

In another 4.3 miles, you'll find yourself driving around the shores of Lake Tahoma, a resort development that was launched in 1924. Like Lake Lure later on this tour, it failed during the Depression and was sold. Homes began appearing around the shoreline by the 1940s. This picturesque lake is 500 acres, and the historic dance pavilion built of native rock still survives, casting a handsome reflection on the water.

Finally the road straightens and passes through a scenic valley. You have made it down the mountain. Soon NC 80 dead-ends into US 70. You are now in Pleasant Garden, a community just outside the larger town of Marion. Remarkably, Pleasant Garden appears in a novel by the French science fiction writer Jules Verne that is discussed in Tour 15. But for now, note the Little Siena Restaurant on your right, a family establishment owned by the Wall family.

Warren Wall met his wife, Erina, in Siena, Italy, when he was stationed there in World War II. They were married there, and then Warren brought Erina back to Pleasant Garden. The Wall family's oral history has been collected by Freddy Bradburn, an award-winning songwriter, storyteller, and instructor at Mc-Dowell Community College in nearby Marion. Bradburn's students published Warren Wall's story, and Bradburn turned Erina's story into a reader's theater piece performed at the college. Beyond the good tales told around the restaurant, Bradburn recommends Little Siena for authentic Italian cuisine.

Turn right on US 70 for the scenic route to Old Fort.

■ OLD FORT

As you come close to this town you may notice the scent of glue in the air. The large Ethan Allen plant on your left marks the outskirts of Old Fort, a small village that in its boom years was filled with a much more unpleasant smell—the effluent of the Union Tanning plant, built in 1904. In those days, trains brought in shipments of fleshy hides from South America. The rank smell of rotting flesh combined with acid used to tan the hides made the air miserable for miles around. Fortunately, by the 1940s a textile manufacturing plant replaced the tannery. More than a thousand workers were employed here at the peak of that enterprise. Layoffs began in 1980, and the sixteen-acre Old Fort Finishing Plant finally closed in 1984. Today Old Fort celebrates its long history as a pioneer outpost and welcomes tourists to learn more about that past, which includes some surprising literary liaisons.

■ THE *OTHER* ANGEL

Just beyond the Ethan Allen plant, begin looking for Cemetery Street on your right. Turn here, and then take the first driveway on your left, which leads you into the Old Fort Cemetery. Here once again we meet up with another larger-than-life legend associated with Asheville's controversial son, Thomas Wolfe.

The story goes that Thomas Wolfe's father once lost a marble angel in a poker game. It was one among the family of angels that W. O. Wolfe had imported from the Carrara Marble Works in Italy, and kin to the angel that inspired the title of his son's first novel. The Old Fort angel, which by now you have probably spotted in front of you, is similar but not identical to the angel in Hendersonville's Oakdale Cemetery, described in Tour 10. Unlike the Oakdale angel, whose arm is raised with a single finger pointing upward, the Old Fort angel seems to be holding an unruly bouquet.

According to Bob Terrell, author of some thirty books about the mountain region as well as a long-running column for the *Asheville Citizen-Times*, S. A.

In Old Fort: W. O. Wolfe's "other angel," which he purportedly lost in a card game with Asheville photographer S. A. McCanless.

McCanless was the man who won the angel. He worked as a photographer on Patton Avenue in Asheville at the beginning of the twentieth century. On a regular basis McCanless played poker after hours with Thomas Wolfe's father, W. O., in the photo studio.

McCanless's gambling, however, did not sit well with his wife, Hattie, so he swore off it for a time. But then, unable to resist a game one evening in 1901, he gambled and won big. The angel he won that night came in handy a little later when his wife died of a ruptured appendix. McCanless placed the angel on his wife's grave in Old Fort.

The story finally came out sometime later when McCanless's second wife complained to her husband that he had never loved her as much as he did his first wife, citing the nine-foot monument as evidence. After all, hadn't she just asked him to go buy her some ice cream in downtown Old Fort? McCanless didn't want to go out that night, saying it was too cold for ice cream. But given his wife's jealousy about the tombstone, he finally found it necessary to confess that the angel had not been purchased but was won in a game of chance. Then he went out for ice cream to keep the peace, so the story goes.

McCanless's niece, Daintry Allison, only a young girl at the time, was in earshot of this confession. Many years later, at the age of eighty-eight, Daintry Allison gave up the story to Bob Terrell for his newspaper column. Terrell in turn sought to verify the tale by consulting an expert associated with the North Carolina Room at Pack Memorial Library in Asheville. He learned that W. O. Wolfe had ordered at least eight monuments from Italy, and that all of them cannot be accounted for, so the story could be true. In any case, it makes another great chapter in the lore of Wolfe.

THE SWANNANOA TUNNEL
I'm going back to the Swannanoa Tunnel
That's my home, baby, that's my home

Asheville Junction, Swannanoa Tunnel
All caved in, baby, all caved in
—From the traditional song, performed by
   Bascom Lamar Lunsford, North Carolina balladeer

From the cemetery, return to US 70 and continue to the right into Old Fort's business district. The town sits at the base of the formidable Old Fort Mountain. Three different museums in town—the Mountain Gateway Museum, Grant's Indian Museum, and the railroad museum in the old depot—tell the story of Old Fort's long history as a way-station to the West. In the 1700s, Old Fort was actually the westernmost outpost in the country and was the site of many skirmishes between the encroaching white settlers and the native peoples of the region. The arrowhead monument in the center of town commemorates Old Fort's status as an outpost. By the 1800s the railway builders who first conquered the steep incline up Saluda Mountain from Spartanburg, South Carolina, to Tryon now faced a more formidable engineering challenge in negotiating Old Fort Mountain to get the train to Asheville.

In the end, it took seven tunnels through solid granite—the longest being the Swannanoa Tunnel, at 1,832 feet—to bring rail service from Old Fort to Ridgecrest and on to Asheville. Unlike many areas in the North Carolina mountains where the African American influence was historically limited, the construction credit for this segment of the railway belongs almost entirely to the black men and boys who gave their lives in the effort to tunnel through this monumental mountain. As Wilma Dykeman explains in *The French Broad*, it was after a series of delays and ultimately a lack of funds that a crew was brought in from prisons in the eastern part of the state and forced to build the railroad. In the Reconstruction South, many of these convicts might well have been jailed for petty crimes or trumped-up charges. A number who came to Old Fort had listed Africa as their birthplace. They worked with heavy picks and handmade dynamite. Accidents were frequent.

Dykeman writes: "It is the human story that is the tragic and half-told portion of this railroad's building. During heaviest construction there were 1,455 men and 403 boys laboring to clear the path up the steep mountain, and over a thousand mules, horses and oxen." Unaccustomed to the cold, wet weather and the altitude, the convicts slept outdoors and were fed navy beans and cornbread, rarely any meat. As the weather changed, pneumonia set in. "One North Carolina resident," Dykeman continues, "remembered where there were four hundred unmarked graves huddled near the last tunnel on the route, filled by victims of pneumonia" (162). In addition, more than one hundred lives were lost in a single rockslide that filled up the unfinished Swannanoa Tunnel.

Remarkably, the railroad track loops up the mountain and makes ten complete circles in twelve miles. The last stretch was the toughest, rising 1,110 vertical feet in only three miles. John Ehle—an Asheville-born novelist profiled in Tour 16—depicted the grisly truth of this construction project in a 1967 novel. Near the end of the book, he provides his own imagined version of the grand opening of the Old Fort/Ridgecrest rail in 1880:

> At the ceremony were many officials from Raleigh, and there was talk about how the Road had been made by the men who, three years before, had had vision enough to pass the bill in the North Carolina legislature. Reporters made notes on all this and wrote feature stories about the unusual manners and ways of the Appalachian mountain people.
>
> One of the reporters on the way home noticed the graveyard above

Babcock station, and while the train was stopped at the station house, he asked a workman who was buried there. The workman said probably they were bodies of workmen who had died. The reporter saw another railroad man working a small gang in the vale below the cemetery, and he approached him. The man said he worked for the Road, but was a preacher, actually. "I'm constructing a fountain here."

"Where's the water for it?" the reporter asked.

"You see that stream high on the mountain? We'll capture it in a pipe or trough and bring it down here and turn it up into the sky. It's an idea for a memorial passed on to me by a friend who sometimes visits my daughter from the college."

"You're making a fountain to whom?"

"To them. To all them," he said waving his hand at Cemetery Hill. . . . "It'll be here near the graveyard, and doubtless it'll be here after all the tomb markers fall over, and maybe after the wolves has got what's left of the corpses, for this is a bad mountain for wolves. I'll capture that stream somehow and bring it here and point it upward, and let it go as high as it wants to into the sky."

—From *The Road*, by John Ehle (New York: Harper & Row, 1967), 400–401.

■ ANDREWS GEYSER

The manmade plume of water that Ehle writes about still exists. The geyser was first built five years after the railroad was finished. Workmen created a spring-fed pond some two miles uphill. At the bottom of the holding pond they placed a six-inch-wide drainage pipe to send water rushing downhill. Near the geyser, the pipe narrows to a couple of inches, causing the water to shoot up in the air between fifty and a hundred feet.

During the same era, developers also built a hundred-bed inn, called the Round Knob Hotel. It was in plain sight of the geyser and the first complete circle that the railroad track makes as it heads up the mountain. Guests stopped here to admire the geyser and contemplate the roundabout journey ahead on the passenger trains that were pulled up the mountain by steam engines.

The Round Knob Hotel burned in 1903 and the area fell into ruin, but in 1911 a wealthy New Yorker moved the geyser, repaired it, and named it in honor of Colonel A. B. Andrews, an engineer and the first president of the Western North Carolina Railroad.

In the 1980s the geyser again required restoration; it is now managed by the proprietor of the Inn on Mill Creek, a bed and breakfast two miles up the hard-

Novelist John Ehle and his wife, actress Rosemary Harris, at the West Branch of the Asheville Library for a reading in 1998. Photo by Deborah Compton. Courtesy of the North Carolina Collection of the Pack Memorial Library, Asheville, North Carolina.

packed dirt road from Andrews Geyser. Calling himself "the geyser geezer," the innkeeper turns off the geyser every night to ensure that his overnight guests at the inn hear an ample rush of water outside their windows. If he didn't shut the water off, the holding pond that supplies the geyser would eventually run dry.

DIRECTIONS

From the arrowhead monument in Old Fort continue on US 70 West to Old Highway 70 and turn right. It's only 2.4 miles to Mill Creek Road, where you'll see the sign for Andrews Geyser. (Straight ahead, Old 70 ends shortly at a gate, though the pavement continues up the mountain. The old road—which was originally NC 10, first paved in 1925—is a popular trail with bicyclists and hikers, though hurricane damage in 2004 compromised the path.) Turn right at the sign for Andrews Geyser and travel 2.1 miles. The plume will be on your left. If you're lucky enough to see a freight train come through, it will completely circle around the geyser, but probably not in the direction you think. The acoustics created by the surrounding mountains are misleading.

Perhaps some day, as locals hope, passenger service on this stretch of historic rail will return, and adventurous tourists can experience the ride up and over

The Andrews Geyser, near Old Fort, figures into John Ehle's novel The Road.

this precarious peak. For now, however, return to Old Fort the same way you came, turn right at the arrowhead monument, and cross the railroad tracks toward I-40. Pass under I-40 and prepare for a beautiful drive down to Tryon. Simply follow the signs to NC 9, which you won't pick up until approximately 13 miles south of Old Fort.

On this slow and scenic old route, bluffs of rhododendron rise on either side of the road, and dogwoods bloom in bursts of white in April. Once you cross into Buncombe County you'll find NC 9, where the road improves. Continue south into Henderson County, and you'll soon be in the lush Broad River Valley, where rich bottom land is cultivated and white boxes containing beehives dot the landscape. NC 9 joins up with US 64 and 74A 17.5 miles from Old Fort. The drive to this point will have taken about 30 minutes.

Turn left toward Chimney Rock and Lake Lure. Soon you'll pass through Bat Cave, where you'll find a few vendors with interesting mountain products. There are also public picnic tables beside the river if you've packed a lunch. At the height of summer, the road from here can be slow going with traffic, but the area has a significant history—both in literature and as an early tourist destination. Margaret Morley, who documents her visit to the region in *The Carolina Mountains* (1913), declared this area "one of the gentlest and most charming valleys one could wish to know" (88).

In the village of Chimney Rock, you'll find old-fashioned souvenirs—taffy, tomahawks, T-shirts, and other trinkets. And you'll be amazed at the size of the rocks that fill the river here and beg for a meditative moment beside the rushing water.

The movies *The Last of the Mohicans* (1992), based on the book by James Fenimore Cooper, and *Fire Starter* (1994), based on the Stephen King novel, were shot here. But the Rocky Broad River and Chimney Rock towering above are the real feature attractions. As in Morley's day, it is possible to climb a long stairway to reach the top of Chimney Rock, but now there is an elevator, too. The park entrance will be on your right as you come into the village of Chimney Rock.

Margaret Morley describes the vista in 1913:

The view from the top of Chimney Rock up the Broad River Valley might be described as that of grand scenery in miniature. It is the atmosphere that makes the mountains here so charming, for, seen near at hand, they are rather forbidding with their stern bare rocks. . . . One can imagine that there might be times when this part of the country would appear less seductive than it appears on a fair spring day.

Because of the natural phenomena, so abundant about Chimney Rock, the rumbling mountain, the caves, the isolated "chimney," it is not surprising that a number of strange legends have collected about it, in which ghostly visitants play their part, although as a rule the mountain people are not superstitious. They go fearlessly through the wilderness alone, even "lying out" with their herds, or for other reasons, with no apprehension of seeing anything more terrifying than a bear or a wildcat, an encounter with either of which would be regarded by the mountain man as a most fortunate adventure.—From *The Carolina Mountains*, by Margaret W. Morley (Alexander, N.C.: Land of the Sky Books, 2002), 100–101.

Postcard of Old Rumbling Bald above Lake Lure, where the author of The Secret Garden *liked to hike. Lake County Discovery Museum, Curt Teich Postcard Archives.*

Children's novelist Frances Hodgson Burnett, whose best known works are *Little Lord Fauntleroy* (1886) and *The Secret Garden* (1888), spent time in the Chimney Rock area. Born in England and raised in Knoxville, Tennessee, Burnett did not become a U.S. citizen until her fifties, and most of her writing reflects the enduring influence of her British heritage. As Margaret Morley tells it, Burnett came to visit the area in the late 1800s, and it was here in a historic lodge that she wrote her play *Esmeralda*. Remarkably, the lodge still exists.

Originally named the Harris Inn, later known as the Logan House, and unofficially called the "Esmeralda Inn" when both Burnett and Morley visited, this property is now called Pine Gables. The historic structure is located at 323 Boys Camp Road, which turns off to the left shortly before you enter the township of Lake Lure. According to the North Carolina Division of Archives and History, the lodge was built sometime between 1782 and 1800 and served as a way station for stagecoach travelers and cattle drovers who were passing through Hickory Nut Gorge. When Burnett and Morley visited, Judge George Washington Logan—a former Confederate congressman, Superior Court judge, University of North Carolina trustee, unionist, and Republican leader during Reconstruction—owned the Logan House. The judge, an outspoken critic of the Ku Klux Klan, lived at the inn until his death in 1899.

Morley describes the lodge and her encounter with Judge Logan:

Crossing a charming, though somewhat deep and rocky ford of the Broad River, you continue on up the beautiful valley, the mountains draw in about you, and you are at "Logan's," a large, old-fashioned farmhouse which was converted to uses of a wayside inn when the road went through to Rutherfordton, connecting the mountains above here with the low country. Logan's is "in the Scenery," so they tell you a good many times while there—and unquestionably it is. A beautiful cultivated valley lies about the house enchantingly surrounded by mountains. The mountains of this region, although so individual in form, so picturesque, or so beautiful, are, according to General Logan, "worth about a cent apiece, there is so little soil on them" (94–95).

Today there are no rooms for rent at the big house at Pine Gables, but the original log structures and several other outbuildings serve as rental cabins, administered by Dream Finders Realty at 828-625-1460 or <http://www.lake-lure.com/pinegables.html>.

◼ OLD RUMBLING BALD

It is still possible to hike the trail that Margaret Morley and Frances Burnett took from Logan's to Old Rumbling Bald, which also begins on Boys Camp Road. In Morley's day, Old Rumbling Bald was "the most noted mountain in this part of the world" (95), she claims, because it rumbled ominously over a seven-year period beginning in 1878. (The rumbling of the bald is not a contemporary phenomenon, but measurable earthquakes in the region still occur from time to time.)

It is this bit of local lore that also informs the opening of the novel *Star Flight* (1993), written by Phyllis A. Whitney, one of the official Grand Masters of Mystery Writing and winner of the coveted Edgar award. Whitney (who was still writing at the age of 103 in 2006) came to the area while *The Last of the Mohicans* was being filmed. Her *Star Flight* protagonist—a Hollywood screenwriter—also visits the set in Chimney Rock and stays for a time at the "Esmeralda Inn." Whitney, who was escorted around the area by librarians from Asheville and Rutherfordton, also manages to get her heroine over to the Grove Park Inn (Tour 8) and the Captain's Bookshelf in Asheville (Tour 9).

Today, the Hickory Nut Gorge area, including Old Rumbling Bald, has been considered for commercial development. However, legislation signed in 2005 may allow the area to become North Carolina's newest state park. Land acquisition in a competitive real estate market is the next hurdle for the effort spearheaded by local rock climbers. Until the park is fully secured, however, hikers may still need to obtain permission to hike the trail to Old Rumbling Bald, which crosses private land.

An old but well-maintained Jeep trail climbs to 4,800 feet and offers views of Rumbling Bald, Chimney Rock, Eagles Rock, and Lake Lure. The trail is 7.5 miles round trip and is considered moderate. On NC 9/US 64/US 74A just before you get into Lake Lure, take a left on Boys Camp Road and proceed one mile. Pass the resort on the right, park, and find the old Jeep trail. For the most current information on the trail and permission to hike, contact the North Carolina Division of Forest Services, 828-887-6527.

■ LAKE LURE

Back on the main road, the village of Chimney Rock seamlessly meets the Lake Lure township. In the mid-1920s, this resort was only a vision on paper created by a group of investors. Among them was Kenneth Tanner, the owner of Stonecutter Mills in nearby Rutherfordton, and his brother Bobo, who would go on to found the Doncaster Collar and Shirt Company, which later became the present-day Tanner Companies, specializing in women's clothing.

Promoted in the roaring twenties as a "National All Year Mountain Lake Resort," the original plans for Lake Lure included a polo field, a horse show arena, a baseball park, an airplane landing strip, several clubs, and an amusement park. The dam and the Lake Lure Inn were completed by 1927.

Bobo and his wife, Millie Tanner, took up residence in the inn with their daughter, Kate, and new baby, Bobo III. As Raleigh novelist Peggy Payne tells it in the company history she wrote for the Tanner family in 1997:

> But perhaps it was emblematic of what was ahead, when, on a lark one windy afternoon in February, Bobo and Millie decided to go for a sail on the brand new lake. The weather was cold and the wind was brisk. Millie, stylish as ever, wore her best fur coat. When the wind intensified, the sailboat went over, but the couple, luckily, were spotted from the shore and rescued from a life-threatening situation. Not long thereafter there could be no rescue. The 1929 stock market crash ruined all immediate prospects for the Lake Lure project. Bobo and Millie lost every dime.—From *Doncaster: A Legacy of Personal Style*, by Peggy Payne (Rutherfordton, N.C.: Tanner Co., 1997), 30.

As you drive by, the Lake Lure Inn and Arcade may look familiar. They served as part of the setting for the 1987 film *Dirty Dancing*. Boat tours are available here, as are kayak and pontoon rentals if you want to get out and see the mountains circling around this body of water.

Lake Lure figures prominently in the writing of Tony Earley. Though Earley now lives in Nashville, Tennessee, and teaches writing at Vanderbilt University, both his fiction and nonfiction draw heavily on Rutherford County. In the autobiographical piece "Granny's Bridge" in *Somehow Form a Family* (2001), Earley tells of his father's brief escape from the area, which was prompted by a woman who broke his heart. She worked as a waitress at a restaurant on the road to Lake Lure.

In Earley's first story collection, *Here We Are in Paradise* (1994), the narrator of "The Prophet from Jupiter" is the dam keeper at the fictional Lake Glen, which strongly resembles Lake Lure. More sites related to Tony Earley's work are described in Tour 13. Any of his books would make good reading on the sands of Lake Lure's public beach.

As you leave Lake Lure, NC 9 parts company with US 74A and 64 and heads off to the right. Stay on 9 and you'll soon be in Polk County. Continue this southward journey through Sunny View, past Lake Adger, and through the valley to the crossroads at Mill Spring, where you should pick up NC 108 to the right. This road leads into Columbus, Lynn, and then Tryon.

■ TRYON

DeSoto, North Carolina, is a village which looks from the air as if it had been carelessly dropped into several small valleys and plateaus between the foothills of the Blue Ridge and the sharp beak of Bald Eagle Mountain. It seems to have spattered as it fell, for bits of it have clung in places at quite a distance from the central town. There are vineyards here and there on clean slopes, an inn on top of a rather remote hill, and stables at the farthest turn of the Branch which idles through the lowlands. The stream is snaky and a dull green color in contrast to the vividly blue, symmetrical swimming pools which dot the local estates.

The place is always being discovered by someone. Travelers from the North have been falling in love with it on sight for a hundred years.

—From *I Took My Love to the Country*, by Margaret Culkin Banning
(New York: Harper & Row, 1966), 1.

Rather than being a summertime resort, Banning's fictional DeSoto, known in reality as Tryon, has historically attracted many winter residents from the coldest parts of the Midwest and Northeast because of its location along a thermal belt that creates a temperate climate year-round. For more than a century Tryon's happy transplants have brought with them a strong appreciation of the performing arts and an affinity for horse breeding. The Blockhouse Steeple Chase is an annual event here, and because of Tryon's proximity to some of North Carolina's and South Carolina's richest game lands, avid hunters—Ernest Hemingway among them—have come here over the years. A first-time visitor might even wonder if there's anyone in Tryon who was actually born here, but in fact, one of the town's most accomplished and gifted citizens was Nina Simone, born Eunice Kathleen Wayman, the sixth child in a family of seven.

Eunice Wayman's gift for music was apparent at age four, when she played piano in the local church where her mother was pastor. She was soon taking lessons from Muriel Massinovitch, a Tryon resident who became her patron. "Mrs. M," as Eunice called her, taught her student to the limits of her ability and then arranged for the child to have lessons in Asheville (see Tour 8). The Eunice Wayman Fund, established by the residents of Tryon, later helped send the teenager to the Juilliard School in New York City.

Having been inspired by Marian Anderson, Wayman hoped to become the nation's first African American female concert pianist; but when her funds ran out, she began playing and singing in clubs in Atlantic City and New York. She took the stage name Nina Simone in 1954. By 1959, Simone's rendition of Gershwin's *I Loves You, Porgy* had reached the Top 40. In the 1960s, Simone became deeply engaged in the civil rights movement and wrote a number of powerful indictments about the struggle, including "To Be Young, Gifted and Black," based on the play of the same name by her friend Lorraine Hansberry; "Mississippi Goddam," in response to the murder of Medgar Evers; and "Backlash Blues," based on a poem that Langston Hughes wrote for her.

Throughout her career, Simone's range of material was extraordinary, including jazz standards, spirituals, folk songs, blues, pop, opera, and classical music—especially her beloved Bach. Her autobiography, *I Put a Spell on You* (1991), details her expatriation to the Caribbean and later Europe and her struggles with the music industry and the IRS.

Simone was ultimately better known abroad than in the United States, and she won many international distinctions and lifetime achievement awards. She was a special guest and sang at Nelson Mandela's eightieth birthday. Upon her death in 2003 at the age of seventy, the BBC declared: "Nina Simone was one

Dr. Nina Simone early in her career as a pianist, composer, and vocalist. In 1959 Simone's recording of "I Loves You, Porgy" reached the Top 40. Photo used with kind permission of Roger Nupie, president of the International Dr. Nina Simone Fan Club <www.high-priestess .com>.

of the last divas of jazz and was considered one of the finest songwriters and musicians of her day." Of her own contributions to the genre, Simone once said: "Jazz is a white term to define Black people. My music is Black classical music."

■ LANIER HOUSE AND LANIER LIBRARY

Heading into Tryon from the east, watch for the Pacolet River. Crossing the bridge, the Mimosa Inn is on the left, and a state historical marker is on the right. The marker stands in front of the private residence where Georgia poet Sidney Lanier succumbed to tuberculosis and died on September 7, 1881. We last left Sidney Lanier ailing on Richmond Hill, in Asheville, in Tour 8. When the poet showed no improvement, his wife moved him south. Zirconia poet Robert Morgan tells the story of this former Civil War prisoner, flute player, and lyric poet:

SIDNEY LANIER DIES AT TRYON 1881

The chill mountain air grew stingy
with oxygen after the long
carriage ride from Fletcher across
the Ridge and down the Thermal Belt
to the house outside Tryon.
Two months of camping on the peaks
only made the world more hazy,
ghostlike, and the summit winds had
sucked away his breath, and stolen
his voice, the form and duration
of English phrasing he'd worked so
to make measurable, to set down.
And the current pouring from his lips
into the flute had vanished
and only turbulence and coughs
and random winds were left gusting,
subsiding in his head. The blood
seemed at times to want to break
out of his heart and through the skin
of his forehead to taste air, to
quench its awful beat. The blood he
spat and blood humming in his ears
and in the manly condition
only Mary understood made
him think of sunrise, the rose-lit
mornings in army camps, in
the prison pits and mud. The one
oratorio, all notes and language,
seemed red as coals, red as his
syllables, while the night he'd married
hovered near, and his son the shadow,
and the world somewhere gaudy and
subtle as Shakespeare drew further
back, swam on the higher oceans.
The black peaks beyond the house looked
down, and there was a certain phrase,
a ripple, a little turn on
the flute he must try to recall,

that ran the same as the dark ridge
looming at the window yesterday,
and he could almost remember
the precise fingering, the pause
and the continuing line, just
as the world became visible.
—From *Sigodlin*, by Robert Morgan (Middletown,
    Conn.: Wesleyan University Press, 1990), 33.

Lanier is still celebrated in Tryon, though the house where he died is not open to the public. (The Mimosa Inn, across the road, where Lanier also stayed briefly, is a spot you can visit.) Eight years after the poet's death, five Tryon women organized themselves in support of civic betterment. One of their agenda items was the establishment of a library. The first two books — Lanier's poetry—were donated to the cause by Lanier's widow, Mary. Still operating today as a private library, open to the public but extending lending privileges only to members, Lanier Library is in the same building on Chestnut Street that it first occupied in 1910. Before it had a home, the library was simply a case of books that moved around Tryon, settling at one point in Misseldine's Drug Store.

Today Lanier is the only private library in the state and one of just a few in the country. It is distinguished by its special collection of Lanier's works and memorabilia. Here, too, is the Morgan Memorial Collection, focusing on the performing and creative arts, and an extensive compilation of fine-art books.

As you come into downtown Tryon, NC 108 merges with US 176 to become Trade Street. The road curves sharply to the left past a row of galleries on your left and continues uphill, parallel to the railroad tracks and into downtown proper. To visit the Lanier Library, turn right on Pacolet and cross the railroad tracks, then take an immediate left on Chestnut. You'll pass the Oak Hall condominiums on your left and come to the Tryon Fine Arts Center and Lanier Library on your right.

Here you are also in the neighborhood frequented by F. Scott Fitzgerald, a big fan of the ice cream served at Misseldine's Drug Store, once located at the corner of Pacolet and Trade, in a building now occupied by a bank. To honor the drug store, Fitzgerald penned this doggerel:

Oh Misseldine's, dear Misseldine's,
A dive we'll ne'er forget,
The taste of its banana splits

View of downtown Tryon from the bluff where the Oak Hall Hotel housed F. Scott Fitzgerald in February 1935. Misseldine's Drug Store was in the white building on the left.

Is on our tonsils yet.
Its chocolate fudge makes livers budge,
It's really too divine,
And as we reel, we'll give one squeal
For dear old Misseldine's.
—From *Poems 1911–1940*, ed. Matthew J. Bruccoli
(Bloomfield Hills, Mich.: Bruccoli Clark, 1981), 144–45.

According to Fitzgerald scholar Michael Cody, Fitzgerald and his daughter, Scottie, spent two weeks in Tryon in February of 1935 before Fitzgerald's wife, Zelda, came down for treatment at Highland Hospital in Asheville. (See Tour 8.)

Fitzgerald took a room at Oak Hall—a hotel that is now the site of condominiums by the same name on Chestnut on a bluff overlooking Trade Street. Scottie stayed with her father's friends, Nora and Maurice "Lefty" Flynn, whose marriage soon became the subject of one of Fitzgerald's short stories, "The Intimate Strangers," published that summer in *McCall's*. Cody writes: "Nora was the youngest of the celebrated Langhorne sisters, one of whom became Lady Astor and another of whom married Charles Dana Gibson and became the model for his 'Gibson Girl.' Lefty had been a football star at Yale and a movie actor" (see <http://www.sc.edu/fitzgerald/facts/facts4.html>).

Fitzgerald returned to Tryon again in January 1937 for another stay at Oak Hall, where he wrote furiously and continued his ice cream habit at Misseldine's, as reported by Margaret Culkin Banning, the Minnesota-born novelist, short-story writer, and early women's rights advocate who was introduced to Fitzgerald on his second stay here.

Margaret Banning lived for many years in Tryon. She wrote thirty-six novels from 1922 to 1979 and more than four hundred essays and short stories, usually concerned with problems of youth, women, and social change. Her 1966 novel, *I Took My Love to the Country*, excerpted above, tells the story of a couple from New York who move to Tryon. The book is dedicated "to my neighbors in North Carolina with great affection." When Banning died in Tryon at the age of ninety-one, she was at work on her thirty-seventh novel.

Two other pathbreaking women writers spent time in Tryon at the opening of the twentieth century. Payne Erskine (a pen name of deliberately ambiguous gender; her first name was Emma) wrote *The Mountain Girl* (1912), *A Girl of the Blue Ridge* (1915), and several other novels published by Little, Brown & Company.

Emma Payne Erskine and her husband, Charles, also introduced Chicago writer Elia Wilkinson Peattie and her son, Donald Culross Peattie, to Polk County, which resulted in many visits by the Peatties to the region. Elia Peattie was a prolific novelist and pioneering journalist. She was the first female reporter to work for the *Chicago Tribune* and later the *Omaha World Herald*. She wrote about subjects controversial in her time, including the Wounded Knee massacre, women's roles in the church, and unwed motherhood. She advocated against Prohibition and for women's suffrage. Her place in the literary history of the Midwest is significant, and many of her books have recently been reprinted online. Her progressive 1914 novel, *The Precipice*, considers the struggle of women to balance independence and family life.

Her son, Donald Peattie, was a naturalist, an editor for *Reader's Digest*, and a popular writer in his day. His work is yet enduring. His 1939 book *Flower-*

ing Earth was reissued by Indiana University Press in 1991. His 1950 classic, *A Natural History of Trees of Eastern and Central North America*, was reissued by Houghton Mifflin the same year.

Two more writers are significant in relation to Tryon. Playwright William Gillette was born in Connecticut, the son of a U.S. senator. He made his New York debut as an actor in Mark Twain's *Gilded Age* (1877). Four years later Gillette mounted his own play, *The Professor*, and then collaborated with Frances Hodgson Burnett on *Esmeralda*, the play written in Chimney Rock and mentioned earlier in this tour. *Esmeralda* ran for over a year and gave Gillette's career a significant boost. He then wrote two plays based on the Civil War. Between these plays, however, Gillette fell ill for several years and was on his way to Asheville for treatment when he stepped off the train in Tryon and fell in love with the village. He bought property here and had a house built in 1891, in what is now known as Gillette Woods.

Fully recovered from his illness by 1897, Gillette secured the rights to adapt Sir Arthur Conan Doyle's *Sherlock Holmes* for the stage. Gillette's play debuted on Broadway in 1899 and in London in 1901. It then enjoyed an off-and-on run in theaters here and abroad for some thirty years. Gillette himself appeared on stage as Holmes more than 1,300 times and was the first to play Holmes on the radio in the 1930s. It was Gillette, not Doyle, who was responsible for the trademark cap and meerschaum pipe that we still associate with Holmes, along with many of the distinctive mannerisms that Basil Rathbone copied for the film version of the story. In his long career Gillette also starred in several works by *Peter Pan* creator J. M. Barrie—including a production with the young Helen Hayes.

Gillette frequently entertained artists and writers in his Tryon home, including the ubiquitous Margaret Morley, also a Tryon resident for many years. For reasons unknown, Gillette boarded up his home in 1910, never to return. He sold the house in 1925, and it was transformed into the Thousand Pines Inn. Today it is a private residence in Gillette Woods, but the public can view props from Gillette's career as Sherlock Holmes at the Depot Museum on Depot Street, which runs parallel to the railroad tracks just off Pacolet.

Mystery writer Lilian Jackson Braun was honored in 2005 by the residents of Tryon for her remarkable string of successful *The Cat Who . . .* books. Braun was the "Good Living" editor for the *Detroit Free Press* for nearly thirty years. She began her detective series in the 1960s with *The Cat Who Could Read Backwards*, *The Cat Who Ate Danish Modern*, and *The Cat Who Turned On and Off*. The *New York Times* called her "the new detective of the year" in 1966. Then

Actor and playwright William Gillette, creator for the stage of Sherlock Holmes's signature pipe and cap, in 1915. He lived in Tryon at the beginning of the twentieth century. Photo by Sarony (NY). Courtesy of the North Carolina Collection of the Pack Memorial Library, Asheville, North Carolina.

Braun abruptly stopped publishing the series until the mid-1980s, when the first books were reprinted along with four new cat titles. They were wildly popular.

Braun and her husband moved to Tryon in 1989. At the pace of one book a year since coming to town, Braun has published more than two dozen titles in the cat series. In her nineties, she still works on a manual typewriter, spinning out the tales of Koko and Yum-Yum, the Siamese cats who always manage to crack the case for their bumbling owner, James Qwilleran, a newspaper reporter.

■ LITERARY LANDSCAPE

The Inn on Mill Creek

3895 Mill Creek Road
Ridgecrest, NC 28770
828-668-1115
877-735-2964 (toll free)
jim@inn-on-mill-creek.com
<http://inn-on-mill-creek.com>

In addition to the constant sound of water and the occasional passing train, this inn has seven suites, a respectable library of local literature, and an orchard with more than 170 peach, apple, apricot, and cherry trees. It is one of only two accommodations in the Andrews Geyser area. The innkeepers are a wellspring of information about other sites, including a monument to an unknown Civil War soldier deep in the woods nearby and hiking trails that offer a closer view of the tunnels.

Round Knob Lodge
2340 Mill Creek Road
Old Fort, NC 28762
828-243-5762
<http://www.roundknoblodge.com>
Very near to Andrews Geyser is the Round Knob Lodge. Originally built in the 1930s for use by executives of the Southern Railway, this large facility was fully restored in 2003 and is decorated with train memorabilia. Constructed with steel bridge beams and railroad timbers, the lodge has five stone fireplaces and six bedrooms. It is available for rent to groups for overnight meetings and retreats.

Noah's Ark Book Attic
31 South Trade Street
Tryon, NC 28782
828-859-5141
noahsarkbookattic@alltel.net
Donald "Noah" Hawthorne was a dealer in antiquarian books in Greenwood, South Carolina, for forty-four years. He moved to Tryon in 2002. His shop, which has a large and friendly resident cat, is located beside the Christian Science Reading Room, just a few doors down from the building where Misseldine's used to serve Fitzgerald his sundaes. A first-rate place to look for out-of-print volumes.

The Book Shelf
90 Pacolet Street
Tryon, NC 28782
828-859-9304
thebookshelf@alltel.net
<http://www.tryonbookshelf.com>
Across the railroad tracks, up Pacolet Street, and across from the post office, the Book Shelf offers national and regional bestsellers, children's books, cards, and gifts. Here since 1952, it's a good place to dawdle and study the facade—

The Swayback Cabin, where Ernest Hemingway stayed while in Tryon on a hunting trip.

a handpainted collection of book spines that parody popular titles and capture the spirited lives of Tryon's citizens.

Goodheart Books

431 North Trade Street
Tryon, NC 28782
828-859-5981

This new enterprise is generally open by appointment and is a veritable museum of rare first editions and collector's items, including first edition poetry collections by Edna St. Vincent Millay and Civil War–era editions of *Harper's* magazine. This shop is highly recommended by Tryon novelist Jeri Fitzgerald Board, whose work will be considered in Trail 6.

Village Book Shoppe

16 Maple Street
Tryon, NC 28782
828-859-0273

The Village Book Shoppe nicely rounds out the bookstore options in Tryon. With a strong selection of used hardcover and paperback books, here's the place to grab something to read at leisure.

Pine Crest Inn

85 Pine Crest Lane
Tryon, NC 28782
828-859-9135
800-633-3001 (toll free)
<http://www.pinecrestinn.com>

Tryon is home to a number of bed-and-breakfast inns, but for literary purposes, you may want to have a look around the Pine Crest Inn, or have a meal and stay the night. From the center of town on Trade Street continue south, but instead of crossing the railroad tracks on Trade, take the left fork, which is New Market Road. This street curves to the left uphill past the Tryon Methodist Church and soon intersects with Pine Crest Lane—a cul-de-sac on the left.

The inn was constructed in 1906 and renovated in 2004. Massive hemlocks and old oaks surround the thirty-five rooms on the grounds. Placed on the National Register of Historic Places in 1982, this complex also has a dining room with a four diamond designation from AAA. In its early days, the Pine Crest literally sat on the edge of the wilderness and was frequented by hunters. Ernest Hemingway and F. Scott Fitzgerald both stayed in the Swayback Cabin, located behind the inn's conference center. Now more than 240 years old, the Swayback is notable for its small doors and windows—built to a human scale different from today. The Woodcutter Cottage and a beautifully constructed stone cottage also provide unusual accommodations on the grounds.

Rutherfordton : Spindale : Forest City : Shelby

Travel through North Carolina's early textile territory to see how cotton shaped the history, people, and literature of this area. Meet two influential writers who disagreed about everything, now buried in the same neighborhood. Visit a children's museum that makes literacy fun.

Writers with a connection to this area: Kathy Ackerman, W. J. Cash, Suzanne Tanner Chitwood, Thomas Dixon, Tony Earley, Kay Hooper, Martha Mason, Lynne Santy Tanner, Tom Tucker

Retrace your route via NC 108 out of Tryon. You'll stay on this road all the way into Rutherfordton. It's a pastoral drive northeast through beautiful fields and farms. Beyond Mill Spring are striking views of the South Mountains, a range of peaks all under 3,000 feet and running more or less parallel to the Black Mountains—the much higher range in the distance. Along this route, you'll pass by the home of Rutherfordton poet Lynne Santy Tanner, and as she describes, you'll do well to be alert for deer if it is early or late in the day:

LAST LIGHT
It's that time of day
when I climb the hill
to hold the sun a moment
longer but caught instead
at my desk I get up
to stretch and see, there
in the shadows of my yard,
a doe and her yearling,
his immature antlers aglow
with the last light.
He darts into the holly

tour 13

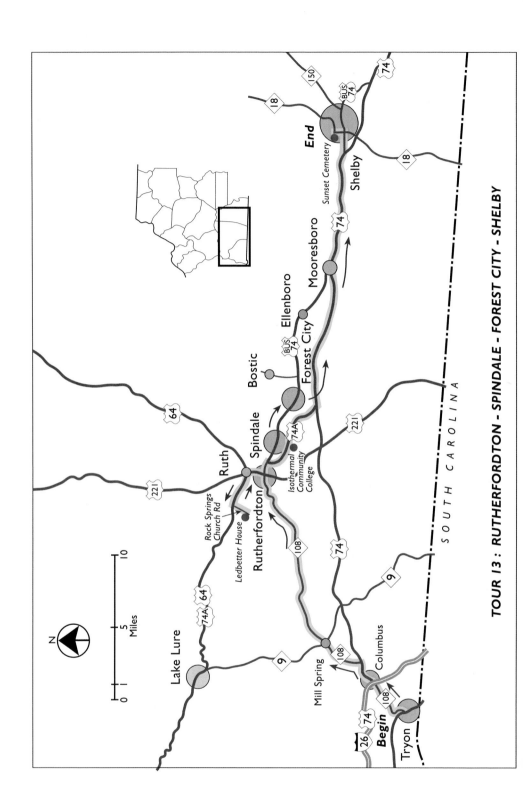

TOUR 13 : RUTHERFORDTON - SPINDALE - FOREST CITY - SHELBY

where two fawns fearlessly
nibble a burning bush.

The room shifts to dark
behind me and the doe, alert,
raises one hoof, her skin
taut over sculpting of muscles
and bronzed with attention.

Barely able to breathe, I
sidle to the window. She
gestures to stamp but halts
an inch from the ground
and becomes quicksilver.
Which of us will move?

I shift my weight only
a whisper but the hoof
drops and four white tails,
like ceremonial prayer flags,
trace arcs into the gloaming.
—From *Where There Is No Night*, by Lynne Santy Tanner
(Georgetown, Ky.: Finishing Line Press, 2004), 20–21.

Tanner is another member of the family mentioned in Tour 12 that helped shape Rutherfordton's identity as a prosperous mill town after the Depression. Today, the Tanner Companies are still headquartered here, along with their original outlet store on Rock Road off of Old Highway 221 north of town.

When you come into the residential outskirts of Rutherfordton, take care to follow 108—there are a couple of turns—before you reach the intersection with US 221, which is Rutherfordton's main street. Turn left on 221 to explore this thriving little center of commerce.

Rutherfordton, and the surrounding communities of Ellenboro, Sunny View, Rock Springs, and Lake Lure are all the province of Tony Earley, whom we first met on Tour 12. Ellenboro—on US 74 Business, west of Forest City—was the model for the fictional town of Aliceville in Earley's novel, *Jim the Boy* (2000), set in the 1930s. Jim, a ten-year-old, lives with his mother and three bachelor uncles on a farm. This debut novel is appropriate for both young readers and adults and followed Earley's first short story collection, *Here We Are in Paradise* (1994).

Since the novel, Tony Earley has largely turned to nonfiction. His voice is fresh, irreverent, and powerful in its recreation of the rural South in a time of profound transition. Here is an excerpt from the essay "Hallways":

I chased my cousin Janet up the front steps. She squealed and opened the front door and ran into the house. We started down the hallway at a dead run. The screen door slammed behind us. A double barreled twenty-gauge shotgun slipped from the top row of hat hooks on the halltree and fell and clattered onto the floor. Janet and I stopped in our tracks. We tiptoed back down the hallway and stared at the shotgun. It hadn't fired.

Paw-paw ran from the living room. Granny came down the hallway at a gallop from the kitchen. The falling gun had split the halltree seat half in two. Janet and I were terrified. We said that we hadn't done it, that we were just running down the hallway and the gun fell. Paw-paw's face flushed red. He began to shake. His fists were clenched at his sides. We could tell he didn't know what to do next. Janet and I held our breath. We had never seen him that angry.

"Damn," Paw-paw said.

"Dan," Granny said. Paw-paw didn't believe in cursing. . . .

Paw-paw was tall as a giant. "How many times have I told you not to run in this house?" he said.

"Please don't whip us, Paw-paw," we said.

"Dan Ledbetter," Granny said, "you're not going to whip anybody. You're lucky that gun didn't go off. I've told you and told you not to keep those guns loaded."

Paw-paw and Granny stared at each other and went out the front door and down the steps and around the side of the house. Janet and I tiptoed into the living room and peeked out the window. We could see them arguing through the gap between the two heating oil tanks at the side of the house."

—From *Somehow Form a Family: Stories That Are Mostly True*, by Tony Earley (Chapel Hill, N.C.: Algonquin Books, 2001), 39–41; originally published in *Home: American Writers Remember Rooms of Their Own*, ed. Sharon Sloan Fiffer and Steve Fiffer (Pantheon, 1995).

The Ledbetter House, with its spectacular view of the South Mountains, is no longer occupied by Earley's grandparents, but it still belongs to the family and is visible from the road. It is a red-roofed, multigabled farmhouse twelve miles outside Rutherfordton. To see it, travel north on 221 from downtown

The Ledbetter House, the farmhouse that belonged to Tony Earley's grandparents, seen from the side yard.

Rutherfordton and soon you'll come to the exit for Highways 74A and 64. At the top of the ramp, turn left and follow 74A west. In approximately twelve miles, watch closely for Rock Springs Church Road on your left. Turn left, cross the river, and proceed uphill for 2.3 miles. Watch for the Rock Springs Church on your left. Just ahead is the Ledbetter House at a fork in the road. Though this is private property, enjoy the view.

On the day we visited, the yard was lush, with Mrs. Ledbetter's peonies blooming large and fragrant in the breeze. A sturdy shag-bark maple, a bed of two-toned purple iris, and a cascade of old fashioned roses filled the side and back yards. It was easy to imagine Paw-paw and Granny Ledbetter arguing right there beside the oil drum about the shotgun that fell off the wall. Note,

A view of the South Mountains.

too, that the Rock Springs Baptist Church is a topic Earley tackles in the essay "A Worn Path," in *Somehow Form a Family.*

Retrace your path to Rutherfordton and continue on 74A through Spindale to Forest City. Enjoy the voices of the region in this passage from Earley's essay "The Quare Gene" — "quare" meaning queer, odd, funny:

Suppose I brought a quare person to Sunday dinner at Granny's house and he ate something that disagreed with him. We would say he looked a little peaked (pronounced peak-Ed). Of course, we might decide he is peaked not because of something he ate that disagreed with him, but because he ate a bait of something he liked. We would say, why, he was just too trifling to leave the table, and ate almost the whole mess by himself. And now we have this quare, peaked, trifling person on our hands. How do we get him to leave? Do we job him in the stomach? Do we hit him with a stob? No, we are kinder than that. We would say, "Brother, you liked to have stayed too long." We would put his dessert in a poke and send him on his way.—From *Somehow Form a Family*, by Tony Earley, 69; originally published in the *New Yorker*, September 28, 1998.

■ SPINDALE AND FOREST CITY

To get a feel for the tri-city area of Rutherfordton-Spindale-Forest City, take US 74A East from Rutherfordton (which is the road you are already on if you're heading back into town from the Ledbetter place).

This region of North Carolina, unlike the higher elevations to the north, has a legacy more closely tied to the plantation South. From the early 1800s, Rutherfordton was the site of the Green River Plantation, which can be visited by appointment by calling 828-286-1461.

Green River was a small enterprise by Deep South standards, but one that nevertheless depended upon enslaved people. Here and across the lower half of North Carolina's Piedmont region to Charlotte and beyond, African Americans represented a larger percentage of the population than in the mountains to the north. The enslaved people contributed their craftsmanship to build elegant homes and public buildings. By the slaves' hard labor, plantation owners grew cotton, corn, and other crops in abundance.

In the 1830s gold was discovered in the hills to the north of Rutherfordton, and enslaved people were also deployed in the mining operations that led to the establishment of a private mint here. The Bechtler Mint out-produced the government mints in Philadelphia and Charlotte during its heyday. By the 1850s the Carolina gold rush was over and the mint was closed, but the significant profits earned by white landowners led to an expansion of their business interests into cotton gins and grist mills and other enterprises. The impact of the Civil War and Reconstruction on the area's economy, social climate, and literature are reflected in the works of W. J. Cash and Thomas Dixon of Shelby and will be considered as we head farther east on this trail. Rutherfordton, Spindale, and Forest City help bring into focus the twentieth-century era of the textile worker in North Carolina.

The name Spindale, of course, reflects the dominance of textile manufacturing in this town until the late twentieth century. Today Spindale is probably best known as home to Isothermal Community College and its regional purveyor of local music and culture: WNCW-FM, 88.7. This public radio station, with its several transmitters that allow the signal to reach broadly across the region, is also simulcast online. It is nationally recognized for its eclectic mix of indigenous music, especially the work of the region's many singer-songwriters and performers of old-time, bluegrass, gospel, spiritual, and Americana music. Isothermal is located on US 74A Bypass, approximately 1.2 miles before you get to the Tri-City Mall.

The college also hosts an annual writing workshop featuring regional guest writers and hosted by Isothermal's two writers-in-residence: book reviewer, science writer, and poet Tom Tucker and Kathy Ackerman, a poet and scholar who wrote *The Heart of Revolution: The Radical Life and Novels of Olive Dargan* (2004). (Dargan was the activist writer discussed in Tours 5 and 9.)

Forest City, just ahead, was originally called Burnt Chimney after the remains of a homesite that marked the crossroads of the Shelby-Rutherfordton and Spartanburg-Lincolnton roads. It was renamed Forest City in 1887, not for any notable stand of trees but for a prominent resident, Forest Davis.

Florence Mills, the town's primary employer for a century, was built in 1897 by Raleigh Rutherford Haynes. In its heyday, this enormous textile operation had some 12,000 spindles and 400 looms. The Cone family bought it in the 1950s. The Florence plant finally closed in 2001, and the building now belongs to the town. Forest City planners are at work to transform this historic property into a multiuse space that will include a textile museum, an art gallery, conference space, a performance pavilion, apartments and condominiums, an arts education center, restaurants, and retail shops.

Bestselling suspense writer Kay Hooper, who lives in nearby Bostic, often comes to town to visit Fireside Books in Forest City. Hooper is faithful to her readers, keeping up with the many requests for autographed copies of her novels that Fireside ships around the world. Hooper is a graduate of East Rutherford High School. After taking some business classes at Isothermal, she turned her attention to history and literature and soon began writing. She sold her first novel, a romance entitled *Lady Thief*, to Dell in 1980. Hooper was only twenty-two. She continued writing in that genre for her next several books, sometimes using the pen name "Kay Robbins." Hooper then turned to psychological thrillers that often involve the paranormal. Hooper's mysteries incorporate a wide array of characters and settings that reappear in subsequent books, which now number near seventy. *Stealing Shadows* (2000) and *Hunting Fear* (2004) are set in fictional small towns in North Carolina.

Another local writer, Martha Mason, lives nearby in the tiny town of Lattimore. She is a 1960 graduate of Wake Forest University, where she completed all of her course work while living in an 800-pound iron lung. As a young child in 1948, Mason was stricken with polio the same year her brother died from the disease. She graduated at the top of her class at Wake and aspired to be a writer. For years Mason's mother helped her daughter by taking dictation, but then Mason's father fell ill and her mother then had two patients to tend. Finally, in 1994, Mason acquired a voice-activated computer, which allowed her to begin her memoir, *Breath* (2003). In it, she tells the story of her mother's dedicated care and then her own role as caretaker of her mother following the older woman's devastating stroke. Mason reportedly holds the record as the longest-living person in an iron lung. When she was first paralyzed, doctors only gave her a year to live.

To reach Shelby, our next stop on this tour, you may take Business 74 out of downtown Forest City and continue on that route if you want to see Ellenboro, the setting of Tony Earley's novel, *Jim the Boy*. For a more direct route, take US 74 Bypass, the larger, divided highway that runs by Fireside Books. Business 74 eventually merges with the 74 Bypass beyond Ellenboro.

▪ SHELBY

Cleveland County is the easternmost county in the foothills of North Carolina, and Shelby is the county seat. Here cotton was the predominant crop for decades. In the 1940s Cleveland reportedly produced the largest yield of cotton per acre of any county in the nation. Some two-dozen textile plants also operated here during that era. Later, dairy farming reached its peak in the 1960s with more than one hundred working dairies in the county. The prosperity of those decades is still evident in many areas of Shelby, where large lawns, shady, tree-lined streets, and elegant homes predominate.

Shelby is the birthplace of bluegrass music legend Earl Scruggs, boxer Floyd Patterson, filmmaker Earl Owensby, and basketball star David Thompson. And it was here at the turn of the century that two influential writers, Thomas Dixon and W. J. Cash—both Shelby natives and Wake Forest College graduates —offered enormously disparate views of the history and prospects of the region.

Preacher, lawyer, state legislator, actor, movie producer, and real estate developer, Thomas Dixon was born just before the Civil War ended. He wrote twenty-two novels and a number of plays and screenplays during his lifetime. In the *Encyclopedia of Southern Culture* (Chapel Hill, N.C.: University of North Carolina Press, 1989), historian James Kinney tells us, "Dixon argued for three interrelated beliefs still current in southern life: the need for racial purity, the sanctity of the family centered on a traditional wife and mother, and the evil of socialism" (880).

Dixon is perhaps best known for the film *Birth of a Nation*, based on his novel *The Clansman* (1905), the second book in his trilogy on the Ku Klux Klan. The film was a manifesto condemning Reconstruction and blaming African Americans for the demise of the Old South. Directed by D. W. Griffith, a Kentuckian who shared many of Dixon's beliefs, it drew large audiences, some say, because it was the first Hollywood film shot outdoors with live action. Condemned by the NAACP, praised by President Woodrow Wilson, and forcefully critiqued by W. E. B. DuBois, the film has been credited by some historians for contributing to the race riots that followed its release and continued for several years across the country.

Dixon eventually modified his rhetoric. He condemned slavery and Klan activities, but he never supported the rights of African Americans to vote or hold elective office. He also opposed women's suffrage. In his last novel, published in 1939, Dixon portrays African Americans as purveyors of communism, working for the overthrow of the United States — a position he promoted well in advance of the similar, inflammatory rhetoric of those who opposed the civil rights movement of the 1960s.

Over the years Dixon gained and lost several fortunes, all the while stridently hoping to change the world through his writing and the new medium of film. At one point he purchased more than a thousand acres on top of Pompey's Knob in McDowell County and founded a colony for writers and artists that he named Wildacres. Dixon lost that property and died a poor man. (See Tour 16.) As James Kinney suggests, "Although his work is seldom read today, both in his themes and as a political preacher seeking a national congregation through mass media, Thomas Dixon clearly foreshadowed the politicized television evangelists of the modern South" (*Encyclopedia of Southern Culture*, 881).

By contrast, Shelby's W. J. Cash published only one book in his short and troubled life: *The Mind of the South* (1941). With a strong narrative voice and using fresh metaphors and colloquialisms, Cash attempted to hold up a mirror to his fellow southern white males, or as he put it, "the man at the center." Cash aimed to portray and critique the habits of thought, complacency, staid values, prejudices, and social standards of the South as he knew it.

Interestingly, Cash had admired Thomas Dixon as a teenager, but his viewpoint dramatically changed as a student at Wake Forest, where he was influenced by liberal theologian and university president William L. Poteat. In the last section of his book, Cash inventories the state of southern literature in his time. He soundly denounces Dixon while lifting up the work of Chapel Hill

Shelby native Thomas Dixon in 1926, outside his Asheville sales office for Wildacres, a retreat for artists and writers he planned near Little Switzerland. The film Birth of a Nation *was based on one of his novels. Photo courtesy of the North Carolina Collection of the Pack Memorial Library, Asheville, North Carolina.*

playwright Paul Green and many others. He suggested that by means of this regional literary renaissance, "the multiplication of Southern writers would go on at such a pace until in 1939 the South actually produced more books of measurable importance than any other section of the country, until anybody who fired off a gun in the region was practically certain to kill an author" (376).

(As an aside, this general idea has since taken on many North Carolina adaptations, including Doris Betts's "Throw a rock in North Carolina and you'll hit a writer," and Lee Smith's "You can't sling a cat without hitting a writer here.")

Ultimately Cash's view of the region's future was guardedly optimistic, though he concludes:

> Proud, brave, honorable by its lights, courteous, personally generous, loyal, swift to act, often too swift, but signally effective, sometimes terrible in its action — such was the South at its best. And such at its best it remains today, despite the great falling away in some of its virtues. Violence, intolerance, aversion and suspicion toward new ideas, an incapacity for analysis, an inclination to act from feeling rather than from thought, an exaggerated individualism and a too narrow concept of social responsibility, attachment to fictions and false values, above all too great attachment

to racial values and a tendency to justify cruelty and injustice in the name of those values, sentimentality and a lack of realism—these have been its characteristic vices in the past. And, despite changes for the better, they remain its characteristic vices today.—From *The Mind of the South*, by W. J. Cash (New York: Random House, 1991), 428–29.

Cash has been criticized over the years for his blind spots—his focus on white men of the region without addressing the plight of white women. He also contributed, critics say, to the perpetuation of stereotypes of African American and Appalachian people. Nevertheless, in his day, the book drew praise as a milestone in southern letters, and Cash received a Guggenheim fellowship in the year of its publication. He went to Mexico with his new bride in July of 1941 to begin a novel, but Cash—who had likely suffered from what we now call bipolar disorder—was overwhelmed by a bout of depression that included paranoid delusions involving Nazi agents. Cash hanged himself in a hotel room with his necktie. His only book still stands as a classic study, revolutionary in its time.

Ironically, Thomas Dixon and W. J. Cash are buried near each other, but on opposite sides of the road, in Shelby's Sunset Cemetery. To get there, take Marion Street as it forks to the left off of US 74 as you are coming into town. In several blocks, turn left on Cora Street. You'll cross Sumter and see the entrance to Sunset Cemetery on your left, opposite a ball field on your right. Turn left onto Woodlawn and follow this narrow lane through the graveyard and around to the right. Look for Memorial Avenue and take this loop bordered by stately maples on either side. Thomas Dixon's tall marker will be on your left about halfway up a rise that is topped by an above-ground tomb. Just a bit farther, around the curve from Dixon and on the right side of the lane, is a darker, weathered marker with "Cash" in Old English letters with deco flourishes.

■ LITERARY LANDSCAPE

KidSenses Children's Interactive Museum
172 North Main Street
Rutherfordton, NC 28139
828-286-2120
<http://www.kidsenses.com>
If you are traveling with kids, your first stop in Rutherfordton could be this colorful and clever repository of activities for children and toddlers. The exhib-

The Alphabet Trail in the KidSenses Museum, Rutherfordton.

its at KidSenses are based on the North Carolina Standard Course of Study used in the public schools. They address literacy, nutrition and health, science, and geography in a playful and instructive way.

One exhibit—the Alphabet Trail—is designed for toddlers and invites them to put on little backpacks and explore a re-creation of the local landscape in search of all the letters of the alphabet, cleverly incorporated throughout the environment. The Alphabet Trail showcases images from *Wake Up Big Barn!* (2002), a book by Rutherfordton-born Suzanne Tanner Chitwood. (Chitwood is the granddaughter of Bobo and Millie Tanner, who went for that accidental swim in Lake Lure described in Tour 12.)

In another area of the museum, children learn about dental hygiene from the mouse dentist made popular in *Doctor De Soto* (1982), a children's book written and illustrated by former *New Yorker* cartoonist William Steig, who was also the creator of the characters in the movie *Shrek*.

KidSenses also sponsors a summer camp that focuses on children's literature. There is an admission fee to the museum.

Anything Southern Books

224 North Main Street

Rutherfordton, NC 28139

828-287-0390

anythingsouthern@bellsouth.net

On the same side of Main Street as KidSenses and a few doors up, this bookstore carries most of the major works cited more than once in Trails One and Two. Proprietors Robin Lattimore and Lesley Bush are serious students of local history and have amassed a respectable collection of rare titles in addition to their sections on the Civil War and Appalachian literature. Their goal for the bookstore is to provide a venue for conversations about the literature and lore of the area—particularly for newcomers just passing through.

Legal Grounds

217 North Main Street

Rutherfordton, NC 28139

828-286-9955

coffee@legalgrounds.net

<http://www.legalgrounds.net/>

On the opposite side of Main Street from Anything Southern and Kid-Senses is this popular hangout. Local thriller writer Kay Hooper recommends this combination coffee shop, sports bar, and restaurant. She says, "Though I've never used it in a book, one of my favorite places in the county is Legal Grounds, in downtown Rutherfordton. They make the best chicken salad I've found anywhere."

Fireside Books

Tri-City Mall

2270 US Hwy 74A Bypass

Forest City, NC 28043

828-245-5188

<http://www.firesidebookstore.com/>

Fireside Books is the center of literary activity in Forest City. Regular readings by regional authors and a large selection of North Carolina literature are a priority here. A local writing group meets here twice a month and a book club once a month. Upstairs is a huge selection of horror and mystery titles. The store also has a strong children's section. Look for the store, which occupies a freestanding A-frame, on the western edge of Tri-City Mall. Take the Highway

74A Bypass (74A Business will take you into downtown) and watch for the mall on your right. Turn right at the traffic light just before the mall and you'll see the A-frame at the edge of the complex.

Cleveland County Memorial Library

104 Howie Drive

Shelby, NC 28150

704-487-9069

<http://www.ccml.org/>

To learn more about Shelby writers and other historic sites in town, this facility is worth a visit. You pass the library coming in on West Marion Street on the way to Sunset Cemetery.

Lincolnton : Hickory : Moravian Falls

Revolutionary and Civil War sites are the inspiration for many of the writers on this tour. Read the journal of the wife of Jefferson Davis's aide. Learn about North Carolina's second official poet laureate, who learned to read from circus posters and only finished one year of school.

Writers with a connection to this area: Dale Bailey, Daniel W. Barefoot, Molly Bass, Rand Brandes, Mary Boykin Chesnut, James Lincoln Collier, Tim Earley, George Fawcett, Kays Gary, Hatcher Hughes, Toni L. P. Kelner, Louis L'Amour, Sallie Nixon, James Larkin Pearson, Tim Peeler, Mary Ellen Snodgrass

If you're coming from Shelby to begin this tour, head northeast on NC 150, a scenic route that could be called the "Strawberry Corridor." Several "U-Pick" strawberry farms along this route offer fresh fruit in April or early May, depending on the length of winter. You'll pass through the villages of Stubbs, Waco, Cherryville, and Crouse. Bear left on Old Highway 150 (not the Bypass). It merges into NC 27 and runs into West Main Street on the way to Lincolnton's town square. As you travel, if it's a clear day you should be able to see King's Mountain in the distance over your right shoulder.

■ LINCOLNTON

Lincolnton has a lively—if eclectic—literary history. One of the early writers to venture here for a time was Mary Boykin Chesnut, the wife of an aide to Jefferson Davis and author of *A Diary from Dixie* (1905; repr. Boston: Houghton Mifflin, 1949). During the Civil War, Chesnut fled her home in Camden, South Carolina, to hide out in Lincolnton while Sherman's army moved through the region. In 1865, she wrote in her diary about Lincolnton: "This is a thoroughly out-of-all-routes place,

tour 14

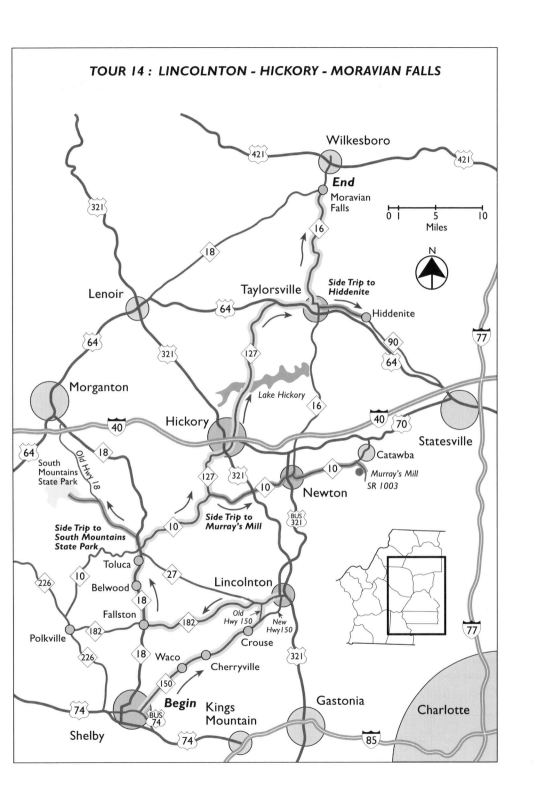

TOUR 14 : LINCOLNTON - HICKORY - MORAVIAN FALLS

Wilkesboro

End
Moravian
Falls

0 1   5   10
        Miles

N

Lenoir

Taylorsville

*Side Trip to
Hiddenite*

Hiddenite

Morganton

Lake Hickory

Hickory

Statesville

South
Mountains
State Park

Catawba

Murray's Mill
SR 1003

Newton

*Side Trip to
Murray's Mill*

*Side Trip to
South Mountains
State Park*

Toluca

Belwood

Lincolnton

Fallston

Polkville

*Old
Hwy 150*

*New
Hwy150*

Crouse

Waco

Cherryville

Begin Kings
Mountain

Gastonia

Charlotte

Shelby

and yet I can go to Charlotte. I am halfway to Kate at Flat Rock, and there is no Federal army between me and Richmond" (478).

Chesnut was opposed to slavery, but she did believe in the right of the southern states to secede from the Union. Her early feminist vision questioned the patriarchy and the Old South way of life. She sympathized with the plight of African Americans. According to historian Elisabeth Muhlenfeld, writing in the *Encyclopedia of Southern Culture*, Chesnut's diary demonstrates "the author's sharp intelligence, irreverent wit, and keen sense of irony and metaphorical vision" (1574). Her 400,000-word diary filled some fifty notebooks and was written between February 1861 and July 1865. It is available online from the University of North Carolina at <http://docsouth.unc.edu/southlit/chesnut/menu.html>.

Another writer of note here: contemporary Lincoln County historian Daniel W. Barefoot is a former member of the North Carolina General Assembly and a graduate of UNC Law School. *General Robert F. Hoke: Lee's Modest Warrior* (2001) is his award-winning biography of the man for whom Hoke County in the eastern part of the state is named. Born in Lincolnton, General Hoke was the youngest Confederate enlistee to rise to the rank of major general, a feat he accomplished in only three years at age twenty-three. He was the hero of the Battle of Plymouth and served as a trusted officer under General Robert E. Lee. After the Civil War, Hoke returned home to Lincoln County to work the land. He eschewed many invitations to seek public office, including the governorship, though he did eventually play a role in local industry.

Dan Barefoot has also written several North Carolina travel volumes and a trilogy of books recounting the best of North Carolina's ghost stories. *Haints of the Hills: North Carolina's Haunted Hundred*, vol. 3 (2002), presents spooky tales from twenty-eight mountain counties. This series, in turn, led Barefoot to investigate a raft of legends about eerie happenings on college campuses across the South. *Haunted Halls of Ivy: Ghosts of Southern Colleges and Universities* (2004) incorporates stories from nearly forty campuses stretching from Florida to West Virginia.

For many years, Lincolnton was also home to poet Sallie Nixon, a past president of the North Carolina Poetry Society. Nixon's work has won both the American Academy of Poets Award and the Vreeland Award for Creative Writing from the University of Nebraska in Lincoln. Her latest collection is *A Kind of Peace—New and Selected Poems* (2006). Nixon's poetry is distinguished by its painterly preoccupation with color and light. She often writes about garden landscapes and natural events:

BLUE HOSANNA

On this last day of June
the fragile morning glories
are giving praise:
here, they reach
to first light, stretch their cups
for earliest grace.

I learn from them:
In this still place
I open my own thin blueness,
take deep into myself.
—From *Working the Dirt: An Anthology of Southern Poets*, ed.
 Jennifer Horne (Montgomery, Ala.: NewSouth Books, 2003), 98.

The Sallie Nixon Collection of North Carolina Writers was a gift from the poet to the J. A. Jones Library of Brevard College in Brevard. The collection is in the College Guest House and provides a good representation of the best of North Carolina's writers, including literature from the southern mountains.

And finally, for science fiction readers, Lincolnton was for many years the home of the 20,000-item Sauceriana Collection of local UFO expert George Fawcett. Fawcett is the author of *Quarter Century Studies of UFOs in Florida, North Carolina and Tennessee* (1975). Although his dream was to build a saucer-shaped museum in town, ultimately he donated his collection to the International UFO Museum and Research Center in Roswell, New Mexico, in 1998. Fawcett is an honorary member of the museum's board and has served as a movie consultant and contributor to many UFO encyclopedia projects. He continues to publish pamphlets and studies on the topic.

■ FALLSTON

Though it may not be the most direct route to our next stop in Hickory, here's a scenic drive with a literary storyline. Head out of Lincolnton on NC 182 West and go eleven miles, to the intersection with NC 18. You are in Fallston, where you will turn left and head north on NC 18. But first notice the lovely rural homes around you. Fallston was the childhood home of the beloved *Charlotte Observer* columnist, Kays Gary. Gary wrote for the newspaper for thirty-eight years. As a high school student he snagged his first job in journalism as the community correspondent for the *Shelby Daily Star*. He attended Mars Hill College and UNC-Chapel Hill. He was a reporter before he began his popular daily column. Gary interviewed Elvis Presley and other luminaries, but for the most part, his daily yarns concerned everyday people. Here's a snippet of Kays Gary from a column titled "Gratitude":

Letty M. Gary is 81, her life spun out in loving and teaching children and her own small family. Like the old man, never a complaint had she and never once a martyr. Her dinner plate commanded only chicken wings. Best pieces were for others.

I went to college on Mama's chicken wings and her make-do in restyling old clothes and reupholstering old furniture. Yet, in beauty and graciousness, she could impress any company.

And so it remained, even when, some years ago, the hardened arteries took all but those qualities and commandments of simple presence.

Sometimes, when the faded blue eyes glimmer with smiling recognition, I wonder how much is still there, because she no longer has words enough. Nor have I.

Then came a fright on a Friday afternoon. She'd had a fall and suffered a deep, ugly and profusely bleeding cut over her right eye. Yet, through all the experience of being lifted in and out of care and being carried to the hospital for injections and stitches, her demeanor was as serene as if guests had dropped in for tea.

Was it possible that Mama, finally, no longer thought or felt anything?

The silent question was answered as I pushed her wheelchair through the hospital's parting electric doors.

The wheelchair went through smoothly but I stumbled and bumped my knee.

Mama said "Ouch!"

—From *Kays Gary, Columnist: A Collection of His Writings*, compiled by his friends (Charlotte: East Woods Press, 1981), 39.

Only a couple of miles west of Fallston is Polkville, the birthplace of playwright Hatcher Hughes. Hughes spent most of his career teaching drama at Columbia University. His mountain melodrama about a North Carolina family feud, *Hell-Bent for Heaven*, won the 1924 Pulitzer Prize for drama. The play had not been the drama jury's first choice, however. They favored *The Show-Off*, a play by George Kelly that had been called "the best comedy which has yet been written by an American," according to critic Heywood Broun. The Pulitzer committee, many of whom were evidently Hughes's Columbia colleagues, overturned the jury's decision, awarding the prize to Hughes. (Kelly won the next year for another comedy.) In the history books, this controversy seems to have had a longer life than either play.

From Fallston north on NC 18, you'll pass through Bellwood and Toluca. Here you'll see the South Mountains dramatically rising in the northwest—the left side of the road. This is orchard country. You may want to stop for a look at one of the few commercial enterprises around—Redbone Willy's Trading Company, at the intersection of Highways 18 and 27. This place is known for its homemade, hand-churned ice cream and homemade pies and cakes. But if you're more curious than hungry, you'll also find clothing, gifts, cookbooks, and antiques in this rambling store. The nearby DeStarté Bed and Breakfast, run by the same family that owns Redbone Willy's, was so named after a character in Louis L'Amour's book *Hondo*. (See <http://www.redbonewilly.com>.)

If you want to stretch your legs before going on to Hickory, you can take a side trip to South Mountains State Park by staying on NC 18. It will soon come to a fork. Here the new NC 18 continues to the right and Old Highway 18 goes to the left toward the park.

South Mountains State Park is the largest of North Carolina's state parks, with more than 18,000 acres and surrounded by another 18,000 acres of game lands. The mountains themselves encompass some 100,000 acres across three counties. Here you'll find a number of trails and campsites. Most popular among hikers is the one-mile hike to High Shoals Falls, an eighty-foot cascade. The Hemlock Nature Trail is a three-quarter-mile, wheelchair-accessible trail. The Chestnut Knob Trail—two strenuous miles—pays off with a dramatic view. There is also an eighteen-mile mountain bike trail that's classified as strenuous.

Resume the journey north on NC 18 to the intersection with NC 10 and head east.

■ HICKORY

To go directly into Hickory stay on NC 10 to NC 127, which eventually becomes Center Street in town. (Note that the north-south routes in Hickory are designated as streets. The avenues run east and west, and Center Street divides east from west.)

Long known as one of North Carolina's furniture manufacturing meccas, with a variety of name-brand furniture outlets, Hickory and Catawba County have a distinguished history in the decorative arts, including textiles and pottery. This town of 37,000 also has a lively arts and literary scene. The place to start is Third Street at the SALT Block (Sciences, Art, Literature Together), where the Catawba Science Center, the Patrick Brewer Memorial Library, and the Hickory Museum of Art are located.

The theater community in Hickory has spawned an abundance of local playwriting over the years. A notable new voice is Davidson graduate Molly Bass, whose work has been produced here nearly annually since she moved back home to Hickory. Bass got her first break in high school when she won a playwriting competition that awarded scholarship funds and a production of her work in New York City at the American Place Theatre. These days she is raising two kids, still writing, and serving as vice president of Bass-Smith Funeral Home, the family business.

Curiously enough, in the same vein (pun intended), another Hickory writer, Dale Bailey, is not only an award-winning fantasy and science fiction writer but also a regular contributor to the *Dodge Magazine*, published by one of the world's leading manufacturers of embalming equipment and chemicals. Bailey's books include *The Fallen* (2002), *House of Bones* (2003), and *Sleeping Policemen* (2006), written in collaboration with Jack Slay Jr. Originally from West Virginia, Bailey holds a Ph.D. in English from the University of Tennessee and teaches at Lenoir-Rhyne College.

Tim Peeler is a Hickory poet and publisher since 1986 of the literary journal *Third Lung Review*. Peeler teaches at Catawba Valley Community College and is winner of the Jim Harrison Award for his contributions to baseball poetry. His collections include *Waiting for Godot's First Pitch* (2001) and *Touching All the Bases: Poems from Baseball* (2000). Peeler also writes about the local landscape. His poem about Ashe County begins Tour 18 later on this trail.

Another poet who teaches in the humanities program at Catawba Valley Community College is Tim Earley, selected by poet Mary Oliver as the Stanley Kunitz Poetry Fellow at the Fine Arts Work Center in Provincetown, Massachusetts. Earley is a native of Forest City and attended Chase High School and Isothermal Community College. He earned his MFA in creative writing from the University of Alabama. His first collection, *Boondoggle*, was published in 2005 by Main Street Rag of Charlotte. This poem speaks to the changes brought by the introduction of mainstream, homogeneous culture to the mountains:

COUNTRY POEM #11: RAPTURE
The lawn is code.
The mulch is code.
The sprinklers are code.

The dogwood trees are code.
The grasshopper is code.
The dandelions are code.
The water moccasin hanging
from the Weeper is code.
The pink dusk is code.
The fire truck's siren is code.
The clink of buggy against buggy
in the Winn Dixie parking lot is code.
The gastrointestinal discomfort.
The drenchings.
The Lord is code and increaseth you.
The car's slack front tire is code.
The loins are code.
The robin come back early from Florida is code.
Open the skies.
Open the sleep white as sleep.
Open Maude's body
and heal her sorrow.
Heal the river in its consort with time.
The mini-mart that keeps changing
its name is code.
The collapsing smokehouse is code.
The poisoned dog is code.
Open the roof and let us ascend.
There is an answer.
There is.
—From *Apocryphal Text* 1, no. 1,
   <http://www.apocryphaltextpoetry.com>.

Though she doesn't live here anymore, mystery novelist Toni L. P. Kelner writes about Hickory in her fiction. In *Trouble Looking for a Place to Happen* (1996), detective Laura Fleming comes back home to Byerly, North Carolina, for a wedding and ends up helping to solve a murder involving a country rock band's tour bus. Laura Fleming's sleuthing covers territory in what Kelner admits is a fictional town that she imagines to be just off of Highway 321 near Hickory. Her characters also take a trip to Statesville in the course of the investigation. Kelner, who lives in Massachusetts, has written a string of Laura Fleming mysteries that celebrate small-town life in North Carolina.

Hickory has another interesting literary distinction. If you've ever wondered who writes those CliffsNotes that students were never supposed to use in preparing book reports for school, Hickory resident Mary Ellen Snodgrass has accumulated an impressive list of publications that includes many, many CliffsNotes volumes. But perhaps more significantly, this prolific writer is also the creator, with Gary Carey, of *A Multicultural Dictionary of Literary Terms* (1999).

To reach our final stop on this tour, continue north on NC 127 out of Hickory and head toward Moravian Falls, in Wilkes County. You'll cross Lake Hickory, created in 1927 by Duke Power Company as one of a series of lakes formed by damming the Catawba River. NC 127 dead-ends into NC 90 and US 64. Turn right and proceed through the rolling countryside to Taylorsville, being careful to stay on 90 as 64 forks off to the right.

■ TAYLORSVILLE / HIDDENITE

This small manufacturing town is the county seat of Alexander County, founded in 1847. It sits at the foot of the Brushy Mountains, where apple orchards dominate. Of literary note here is an extraordinary mural that is thirty-three feet long, located in the children's area of the Alexander County Public Library. It was created by artist Tamara Scantland Adams to celebrate the sesquicentennial of the county and depicts local children as they have lived over the past 150 years here. The library is one block from the courthouse and post office at 77 First Avenue.

For a short side trip, follow NC 90 east to the village of Hiddenite, so named for a green, transparent mineral that was discovered in the nineteenth century and believed to exist only in Alexander County. It was many years before additional specimens of hiddenite were found in Madagascar and Brazil. As a gemstone, hiddenite is reportedly challenging to jewelers because it splinters easily when cut. Hiddenite is home to an annual festival featuring storytellers and regular exhibitions on local history at the Hiddenite Center.

■ MORAVIAN FALLS

To reach Moravian Falls, take NC 16 due north from Taylorsville. (If you've been to Hiddenite, you'll have to backtrack five miles.) It's a fourteen-mile ride through rolling apple orchards, and then the road climbs to the quiet village of Moravian Falls. Watch for South Wilkes Elementary on your right, then turn left at the stoplight (Country Club Road) and you'll have reached your destination.

Admittedly, there's not much for the literary tourist at this historic crossroads except the grave of North Carolina's second official poet laureate, James Larkin Pearson, appointed by Governor Umstead in 1953. (At that time the appointment was for a lifetime; today the appointment is only for two years.) Pearson, who died just short of his 102nd birthday, once wrote:

> As a poet, I have written a great deal of stuff that is perishable and soon to be forgotten. But if I have written just one poem that will live, I will go out of this world rejoicing. I am fully aware that some day—or some night—my good health will come to an end and they will take me over to the cemetery at Moravian Falls and lay me down beside Cora and the baby, where I will sleep for—who knows how long. The Moravian Falls cemetery is a beautiful place to sleep and it is not very far from the mountain-top where I was born so long ago. So after all my restless goings and comings here in this work-a-day world, I will not be very far from home.
> —From *Wilkes Journal Patriot*, September 3, 1981.

Pearson was born in a cabin on nearby Berry Mountain and went to school for little more than a year in a one-room schoolhouse. He was nevertheless a lifelong reader and self-taught poet. He claimed to have learned his ABCs from the circus posters that papered the walls of the family cabin. His mother could not read cursive handwriting, but she could read print, he once explained. Pearson believed that his penchant for poetry began in vitro. While she was pregnant, Pearson's mother read the hymnbook aloud every day. "Almost as soon as I could talk at all it was noticed that my baby words fell into a rhymed and measured pattern," Pearson told journalist Bernadette Hoyle for her book *Tar Heel Writers I Know* ([Winston-Salem: John Blair, 1956], 137).

Pearson published his first poems at the age of sixteen and then went to work for a local newspaper. He eventually decided he'd make his living as a printer, a trade he learned over in West Jefferson as a young man. In 1910 he launched his own newspaper, the *Fool Killer*, dedicated to humor. The paper was written in what Pearson called "cornfield English." At its peak, it had some 50,000 readers nationwide. Remarkably, seventeen newspapers were being published in Moravian Falls at the time, the largest of which was the *Yellow Jacket*, a Republican weekly with a readership of 200,000 across the country.

Pearson's first poetry collection came out in 1908 and his last in 1971. He was "discovered" by Upton Sinclair, who wrote a story about the poet for the *New York Times* and quoted Pearson's poems in two of his books. Sinclair also reportedly said, "When the great anthology of American poetry is made there will be something in it from James Larkin Pearson."

Tombstone of James Larkin Pearson, North Carolina's second poet laureate.

Pearson's first wife, Cora, died in 1934, and with his second wife, Eleanor Fox, he moved for a time to Guilford College; but he returned home to Wilkes County for his later years. He kept his print shop in a cinder block building behind his daughter's house. His most famous poem, *Fifty Acres*, was published in the *New York Times*, which led to a popular 1937 collection by the same name.

FIFTY ACRES (EXCERPT)
I've never been to London,
I've never been to Rome;
But on my Fifty Acres
I travel here at home.

The hill that looks upon me
Right here where I was born
Shall be my mighty Jungfrau,
My Alp, my Matterhorn.

A little land of Egypt
My meadow plot shall be,

With pyramids of hay-stacks
Along its sheltered lee.

My hundred yards of brooklet
Shall fancy's faith beguile,
And be my Rhine, my Avon,
My Amazon, my Nile.

My humble bed of roses,
My honeysuckle hedge,
Will do for all the gardens
At all the far world's edge.

In June I find the Tropics
Camped all about the place;
Then white December shows me
The Arctic's frozen face.

My wood-lot grows an Arden,
My pond a Caspian Sea
And so my Fifty Acres
Is all the world to me.

Here on my Fifty Acres
I safe at home remain,
And have my own Bermuda,
My Sicily, my Spain.
—From *Fifty Acres, and Other Poems*, by James Larkin Pearson
   (Wilkesboro, N.C.: Pearson Publishing Company, 1933).

When asked his advice to young writers, Pearson told his interviewer: "Don't be a poet if you can possibly help it. It is the poorest paid profession in the world. If you are rich and have no poor kinfolks, you might try it awhile just for fun. But don't depend on it for a living" (*Tar Heel Writers I Know*, by Bernadette Hoyle, 143). Pearson's grave is in the Moravian Falls Cemetery, which is at the highest point in town and easy to find. With the water tower at your back, count the rows of gravestones. Pearson's grave is in the twelfth row counting from the front.

Charles R. Jonas Public Library

306 West Main Street

Lincolnton, NC 28072

704-735-8044

<http://www.glrl.lib.nc.us/docs/jonas.htm>

As part of the large Gaston-Lincoln Regional Library System, the Jonas Library, just west of the Lincolnton square, is home to an excellent poetry and genealogy collection. The librarians here still remember their thrill when the prolific children's-author-turned-jazz-critic James Lincoln Collier visited their stacks to do research for *Duke Ellington: The Life and Times of the Restless Genius Of Jazz* (1987). James Edward Ellington was born in Lincolnton in 1879 and moved with his parents to Washington, D.C., in 1886. He was the father of pianist Duke Ellington.

North State Books

109 Court Square SE

Lincolnton, NC 28092

704-732-8562

norstat@vnet.net

This bookshop is a rare find, right on the square in Lincolnton. You might not make it past the check-out counter inside the front door, however, so large is the collection of books about North and South Carolina here. Right away, we found a 1949 paperback version of Mary Boykin Chesnut's *Diary from Dixie* and countless other hard-to-find classics. The proprietors are a great resource — generous with information about writers in the region, including those from upstate South Carolina, nearby.

Annual Catawba Valley Storytelling Festival

c/o Catawba County Museum of History

30 North College Avenue

Newton, NC 28658

828-465-0383

<http://www.catawbahistory.org/catawba_valley_
   storytelling_festival.php>

The Catawba Valley Historical Society maintains a museum in the Newton courthouse with local artifacts and pottery. They also oversee several other historic sites in the area, most notably the Murray's Mill Historic District, site of the annual storytelling festival held in May. You can reach Murray's Mill by staying on NC 10 beyond the junction with NC 127. The road to the historic site is well marked, about eleven miles from this intersection.

Patrick Beaver Memorial Library

375 Third Street NE
Hickory, NC 28601
828-304-0500
<http://www.ci.hickory.nc.us/library>
It seems that just about everything in Hickory is on the SALT Block, so while you're in the neighborhood, check out the new Patrick Beaver Library, a large and busy place with a local history and genealogy room.

Hickory Community Theatre

30 Third Street NW
Hickory, NC 28601
828-327-3855 (office)
828-328-2283 (tickets)
<http://www.hct.org>
HCT is the third-oldest community theater in North Carolina, mounting some eight productions every year. It has two performance spaces—the Fireman's Kitchen (named after its first use) and the Jeffers Theater, renamed by the city council in honor of the theater's former artistic director, Charles Jeffers. Jeffers directed more than 200 plays and musicals and has won several major awards, including the American Association of Community Theaters Distinguished Merit Award.

McGuire's Pub

46 Third Street NW
Hickory, NC 28601
828-322-7263
According to poet Tim Peeler, this pub in downtown Hickory is "the one place that stands out the most. The theater arts and writing crowd has met there since the 70s." There's a Fitzgerald sandwich on the menu.

Lenoir-Rhyne College

625 Seventh Avenue NE
Hickory, NC 28601
828-328-1741
<http://www.lrc.edu/visitingwriters/>

Since 1988 Lenoir-Rhyne has played a key role in the literary life of Hickory by hosting an annual visiting writers series called In Their Own Words. Seamus Heaney scholar Rand Brandes, who is Martin Luther Stevens Professor of English, directs the program. The series has brought writers ranging from Pat Conroy to Luis Rodriquez to Alice Walker. This liberal arts institution serves some 1,500 students and is affiliated with the Lutheran Church.

The Writer's Stage

c/o Taste Full Beans Coffeehouse
29 Second Street NW
Hickory, NC 28601
828-325-0108
tfbcoffeehouse@charter.net

This coffee shop in downtown Hickory becomes a literary venue every other month. Usually these events begin with a featured writer, followed by an open microphone for writers of fiction, songs, poetry, essays, and creative nonfiction.

Hiddenite Center, Inc.

316 Church Street
Hiddenite, NC 28636
828-632-6966
info@hiddenitecenter.com
<http://hiddenitecenter.com>

The Lucas Mansion, home to the Hiddenite Center, is a large nineteenth-century Victorian house with galleries featuring contemporary and historic art, period clothing, and artifacts related to local history. The center is three blocks north of NC 90 on Church Street and is open Monday through Friday from 9:00 A.M. to 4:30 P.M. There is a small admission fee for the museum; the galleries are free to visitors. The annual Hiddenite Celebration of the Arts takes place on the fourth Saturday in September each year and features storytelling, music, dance, and demonstrations of folklife and folk art by local practitioners.

Wilkesboro : Happy Valley : Blowing Rock : Linville Falls : Morganton

From the legend of Tom Dula in Happy Valley to Jan Karon's wildly popular tales of Mitford, this tour includes mystery, murder, mountain myth, and even a fantasy by Frenchman Jules Verne.

Writers with a connection to this area: John Ehle, Sam Ervin, Marita Garin, Robert Inman, Jan Karon, Sharyn McCrumb, Michael McFee, Margaret Mitchell, Kathleen Moore Morehouse, Margaret Morley, Scott Nicholson, John Parris, James Larkin Pearson, Marjorie Kinnan Rawlings, Christian Reid, Donald Secreast, Sequoyah, R. T. Smith, Jules Verne, Manly Wade Wellman, John Foster West

■ WILKESBORO

If you're coming from Moravian Falls, continue up NC 16 (which joins with 18) and in a few miles you'll pass under US 421 to reach Wilkesboro and North Wilkesboro. According to local historians, the first white man to settle in what would become Wilkes County was Christopher Gist. He built a home on the north side of the Yadkin River, just a mile west of what is Wilkesboro today. Gist befriended the Cherokee people who lived here. He also reportedly showed Daniel Boone the route to Kentucky. (Boone also lived in Wilkes for a time.) Nathaniel Gist, one of Christopher's three sons, married a Cherokee woman named Wurteh, a sister of Cherokee chiefs Old Tassel and Doublehead. Wurteh and Nathaniel gave birth to a son they named George, the man who later became known as Sequoyah, inventor of the Cherokee alphabet. (See Tour 6.)

Wilkesboro is rich in early American history. The Old Wilkes Heritage Walking Tour is a good way to learn more about this storied town. The self-guided walk begins at 202 Bridge Street,

tour 15

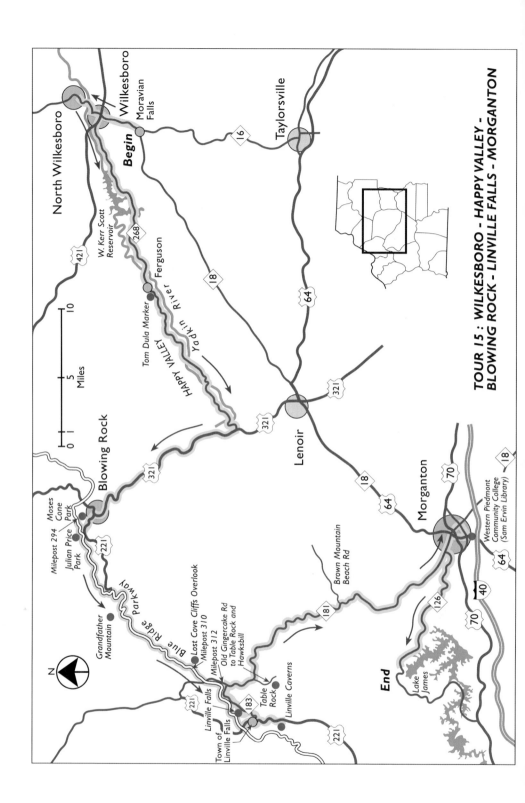

TOUR 15 : WILKESBORO - HAPPY VALLEY -
BLOWING ROCK - LINVILLE FALLS - MORGANTON

North Wilkesboro

Wilkesboro

Begin

Moravian Falls

Taylorsville

16

64

18

268

W. Kerr Scott Reservoir

421

Ferguson

Tom Dula Marker

Yadkin River

HAPPY VALLEY

10

5
Miles

0

321

321

Lenoir

321

Blowing Rock

Moses Cone Park

Milepost 294

Julian Price Park

221

Blue Ridge Parkway

Grandfather Mountain

N

Lost Cove Cliffs Overlook
Milepost 312
Milepost 310
Old Gingercake Rd
to Table Rock and
Hawksbill

Linville Falls
Town of Linville Falls

221

183

Table Rock

Linville Caverns

221

181

Brown Mountain Beach Rd

18

64

Morganton

70

Western Piedmont Community College
(Sam Ervin Library)

18

64

40

126

70

End

Lake James

Old Wilkes Jail in Wilkesboro, where Tom Dula was held for the murder of Laura Foster.

where maps are available. As you are coming into town on NC 16 and 18, take a right where the road dead-ends onto Main Street. In several blocks, watch for Bridge Street on your left and signs for the Old Wilkes Jail.

The Old Wilkes Jail, built in 1859, housed both Confederate and Union prisoners during the Civil War. It was also the place where Tom Dula was first brought in for the murder of Laura Foster. Dula was held here until his trial venue was changed to Statesville. The legend of Tom Dula has been told and retold as both story and ballad. It became the basis for the song "Hang Down Your Head, Tom Dooley," recorded by the Kingston Trio in the 1950s. When we get to Happy Valley a bit later in this tour, you can read Manly Wade Wellman's version of the story. The jail is open Monday through Friday and weekends by appointment.

Also on the walking tour is St. Paul's Episcopal Church, just uphill from the jail. The church, on a beautiful knoll overlooking the Yadkin River Valley, is home to more of Ben Long's fresco work, which is also described in Tours 1 and 18.

For cyclists looking for a good ride, behind the Old Wilkes Jail is the Benjamin Cleveland Home, a reconstructed cabin. It marks the entrance to the Yadkin Greenway—a four-mile trail that goes down the bluff, crosses the Yadkin River, and proceeds along the Yadkin to its confluence with the Reddies River. Details on the trail are available at <http://www.yadkinrivergreenway.com>.

To visit North Wilkesboro, continue on NC 18 and 268 beyond Bridge Street, and turn left on Oakwoods Road. You'll cross the Yadkin River; North Wilkesboro, built on a steep mountainside, is straight ahead.

North Wilkesboro was home to Kathleen Moore Morehouse, who wrote *Rain on the Just* in 1936. As noted on the 1980 edition's flyleaf, Ray Erwin of the *Charlotte Observer* nominated the book for a Pulitzer Prize, calling it "the finest novel produced in North Carolina in this generation." Some local readers, however, condemned Morehouse and her characterizations of mountain people. They found the book vulgar and ill mannered, and its author was roundly criticized in much the same way that Muriel Earley Sheppard had been for her nonfiction work, *Cabins in the Laurel*, published just a year before. However, like Sheppard's work, *Rain on the Just* was eventually reissued. Southern Illinois University Press reprinted it in 1980 as part of its Lost American Fiction series.

The novel tells the story of Least Dolly Allen, who at nine "was uncommon tinsy, but Dolly was a smart young un, so Mammy said, for all her pindling size, her puny ways" (*Rain on the Just*, by Kathleen Moore Morehouse [Carbondale: Southern Illinois University Press, 1980], 13).

Encouraged by her sister to write down the tales and speech patterns of her neighbors, Morehouse recorded the language and lore of the Brushy Mountain region by listening to local elders and adapting it to her fiction. As a result, the book has a musical quality. The rhythms of the narrative take the reader into a wholly different world. The language is vivid and poetic. One character is described as wearing "a draggle-tailed shirt and scuffly shoes." Least Dolly goes looking for "the twistiest way out" of the brush. Another character owns "a bench leg beagle."

The 1980 edition of the novel has an afterword by Morehouse, a Massachusetts-born and Wellesley-educated writer who moved to Wilkes County as a young woman with her husband. After nearly fifty years, she reflected on how much change had come to "the Brushies" since she was "in the presence as the talk was passed" and faithfully recorded the speech patterns of her neighbors. She explains:

> The dark woods are not as dark nor as thickly wooded as once upon that imagined night. We are becoming a suburban cultured community as doctors, lawyers, teachers, preachers have come to enjoy the beauty of this land of the sky. So the peace of the little hills is not eternal as of old. And darkness, even dark-of-the-moon darkness or cloud-cover thickness to the north, west, and east of us is no longer black dark. The night is suffused with the illumination of more and more street lights, reflected from the valley towns and villages. —From *Rain on the Just*, by Kathleen Moore Morehouse, 325.

Although the initial reaction to Morehouse's book included a discussion among some Wilkes residents of "hanging Massachusetts witches," feelings about the book have changed. Morehouse wrote in her afterword that many of her neighbors were grateful for the novel's preservation of the oral traditions. Today twelve copies of the book are available at the Wilkes County Library.

Once you've had a good look around North Wilkesboro and Wilkesboro, head back the way you came, following NC 18 and 268 once more through the historic district of Wilkesboro, but this time, instead of heading south on 18, go straight on NC 268.

Poet Laureate James Larkin Pearson (Tour 14) donated his personal library and memorabilia to Wilkes Community College, which named its library for Pearson shortly after his death. The campus is located on the way out of Wilkesboro, just off NC 268. Beyond the intersection with US 421, watch for signs to the college and turn left on Collegiate Drive if you'd like to learn more about Pearson and see the college.

Heading south on NC 268 to Happy Valley, we come to the area where Tom Dula lived, courted Laura Foster, and was buried.

Chapel Hill writer Manly Wade Wellman offers this account:

The Civil War was over, in Wilkes County as in a lot of other places, and some of those who had marched away marched back again. Among those very lucky ones was handsome young Tom Dula, who lived in Happy Valley and, you may be sure, had every reason to be happy. . . .

Happy Valley had its contrasts, cultural and ethical, as well as scenic. Vividly, even luridly, these contrasts were set forth by a contemporary journalist:

"The community . . . is divided into two entirely separate and distinct classes. The one occupying the fertile lands adjacent to the Yadkin River and its tributaries is educated and intelligent, and the other, living on the spurs and ridges of the mountains, is ignorant, poor and depraved. A state of immorality unexampled in the history of any country exists among these people, and such a general system of free-lovism prevails, that it is 'a wise child that knows its father.'"

One must take note that these words were written by a northern correspondent for the New York *Herald* and remember the tendency of outsiders, already here recognized, to misjudge North Carolina's mountain folk. Not all the cove dwellers above Happy Valley were unlettered. . . . Poverty they may have known, for the land was poor and sometimes almost per-

pendicular, but they worked that land and from it gained their living. . . .
As to what the *Herald*'s representative referred to as "free-lovism"—well,
Tom Dula was back home, and he liked the girls and the girls liked him.

He was a good-looking young man in his early twenties. Nearly six feet
tall, with dark eyes and dark curly hair, he moved gracefully, paid smiling
compliments, and he was a fiddle-scraping, banjo-picking caution. . . .
Tom Dula began his conquests on a sensibly modest scale, with Laura
Foster, the pretty but more than formally hospitable daughter of Wilson
Foster.—From *Dead and Gone: Classic Crimes of North Carolina*, by Manly
Wade Wellman (Chapel Hill: University of North Carolina Press, 1954),
172–73.

As Wellman goes on to explain, Tom Dula had many girlfriends. Meanwhile,
Laura Foster—who also apparently had many suitors both before and after
Tom came home from the war—said she wanted to be with no one but Tom.

Laura mysteriously disappeared one morning, and the entire Happy Valley
community set out to find her. When Laura's body, stabbed through the heart,
was found in a shallow grave near Elkville, five men—all suitors of Laura's
at one time or another—suddenly disappeared. Among them was Tom Dula.
Three of the five men returned days later with Tom Dula and another suitor
under arrest. They had been found in Tennessee. Another of Tom's girlfriends
—a married woman named Ann Melton—was also rounded up and put in jail.
One man proved his alibi and was set free, but Melton and Dula were held on
the charge of murder.

Wellman tells us: "Into Wilkesboro then rode a striking figure, burning-eyed
and fierce-moustached, who was immediately recognized and cheered from
both sides of the street" (179).

The striking figure was thirty-six-year-old Zebulon Vance, future governor
of North Carolina, but for now the first colonel of the Confederate regiment in
which Tom Dula had served as a private. Vance had come to defend Dula as
his legal counsel. (For more on Vance, see Tours 7 and 8.) Vance successfully
argued to have the trial moved to Statesville, where he essentially blamed the
victim's character for her demise and tried to dismiss as hearsay the testimony
from several locals that Tom Dula was seeking revenge for a disease he had
contracted from Laura Foster. Some in the community suspected that the other
defendant, Ann Melton, had actually killed Laura Foster when she learned that
Dula and Foster planned to elope.

Tom Dula was found guilty and sentenced to hang. Vance appealed to the
Supreme Court, and there new evidence was presented that Dula and Melton

Happy Valley is where Tom Dula and Laura Foster lived.

were coconspirators. The guilty verdict held, however, and Dula was scheduled to hang on May 1, 1868. Melton's trial had still not been scheduled. According to Wellman, Zeb Vance believed that Tom Dula was protecting Melton, who had probably committed the murder alone.

On the day of the hanging in Statesville, Tom Dula was baptized and then invited to address the large crowd that had gathered to witness the execution. His coffin waited nearby. Wellman describes the scene: "This address, which lasted nearly an hour, must have rambled extensively but was heard with the utmost attention. When Dula had finished, the time was past two o'clock. He took an affectionate farewell of his sister. Sheriff Wasson lowered the noose over his curly head, and he made a last joke. 'You have such a nice clean rope,' he observed. 'I ought to have washed my neck'" (185).

NC 268 out of Wilkesboro runs alongside the placid W. Kerr Scott Reservoir, created from the Yadkin River. As you go beyond the banks of the reservoir on 268, watch for Underwood Road on your right and then Beaver Creek on your left. Just a short distance beyond these roads is the Whippoorwill Academy and Village on the left. (If you get to Champion Road at Ferguson, you've gone too far.) This historic site includes the one-room schoolhouse that North Carolina poet laureate James Larkin Pearson attended. The Whippoorwill Academy, built in 1880, was so named because it was located so far back in the woods that not even the whippoorwills could find it. It was later moved and restored on this site. The loft of the schoolhouse is home to the Tom Dula Museum, where memorabilia associated with the Dula legend is on display, including what is purported to be a lock of Laura Foster's hair. A gallery featuring the work of local artists and a country store, chapel, weaving studio, and blacksmith shop are also part of the complex. Hours are limited; contact 336-973-3237.

When you get to Ferguson, just beyond the Whippoorwill Academy, take note of Champion Road coming in on your right. Up the road is the town of Champion, birthplace of another Wilkes County writer, John Foster West, who served many an aspiring student writer at Appalachian State in nearby Boone, where he taught for many years. West wrote *The Ballad of Tom Dula* (1977) and *Lift Up Your Head, Tom Dooley* (1993).

A little farther down NC 268, where the Yadkin River crosses under the highway, there's a state historic marker commemorating Tom Dula. Dula's sister and her husband carried Tom's casket back to this area, and he was buried on the farm of his cousin Bennett Dula III, beside the Yadkin River on what is now known as the Tom Dula Road, or County Road 1134.

Once across the Yadkin, you are in Caldwell County, and NC 268, an official Scenic Byway, gets even more spectacular. All through Happy Valley, antebellum homes and old churches are visible on either side of the road amid broad, cultivated fields. You might want to stop at the Chapel of Rest, on your right less than three miles before you reach US 321. The chapel is a hundred-year-old restored Episcopalian church. In the cemetery there are a number of Civil War soldiers. Charles Frazier's *Cold Mountain* protagonist, Inman, walks through Happy Valley on his journey home, though his description of the place is not flattering, occupied as the valley was by the Home Guard at the time.

When you reach US 321, the town of Lenoir (birthplace of novelist Jan Karon) is to your left. Lenoir was also the childhood home of writer Donald Secreast, whose two story collections, *The Rat Becomes Light* (1990) and *White Trash, Red*

Velvet (1993), capture factory life in this pleasant town where furniture manufacturing has for so long been the mainstay. Secreast now teaches English at Radford University in Virginia.

Our tour, however, goes up US 321 to the right and into the town of Blowing Rock, one of North Carolina's earliest tourist destinations, where the first boardinghouse for visitors was established in 1875. As you get close to the summit, be sure to pull out and look back at the dramatic St. John's Gorge below.

■ BLOWING ROCK

Blowing Rock—the landmark, not the town—is just off US 321 to the left before the road forks into separate business and bypass routes. *Asheville Citizen-Times* journalist John Parris tells the story behind the name:

> Long the legendary haunt of lovers, the Blowing Rock is etched in Indian legend and lore.
>
> There is the story that two Indian braves once stood on the summit of the rock and fought for a chieftain's daughter.
>
> They struggled all day up and down the narrow ridge until finally the stronger warrior cast his opponent over the cliff.
>
> In that moment, the Indian maiden realized that the defeated warrior was the one she loved and she implored the God of the Winds to save him.
>
> The wind caught up the warrior as he fell through space and tossed him through the air to safety.
>
> And since that day, the wind has returned any object tossed over the gorge.
>
> The Blowing Rock got its name because the rocky walls of the gorge form a flume through which the northwest wind sweeps with such force that it returns to the sender light objects cast over the void.
>
> This current of air flowing upward prompted the late Robert L. Ripley to call it "the only place in the world where snow falls upside down."—From *Roaming the Mountains*, by John Parris (Asheville: Citizen-Times Publishing Company, 1982), 62–63.

For her part, travel writer Margaret Morley was taken with the shifting mood of this mountaintop in accord with the weather:

> The view from Blowing Rock changes continually. The atmospheric sea that encloses mountain and valley melts the solid rocks into a thousand

enchanting pictures. Those wild shapes in the great basin which at one time look so near, so hard, and so terrible, at another time recede and soften, their dark colors transmuted into the tender blue of the Blue Ridge, or again the basin is filled with dreamlike forms in an exquisite sea of mystical light. . . . Blowing Rock at times lies above the clouds, with all the world blotted out excepting the Grandfather's summit rising out of the white mists. —From *The Carolina Mountains*, by Margaret W. Morley (Alexander, N.C.: Land of the Sky Books, 2002), 351–52.

As if the meteorological charms of Blowing Rock weren't enough as described by Margaret Morley more than a hundred years ago and by John Parris in the mid-twentieth century, we also have Jan Karon, who recreated this resort village in the imaginations of thousands of contemporary readers through her Mitford series of novels.

Autumn drew on in Mitford, and one after another, the golden days were illumined with changing light.

New wildflowers appeared in the hedges and fields. Whole acres were massed with goldenrod and fleabane. Wild phlox, long escaped from neat gardens, perfumed every roadside. And here and there, milkweed put forth its fat pods, laden with a filament as fine as silk.

There were those who were ecstatic with the crisp new days of autumn and the occasional scent of woodsmoke on the air. And there were those who were loath to let summer go, saying it had been "the sweetest summer out of heaven," or "the best in many years."

But no one could hold on to summer once the stately row of Lilac Road maples began to turn scarlet and gold. The row began its march across the front of the old Porter place, skipped over Main Street and the war monument to the town hall, paraded in front of First Baptist, lined up along the road of Winnie Ivey's small cottage, and ended in a vibrant blaze of color at Little Mitford Creek.

When this show began, even the summer die-hards, who were by then few enough in number to be counted on the fingers of one hand, gave up and welcomed the great spectacle of a mountain autumn. —From *At Home in Mitford*, by Jan Karon (Elgin, Ill.: Lion Publishing, 1994), 121.

Born just down the mountain in Lenoir, Jan Karon was actually named Janice Meredith Wilson, after the 1899 novel *Janice Meredith*, written by Paul Leicester Ford. The book—set during the Revolutionary War—was so popular at the time of its publication that women adopted the heroine's hairstyle as it was illustrated on the book jacket. The hairdo came to be known as the "Janice Meredith curl."

Karon grew up in the care of her grandparents on a Caldwell County farm and wrote her first novel in a Blue Horse notebook, she says, at the age of ten. She married early and had one daughter, Candace Freeland, a former photo-journalist for the *Charlotte Observer* who now lives in Hawaii. Karon made a forty-year career for herself in advertising before she retired to Blowing Rock to write. Her first book, *At Home in Mitford*, was released by a Christian publishing house without great fanfare, but the story caught on. Noticing the book's popularity with her customers, Nancy Olson, the owner of Quail Ridge Books in Raleigh, called her friend, literary agent Liz Darhansoff, to tell her how well the book was selling. Darhansoff took on Karon as a client, and soon Viking Penguin editor Carolyn Carlson knew that Karon was onto something. The series has continued with enormous success.

In the first book, Karon's affable hero, Father Tim, rises every morning to pray, takes his dog, Barnabus, for a walk around Mitford, and has his breakfast at The Grill before beginning his rounds at the hospital and tending to other parishioners of Mitford's Chapel of Our Lord and Savior.

Sonny's Grill, on Main Street (Business 321) in Blowing Rock, is, Karon admits, one of the settings that inspired her. Sonny's has been in business for more than fifty years and is the place to try livermush—a native concoction of pork liver and corn meal that is best when fried into crisp squares—if you've never had it. It's a favorite of one of Father Tim's fictional parishioners.

Throughout the series, Karon captures the easy pace of Blowing Rock, with its upscale shops and tourist haunts. The Oxford Antique Shop (which could be based on any of several fine antique purveyors in town) figures prominently in the first book. Memorial Park, at the heart of Blowing Rock, will also be familiar to Mitford fans.

Blowing Rock is a good place to explore on foot—you can window shop, eat fresh local trout, have an ice cream or some homemade candy, and generally knock around and enjoy the cool elevation. The grassy park in the center of town has plenty of benches when you tire.

In 1936, Blowing Rock was a literary hotbed. According to *Rain on the Just* author Kathleen Moore Morehouse, Blowing Rock at that time was the site of Edwin Osgood Grover's "Blowing Rock School of English." (Grover was a beloved librarian at Rollins College in Florida, and his sister, Eulalie Osgood Grover, was the creator of the "Sunbonnet Babies" and "Overall Boys"—a series of children's books popular at the beginning of the twentieth century.)

Sonny's Grill, where Jan Karon's Mitford characters eat livermush.

Grover invited Morehouse, whose novel was published in April 1936, to lecture in Blowing Rock that summer. While visiting Morehouse met two other women novelists of the era—Margaret Mitchell and Marjorie Kinnan Rawlings.

Apparently Margaret Mitchell had just arrived in Blowing Rock on the lam that summer. She had been invited by *New York Sun* book reviewer Edwin Granberry to come hide out in the mountains that July. Readers had easily found Mitchell's home phone number in the Atlanta directory and had been calling with praise and questions ever since the June publication of *Gone with the Wind*. Mitchell apparently fled Atlanta for Blowing Rock just after the contract for movie rights to the novel had arrived from David O. Selznick, leaving her husband to attend to the business deal. (Her novel would win the Pulitzer in 1937.)

Meanwhile, Floridian Marjorie Kinnan Rawlings was in town to provide the keynote speech at an assembly of writers—probably the one hosted by Grover. According to Anne Pierce of the Marjorie Kinnan Rawlings Society, Rawlings discovered that Lees-McRae College in Banner Elk had cabins for rent. Rawlings quickly booked a spot where she could work in peace through the fall on the draft of her novel in progress.

Novelists Margaret Mitchell and Marjorie Kinnan Rawlings visited Blowing Rock in 1936 to speak at a summer writing conference. Both won the Pulitzer Prize for their work. Photo courtesy of the Marjorie Kinnan Rawlings Collection, Department of Special and Area Studies Collections, George A. Smathers Libraries, University of Florida.

The novel, as it turned out, was *The Yearling*, which won the Pulitzer in 1939. (We'll visit the memorial to Marjorie Kinnan Rawlings in Banner Elk in Tour 16.)

From the middle of Blowing Rock on US 321, follow signs to the Blue Ridge Parkway and head south. The next stop on this tour is the Craft House in Moses Cone Park, which is two miles south of US 321 at milepost 294. The entrance to the parking area for this stop is on the left side of the Parkway as you are heading south.

Greensboro textile magnate Moses Cone and his wife, Bertha, bought 3,500 acres outside Blowing Rock and built this 13,000-square-foot mansion in 1901. The Cone estate was eventually donated to the U.S. Park Service in 1950, and today hikers, mountain bikers, and horse enthusiasts frequent the grounds. Twenty-seven miles of carriage trails and active stables near the Cone Manor House make it possible for visitors to travel the grounds by horse-drawn carriage. There is also a twenty-mile walking loop around the estate known as the Craftsman's Trail, with excellent specimens of wildflowers and plants native to this elevation.

By his own admission (as if you couldn't guess from the book jacket), writer Scott Nicholson of Boone has set his 2004 horror novel, *The Manor*, in a house that looks like the one the Cones built:

Moses H. Cone Manor House, called Korban Manor in novelist Scott Nicholson's 2004 thriller,
The Manor.

The forest ended and Korban Manor stood before them like something out
of an antique postcard. The open fields fell away to a soft well of orchard,
a patchwork of meadows, and two barns stitched together with fencing.
The manor itself was three outsized stories high, tall the way they were
built in the late 1800s, six colonial columns supporting the portico ceiling
at the entrance. Black shutters framed the windows against the white sid-
ing. Four chimneys puffed away, the smoke swirling through the giant red
oaks and poplars that surrounded the house.

　　Atop the roof was a widow's walk, a flattened area with a lonely railing.
He wondered if any widows had ever walked those boards. Probably. One

thing about an old house, you could be sure that somebody had died there, probably a whole lot of somebodies.—From *The Manor*, by Scott Nicholson (New York: Pinnacle Books, 2004), 14.

In Nicholson's story, the Manor is a retreat for artists and writers who come to do their work in the company of other talented artists, but without benefit of electricity. The central character, Mason Jackson, is a young sculptor who has just won a grant from the North Carolina Arts Council to be in residence at the Manor. Among the guests is Anna Galloway, a woman with psychic powers who believes that Korban's ghost haunts the house. Nicholson's writing is witty and vivid. He has been compared to Stephen King and Sharyn McCrumb.

Though there may be a ghost or two in this manor house, you're more likely to find something handcrafted that you'll want to take home. Here the Southern Highland Craft Guild maintains an extensive collection of crafts from a nine-state region. Visiting this elegant storehouse of take-home treasures also gives you a chance to take in the exceptional views from the porch that Nicholson describes. For hours of operation, call 828-295-7938.

Continue south down the Parkway. On the left you'll soon pass Sims Creek Pond (just before milepost 296), where there is an excellent hike if you're so inclined. Just a bit farther is Julian Price Park, where there is a serene fishing pond and easy camping. On down the road a ways on the southeast side of Grandfather Mountain, you'll drive over the Linn Cove Viaduct, the last section of the 469-mile Parkway to be built. Engineering technology had to catch up with the rugged mountain ledges that required a cantilevered road. This dizzying stretch was not completed until 1986.

As you make your way, watch for milepost 310 and the view there of Lost Cove cliffs. Pull off the Parkway here to read about the Brown Mountain Lights, which have a most remarkable literary connection.

■ BROWN MOUNTAIN LIGHTS

As John Parris tells it: "Jutting out of the Catawba Valley like a grim prophecy is the mountain that provided the locale for a best selling mystery novel, *Kill One, Kill Two.* It is the famous Brown Mountain where mysterious balls of fire gambol across its summit in the night when the moon is down and the stars are too sleepy to wink" (*Roaming the Mountains*, 50).

The occurrence of roaming lights over Brown Mountain has spawned many theories. Could it be the result of the phosphorescent fungus known as foxfire that grows in rotting wood? Is it the reflection of automobile or locomotive headlights in fog? Perhaps the best theory is offered by William G. Lord in the *Blue Ridge Parkway Guide* (New York: Eastern Acorn Press, 1982). He suggests that "Percey Slewfoot, a mythical moonshiner, is brewing a batch of incandescent mountain dew" up there.

The Brown Mountain Lights, whatever their source, gained the attention of Jules Verne, the enormously popular and prophetic science fiction writer who penned *20,000 Leagues Under the Sea* (1869) and *Around the World in Eighty Days* (1872). Verne, who wrote a book a year for some forty years, lived his entire life in France and visited the United States once, for only a week in 1867. Though he never set foot in North Carolina, he did perform extensive research for all his books. At some point in his library excursions, he must have run across an account of the Brown Mountain Lights, which became the jumping off point for his 1904 novel *Master of the World*:

> The strange occurrences began in the western part of our great American State of North Carolina. There, deep amid the Blueridge Mountains rises the crest called the Great Eyrie. Its huge rounded form is distinctly seen from the little town of Morganton on the Catawba River, and still more clearly as one approaches the mountains by way of the village of Pleasant Garden. . . . A glow in the sky had crowned the height at night.
>
> When the wind blew the smoky cloud eastward toward Pleasant Garden, a few cinders and ashes drifted down from it. And finally one stormy night pale flames, reflected from the clouds above the summit, cast upon the district below a sinister, warning light. . . .
>
> In presence of these strange phenomena, it is not astonishing that the people of the surrounding district became seriously disquieted. And to the disquiet was joined an imperious need of knowing the true condition of the mountain. The Carolina newspapers had flaring headlines, "The Mystery of Great Eyrie!" They asked if it was not dangerous to dwell in such a region. Their articles aroused curiosity and fear — curiosity among those who being in no danger themselves were interested in the disturbance merely as a strange phenomenon of nature, fear in those who were likely to be the victims if a catastrophe actually occurred. Those more immediately threatened were the citizens of Morganton, and even more the good folk of Pleasant Garden and the hamlets and farms yet closer to the mountain. — From *Works of Jules Verne* (1911), <http://jv.gilead.org.il/vt/world/world.chp01.html>.

Verne's character John Strock, a top U.S. government investigator, is sent to solve the mystery, and things get worse before they get better. Ultimately the setting bears little resemblance to the Brown Mountain area. A film adaptation of the book was made in 1961 starring Vincent Price, but it conflates the incidents in *Master of the World* with another Verne novel, resulting in a story even more fantastical and removed from North Carolina as we know it.

Our next destination is Linville Falls, between milepost 316 and 317 on the Parkway.

▓ LINVILLE FALLS

The Linville River Gorge is remote and rugged. The Linville River flows through the steep walls of the gorge, dropping 2,000 feet over the course of its journey. Here is Salisbury writer Christian Reid's elegant description from the late 1800s:

> The gorge is fifteen miles in length, and the heights, which overshadow it, are in many places not less than two thousand feet high. The river plunges into its dark depths in a beautiful fall, and then rushes forward over a bed of rock. Cliffs worn by the ceaseless action of the water into the most fantastic shapes lean over it; detached masses of granite strew its channel, and the tumult of its fretted water only ceases when it falls now and then into crystal pools of placid gentleness. Along its course the Table-Rock rises with perpendicular face, the Hawkbill stands with curved beak of overhanging rock, and Short-off Mountain looks down on dancing water.—From *The Land of the Sky*, by Christian Reid (Alexander, N.C.: Land of the Sky Books, 2001), xii.

Park at the Linville Falls turnout on the Parkway and take the short hike down to see the dramatic falls. Black Mountain poet Marita Garin offers this companion poem for your hike:

CLIMBING TO LINVILLE FALLS
1
Air over the mountain rises
shaping itself into someone's dream

Beside the path
soft green thorns brush our skin
rhododendron twist toward light

in that cage
their branches locked

2
At the falls the children run
toward noise

their screams flatten
against the torrent gathering
everything into itself

We climb the massive rocks
edges smoothed away
by the clear purpose
of water

3
If you could feel water
cutting through layers
leaving mark after mark

If your body were rock
and water could ridge your flesh
the way time has wrinkled this rock
into folds

you would close your eyes
Nothing else would matter

4
High on the trail
your husband and children call
empty voices drifting
among the hemlock props

You're not ready
to leave
Something waits for you here

where nothing holds back
and everything returns to itself

5
Near the falls eyes watch you
from inside rock
a shadow moving inside a shadow
snake or some thin thing
living in a hollow

In such darkness life begins
or ends

asleep as deliberate
as earth turning to rock

Indifferent to your body
water churns over ledges

6
At night the stars
are tiny threads of light
knotted in place

Your family gathers on a hillside
around a cone of flame
You reach for them
Your hands are shadows

Trying to touch them
the way water moves against rock.
—Used by permission of Marita Garin

The town of Linville Falls is less than a mile down the Parkway from here. Exit the Parkway onto US 221 South. You'll find several eateries, including Famous Louise's Rockhouse Restaurant. This historic roadhouse, built of river rock and popular with tourists for decades, serves homestyle meals. You can choose to dine in one of three counties—Avery, McDowell, or Burke. The county lines run through the building and are so noted above the tables. Call for hours: 828-765-2702.

■ LINVILLE CAVERNS

From here you may want to drive a few more miles down US 221 to visit Linville Caverns, North Carolina's only natural limestone caverns and a memory-in-waiting for children. Poet Michael McFee offers his take on this historic tourist attraction:

LINVILLE CAVERNS

Our guide's a walking stalagmite, a pale kid
with his certificate in Creative Geology.
He swipes a flashlight at nicknamed formations—
Franciscan Monk, Taco Meat, The Capitol Dome.
We can't see a thing, so we make up our own:
Revival Preacher, Indigestion, The Senator at Play.

He infects the mountain's sinus with his drone:
the cave-stream trout that are "98 percent blind,"
the fate of the Union and Confederate deserters
who hid in this chilly hell during the War,
the star-crossed Linville Lovers. . . . We gasp
with laughter as he hurtles us along, passing

The other shivering tour groups, squeezing
deeper and deeper into the dripping caverns.
"Please don't touch the formations," he warns.
"There are salts and oils on the human skin:
if you touch them, they'll stop growing forever."
"Don't touch," we echo. "Human skin. Forever."

Suddenly we're alone, wedged in a cul-de-sac.
"Have you ever experienced Total Darkness?" he asks,
then hits the lights and leaves us suffocating
there in the black too absolute for metaphor.
And then we hear a distant voice, a curse:
"You might go blind, but you'll go crazy first."
—From *Colander*, by Michael McFee (Pittsburgh:
   Carnegie Mellon University Press, 1996), 73.

■ TABLE ROCK AND HAWKSBILL

To continue this tour come back up 221 and then take NC 183 to the right out of Linville Falls. At the junction of 183 and 181, follow 181 south, down the mountain. If you're in the mood for a good hike, watch for Old Gingercake Road coming in on your right just three miles down NC 181. Turn right on Old Gingercake and go 0.3 miles to the fork. Then turn left on Gingercake Acres Road, which will become Forest Road 210. Along this road you'll pass the Devil's Hole Trail parking area in 2.6 miles, then come to the steep Hawksbill Mountain Trail in another 1.3 miles. Here you can park on the left; the trail is on the right. Hawksbill (4,020 feet) is popular with rock climbers but is a much more rigorous climb than the path to the summit of Table Rock, which is just ahead.

In another couple of miles watch for Forest Road 210B, which leads to the Table Rock picnic area and the mile-long rocky trail to the top of Table Rock (3,909 feet). It's not a tough hike for the rewards of a 360-degree view and a fresh appreciation for the rugged landscape of the Linville Gorge.

From this point retrace your route and continue down the mountain on NC 181 to reach the final stop on this tour.

■ MORGANTON

In the 1800s, Morganton was the center of commerce for settlers who lived and farmed much higher up in the hills from which you've just come. Morganton was the place where John Ehle's hardscrabble farmer, August King, made his regular trips down the mountain to sell ginseng and buy provisions and stock animals in the novel *The Journey of August King* (1971). Set in the mid-1800s, the novel describes August King's encounter with an enslaved woman who is attempting to escape north. King helps her and, in the process, finds a new identity for himself.

Morganton is also the setting for much of Sharyn McCrumb's novel, *The Ballad of Frankie Silver*—a masterful mystery that weaves a contemporary story of domestic violence with the legend of Frankie Silver. Silver was hanged in 1833 for killing her husband with an axe and, with the help of her mother and brother, attempting (unsuccessfully) to burn the body in the fireplace of their cabin. More on this story and novelist Sharyn McCrumb in Tour 16, when we visit the grave of Frankie's husband, Charlie. But for now, here's an excerpt from the novel:

> Frankie Silver and her mother and brother were under lock and key in
> the wooden house that served as Morganton's jail, and all the town was
> talking about the dreadful crimes that had happened in the wild land
> beyond the mountains. . . . It would be two months before that fair-haired
> girl and her kinfolk would answer for the crime, and I wondered where
> an impartial jury could be found in all of Burke County, and who among
> my colleagues would be fool enough to defend them. . . . The morning

after Constable Charlie Baker brought his prisoners down the mountain to Morganton, he headed home again, back past Celo Mountain and into the valley of the Toe River, named for the legendary Cherokee maiden Estatoe, a star-crossed Juliet of the Indian nation. It was a good day's ride up the Yellow Mountain Road even in high summer. Now, with a foot of snow on the trail, and winds like knife blades slicing through the passes it was bound to be a bitter journey, but at least the constable could travel faster and easier in his mind without three dangerous prisoners in tow.—From *The Ballad of Frankie Silver*, by Sharyn McCrumb (New York: Signet Books, 1998), 64–65.

Around the time of Frankie Silver's incarceration, as journalist John Parris describes it,

Morganton was a budding settlement of log cabins then, seat of government of the westernmost county of the State of North Carolina, and her domain stretched all the way to the Mississippi River. . . . The town's streets had been named for the streets of Charleston, the city to which early mountain dwellers went for their loaf sugar and Jamaican rum, and later for slaves brought from Africa.—From *Roaming the Mountains*, by John Parris, 33.

Until the Civil War, the North Carolina Supreme Court met in Morganton for its summer sessions. Perhaps because of that legacy as a spot for important state government functions, Morganton was later chosen toward the end of the nineteenth century as the site for the North Carolina School for the Deaf and for Broughton Hospital, serving patients with mental illness. In recent years Morganton has been adopted by a growing Hmong community—political refugees from Southeast Asia—and by significant numbers of people from Central America.

Morganton was also the birthplace of one of North Carolina's most distinguished public servants, Senator Sam Ervin Jr. Ervin, who achieved national stature as the steady but outspoken chair of the Senate Watergate Committee in the 1970s, was also a masterful storyteller. His books include *Quotations from Chairman Sam: The Wit and Wisdom of Senator Sam Ervin* (1973), *The Whole Truth: The Watergate Conspiracy* (1980), *Humor of a Country Lawyer* (1983), and *Preserving the Constitution! The Autobiography of Senator Sam J. Ervin* (1984).

The Senator Sam J. Ervin Jr. Library and Museum are located on the campus of Western Piedmont Community College on US 64 between I-40 and Business

Senator Sam Ervin, a prolific writer and statesman, made Morganton famous. The portrait is in the Senator Sam J. Ervin, Jr. Library and Museum.

70. The re-creation of Ervin's office in a special area in the main library feels as if Senator Sam has just stepped out for a moment. Visitors can peruse the books that surrounded and inspired him and examine the collection of memorabilia from his long career as a lawyer and statesman.

DIRECTIONS

Coming in on NC 181, take Sanford Drive to the right, cross West Union and continue on Sanford until you come to US 64. Turn right on 64 and watch for the entrance to Western Piedmont Community College on your left. Follow signs to the Phifer Learning Resources Center (828-438-6195), which houses the college library upstairs. Here you can also get a brochure that will lead you to the senator's childhood and adult homes on Lenoir Street just north of downtown Morganton and to the Forest Hill Cemetery, where he is buried.

To visit downtown Morganton from Western Piedmont Community College, follow US 64/Burkemont Avenue back the same way you came. Cross US 70, and soon you will run into West Union Street. Turn right toward town. Here you'll find books, good food, and interesting architecture.

While you're downtown you may want to pay your respects to the Muses. *Sacred Dance and the Muses*, by fresco artist Ben Long, depicts the earthly representations of the goddesses of arts and literature. It is in the City of Morganton

Memorial Auditorium, best known as COMMA, located at the intersection of West Union and South College Streets. COMMA is a highly regarded venue for concerts and dramatic productions. Call 828-433-7469 for hours.

As the largest county in western North Carolina, Burke is also well known for Lake James, one among several Duke Power reservoirs created by damming the Catawba River. To see the lake, head out of town on NC 126 toward Marion.

Poet R. T. Smith concludes this tour with a vivid poem about the lake. Smith was born in Washington, D.C., and raised in North Carolina. He studied at the University of North Carolina and Appalachian State, where he founded the literary magazine *Cold Mountain Review* in 1973. He then taught at Auburn University for nineteen years and now edits the literary journal *Shenandoah* at Washington and Lee University in Virginia. This poem captures the still-rugged quality of Burke County:

SUPPOSE A MAN
Has backpacked to the low shoals of Lake James
below where the Linville River cuts its gorge
to fish alone

and has spread his camp by a shallow stream
where the white pulse feeds the lake
and has stepped into the lake to wash

and he has stepped on a ledge of shale and shell
that opens a seam in his right sole
where the red threads of life seep out
and head for the lake's calm heart.

And alone by the Coleman lantern
where silk mantles whisper white light
he finds the rip deep and knows somewhere before
time he has lived in

that he must take a risk to mend

that he must sew up the flesh
with fifteen-pound test line to walk out,
that he must soak the black cord in boiling bourbon
to sterilize, to save his life.

Suppose a man
down on his luck and alone by the lake's dark shiver

lies backed against poplar and leads the line
with an unbarbed hook through his foot
as the threads of his own life sort out and swim
as the red blood spreads to feed the fish
as the river flows into a lake
the color of his eyes

and the red threads salt the water

and he knots the cord that splices him and dreams
of the grandfather fading into ground fog
of the neglected son sleeping in his cowboy bunk
of the sun shimmering the lake to fire-dazzle
as the nightjars whisper
and game creeps to the lake edge to sip water
wry with his raveled blood

and in dreams he feels the right leg jump as if a great
beast has struck the bait
and feels the tense draw on his stitching and the deep fight

and the pulse humming through the sole
and eyelids surrender all hope of sight

Then the wild bass appear leaping
high in the tidelight of dream

and suppose he can cut a crutch from the pale maple
and limp for three days back up the laurel path
sleeping in the mercy of the wood
and find the ranch wagon and drive
with a limb pressing the accelerator
and suppose he can find a doctor
and lockjaw shot in time and can step whole

from the delirium of seeing the Big Dipper
pour his history into water.

And suppose he can survive his own death
in some private and behind-the-heart sense

and can rattle the ice in his sweating tumbler
and feel his tongue thicken with gin,

can sit across the table where one lamp's light
is pooling deep,
look hard and long at you
and tell you this story of small terror
where the watersnakes whipped in the riversilt
and the boomer quaked across the night
and the wild owl spoke his insatiable hunger
against all motion

and suppose he
looks into your centercut bole of brown eye and says:
this is how it unfolds, the line unreeling as fast as the
catch sounds
and the high whine of the wobbling spinner
until you grasp the crank and roll it up
like a man pulling clear water from the red clay source
of the only well within miles, artesian and magical.

And suppose he can give you the smile sudden as a
slice into flesh
with the unselfish blood pouring
like a drought-ending deluge.

Suppose he can give you this gift,
can catch you in his survivor's tense rhythm—
will you feel your heart and his tethered,
your blood go to water, then wine?

Will you know that to live by other than bread
you must surpass your own breath,
let the barb of belief snag you
and the line cut across your life,

know that just receiving the story cannot purify
unless you share the solitude
and feel the pain ignite in your step
like the moon seen burning in the lake
by one man wildly wounded and fighting to survive?

And will you testify?
—From *From the High Dive*, by R. T. Smith
     (Huntington, N.Y.: Water Mark Press, 1983), 10–12.

Wilkes County's sleek new public library.

Wilkes County Public Library

215 Tenth Street

North Wilkesboro, NC 28659

336-838-2818

<http://www.arlibrary.org/index.php?page=8>

This expansive library is a rightful source of pride for Wilkes County. Literature lives here with regular meetings of a book club, guest speakers, and a lively forum for community exchanges. Extensive genealogical information and files on local writers are part of the collections.

Wilkes Playmakers

Benton Hall

300 D Street

North Wilkesboro, North Carolina 28659

336-838-7529

<http://www.wilkesplaymakers.com>

Tom Dooley: A Wilkes County Legend is a popular play presented annually in summer by the Wilkes Playmakers. The production includes local musicians and square dancing. The Playmakers also present other community productions year-round.

MerleFest

P.O. Box 120

Wilkesboro, NC 28697

800-343-7857

merlefest@wilkescc.edu

<http://www.merlefest.org>

Every April, the Wilkes Community College hosts MerleFest—one of the largest bluegrass/country music festivals in the United States. The annual singer/songwriter competition is a popular feature of the festival that was named for Watauga County native Merle Watson, the late son of the guitarist/singer Doc Watson.

Blowing Rock Stage Company

152 Jamie Fort Road

Blowing Rock, NC 28605

828-295-9627 (tickets)

info@blowingrockstage.com

<http://www.blowingrockstage.com/>

For more than twenty years, this professional theater has produced popular classics and premiered the work of North Carolina writers, including several works by Charlotte novelist Robert Inman.

Tucker's on Main

1116 South Main Street, Unit 5

Blowing Rock NC 28605

828-295-4231

Tucker's on Main is set back from Main Street, close to Memorial Park. This store places an emphasis on regional writers and regularly hosts readings and book signings. The Internet café here is a nice addition to their selection of books.

Gideon Ridge Inn

202 Gideon Ridge Road

Blowing Rock, NC 28605

828-295-3644

<http://gideonridge.com/>

This elegant, slate-roofed inn has had a long association with the Creative Writing Program in the English department at Appalachian State University and plays host to the writers who come to teach and read in nearby Boone. Signed copies of dozens of visiting writers' works are a significant part of the inn's library. The inn's owners, Cobb and Cindy Milner, won a Governor's Business Award in the Arts and Humanities in 2000 for their years of support for the writing program at ASU.

The Muses

820 West Union Street

Morganton, NC 28655

828-433-1314

Morganton's premier bookstore, The Muses, began in 1972. Shirley Sprinkle and her daughter, Kelly Treiber, manage the operation. Here you can find out-of-print copies of several notable works, including Jules Verne's *Master of the World* and Anne Hall Whitt's autobiographical story, *The Suitcases*, which is discussed in Tour 17. This feisty independent bookstore has hosted many nationally recognized writers, including Jean Auel, John Jakes, and David Balducchi, among others.

Marion : Little Switzerland : Spruce Pine : Penland : Bandana : Kona : Bakersville : Roan Mountain : Banner Elk

Visit the three graves of one man. Explore indigenous crafts that have been practiced and written about for decades. Take in the vistas from the Roan and try to imagine the luxury hotel that once straddled the state line between Tennessee and North Carolina.

Writers with a connection to this area: Doris Betts, LeGette Blythe, Bill Carson, Thomas Dixon, Hilda Downer, Louisa Duls, Julia Nunnally Duncan, John Ehle, the Hicks Family, Gloria Houston, Elizabeth Hunter, Jennifer Bauer Laughlin, Sharyn McCrumb, Robert Morgan, Margaret Morley, Marjorie Kinnan Rawlings, Christian Reid, Carolyn Sakowski, Muriel Earley Sheppard, Jonathan Williams, Perry Deane Young

■ **MARION**

Since the cotton mills have closed, Marion now depends on the sale of native stone, lumber milling, a thread plant, and many small businesses. The town also serves as a gateway for tourists to the highest part of the Blue Ridge Mountains. In recent years, downtown redevelopment has created new venues for entertainment in Marion. Local musicians regularly perform in coffeehouses and in several restaurants that have moved in to occupy historic buildings.

Marion is also home to novelist and short story writer Julia Nunnally Duncan, who grew up here. Duncan earned her MFA at Warren Wilson College and teaches writing at McDowell Technical Community College. Her short stories are collected in *Blue Ridge Shadows* (2002), and her first novel is *The Stonecutter* (2005). Duncan's fiction reflects the cotton mill culture

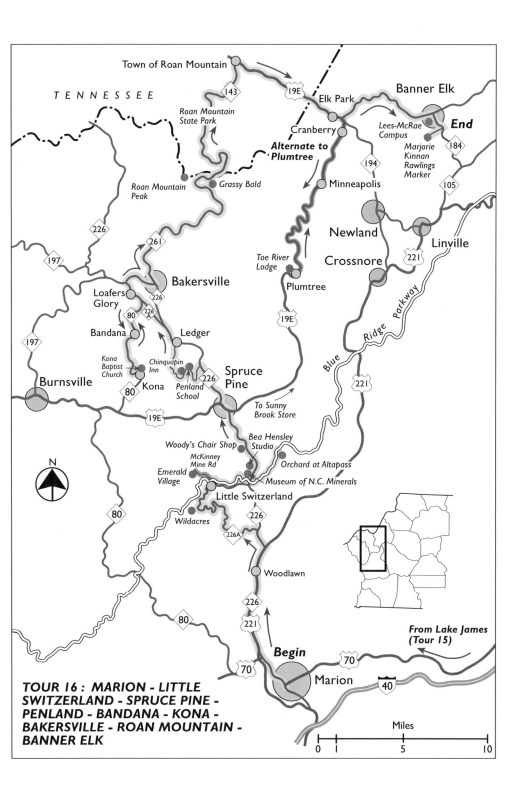

TENNESSEE

Town of Roan Mountain

143

19E

Elk Park

Banner Elk

Roan Mountain
State Park

Cranberry

Lees-McRae
Campus

End

184

Alternate to
Plumtree

194

Marjorie
Kinnan
Rawlings
Marker

105

Roan Mountain
Peak

Grassy Bald

Minneapolis

226

261

Newland

Crossnore

Linville

197

Bakersville

Loafers
Glory

226

80

226
A

Bandana

Ledger

Kona
Baptist
Church

Chinquapin
Inn

Toe River
Lodge

Plumtree

19E

221

221

226

Spruce
Pine

To Sunny
Brook Store

Penland
School

Burnsville

80

Kona

19E

Bea Hensley
Studio

Woody's Chair Shop

McKinney
Mine Rd

Orchard at Altapass

Emerald
Village

Museum of N.C. Minerals

Little Switzerland

N

Wildacres

226

226A

80

Woodlawn

226

221

Begin

From Lake James
(Tour 15)

80

70

70

Marion

40

Miles

0   1   5   10

**TOUR 16: MARION - LITTLE
SWITZERLAND - SPRUCE PINE -
PENLAND - BANDANA - KONA -
BAKERSVILLE - ROAN MOUNTAIN -
BANNER ELK**

and colorful small town characters in and around Marion, which she calls "Milton" in her books.

From Marion, we travel to the picturesque village of Little Switzerland, which sits on the line between McDowell and Mitchell Counties. Follow the combined US 221 and NC 226 approximately five miles out of town and through the community of Woodlawn. Watch for the turn to Little Switzerland on NC 226, which goes off to the left just beyond a large sawmill on the right. It is 1.3 miles from this turn to the intersection where 226 turns right and climbs four miles to the Blue Ridge Parkway at the Museum of North Carolina Minerals. However, the literary tourist may be more interested in following 226A straight ahead. This slower, winding road climbs directly to Little Switzerland.

■ WILDACRES

About halfway up the mountain on 226A, watch for Wildacres Road on your left. This property of more than a thousand acres once belonged to writer Thomas Dixon, who made and lost several fortunes over his lifetime. Dixon, a Shelby native whom we first met in Tour 13, was best known for his advocacy of racial purity as expressed in his novel *The Clansman*, the book upon which the controversial film *Birth of a Nation* was based. With royalties from the film, Dixon bought the acreage on Pompey's Knob right here in McDowell County and named it Wildacres. He then set about to create a colony where writers and artists might do their work in the isolated beauty of the Blue Ridge.

Dixon built a dormitory and assembly hall, a dining hall, and several other buildings. He also planned to sell private lots for artists to build studios and summer homes. He published an elaborate sales brochure in 1926, and when the artists did not materialize he opened Wildacres to the general public, bringing busloads of prospective buyers to the mountain. The effort bore little fruit. With the stock market crash of 1929, Dixon was forced to declare bankruptcy, and the property went into receivership through a bank in Austin, Texas. The mortgage was valued at $190,000.

According to historian Louisa Duls, the Texas bank itself went under in 1932, and by 1936 the property was up for sale at auction. I. D. Blumenthal, a business owner in Charlotte, heard about the Wildacres tract from his real estate agent and was told he could probably make a bid as low as $6,500 on the property and win the auction because no one else knew about it. After attending the National Conference of Christians and Jews at nearby Ridgecrest that summer, Blumenthal visited the property, accompanied by his rabbi. He was excited by the possibilities and put in a bid as the realtor had suggested.

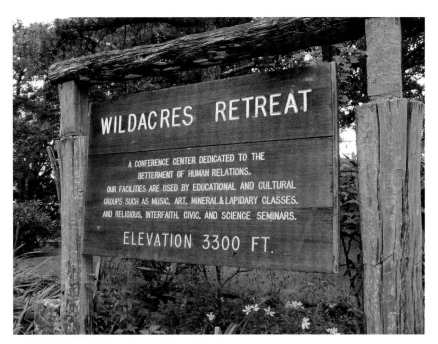

Wildacres Retreat is now dedicated to the betterment of human relations and hosts an annual writing workshop for writers at all stages of development.

Blumenthal's offer was the only one tendered at the auction, but the judge in Texas was wary. How could so many acres be worth so little? He sent an appraiser to North Carolina to see the property and determine its worth. Blumenthal met the appraiser in Asheville on a beautiful day, but as they drove up the mountain, a deep fog began to roll in. As Duls describes it: "They went through the buildings by flashlight but could see almost nothing. And, of course, the appraiser was unaware of the magnificent views from the knob. He must have told the judge that the property was overvalued" (*The Story of Little Switzerland*, by Louisa DeSaussure Duls [Richmond, Va.: Whittet & Shepperson, 1982], 165).

Blumenthal won the auction and declared Wildacres a gift from God. He later dedicated the retreat to "the betterment of human relations and interfaith amity"—a purpose that profoundly contradicted Thomas Dixon's separatist vision. Today, dozens of cultural, religious, civic, and nonprofit groups regularly use Wildacres for retreats, conferences, and concerts, always with an emphasis on encouraging better understanding among diverse peoples. The old structures that Dixon built were gradually replaced with new buildings in the 1970s, and Wildacres is now open to groups from April to October. Among several literary programs, the annual Wildacres Writers Workshop brings more than a hundred writers to the mountaintop to study fiction, poetry, nonfiction, and playwriting each summer. See <http://www.wildacres.com/>.

Administered by the Blumenthal family of Charlotte, Wildacres also offers a residency program for writers and artists who may come free of charge to the mountaintop to live in an isolated log cabin and work on a project for a week at a time. While the grounds are not open for public tours, some concerts and lectures are available to the public. For more information, visit: <http://www.wildacres.org>.

◼ LITTLE SWITZERLAND

You'll know when you reach the top of the mountain that you are in Little Switzerland. This small community at the intersection of NC 226A and the Blue Ridge Parkway includes some 300 houses scattered in the woods, two restaurants, several shops, a post office, an ice cream store, a gallery, and an Alpine-themed inn. It was originally developed by a group of Charlotte attorneys and businessmen in 1906, and some of the original cottages remain in use from that era. The developers bought more than 1,000 acres on Grassy Mountain to create this resort, designed as an escape from the summer heat of the Queen City. Upon visiting the spot for the first time back in the early 1900s, one of the visitors from Charlotte declared that the spectacular views here reminded her of the Jura Mountains in Switzerland. The idea stuck, and Little Switzerland has been its name ever since. Today Little Switzerland is the only commercial village that is immediately adjacent to the 469-mile Blue Ridge Parkway, permitted here because it preceded the construction of the Parkway.

For the literary tourist, the Little Switzerland Book Exchange is home to one of the best collections of used and rare books in the state. The store is particularly strong in southern literature and books by North Carolina writers in all genres. In fact, a number of the more obscure, out-of-print titles cited in these trails can be found at the "LSBX," as it has come to be known under the ownership of Thomas and Donna Wright. The proprietors have an amazing ability to help customers find just what they are looking for among more than 100,000 wide-ranging titles—all without a computerized index system. The café next door—and especially the smoked trout BLT—come highly recommended by the writers who regularly visit here to give readings and sign books.

Little Switzerland appears in *Heading West* (1981), a novel by University of North Carolina at Chapel Hill professor emerita Doris Betts. In the ominous first chapter excerpted below, Betts introduces the man who will soon kidnap librarian Nancy Finch while she is traveling on the Blue Ridge Parkway with her sister and brother-in-law. Their journey west as kidnapper and victim is the basis for the entire novel.

He ate Sunday lunch in Little Switzerland. His waitress in the rustic inn was young and energetic; winters as a majorette she marched in Christmas parades. "We're always glad to have you northerners see our mountains," she prattled. He was not a northerner. She served small bowls of vegetables. "And the rain is over at last. One of the rangers claimed that the animals were lining up in the park two by two—you get it? For the new ark?"

Though the man said nothing, she chattered about a highway washout, the mineral show in Spruce Pine, the sourwood honey for sale down the road. The man thought briefly of taking her with him to Florida just to listen to her soft southern voice run on about nothing. Better than the radio. . . .

In the mid-afternoon, driving toward Asheville, he saw ahead the blinking blue light that meant police, so with a U-turn at Craggy Gardens he sped back the other way. Perhaps he should get off the main road until dark. He could have driven to Mount Mitchell Tower or blended with the crowd at the mineral museum but opted for distance and, at last, a rough unpaved road that promised picnic areas and Lake James at its far end.

Once off the manicured parkway he found the rocky road steep, curving, hemmed in by chokeberry and dog hobble. On one side lay Linville Gorge, twelve miles of wilderness where Marines practiced survival tactics and Boy Scouts sometimes died. He had never cared much for woods or mountains. Cursing, he bounced on the seat and fought the steep grade until he came finally to an empty parking area with three stone platforms built over the great ravine. Deep under clotted trees he parked, stood impassive in the cool shade. Everything smelled of black dirt and worms.

He walked down the huge granite stairs to sit on the stone wall of the overlook. Far below, the Linville River, brown with silt, ran between steep walls and hemlocks as blue green as the sea. Across the gorge were sheer gray cliffs with galax and myrtle clinging in the cracks. None of it interested him. He lay back on the stone, folding his jacket for a pillow. By accident the gun barrel rested in the groove behind his neck like an extended spine. He liked the danger and was soon asleep.—From *Heading West*, by Doris Betts (New York: Alfred A. Knopf, 1981), 7–8.

Note that Betts also mentions the Museum of North Carolina Minerals, which is three miles north of Little Switzerland on the Blue Ridge Parkway. As described in Tour 11, Mitchell and Yancey Counties have long been recognized for the wide range of gems and minerals found here. Today, the area's extraction industry revolves around feldspar, an inexpensive byproduct of the mica that was key to the local economy beginning in the late 1800s. You can see evidence of feldspar mining on the tops of the mountains above Spruce Pine, which appear to be snow-covered at first glance. "Spar," as it is called here, is ground into a fine powder and used in the production of sinks, toilets, and other porcelain products. It is also an abrasive often used in scrubbing powders.

Spruce Pine hosts an annual gem show in August every year, and rock hounds from around the country drive in to show and share their collections. But before you head into Spruce Pine, a good place to have a hands-on experience of the history of local mining is Emerald Village, on the west side of the Parkway, 3.1 miles from Little Switzerland.

Emerald Village is a historic mine that now caters to visitors. Blue signs posted at the main intersection in Little Switzerland will direct you along Chestnut Grove Church Road to McKinney Mountain Road, where the Big McKinney and Bon Ami Mines once operated. For more information and hours call 828-765-6463.

In addition to panning for gems and touring the old mining facility, you many wander freely in a massive rock pile of native quartz, feldspar, and mica while reading this poem (a pantoum) by Robert Morgan, who hails from Zirconia—a small village in Transylvania County to the west, also named for an unusual mineral.

MICA COUNTRY
Here in the poorest mine country
in the dust of Dog Day drought,
the road itself glitters and weeds
along the bank and meadow sparkle.

In the dust of Dog Day drought
dirt of fields and spoil heap sides
along the bank and meadow sparkle,
and mud in the stream, all gilded.

Dirt of fields and spoil heap sides
and manure piles show millions,

and mud in streams, all gilded
with little mirrors, like fish scales,

and manure piles show millions,
where a farmer plows a milky way
of little mirrors, like fish scales,
and each mote and grain is brighter

where a farmer plows a milky way
than dew or facet or window,
and each mote and grain is brighter
to reflect in luminous soil

through dew or facet or window,
the glare of blinding poverty
reflected in the luminous soil
here in the poorest mine country.
—From *Sigodlin* (Middletown, Conn.:
    Wesleyan University Press, 1990), 53.

To get back to the Blue Ridge Parkway from Emerald Village, return to Little Switzerland the way you came. From here, it is three miles north on the Parkway to the Museum of North Carolina Minerals and the Parkway Visitor Center at NC 226.

While you are on the Parkway and before heading into Spruce Pine, you may want to drive three more miles north from the Museum of North Carolina Minerals to visit the Orchard at Altapass, just beyond milepost 328 on the right. Bill and Judy Carson have fastidiously maintained this 3,000-tree orchard at an elevation of more than 3,000 feet. Whether the many varieties of apples grown here are ready to pick or not, the orchard offers hayrides hosted by a local storyteller who provides the colorful history of the nearby community of Altapass. Take a stroll through the butterfly garden outside and study a working honeybee hive encased in glass inside the orchard headquarters. Live music on weekends often brings out dozens of cloggers from the area who fill the store with the rhythmic chatter of tap shoes. Local crafts, jams, fudge, ice cream, apple butter, and honey are always on sale here.

The Orchard at Altapass store also offers a good selection of local literature, including Bill Carson's collection of stories about the region. The Orchard often sponsors readings and performances by area writers. East Tennessee's Jo Carson, cousin to orchard owner Bill Carson, is an award-winning playwright and founder of the grassroots theater group, Alternate ROOTS. She periodically performs her work here based on oral histories she has collected in the area. For more information, call 828-765-9531 or visit <http://www.altapassorchard .com>.

■ SPRUCE PINE

To reach Spruce Pine, leave the Parkway at the intersection with NC 226 and head north. You may want to stop in the Museum of North Carolina Minerals and Visitors Center, where books on the area are available for purchase. Also check out the recently refurbished exhibit of local gems and minerals, under-written by the Blumenthal Foundation (proprietors of Wildacres). From here, Spruce Pine is six miles north on NC 226.

As you head toward town, just beyond the minerals museum, watch for the intersection with Dula Road immediately on your left. Here a sign directs visitors to the foundry and studio of Bea Hensley, a natural-born storyteller, who learned to produce ornamental ironwork from Daniel Boone VI and has been making wrought iron pieces on commission for presidents, Hollywood celebrities, and many others. Born in 1919, Hensley was the recipient of a 1995 National Heritage Fellowship Award, presented by the White House. He is featured in Robert Isbell's *The Keepers: Mountain Folk Holding on to Old Skills and Talents* (1999). North Carolina poet Jonathan Williams, profiled in Tour 3, also captured Hensley's distinctive storytelling voice in this poem:

BEA HENSLEY HAMMERS AN IRON CHINQUAPIN
LEAF ON HIS ANVIL NEAR SPRUCE PINE & COGITATES
ON THE NATURE OF TWO BEAUTY SPOTS

in the Linville Gorge I
know this place

now it's a rock wall
you look up
it's covered in punktatum all
the way to Heaven.

that's a
sight

.

up on Smoky
you ease up at daybust
and see the first
light in the tops of the tulip trees

now boys that just naturally
grinds and polishes
the soul

makes it
normal
again

I mean it's really
pretty!
—From *Blues and Roots/Rue and Bluets:*
   A Garland for the Southern Appalachians,
   by Jonathan Williams (Durham, N.C.:
   Duke University Press, 1985).

In another 2.5 miles look for Dale Road on your left, just around a blind curve. Here is Woody's Chair Shop, where Arval Woody, another of Mitchell County's living treasures, first learned his trade shortly after World War II. In *Cabins in the Laurel* (1935), Muriel Earley Sheppard describes the four generations of chair-makers before Arval:

The Woodys on Grassy Creek, who turn chairs on a lathe run by a water wheel when they are not grinding meal, will charge you at the same rate for one or two chairs as for ten, because they are all made as cheaply as it is possible to do it. Charlie Woody, the son, has been making chairs for twenty years. Art'ur, his father, has made them for forty. The grandfather, Henry Woody, made them before that, and so did the great-grandfather, Wyatt Woody, back in the days when John Strother was surveying the North Carolina–Tennessee line. The Woody chairs are fashioned in simple mountain style with comfortably curved two-slat backs. —From *Cabins in the Laurel*, by Muriel Earley Sheppard (Chapel Hill: University of North Carolina Press, 1991), 238.

Today Arval Woody represents his family's fifth generation of talented craftsmen. In the shop he proudly displays one of the original pieces made in

Arval Woody is a fifth-generation chairmaker in Mitchell County.

the fashion Sheppard describes. The slat-back chair, also known as a "mule ear chair" for the distinctive slant of the back, is perhaps the most comfortable in the shop and has been displayed at the Smithsonian Institution in Washington, D.C. Because the Woody family originally sold many of these chairs over the years at three for a dollar, it is still possible to find them in local antique shops. Arval Woody will quickly tell you, however, that the rocker his family made for President John F. Kennedy sold at auction not so long ago for $96,000. Today the new chairs in Woody's shop, made to order, sell for around $250, and each style has its own story.

Continue straight ahead on 226 through all the traffic signals. At the top of the last hill before you descend into Spruce Pine, notice the open feldspar veins in the mountains above town. This road crosses US 19E to become Oak Avenue. Continue across the bridge over the Toe River where the road comes to a "T." To the right are the upper and lower streets that compose downtown Spruce Pine. Head toward the train depot on the lower street and park for a look around town. The astute literary tourist may be wondering where the bus station is that was made famous in Doris Betts's most anthologized short story, "The Ugliest Pilgrim." This celebrated tale was adapted for television and later for *Violet* —the first Off-Broadway musical ever to win a Drama Critics Circle Award, in 1998. The story later served as the basis for an Academy Award–winning short film, also known as *Violet*.

In the story, Betts's character, Violet Karl, leaves her father at their home near Roan Mountain and travels down to Spruce Pine to catch a bus. As Betts reveals, Violet had been accidentally disfigured by a flying axe blade that struck her in the face as a child. As the story begins, she climbs aboard a Greyhound bus, hoping to be healed by the touch of a radio preacher in Tulsa, Oklahoma, whom she is determined to meet. What happens to Violet on her journey is not exactly what she planned.

"There is no bus station in Spruce Pine!" admits Shirley Hise, director of the Mitchell County Chamber of Commerce and a former English teacher at Mitchell High. "Doris Betts made that up."

What *is* in Spruce Pine—a town of about 2,000 residents—is the handsome old train depot and two busy streets where several new businesses and restaurants have been established in recent years. The antique shops and galleries featuring local art and crafts are definitely worth a visit. The annual Toe River Storytellers Festival takes place here in mid-July.

Judging by this description of Spruce Pine offered in *Littlejim*, a children's book by distinguished local writer Gloria Houston, the town hasn't changed much since the beginning of the twentieth century except for the preferred means of transportation:

> Littlejim had been into town twice in the past, but he had forgotten the bustle of the place. It seemed to him that everybody was in a hurry. He and his father approached the spot where the main road divided into Upper Street, higher up the hill parallel to the river, and Lower Street, lower on the hill parallel to the river. The number of wagons and carriages increased. Here and there, an automobile added its noise to the confusion.—From *Littlejim*, by Gloria Houston, illustrations by Thomas B. Allen (New York: Philomel Books, 1990), 119.

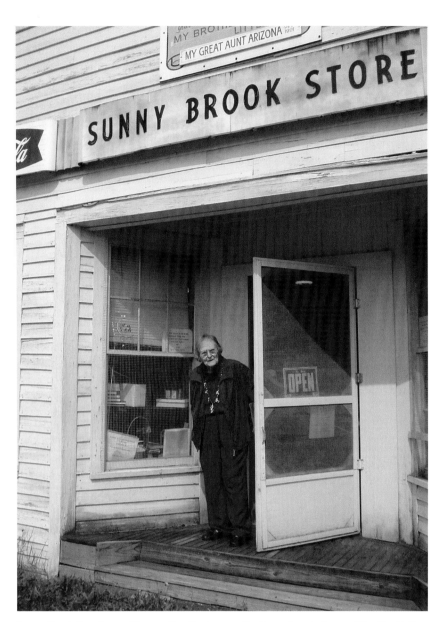

Sunny Brook Store beyond Spruce Pine (just across the Avery County line on US 19E) sells the works of children's author Gloria Houston. Her mother, Ruthie Houston, pictured here, is Gloria's biggest fan.

Beloved in Spruce Pine, Gloria Houston wrote *Littlejim* for and about her father, the late James Myron Houston, who in 1937 with his wife, Ruthie, opened the Sunny Brook Store, just up the road from Spruce Pine in Avery County. Myron Houston attended a log schoolhouse and aspired to be a writer, a dream his daughter has realized in spades. Gloria Houston's most successful work to date, *The Year of the Perfect Christmas Tree* (1988) is a picture book about her mother Ruthie's childhood that has sold nearly four million copies. Spruce Pine has, in turn, dubbed itself the "Home of the Perfect Christmas Tree" to celebrate Houston, a college professor who has now retired to Asheville.

Gloria Houston's mother, now in her nineties, still holds court at the Sunny Brook Store five miles north of Spruce Pine on US 19E. Ruthie Greene Houston has transformed the old grocery into a bookstore and museum celebrating her daughter's career. Autographed copies of Houston's work are available here, along with maps that point out various locations that Houston has written about in her books. Ruthie regularly entertains busloads of schoolchildren, who come to learn about a local-girl-made-good as a writer and to hear tales of the old ways of commerce in the early twentieth century.

Ruthie is fond of telling about her husband's job as a school bus driver. "He carried sixty children every day over sometimes treacherous mountain roads, for which he earned exactly one dollar a day," Ruthie says. She also explains how Sunny Brook Store let their customers buy groceries on credit during hard times, and how today she sells several thousand books to visitors and through mail order every year. Gloria Houston's extraordinary mother also awards "Ruthie" medals to outstanding young writers from Mitchell, Avery, and Yancey Counties each spring.

Though she now lives in Virginia, novelist Sharyn McCrumb's family roots are also in Mitchell County, dating back to the 1700s. Her great-grandfathers were circuit preachers here. An alumna of the University of North Carolina at Chapel Hill and Virginia Tech, McCrumb returned to her roots in her fiction. On her website, she explains: "My books are like Appalachian quilts. I take brightly colored scraps of legends, ballads, fragments of rural life, and local tragedy, and I piece them together into a complex whole that tells not only a story, but also a deeper truth about the culture of the mountain South" (see <http://www.sharynmccrumb.com>). McCrumb has written seven "ballad novels" as she calls them, that incorporate local legends, one of which will be considered later in this tour.

◼ PENLAND

Heading out of Spruce Pine on NC 226 North toward Bakersville, watch for Penland Road on the left in about two miles, marked by a large sign. Turn left. From here it is one mile to the sharp right turn marking the entrance to the internationally acclaimed Penland School of Crafts, founded in the 1920s by Lucy Morgan, whose life story was recorded by Charlotte journalist LeGette Blythe in *Gift from the Hills* (1958). Morgan, born in Franklin, North Carolina, was related to the Siler family described in Tour 4. "Miss Lucy" came to Penland in 1920 to obtain her teacher training at the Appalachian School run by her brother. At her brother's urging, Lucy took up weaving under the guidance of a ninety-year-old-woman named Aunt Susan Phillips. Then, after visiting the Berea School in Kentucky, where handicrafts were being taught and techniques preserved as part of the curriculum, Lucy Morgan came to understand her life's work. As she described it, "There were two things I very much wanted to do. The first was to help bring about a revival of hand-weaving, which in our country—I'm speaking of the nation now—had become all but a dead art. . . . The other thing I wanted to do was provide our neighbor mothers with a means of adding to their generally meager incomes without having to leave their homes" (*Gift from the Hills: Miss Lucy Morgan's Story of Her Unique Penland School*, by LeGette Blythe [New York: Bobbs-Merrill, 1958], 50).

Lucy Morgan dedicated her life to the school, which now covers 400 acres and has more than forty buildings. Some 1,200 students come here each year to take classes in ten craft media, including fiber arts, glassblowing, photography, metalworking, book and papermaking, pottery, and printmaking. The Penland Gallery—which is the first building you come to on your right after climbing 0.7 miles up the road to the school—offers the work of faculty, resident artists, students, and community artists in exhibition and for sale. Here you may also want to pick up a map of the dozens of local studios owned by area artists, many of whom have been associated with Penland through the years. Continue beyond the gallery, and in a half-mile you'll drive past the historic Craft Building, the Dye Shed, and the Dining Hall. Continue to the corner of Conley Ridge Road and Bill Brown Way. Turn right here where the Chinquapin Inn, a year-round bed and breakfast, is on your right.

This well-maintained gravel road will take you past the summer home of distinguished North Carolina writer and public servant John Ehle, whose works are cited in Tours 6, 12, and 15. Ehle served as an adviser to North Carolina governor Terry Sanford and helped to establish the North Carolina School of the Arts, the North Carolina Film Board, and the Institute for Outdoor Drama, among other important cultural resources in the state during the 1960s and 1970s. Born and raised in Asheville, he has written seventeen books, eleven fiction and six nonfiction. He has received the North Carolina Award for Literature, the John Tyler Caldwell Award for the Humanities, the Thomas Wolfe Prize, the Lillian Smith Award for Southern Fiction, and, on five occasions, the Sir Walter Raleigh Award for Fiction. Ehle's rambling old farm house, beyond Barking Spider Pottery and visible from the road, is not open to visitors and is a protected property on the National Register of Historic Places.

Soon you'll once again reach pavement and pass through dense plantings of Christmas trees. At Snow Creek Road, turn right. In another 0.1 miles turn right again on Wing Road, which will take you back to NC 226. Proceed north (left) toward Bakersville. Watch for NC 226A on the left in 1.6 miles and turn left here to visit our next stop of literary significance. Look for a state historical marker commemorating the Sink Hole Mine as a landmark for the turn.

■ BANDANA / KONA

To reach the little communities of Bandana and Kona, follow 226A for 1.5 miles and then turn left on NC 80. In 2.7 winding miles you will be in the Bandana community, home of writer and naturalist Elizabeth Hunter, coauthor, with photographer J. Scott Graham, of *Blue Ridge Parkway: America's Favorite Journey* (2003). Hunter's feature stories about the mountains have often appeared in *Our State* magazine. In addition, the poet Hilda Downer, who now lives near Boone, was raised here. In an essay called "Mutant in Bandana," Downer speaks of her roots in this community named

> ... for the red bandana Clinchfield Railroad tied to a laurel branch to denote an imaginary train station. The train, often rattling baggage in my sleep and offering a prediction of snow for the next morning by the strange way its whistle sounded, never tunneled through my door with ballet slippers, but there was paper and pen.
>
> Since the roots of poetry for me dig into the place I come from, I cannot separate my love of writing from my love of Bandana. *Bandana*—I love the very word. When I write, my thoughts travel from the Sink Hole Mine to the varied blue of distant mountain ranges. In these mines next to my grandfather's house, I collected pretty rocks—the ones I have always known the names of as though I had named them myself: garnet,

Poet Hilda Downer's hometown of Bandana today.

mica, feldspar, aquamarine, burle. I could sing as loudly as I wanted. I could write poetry there. Even now I must write from that spiritual spot of feldspar purity and complete freedom. Those cataracts and creeks, the banks glinting mica in Morse code, are the physical wording of my poetry and spirit.—From *Bloodroot: Reflections on Place by Appalachian Women Writers*, ed. Joyce Dyer (Lexington: University Press of Kentucky, 1998), 99.

Downer studied at Appalachian State University with John Foster West, whose work is described in Tour 17. Her first book was published when Downer was in her twenties. This sample from that collection captures the voice and tone of the people who live in this spectacular countryside:

HILLS SO BEAUTIFUL, THEY STING
The Johnson boys
were headed up Conley Ridge
when the least 'un got copperhead bit.
Arching like a pitcher handle
against his thigh,
the snake shuddered there.
Breaking off in a scream,
the oldest 'un spurted
back up the hill, losing
himself in the creek,
finding himself on the opposite bank,
slapping through woods.
Trees seemed to swat back.
Distance erased all but one hill
before home.
Clutching breath,
his back measured up to an apple tree,
he slunk to somniferous ground
where snakes might think he was one of them.
Eyes patted closed.
Respiration heaved like tractor wheels,
heavy as thighs after running.
Feeling like cornbread softening in milk,
or the gathered top of gravy stagnant in a bowl,
his mind snapped stringbean alert,
pricked like ears of distant grass,
heart almost leaping over the darkening hill.
Twenty years would find a lot of people dead.
Slithering over the blind of hill,
he tasted the wet kerosene smell of light,
slid through the back screen door,
and seeing his brother lying safe on a tick,
his face narrowed into a grin.
—From *Bandana Creek*, by Hilda Downer
   (Charlotte: Red Clay Books, 1979).

From Bandana it's only two more miles on NC 80 to Kona, where you can visit the graves of Charlie Silver in the old Kona Baptist Church. Yes, *graves*, be-

Three old stones mark the three burial sites of Charlie Silver's dismembered body behind the Kona Church.

cause as novelist Sharyn McCrumb writes in *The Ballad of Frankie Silver* (New York: New American Library, 1998): "They never did find all of him. The snow was still deep, and general opinion was that bits of the corpse would continue to turn up well into the April thaw, when the last of the spring snowmelt revealed the most deeply covered pieces. 'They buried what they found,' one traveler remarked" (65).

In her earlier account of this long-lived local legend, Muriel Earley Sheppard characterizes the story of Frankie and Charlie Silver as "the most sensational murder case in the history of the Toe River Valley" (*Cabins in the Laurel*, 24).

Three old, unmarked stones and a newer slab of engraved granite mark the final resting place of nineteen-year-old Charlie Silver, who was killed by his eighteen-year-old wife, Frankie, just before Christmas in 1831. The story goes that Frankie chopped her husband into pieces with an axe and then attempted to burn the body in the fireplace of the couple's small cabin. The next year, Frankie Silver was tried and hung in Morganton for murder, popularly reported to be the first woman hung in North Carolina, though historians have proved otherwise.

According to Sheppard and to Manly Wade Wellman, writing in *Dead and Gone* (1954), Frankie was simply a jealous wife seeking revenge for her husband's frequent desertions of their tiny cabin home. But when Sharyn McCrumb takes her turn with the tale, combining fact and fiction with historic and contemporary characters, the story becomes a chronicle of Frankie's frustration and, finally, self-defense. In McCrumb's version, Charlie Silver is characterized as a drunk who was likely abusive to both his wife and infant daughter, Nancy.

Yet another version of the story has been created by Perry Deane Young, the Asheville-born writer who is the great-great-great grandnephew of George Young, who reportedly sold Charlie Silver whiskey from time to time. Young conducted extensive research on the murder for his book *The Untold Story of Frankie Silver* (1998). He then joined forces with Bill Gregg, of the Southern Appalachian Repertory Theatre (SART), to write the play *Frankie*, which premiered in Mars Hill in 2001. Young credits the careful research of Morganton native Carolyn Sakowski in helping to dispel some of the myths surrounding the story. (Sakowski wrote about the Silver case in her master's thesis at Appalachian State University and went on to become editor-in-chief of John F. Blair Publisher in Winston-Salem.)

In Young's account, he pays particular attention to the mysterious events surrounding Frankie's trial in Morganton and the all-male jury's first vote for acquittal, which was then quickly reversed. Later on, public sentiment called for a pardon for Frankie. But North Carolina's Governor Swain was unmoved.

After the hanging, Frankie Silver's father spirited his daughter's body away in darkness. She was hastily buried in a grave that is now on private land near Lake James in Burke County.

As you climb the hill behind the Kona church to the Silver family graveyard, you're likely to feel a brisk wind. The dramatic views of Celo Knob and the still sparsely settled valley below are not so very different than they were more than a century ago. Walking among the dozens of stones, you can't help but wonder at all the other stories of hardship and joy that are buried here.

■ BAKERSVILLE

To reach the town of Bakersville, retrace your route along NC 80, and when you reach the "T" at Mine Creek Road, turn left toward Loafers Glory, a little crossroads you'll reach in about two miles. Turn right on 226 South and you'll come to the town limits of Bakersville in 2.4 miles.

Bakersville, the county seat in Mitchell, is home to several craft galleries and a handsome riverwalk along the banks of Cane Creek, which flows alongside NC 226 south of the main intersection where the courthouse sits. Muriel Earley Sheppard devotes an entire chapter of *Cabins in the Laurel* to dramatic events at Mitchell Superior Court during her visits in the 1930s.

Bakersville also figures in the work of contemporary writer Elizabeth Hunter of Bandana, whose essay on Bakersville's history appears in *Voices from Home: The North Carolina Prose Anthology* (1997). As the closest town of any size in North Carolina to Roan Mountain, Bakersville serves as the gateway to this natural wonder and hosts the Rhododendron Festival each June as the mountainsides fill with elegant blooms.

■ ROAN MOUNTAIN

To reach the Roan fourteen miles north, take NC 261 from the main intersection in Bakersville. At one time this pastoral road alongside Rock Creek was one-way up the mountain in the morning and one-way down the mountain in the evening. The Tennessee state line runs across the Roan's summit, and travel over the peak was often precarious in horse-and-buggy days. It can still be tricky in winter weather.

Salisbury travel guide Christian Reid, writing in 1877, puts Roan in the context of its neighboring peaks:

Northward of the Black Mountain stand two famous heights, which Professor Guyot calls "the two great pillars on both sides of the North Gate to the high mountain region of North Carolina." These are the Grandfather Mountain in the Blue Ridge, and the Roan Mountain in the Smoky. Both of these command a wide view, but the Roan is especially remarkable for the extent of territory which it overlooks. The traveler on its summit is always told that his gaze passes over seven States—to wit, North Carolina, Virginia, Tennessee, Kentucky, Alabama, Georgia, and South Carolina—but since states are not laid off in different colors, like the squares of a chessboard, he may be pardoned for perceiving no great difference in the imaginary lines which divide the vast expanse.—From *The Land of Sky*, by Christian Reid (Alexander, N.C.: Land of the Sky Books, 2001), xii.

Writing some forty years after Reid, at the beginning of the twentieth century, Margaret Morley provides an account of the drive from Bakersville that is still accurate, though the legendary but long-gone Cloudland Hotel is now designated only by a narrative sign adjacent to the parking lot on the peak that bears its name.

The ascent of the Roan from either side is delightful. From Bakersville the road leads up the picturesque Rock Creek Valley that lies squeezed between the Pumpkin Patch Mountain on the south and the slopes of the big Roan on the north. The Roan, standing boldly out in the landscape, is remarkable as being without trees excepting in the ravines and a narrow belt of firs towards the top. For this reason it is a mountain of pastures, as are Grassy Ridge Bald and the Big Yellow Mountain connecting with it to the east. Near the top of Roan, which is over sixty-three hundred feet high, is Cloudland Hotel where one dines in North Carolina and sleeps in Tennessee, the hotel being cut in two by the state line.

Roan Mountain has long been famous for two things, the circular rainbow sometimes seen from the summit, and the variety of wild flowers that grow on its slopes, it being reported that more species are found here than on any other place on the continent.—From *The Carolina Mountains*, by Margaret W. Morley (Alexander, N.C.: Land of the Sky Books, 2002), 334–35.

Usually in late June, deep magenta rhododendrons here clash with the bright orange of native flame azalea. You can drive to the very top of Roan by turning left off of NC 261 at the road's summit. Or you can park in the lot at the base of the summit road and hike to the top of Grassy Bald on the well-marked trail that ascends to your right near the sign marking the Tennessee state line. The views are actually more dramatic from the bald. Both options offer great picnic spots.

Jennifer Bauer Laughlin's *Roan Mountain: A Passage of Time* (Johnson City, Tenn.: Overmountain Press, 1991) tells the amazing story of Roan Mountain's botanical wealth and the many scientists who have come to study it. She also details the era of the Cloudland Hotel, which was "quite possibly the highest human habitation east of the Rockies" (83). Here guests would find cool nights and cold water "only thirteen degrees above freezing" (99), and a respite from hay fever, asthma, and countless other ailments, according to their testimonials. Following his 1885 visit shortly after the grand hotel opened with its hundred-plus rooms, Mark Twain's friend Charles Dudley Warner (who also visited Hot Springs, as described in Tour 7) complimented the Cloudland on its food and accommodations but wrote that the hotel "rocked like a ship at sea when the wind blew" (98).

Laughlin tells us that the Cloudland offered bowling, croquet, and golf, with special balls for the latter since the altitude caused them to fly wildly farther than in the flatlands. The hotel itself was built of native balsam, and the furnishings were crafted from local cherry trees. The whole place was heated with steam, an innovation at the time. Alcoholic beverages could only be served on the Tennessee side of the hotel, so designated by a bold white line painted down the middle of the dining room and across one large dining table. (Because North Carolina prohibited alcohol, the local sheriff often appeared hoping to catch a guest or two who crossed the line, drink in hand.) Of all these amenities, only the plumbing fell short. Incredibly, the entire hotel had only one bathroom, Laughlin reports. The Cloudland was abandoned in 1910 and quickly fell to ruin in the harsh winter weather.

Rather than backtrack to Bakersville, you may want to continue down the other side of the Roan on Tennessee Highway 143 for a short jaunt through Tennessee's manicured Roan Mountain State Park, where camping, tennis, outdoor concerts, and a swimming pool make for a nice stopping place. At the base of the mountain, turn right on US 19E, which will shortly cross back into North Carolina. Turn left at the intersection with NC 194 to reach Banner Elk.

Or, if you wish to loop back toward Spruce Pine, follow scenic 19E though the charming communities of Cranberry, Minneapolis, and Plumtree. Plumtree was once home to a thriving mica plant and Vance's Store, which figures prominently in the children's books of Gloria Houston. It was also the site of Dr. Eustace Sloop's first medical practice at the beginning of the twentieth century (see Tour 17), and was the original home of the "boys' department" of Lees-McRae Institute, now a coeducational four-year college in Banner Elk. Today, tiny Plumtree is likely to be clotted with visitors to the Toe River Lodge, where weekend meals are plentiful and old-fashioned accommodations are available to families and larger groups. Sunday brunch buffet is a feast that, weather permitting, can be consumed right alongside the shimmering rush of the Toe River. You'll know you have arrived in downtown Plumtree by the wooden planters that flank both sides of the Toe River bridge. In the late 1980s, the film version of John Ehle's novel *The Winter People* was shot here over a

On the back side of the Lees-McRae College campus is a monument to Marjorie Kinnan Rawlings, author of The Yearling. *She drafted the novel here in the fall of 1936.*

three-month stretch. Kurt Russell, Lloyd Bridges, and Kelly McGillis starred in the adaptation.

■ BANNER ELK

For literary tourists bound for Banner Elk on NC 194, know that you are in the vicinity of the famous Hicks family of Beech Mountain. Beyond Banner Elk up a country lane off 194 the homeplaces of the Hicks family of storytellers are scattered about the hillside. Stanley, Ray, Rosa, Ted, and Orville Hicks are documented in *The Last Chivaree: The Hicks Family of Beech Mountain,* by Robert Isbell (1996). Best known for their Jack tales, Ray, Rosa, and son Ted Hicks lived proudly without electricity and indoor plumbing until Ray's passing in 2003 at the age of eighty. Today Orville Hicks carries on the family tradition of tall-tale telling at festivals and schools—sharing stories that harken back to the earliest European settlers in these mountains.

In Banner Elk we also pick up on the story begun in Tour 14 about the novel *The Yearling,* which was written here. In the summer of 1936, Florida writer

Marjorie Kinnan Rawlings had come to Blowing Rock to speak at a gathering of writers and to escape the hot and humid summer days in Florida. At the time Rawlings was suffering from malaria. According to Anne Pierce of the Marjorie Kinnan Rawlings Society, when Rawlings learned that Lees-McRae College had cabins for rent at $15 a month,

> ... she booked a place to work on a draft of a novel she described to editor Max Perkins as "a book about a boy and the life in the scrub." As part of her rental, she was promised a helper from the nearby orphanage, the Grandfather Home for Children, to chop wood and take care of other chores. She specified a 12-year-old boy since that was the age of the boy in her planned book. That boy was Dave Wills, an excellent wood chopper and a willing companion for her pointer, Moe. Rawlings worked there from late-September until mid-November, making significant progress on the book and recovering from her malaria. As the days passed, she grew quite attached to the boy and wrote her aunt that she would like to take him back to Florida. However, in conversation with Dave, she learned he had a mother in Bristol. Rawlings was very disappointed, as she had been seriously thinking of adopting him. She wrote a poignant story based on this experience titled "A Mother in Mannville." It first appeared in the *Saturday Evening Post* and is included in various collections of her short stories.
> —From *News from the Creek* 7, no. 4 (Summer 2004), <http://www .marjoriekinnanrawlings.org/newsletters.php>.

In 2004, a granite marker commemorating Rawlings's relationship to the Banner Elk community was placed on the campus of the Grandfather Home. To visit the site, continue on NC 194 past the main entrance to Lees-McRae College. Turn right at the intersection with NC 184. In the next half-mile you'll pass by a number of shops and restaurants before the road descends and Hickory Nut Gap Road comes in on your right. Turn right on this road and watch for the campus of the orphanage on your right. Turn right into the campus at the Grandfather Academy sign. Follow the circular drive beyond the gymnasium and turn right again on a narrow steeply climbing lane. On your right you'll see the large granite marker and a bench set out on the grassy hillside. Note also the enormous maple trees around you, some of the largest in North Carolina.

Blue Moon Books

271 Oak Avenue
Spruce Pine, NC 28777
828-766-5000
<http://www.bluemoonbookstore.com>

This shop on "Upper Street" in Spruce Pine hosts writing classes, a book club, and the Mayland Writers Group. Next door to the Toe River Arts Council's gallery, featuring rotating exhibitions of work by local artists, Blue Moon also carries a wide selection of trade books and works by local authors including mystery writer Marian Coe, humorist Taylor Reece, and novelist Jack R. Pyle. Blue Moon is an excellent source for the works of Sharyn McCrumb, whose best-selling "ballad novels" about the region are always in stock here.

Spruce Pine Library

142 Walnut Avenue
Spruce Pine, NC 28777
828-765-4673
<http://www.youseemore.com/amyregional/branch.asp?branch=4>

This writer-friendly library has two special collections—a sampling of local minerals and gems and an exhibition of handcrafted baskets from around the world.

Grandfather Mountain : Crossnore : Valle Crucis : Vilas : Boone

Consider the dramatic visage of Grandfather Mountain, the place that journalist Charles Kuralt said he'd rather be in the month of May than anywhere else on the planet. Learn the dark secrets of Valle Crucis through the work of native son Romulus Linney.

Writers with a connection to this area: Joseph Bathanti, LeGette Blythe, Susan Fenimore Cooper, Robert Crutchfield, Grace DiSanto, Lynn Doyle, Kermit Hunter, Kathryn Kirkpatrick, Charles Kuralt, Romulus Linney, John Muir, Scott Nicholson, Susan Weinberg, John Foster West, Anne Hall Whitt, Isabel Zuber

To begin this tour from Banner Elk, continue on NC 184 south past the entrance to Beech Mountain ski resort on your right. The road comes to "T" at NC 105. Turn right toward Grandfather Mountain and Linville. In Linville, take US 221 to the entrance of Grandfather Mountain, which is privately owned and charges an entrance fee.

tour 17

■ GRANDFATHER MOUNTAIN

Grandfather Mountain has captured the imaginations of many environmental writers with what is perhaps the most visually distinctive profile of any mountain in the Blue Ridge. Heading south on NC 105 it appears to be the head of a bearded old man taking a nap on his back. Grandfather was a favorite getaway spot for the lyrical writer and television journalist Charles Kuralt, who often came here to visit his friend, the late Hugh Morton, a photographer and the heir to the Grandfather property. According to Morton, Kuralt spent three weeks at Grandfather immediately after his retirement from CBS.

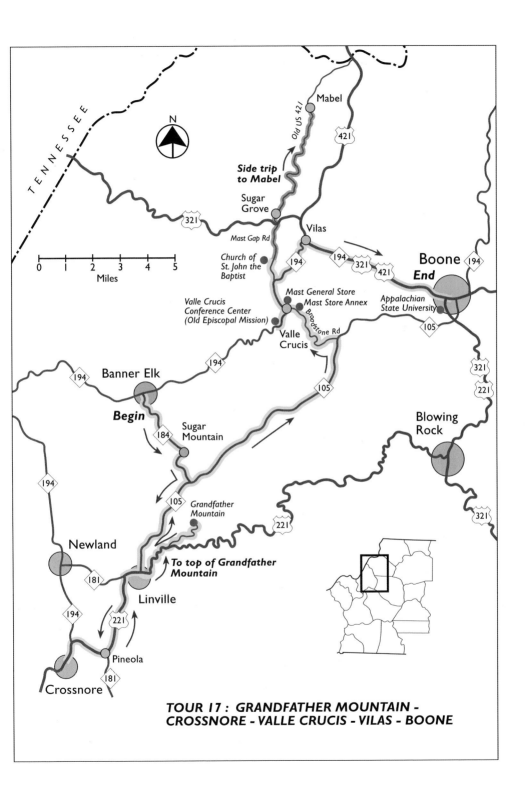

TENNESSEE

N

Mabel

Old US 421

421

Side trip
to Mabel

Sugar
Grove

321

Vilas

Mast Gap Rd

194

194

321 421

Boone
End

194

0 1 2 3 4 5
Miles

Church of
St. John the
Baptist

Mast General Store
Mast Store Annex

Appalachian
State University

105

Valle Crucis
Conference Center
(Old Episcopal Mission)

Broadstone Rd

Valle
Crucis

194

Banner Elk

194

105

321

221

Begin

184

Sugar
Mountain

Blowing
Rock

194

105

Grandfather
Mountain

221

321

Newland

To top of Grandfather
Mountain

181

Linville

194

221

Pineola

181

Crossnore

**TOUR 17 : GRANDFATHER MOUNTAIN -
CROSSNORE - VALLE CRUCIS - VILAS - BOONE**

Grandfather Mountain's mile-high swinging bridge and craggy visage are visible from NC 105. North Carolina–born writer and television commentator Charles Kuralt always said Grandfather was the best place on the planet to be come May.

Over the centuries, this 742-million-year-old mountain with its jagged visage has inspired many writers in addition to Kuralt. On his visit to Grandfather in 1898, nature writer and Sierra Club founder John Muir reportedly wrote to his wife: "The air has healed me. I think I could walk ten miles and not be tired" (see <http://www.grandfather.com/about/history.php>).

Morganton poet Grace DiSanto, recipient of the 1982 Oscar Arnold Young Memorial Award from the North Carolina Poetry Society, takes a metaphorical approach to the cloud-swept summit:

YOU SALOME! ARE THE CLOUD DANCING
ON GRANDFATHER MOUNTAIN

You tiptoe across the
sleeping giant,
Grandfather's chest.

In your chiffon dress,
playful-swayer,
you jeté, jeté and
pirouette.

Dropping a veil
you shield Grandfather's
shoulders, wrap them warm
in winter cold.

As if to ease a headache,
next cloth you unfold
binds his brow.

In fascination, I watch
your kiss; it bandages
his lips with frothy gauze.

Teasing seduction
weaves a shroud:
Grandfather's face disappears
in silk.

The tempo quickens.

When more layers fall,
braid tight his throat,

I know your aim: it's
off with His head.

For shame! Salome
Is not one head—
John the Baptist's—
Omnipotence enough
for your harlot's plate?
—From *North Carolina's 400 Years: Signs Along the Way*—
    An Anthology of Poems by North Carolina Poets to Celebrate
    America's 400th Anniversary, ed. Ronald H. Bayes with
    Marsha White Warren (Durham, N.C.: Acorn Press, 1986), 59.

In the shadow of Grandfather Mountain, Dr. Mary T. Martin Sloop lived a life of service to the surrounding mountain community. In her autobiography, *Miracle in the Hills* (with LeGette Blythe [New York: McGraw-Hill, 1953]), Sloop provides not only an account of her distinguished career but also gives a glimpse of the region from the opening of the twentieth century forward. As she tells us early on in the book: "My old bones may be aching, for I'm an ancient rock myself—though I insist I'm no fossil. But even eighty years, by some standards of measurement, is a mighty short period. And when I look upon Grandfather, I feel young, and transient. And very humble" (7).

Sloop was born in Davidson, North Carolina, where her father taught geology and chemistry at Davidson College. (Before her birth, Mary's father had taught at the University of North Carolina at Chapel Hill, where he replaced Elisha Mitchell after Mitchell fell to his death attempting to measure the height of the mountain that came to bear his name.) Mary Martin studied medicine in Philadelphia and soon married Dr. Eustace Sloop, whom she had met at Davidson when he was a freshman in 1893. Told that she was "too old" for foreign missionary work as a woman in her late twenties, Sloop and her husband decided to settle in the North Carolina mountains instead. The Sloops would go on to build a hospital, dental clinic, and boarding school for children who were orphaned or abused. With these institutions the Sloops brought the first electricity, telephone, and paved road to Avery County. Mary Martin Sloop also established a weaving room at Crossnore School where local women could practice and preserve their native craft and sell their woven goods on site. The facility is open today, and students at Crossnore School have a cottage industry in "bobbinscopes"—kaleidoscopes made from antique bobbins collected from abandoned cotton mills.

In her 1982 memoir, *The Suitcases*, writer Anne Hall Whitt tells of her years as a student at Crossnore School, where her foster mother enrolled her in the ninth grade in 1944. (After the death of their mother in 1936, Whitt and her two sisters had gone from one orphanage to another and through several foster families.) When Anne Whitt arrived at Crossnore, Mary Sloop became her mentor. (Whitt's book became well known when Reader's Digest Condensed Books issued the story in twenty-one countries. The most recent version of the book has been issued by Crossnore School.)

To come full circle, *The Suitcases* includes a foreword by Charles Kuralt. In it, Kuralt explains that as a twenty-one-year-old journalist he wrote a profile in the *Charlotte News* of a certain destitute man who lived in the county home and often sat on a bench in front of the Presbyterian Church in downtown Charlotte, quoting easily from Shakespeare and Robert Burns. In the late 1950s Kuralt's daily column was called "People," and the troubled man he profiled that day turned out to be Malcolm Whitt, Anne's father, who had never been able to care for his daughters after the death of his wife.

To visit Crossnore from Grandfather Mountain, take 221 South through Linville and follow the signs to the village of Crossnore. The Weaving Room and Gallery are less than a half-mile to the right off US 221 at the flashing light. There's also a Ben Long fresco here, entitled "Suffer the Children."

■ VALLE CRUCIS

Heading back up NC 105 from Linville, you'll pass through a corridor of antique shops, landscaping nurseries, restaurants, and other upscale stores that serve the burgeoning residential and resort developments that stretch from Banner Elk, at the base of Grandfather Mountain, all the way up to Boone. Before you reach Boone, however, take a left at the traffic light that marks the beginning of Broadstone Road. Broadstone runs through the extraordinary "Vale of the Cross," or Valle Crucis, so named by the second Episcopal bishop of North Carolina, Levi Silliman Ives, who noted that three creeks flow together here in the shape of a cross. Like Crossnore, Valle Crucis was adopted by outsiders with a missionary zeal to improve living conditions among mountain folk.

The Episcopal Diocese set out in 1844 to build a mission and a school for boys in Valle Crucis, where at the time only a single cabin belonging to a miller stood. At first the going was rough. The winter weather came in hard that year before the student housing was finished and "a number of lads had been sent to Valle Crucis by their friends as to a Reformatory," writes Susan Fenimore Cooper, whose account of the founding of the Episcopal mission was first published in 1889 and reissued by the Valle Crucis Conference Center in 1992. (Susan was the daughter of James Fenimore Cooper, who wrote *The Last of the Mohicans*.) Also in that first year, the mission school's clergyman in charge died. Soon a new recruit, William West Skiles, the primary subject of Cooper's history, came to Valle Crucis to assume responsibility for the agricultural program of the school. In a short time he became the general superintendent, was ordained, and remained in Valle Crucis for the rest of his life, even after the diocese cut off support because of a controversy about rumored liturgical practices at the mission.

Today the Episcopal Church runs the Valle Crucis Conference Center at the site of the historic mission school. To visit this landmark, watch for NC 194, coming in on the left shortly before you reach the original Mast General Store. Turn left on 194. The highway climbs to the historic Holy Cross Chapel and a beautiful view of the surrounding valley.

The story of this mission served as the inspiration for Romulus Linney's widely reviewed novel *Heathen Valley*, first published in 1962 and named a Book-of-the-Month-Club alternate. The novel was reissued in 2004. Linney is now best known as the author of some three-dozen plays for which he has earned two Obies and two National Critics Awards for Best Play of the Year, including his 1987 adaptation of *Heathen Valley* for the stage. As a member of the American Academy of Arts and Letters, Linney also won both the Award in Literature and the Award of Merit Medal for Drama. *Heathen Valley*, the first of his three novels to date, presents a dark and sometimes brutish portrait of the years in which the church struggled to gain a foothold in the spiritual lives of Watauga County residents.

Come back down NC 194 from the conference center and turn left to proceed on this tour. Soon you'll come to the original Mast General Store, which was first opened in 1883 and continually strives to be the "the store that has everything," including local literature. Once a remote trading post, the store today celebrates its roots while offering an impressive array of drygoods, including shoes and cast-iron cookware. The nearby Mast Annex offers clothing, candy, and outdoor gear.

Continuing beyond Mast General Store, you can also visit the Church of St. John the Baptist, which was consecrated in 1862. William West Skiles is buried there. To visit this site, watch for Mast Gap Road and turn left, then take the first left onto Herb Thomas Road. St. John's — now used only for weddings and occasional services — is 1.5 miles down this road.

Devoted readers of horror novelist Scott Nicholson (also discussed in Tour 15) will recognize St. John's as the church pictured on the cover of the 2002 mass-

The Valle Crucis setting for Romulus Linney's novel Heathen Valley.

market paperback version of Nicholson's first novel, *The Red Church*. This brisk and keenly felt novel was a Bram Stoker Award finalist. Nicholson, who was born in Mooresville, North Carolina, has lived in a number of towns across the state and now makes his home in nearby Boone, where he studied creative writing at Appalachian State.

Novelist and poet Isabel Zuber also had St. John's in mind when she was writing her family saga, *Salt* (2002). In an interview Zuber explained: "The Salt area is around Mabel, North Carolina, which is named Faith in my book. It is less developed than some other parts of Watauga County (at least for now) and much of it is lovely. The church that Anna and Nell walk to near Valle Crucis (St. John's) is still there. John's barn in the community I called Faith also still stands, as well as the house where Roland picked up the mail."

Church of St. John the Baptist, consecrated in 1862, is the "Red Church" in Scott Nicholson's novel by the same name. It also figures in the novel Salt, *by Boone native Isabel Zuber.*

Born in Boone, Zuber served as a librarian at Wake Forest University for many years and still makes her home in Winston-Salem. She earned Virginia Commonwealth University's First Novelist Award for *Salt*. Her poetry collections are *Oriflamb* (1987) and *Winter's Exile* (1997).

Zuber enthusiasts can visit the Mabel area by continuing up Mast Gap Road to US 321. Turn left on 321 and watch for Old Highway 421 soon coming in on your right. Carefully follow Old 421 north as it winds through the communities of Sherwood and Mast, finally reaching the Mabel community where Old 421 crosses the North Fork of Ellison Branch and continues on to Zionville, a town perched on the Tennessee state line. Zuber explains more about the sites in *Salt*:

"The second house the family lived in is next to Mabel School and was occupied the last time I looked. The cemetery above Union Baptist Church is on
North Fork Road out of Mabel where John sat to watch Jenny climb the hill
toward him and where the people my characters are based on are buried. The
cemetery at the Baptist church in Zionville was the site of the big Mabel vs.
Trade brawl. The Revolutionary soldier's monument mentioned in that scene
in the book is in the lower right hand corner as one stands behind the church
facing away from it."

From Mabel, backtrack to US 321 and turn left toward Boone. If you want
to continue on the tour without visiting Mabel, return to NC 194 the way you
came to St. John's Church and turn left, continuing north to the intersection
with US 321. Either way, you will soon be in the town of Vilas, home to poet
Kathryn Kirkpatrick, winner of North Carolina's Brockman-Campbell Prize for
her first collection, *The Body's Horizon* (1996). She is associate professor of English at Appalachian State.

Vilas is also home to one of North Carolina's most versatile writers, Joseph
Bathanti. By turns poet, playwright, and novelist, Bathanti is professor of English at Appalachian State University. Born in Pittsburgh and transplanted to
North Carolina as a VISTA volunteer in 1976, Bathanti has written poetry inspired by many places in North Carolina, including Vilas:

HOUSE HUNTING AT FOUR THOUSAND FEET
The road's not but a ledge,
near straight up shale and millstone.
Mud. Good God, come winter.
Three slough-bellied brown and white
bangtail paints cleat to a shelf in the mist,
then a bouquet of pink plastic roses stabbed
in the scarp ahead of the fall-off.
By the time we find the house,
fog's set in and we can't see to turn around.
Sheer on both sides.
The children wear those silent worried looks.
They don't want to live in the sky
where a thing mishandled plummets
the better part of a mile;
and all there is for it is to cock an ear
and reckon altitude by the *whump*.
Pray each time your foot touches earth.

Hold on like Hades.
Folks up here are born cloven and slouch.
Purchase is bred well-deep into them.
The house is slant, lank, with enough give
to weather gravity, and thus plumb.
Appalachian physics.
We creep up and beam the brights on it.
It eyes right back, querulous
like a bedridden crone, but old man too,
finicky, the tin roof a rusted skullcap.
Thick watery glass windows, cataracted
with silica, yellow dauber nests
like sleep mortised into the panes.
Up here is odd enough to make a house
not just thingful, but a someone
with blood and breath. Secrets.
Voices. Some say
you get used to it:
catamounts, fog, rime-ice, the wind
like Deuteronomy when it gets het up,
snow beading down, shrinking everything
in its alabaster clout.
We venture no farther than the spinney
gnarling the busted porch,
demur like the beholden Israelites
and wait for a sign, our eyes
discomfited by everlasting up.
—Used by permission of Joseph Bathanti

Continue from Vilas on US 321 into downtown Boone, which Boone native Isabel Zuber tells us "is far different from when I was growing up. The house I was born in is still standing, but the town is ten times bigger than it was. The old post office with its WPA mural is there, and the movie theater and hardware store and Boone Drug are still in the same places, but much has been lost."

Though Boone has substantially changed in the last half-century, *Horn in the West*, an outdoor drama, has been seen by generations of North Carolinians and out-of-state tourists since its debut in 1952. Kermit Hunter, whose biography is presented in Tour 6, wrote the drama after *Unto These Hills*, the Cherokee story he wrote as his master's thesis at the University of North Carolina at Chapel Hill. The play, presented in the 2,500-seat Daniel Boone Theatre, chronicles the story of Daniel Boone and settlers in the Blue Ridge Mountains during the Revolutionary War.

Today Boone is a booming university town with a vibrant literary community. Parkway Publishers is a local company that specializes in regional literature and has published many local writers. Notable among them is novelist and poet John Foster West. Born in Wilkes County in 1918, West is best known for his mentorship of many young writers studying at Appalachian State, where he served on the faculty for twenty-two years. West's early novels, which are still in print thanks to Parkway, are *Time Was* (1965), *The Ballad of Tom Dula* (1977), and *The Summer People* (1989)—all of which are set in the region. Parkway also published West's 2005 novel, *Going Home to Zion*.

The campus of ASU, which flanks the town, has a raft of talented writers in the English Department. In addition to Joseph Bathanti and Kathryn Kirkpatrick, the faculty includes poet Lynn Doyle, Writing Center director; Watauga native John Crutchfield, who is a playwright, poet, and performer; and fiction writer Susan Weinberg. The English Department is also home to the literary journal *Cold Mountain Review* (which Crutchfield edits), and a flourishing Visiting Writers Program that annually augments the university's own writers with nationally and internationally recognized authors who come to teach and read from their works. *Appalachian Journal* is also headquartered at the university. This multidisciplinary publication accepts some poetry but primarily presents scholarly writings about the culture and history of the region.

In the Department of Philosophy and Religion, Professor William M. Hutchins has also brought literary acclaim to ASU with his translations from the work of Arabic poets, novelists, and playwrights. Most notably, Hutchins was the lead translator of *The Cairo Trilogy*—three novels written by 1988 Nobel laureate Naguib Mahfouz and collected in a single, 1,500-page volume.

■ LITERARY LANDSCAPE

Watauga County Library
140 Queen Street
Boone, NC 28607
828-264-8784
<http://www.arlibrary.org/index.php?page=10>
This local institution is an official site in the National Storytelling Network's Tellabration events and hosts the High Country Writers group, among other community events.

High Country Writers

<http://highcountrywriters.tripod.com/

This group, founded in 1995 to support a small body of aspiring romance writers, is now a much larger, multigenre organization that sponsors an annual book fair and an awards program. The group meets twice a month at the Watauga County Library.

Black Bear Books

2146 Blowing Rock Road

Boone, NC 28607

828-264-4636

Black Bear Books, located on the right side of US 321/221 as you are headed toward Blowing Rock, is Scott Nicholson's recommended choice for a local bookstore. With its expansive selection of regional literature and comfortable reading areas, Black Bear is one of the larger booksellers in the region.

Todd : West Jefferson : Jefferson : Crumpler : Sparta : Roaring Gap

Visit an international publishing house tucked away in the mountains. Hear authentic old-time music favored by novelist Clyde Edgerton. Follow National Public Radio commentator Noah Adams's narrative about the New River.

Writers with a connection to this area: Noah Adams,
Leland Cooper, Mary Lee Cooper, Chris Cox, Hal Crowther,
Clyde Edgerton, Zetta Barker Hamby, Frank Borden Hanes,
Tim Peeler, Lee Smith, Tom Wolfe, T. J. Worthington

IN ASHE COUNTY, NC
Hills are still paved by pasture grass
and the hiss and roar of travel
has not yet blundered the beauty.

Narrow blue roads twist through
ancient valleys; unlike neighbors
to the west, no writer has imagined

a place that it has never been
to thrust this country out to
those who view people as an experience

and land like a butcher handling
fresh meat. For now, the history resides
in the small down towns and

in the shapes of old churches, in the
way a park can fold out from a hill
between two pristine streams.

A photographer leaves, wanting
to be a fish or a bird here; the poet
leaves in fear that somewhere

tour 18

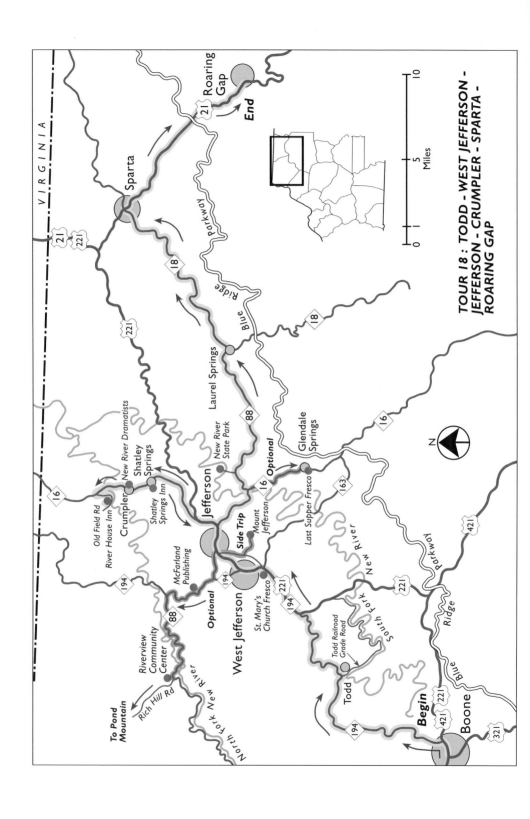

TOUR 18: TODD - WEST JEFFERSON -
JEFFERSON - CRUMPLER - SPARTA -
ROARING GAP

a baron with a face like a brick
brings his push pins to this map.
—From *Amarillo Bay Literary Magazine* 6, no. 4
(November 2004), <http://www.amarillobay.org/>.

Hickory poet Tim Peeler captures the feelings of many longtime and newer residents who zealously want to preserve the pastoral beauty of Ashe County. Unlike the more rugged mountains to the south, the rolling fields and rounded green hills of Ashe are no less dramatic but somehow more serene. Ashe is the northwestern-most county in North Carolina, and perhaps best known as home to the New River, which is one of the three oldest rivers on the planet. The others are the French Broad River, farther west in the state, and the Nile. Unlike other rivers in the state, the New flows north. The scenic route into Ashe County from Boone is NC 194. Head east from downtown Boone on US 221/421 past the Daniel Boone Inn and watch for 194. It turns off to the left before you reach Cheap Joe's Art Stuff.

■ TODD

NC 194 parallels the South Fork of the New River, which comes close to the road as you cross the county line from Watauga into Ashe County, some eleven miles north of Boone. Watch for the signs to Todd, a village that sits right on the riverbank. Turn right off 194 onto Todd Railroad Grade Road to reach the town center.

Once the largest town in Watauga and Ashe Counties, Todd now serves as the postal address for a scattering of some 2,200 residents, many of whom are farmers. In Todd, you also just might run into novelist Lee Smith and her husband Hal Crowther, a nationally celebrated essayist and political curmudgeon. Smith—who is originally from Grundy, Virginia, in the southwest corner of the state—worked on her 2006 novel, *On Agate Hill*, in Ashe County. The one-room Bobcat School, which is described in the novel as being in the "Lost Province" of western North Carolina near the Tennessee border, might well have been near here. Smith and Crowther have a getaway cabin in the vicinity and often bring along other writer friends to poke around Todd.

In Todd you'll find a charming old train depot, Appalachian Adventures (a company that conducts river trips on the New), and Todd Mercantile, where local crafts and fresh baked goods are for sale. Todd General Store (dating back to 1914) sells groceries, baked goods and jellies, deli sandwiches, crafts, and antiques. On most Friday nights, an old-time music jam starts at seven. On most

Todd General Store is a regular gathering place for local residents, tourists, storytellers, musicians, and writers.

Saturday mornings at ten during the tourist season the store presents an author or artist talking about his or her work. On Tuesday nights at six, the store hosts a storytelling session, and once every other month or so is "Liar's Night" where folks tell the tallest tales they can summon. In the summer, there's also a music series on the lawn beside the river. For more than a dozen years, Todd has also hosted a New River Arts Festival in October.

And what are all those cars parked alongside the road just beyond Todd? People park and pedal along a ten-mile bicycle route along the scenic New River on Todd Railroad Grade Road to Fleetwood. There are virtually no other bike trails in the mountains that are flat and afford such extraordinary views of the countryside. This trail is considered one of the top ten in the state.

From Todd, continue up NC 194 until it meets up with US 221—the road that will carry you toward West Jefferson, a town that has recently been transformed in large measure by the presence of many artists and gallery owners.

Turn left where NC 194 heads into town proper. At this intersection you will see signs leading to the St. Mary's Frescoes by Ben Long. To visit, turn left on Beaver Creek Road. St. Mary's Church is approximately one half-mile from the Nations Inn. Long, whose work is also considered in Tours 1 and 15 in this volume, painted several images for St. Mary's here in West Jefferson, including a very pregnant Virgin Mary.

The literary tourist may be interested to know that in his college years at UNC-Chapel Hill, where he was enrolled in the writing and literature program, Ben Long was enormously influenced by one of the state's most prolific writers:

In January of 1965, the second half of his sophomore year, he [Long] took a writing class taught by a young visiting professor from Duke University in nearby Durham. Reynolds Price had written *A Long and Happy Life*, his first novel, and *The Names and Faces of Heroes*, a book of short stories, the initial steps in a distinguished career. It was his practice to invite students to his home for a picnic-type meal and informal socializing. Price's home was filled with paintings and drawings, the kind of figurative work he liked. . . . Seeing Price's art collection and sensing he was a kindred spirit, Long told Price he was interested in painting and drawing. Price asked to see some of his work. Price was amazed that a shy, almost taciturn young man who looked like a football player could produce such "enormously impressive drawings." —From *Wet-Wall Tattoos: Ben Long and the Art of Fresco*, by Richard Maschal (Winston-Salem: John F. Blair, 1993), 120.

If you have time, you may also want to follow NC 16 south out of Jefferson (later in this tour) to Glendale Springs, where the Ben Long fresco *The Last Supper* is located in the Holy Trinity Church. The subjects in this fresco were modeled after Ashe County residents, and the dog that sleeps at the foot of the table in the painting belonged to one of Long's helpers on the project. After the local priest would not allow the pet to come into the chapel as the artists worked,

Detail of the sleeping dog in Ben Long's fresco The Last Supper *in Holy Trinity Church at Glendale Springs near the Blue Ridge Parkway and the Inn at Glendale Springs.*

Long mischievously painted the dog into the fresco, guaranteeing him a spot in the church for eternity.

■ WEST JEFFERSON

Follow 194 into West Jefferson. At last count, some thirteen galleries and another seven gifts and crafts stores keep this downtown district hopping. In addition to North Carolina's only cheese factory, you'll also find a half-dozen cafés and a collection of indoor and outdoor public art here that rivals those of much larger towns.

■ JEFFERSON

Jefferson, the Ashe County seat, is located just beyond the downtown business district in West Jefferson. Watch for Business 221, which you can pick up in West Jefferson as you come all the way through town on NC 194. The literary tourist has a rare opportunity in Jefferson—namely, to visit a publishing house that also happens to have an impressive collection of art in its headquarters.

Launched in 1979, McFarland and Company publishes some 275 scholarly and reference works and textbooks a year, including titles on the Civil War (such as those in Thomasville writer Christopher M. Watford's 2003 series, *The Civil War in North Carolina*), performing arts (such as Hickory writer Mary Snodgrass's *August Wilson: A Literary Companion* [2004]), and sports. In the last category, Hickory poet Tim Peeler has published two poetry collections that exclusively deal with baseball.

McFarland welcomes visitors. To get there, continue on 221. You'll pass Mt. Jefferson Road and Long Street. At the next traffic light, turn left on NC 88. From this intersection, McFarland is only 0.9 miles on the right, at number 960. Watch for a small white sign on the right for McFarland. Two designated visitor parking spaces are at one end of the building and the entrance is near an impressive stone sculpture.

McFarland has also published local histories, including a collection of oral histories from residents of the Pond Mountain community in Ashe, where North Carolina meets up with both Virginia and Tennessee. The book explores mountain life at the beginning of the twentieth century and offers a powerful glimpse into the traditions of Ashe County. Lockie Richardson told her story in 1992 at the age of ninety-four:

I said there wasn't much to say about the old days, but I guess there is a lot to talk about. Those were hard times back when I was raised up. Oh, times were so hard. I lived on the farm. I was married in 1911 when I was 14. I had nine children. Four of them are dead. I lost my husband in '48. . . . Things have changed. Things are not like they used to be. If things were now like they were back then, the young people would starve to death.—From *The Pond Mountain Chronicle: Self-Portrait of a Southern Appalachian Community*, by Leland R. Cooper and Mary Lee Cooper (Jefferson, N.C.: McFarland, 1998), 14–15.

Beyond McFarland headquarters, depending on the time of year and day of your visit, you may be able to find some authentic mountain music a bit farther up NC 88, according to novelist Clyde Edgerton. Originally from Durham and now teaching at the University of North Carolina at Wilmington, Edgerton also has a getaway in Ashe County. He recommended the following:

"Friday nights at the Community Center at the intersection of Route 88 and Rich Hill Road in Ashe County—about twenty minutes north of Jefferson—you can find good pie and informal bluegrass music. And then on Saturday nights about a mile north of this location at the drive-under filling station there's also informal bluegrass music, outside in the summer. (I don't know about winter)." The first location Edgerton is referring to is the Riverview Community Center at 11719 Highway 88 West, in Creston. The Friday night gathering is a year-round activity—weather permitting.

In addition to his North Carolina–based novels, considered in the next volume of this series, Edgerton describes his fondness for Ashe County in a coffee-table book simply called *North Carolina* (2003), featuring the photographs of George Humphries.

If Clyde Edgerton's recommendations pique your curiosity, you can take NC 88 all the way to Trade, Tennessee, visiting the more remote communities of Warrensville, Clifton, Creston, and Ashland, dotted along NC 88 to the west. The road is winding and gorgeous. The Pond Mountain community described in the oral history published by McFarland is to the right off NC 88 on Big Laurel Road (the next intersection after Rich Hill), which will carry you northeast all the way to Hemlock and the state line. Otherwise, backtrack on 88 to Jefferson to continue this tour.

While in Jefferson, you may also want to drive up Mount Jefferson, a distinctively dark peak among the greener slopes of Ashe County. It rises some 1,600 feet above the towns of Jefferson and West Jefferson. On a clear day you can see into Virginia and Tennessee. As National Public Radio's Noah Adams put it in his travelogue, *Far Appalachia: Following the New River North* (New York: Delacorte, 2001): "Stand at the top of Mount Jefferson, at 4,683 feet, and you'll see the Ashe County Christmas trees, arrayed in dark evergreen smudges on the hills below" (39). Noah Adams's book is a handy companion as you travel in the vicinity of the New River. He begins in Ashe County and follows the fabled river all the way into West Virginia.

To get to Mount Jefferson State Park, retrace your route on NC 88 to 221 and watch for Mt. Jefferson Road on your left, which will lead you to the park.

■ CRUMPLER

Next we head to the northernmost point in Ashe County. Go north on NC 16 from Jefferson to reach the little town of Crumpler, just off 16 on State Road 1560. What could possibly be of interest to the literary tourist here? Amazingly, an international retreat for writers is hidden down Healing Springs Road. The old schoolhouse and a number of frame cottages that once housed pilgrims seeking the curative waters of the local springs sit amid old plantings of lilacs, roses, yuccas, and towering hemlocks. But only a new sign gives away the presence of the New River Dramatists (NRD).

With the sole ambition of raising the standards of storytelling in theater, film, and television, Mark Woods created New River Dramatists, a nonprofit organization that serves writers and, eventually, their audiences. The playwrights who come to Healing Springs are able to work in seclusion in the cottages and are paid an honorarium for their time on site.

"We never bring a writer here on the basis of a piece we think they should work on," says Woods. "Our interest is not in the piece but in the strength of the writer's talents."

Actors are also brought in to stage readings of the playwrights' works-in-progress. NRD makes no financial claim on works written at the retreat, but the organization does invite producers to meet the writers, and they make works available online to theaters in search of new material. Among the writers in residence here have been Native American writer N. Scott Momaday, Billy Aronson, who conceived the play *Rent*, North Carolina playwright and actress Phyllis MacBryde, and poet and novelist Ian McHugh. Before he founded NRD, Mark Woods was a cofounder of the North Carolina Theatre Ensemble, founder of the North Carolina Shakespeare Festival, and a producer with the Charlotte Repertory Theater.

One more notable writing retreat is nearby. Beyond Crumpler on NC 16, just before you reach the Virginia state line, the River House Inn and Restaurant

These historic cottages house playwrights who come to work and observe staged readings of their plays in progress at the Healing Springs headquarters of New River Dramatists.

will be on your left, accessible by Old Field Road. Proprietor Gayle Hamby Winston owns the inn that overlooks the North Fork of the New River and the 180 acres it sits on. Not only does Winston feed the writers at NRD, but the River House has had many literati under its roof. Over the years, Winston has hosted the likes of cartoonist and writer Gary Trudeau, Raleigh novelist Angela Davis-Gardner, Charlotte poet and columnist Dannye Romine Powell, NPR's Noah Adams, novelist Lee Smith, and essayist Hal Crowther. Winston's friend Annie Dillard also stayed for a week once and fed the cat when Winston took a rare vacation.

Gayle Winston's affinity for writers comes naturally. After stints as a journalist, Broadway producer, and political fundraiser, she returned home to Ashe County more than two decades ago to run the Inn at Glendale Springs and a pub in Winston-Salem before moving back here to her home community of Grassy Creek in 1988. At Winston's urging, her mother, Zetta Barker Hamby, born in 1907, wrote a compelling memoir of her life here.

Zetta Hamby, with her characteristically understated wit, describes the "writing schools" that were held in the region when she was a youngster. The subject matter was actually not literature but how to improve penmanship,

The New River at sunset, as seen from the porch of Gayle Winston's River House Inn.

which was especially important in the recording of legal documents, particularly in reference to property lines:

> Some of the old deeds are interesting to read. They often began, "Beginning at a white oak tree at the road and running 32 poles to a stake on the wagon road near the top of a ridge near a barn." A pole was a rod length or 16½ feet used in measuring land.
>
> An elderly man, who had been the recorder of deeds in Grayson County [Virginia] for a number of years, told us of one deed that began, "From where I am now standing." — From *Memoirs of Grassy Creek: Growing Up*

in the Mountains on the Virginia–North Carolina Line, by Zetta Barker Hamby (Jefferson, N.C.: McFarland, 1998), 119.

Zetta Hamby lived long enough to see her lively manuscript edited but not printed in its final form. Her daughter's River House serves dinner nightly. The range of accommodations is eclectic but elegant, as are the guests. (The bed and breakfast has been featured in *Martha Stewart Living*.) Winston hosts wine tastings, cooking classes, a music festival on the banks of the river, and salon evenings with local performers. For more information, call the River House Inn and Restaurant at Grassy Creek at 336-982-2109 or visit <http://www .riverhousenc.com/>.

Heading back down NC 16, if the time is right and you need a more down-home meal, you may want to take a turn into Shatley Springs. This regionally famous inn is celebrated for its country-style dining. It is open every day from seven A.M. to nine P.M., except from early December through mid-April. The food is favored by church groups and bus tours and there can sometimes be a wait, but there's always room for plenty of diners. Noah Adams describes the scene:

> The dining was family-style—sit down with happy strangers. One of them said, 'I tried not to eat all day,' and started passing the platters: fried chicken and piled high slivers of dark, salty ham. Mashed potatoes and brown gravy and green beans and fried apples and slaw and biscuits. Young women and men waiting to pour iced tea and coffee and bring ice cream or pie or cobbler. You have to remember to sit up straight and take slow breaths.—From *Far Appalachia*, by Noah Adams, 35.

For more information on the Shatley Springs Inn, call 336-982-2236.

If you follow NC 16 south from Shatley Springs, it will soon join up with NC 88. You may continue on 16 south to Glendale Springs to visit the Ben Long fresco of the Last Supper mentioned earlier, or you may head east on NC 88 to experience New River State Park.

Just off NC 88 to the left at Wagoner Road, shortly after NC 16 forks south, New River State Park encompasses 1,500 acres and offers access to boaters and picnickers. (There is also an access point three miles west of Scottville off US 221 where the New River General Store offers camping supplies and regional reading material.) From here, we head into Alleghany County, the final stop on Trail 2.

Alleghany County is perched so high up in the hills of western North Carolina that golfers intrepid enough to go up there to play golf call it mountain golf. The county's only big cash crop is Christmas trees. Fraser firs mostly, and the main manufacturing that goes on is building houses for summer people. In the entire county there is only one town. It is called Sparta.

The summer people are attracted by the primeval beauty of the New River, which forms the county's western boundary. "Primeval" is precisely the word for it. Paleontologists reckon that the New River is one of the two or three oldest rivers in the world. According to local lore, it is called New because the first white man to lay eyes on it was Thomas Jefferson's cousin Peter, and to him its very existence was news.... Not long ago the mountains were a wall that cut Alleghany County off from people in the rest of North Carolina so completely they called it the Lost Province, when they thought of it at all. Modern highways have made the county accessible, but an air of remoteness, an atmosphere primeval, remains, and that is what the summer people, the campers, the canoers, the fishers, hunters, golfers and mountain craft shoppers love about it. There is no mall, no movie house, and not one stockbroker.—From *I Am Charlotte Simmons*, by Tom Wolfe (New York: Farrar, Straus, Giroux, 2004), 13–14.

By our informal reckoning, not many Alleghany residents were thrilled with Tom Wolfe's portrayal of their county. You can strike up a conversation with most anyone in the town of Sparta and get an opinion on the subject. The author of *The Right Stuff* (1979), *The Electric Kool-Aid Acid Test* (1968), and *The Bonfire of the Vanities* (1987) set about to create a portrait of contemporary college life. For his main character, he invented Charlotte Simmons, a resident of Alleghany County. Wolfe visited here several times while working on the book and declared the county the most beautiful in all of North Carolina. It is also remote and undeveloped. Here, scenery is the main event.

To reach Sparta, pick up NC 18, which connects with NC 88 in Laurel Springs. The countryside is a bit steeper than in Ashe County, but there are no fewer Christmas trees.

Sparta's hometown-boy-made-good as a writer is Chris Cox, a weekly newspaper columnist whose work is collected in *Waking Up in a Cornfield* (1999). Cox teaches now at Southwestern Community College in Sylva and writes for the *Asheville Citizen-Times*.

Farmers Hardware is community headquarters in Sparta.

Farmers Hardware, in downtown Sparta, is run by Marsha Wagner, a classmate of Chris Cox and the third generation in her family (and the first female) to manage the hardware store. She is a font of local knowledge. Farmers is an upscale purveyor of everything from gourmet gadgets to snow shovels and has been known to host a book signing once in a while. The store sells a few cookbooks and one local title—a history of the county by local deejay, bluegrass musician, and music store proprietor T. J. Worthington.

In *Mountain Heritage: Alleghany Style* (2005), Worthington considers the relative merits of Tom Wolfe's take on the county and declares Charlotte Simmons a person of authentic character, though he admits that Wolfe's attempt at a mountain-sounding dialogue and his knowledge of local geography is a bit off.

If you want to go book hunting here, the Alleghany Public Library is right downtown on Main Street, and across the way is Books 'N Friends, a used bookstore that benefits the Friends of the Library.

If you are hungry, the local general store serves hot dogs and an excellent chicken salad on a croissant.

Slated to become the home of an amazing collection of teapots, to be housed in a museum here, Sparta is a haven for mountain music and storytelling, and if you hang around long enough, you'll hear some tales.

■ ROARING GAP

To finish our tour, we head a little farther down US 21 from Sparta to Roaring Gap, where refugees from the summer heat of Winston-Salem have weekend homes and play a good bit of golf in Alleghany County. Among this group for years has been Frank Borden Hanes. As a member of the textile family of hosiery fame, Hanes studied at UNC-Chapel Hill and worked for a time as a columnist and reporter. Then he won the very first Roanoke-Chowan Prize for Poetry in 1953 for his verse novel *Abel Anders*. Undoubtedly inspired by Hanes's trips to the mountains, the book is an engrossing story of a precocious boy who grows up and leaves the remote mountains of North Carolina to attend college and go far beyond his raising:

> The folks along the Roan called Abel "bryte."
> They said that he was "offish," too, and "selfly."
> He was two years gone in high grades,
> jumping classes in the grammars.
>   Dreams were things he reckoned with
> but termed them each a purpose and a pledge,
> high views unrelenting and secure
> from which he drew a needy sustenance.
> His mind etched altars in the valley mist,
> vague prophecies of a distant strength
> laid hard athwart both wishing and the will.
> —From *Abel Anders*, by Frank Borden Hanes
>   (New York: Farrar, Strauss and Young, 1951), 6–7.

Hanes wrote two other novels (in prose), *The Bat Brothers* (1953) and *The Fleet Rabble* (1961), both set in the American West. The latter was nominated for a Pulitzer and won the Sir Walter Raleigh Award for Fiction in 1961.

And now, facing east, we have come to the end of Trail Two. The next volume in this series of literary guidebooks will take up the journey in Yadkin County and cover the prodigious literary talents and sites in North Carolina's Piedmont.

Ashe County Arts Council

303 School Avenue
West Jefferson, NC 28694
336-846-2787
<http://www.ashecountyarts.org/>

Just one block off Main Street, near the Ashe Cheese outlet, and located in a stone house built by the Works Progress Administration in the 1930s, the Ashe County Arts Council maintains a gift shop with local crafts, music CDs, and a number of poetry volumes from local writers. The council also sponsors a range of literary events throughout the year.

Ashe County Public Library

148 Library Drive
West Jefferson, NC 28694
336-846-2041
<http://www.arlibrary.org/index.php?page=9>

Besides its excellent collection of regional literature, the Ashe County Library, on a hill overlooking downtown West Jefferson, is the monthly meeting spot for the Blue Ridge Writers Group.

Skyland Books

8-A South Jefferson Avenue
West Jefferson, NC 28694
336-846-2660

This bookstore carries regional titles that may not be so easy to find elsewhere, such as the Southern Appalachian Studies Series published by McFarland Books in the neighboring town of Jefferson.

Browse About Book Exchange

3 North Jefferson Avenue
West Jefferson, NC 28694
336-246-3502

Just a few doors down from Skyland Books, this bookstore offers used and out-of-print titles, some rare.

ACKNOWLEDGMENTS

First thanks go to the staff and board of the North Carolina Arts Council for imagining this project and issuing an invitation to carry the idea into print. Over many years, North Carolina's arts and literary community has been fortunate to have the steady leadership of Mary Regan and Nancy Trovillion. The Literary Trails concept is one more example of the vision and creativity that has led to North Carolina's national reputation as the "State of the Arts." Any shortcomings or mistakes in this book are mine alone. The opportunity to devise these tours according to my own lights is characteristic of the artistic freedom that the council always encourages.

The council's marketing experts—at the beginning of the project, Maryanne Friend and Joe Newberry, and now Rebecca Moore and Jessica Orr—have been enthusiastic cheerleaders and skilled partners in getting the word out.

Mountainous thanks go to marketing program assistant Jan Ruiz, Duke intern Marisa Bossen, and literature program assistant Burdette Southerland, who have contacted writers and publishers and acquired permissions where needed with diligence and diplomacy. The council's web wizard, Adam Lord, has done an astonishing job in conceiving an Internet version of this guide with links to other useful resources. Special credit must also go to Cindy Mixter for sorting out the numbers.

The council's literature director, Debbie McGill, has been a steady champion and first reader/editor throughout this process. For me personally, Debbie holds the distinction of crafting the nicest rejection letter I have ever received more than twenty years ago when she worked as an associate editor at the *Atlantic Monthly*. To avoid holding up my short story from submission elsewhere, Debbie not only had the rejection and manuscript returned to me by Federal Express, but she recommended that I shoot the story on to the magazine that did ultimately publish it. Such is the extra measure of care and respect that our literary community possesses in Debbie McGill.

At the University of North Carolina Press, David Perry, Paul Betz, Rich Hendel, Gina Mahalek, and Zach Read have all been patient shepherds. Copyeditor Liz Gray clearly has the "proofing gene" that I do not have, in addition to her finely tuned sense of a clunky sentence. I am indebted to her hundreds of times over for her wise revisions and catches. The project has also been fortunate to receive the savvy counsel of Nicki Leone, current president of both the

North Carolina Writers' Network and the Southern Independent Booksellers Association.

For their enthusiastic assistance with photographic research, thanks to Zoë Rhine at the Pack Memorial Library in Asheville, Flo Turcotte at the Smathers Libraries at the University of Florida, and Roger Nupie in the Netherlands. Beyond these specific individuals, I applaud the dozens of local public librarians who persevere in our service, keeping books in the hands of children and promoting new titles every day to adult patrons. They have been an enormous help here.

On the road, Donna Campbell and I encountered many other helpful guides—bookstore owners, proprietors of gas stations and grocery stores, folks on the street, restaurateurs, innkeepers, cultural mavens, and literary lions. Our gratitude is extended to many new and old friends: Bob Anthony, Frannie Ashburn, Dale Bartlett, Joseph Bathanti, Sallie Bissell, Jeri and Warren Board, Gary Carden, Bill Carson, Michael Chitwood, John Cooper, Jan Davidson, Pam Duncan, Clyde Edgerton, George Ellison, Marita Garin, Kay Hooper, Jane Lonon, Michael McFee, Joan Medlicott, Robin Merrell, Teri and Jimmy Milhous, the late Hugh Morton and his daughter Catherine, Scott Nicholson, Peggy Parris, Peggy Payne, Tim Peeler, Dannye Romine Powell, Anne Rawson, Ann B. Ross, Tim Silver, Nancy Simpson, Lee Smith and Hal Crowther, Dykeman Stokely, Judy Teele, Bob Terrell, the indefatigable Marsha Warren, arts evangelist Karen Wells, Gayle Winston, Thomas and Donna Wright, Perry Deane Young, Isabel Zuber, and most especially Professor Allison Ensor at the University of Tennessee for so generously sharing his research on Henry James and Edith Wharton.

I would also like to thank my mother, Virginia Reed, who traveled with us during part of the research phase of this project. I am grateful for the inheritance of her good sense of direction and her indefatigable love of travel.

In her essay "Place in Fiction," Eudora Welty argues that "every story would be another story, and unrecognizable as art, if it took up its characters and plot and happened somewhere else." The significance of place in any kind of creative writing is immeasurable. Who can imagine *Look Homeward, Angel* set in another town besides Asheville, or the finely tuned voice of Robert Morgan without his birthright perch atop the Blue Ridge?

The greatest thanks of all, then, go to the writers who have given us their vision of a place—western North Carolina. In particular, I have been appreciative of that very tall woman, the late Wilma Dykeman, who followed a river through this region and set a very high bar for such a guidebook. To Wilma's family and to all the writers who have given permission here to excerpt their works, thank you for the inspiration that continues to invite deeper investigation into the region's natural and human wonders.

PHOTOGRAPHER'S NOTE

One night in 1961, poet Carl Sandburg was on CBS television talking about his biography of Abraham Lincoln. Then, right there in our living room, he talked about how much he loved the mountains of North Carolina! My daddy was thrilled. And the next summer, when we loaded up in the Rambler station wagon and headed for the mountains, my four siblings and I heard a lot about Mr. Sandburg: how he had won the Pulitzer Prize, how he wrote about the working man. We would be camping right in his neighborhood, our daddy told us, and we might even see the great writer in the grocery store. It rained the whole weekend we were in Flat Rock. We drove down a few roads looking for what might be the poet's home. Then the fog came in on its little cat feet. So we played a lot of Monopoly in our tent. We never saw Carl Sandburg.

That wasn't our only failed attempt at literary tourism. We didn't find Thomas Wolfe's house when we were in Asheville. We just missed the Brown Mountain Lights. And we never saw where Tom Dula was jailed. But we did like singing that song, over and over, while we rode down all those winding roads. Later we would find out that we were in the wrong county.

Now, more than forty years later, I have stood in these and many dozens of other places of literary significance for my home state. And it has been a joy to photograph them.

Of course, the photos are included here only as reference. You really should see these places for yourself. The majesty that inspired Charles Frazier, the "laurel hells" of Horace Kephart, the green valleys that must have looked like home to the Scot ancestors of Sharyn McCrumb. Other regions have paved over their inspirational history, but in westernmost North Carolina, the places of literary significance mostly still exist. And with this guide in hand, you can find them. We did.

Georgann Eubanks and I traveled more than a thousand miles to document the tours and trails in this book. In addition to cameras and notebooks, we carried an atlas, a stack of maps, and a back seat filled with poetry books, biographies, and novels. We stopped in every library and bookstore, and more than a few gas stations, asking for directions and information about writers. We hiked to the top of scenic peaks to read Robert Morgan and Wilma Dykeman out loud. We watched sunrises and sunsets. We ate biscuits at the Nu Wray and drank bourbon at the Grove Park. We spent a lot of time in cemeteries. All in pursuit of authenticity and accuracy.

And when we finally visited Connemara, Sandburg's home in Flat Rock, I called my daddy on the cell phone. We had just missed the turn by the lake, I told him. We had been so close.

Donna Campbell

A NOTE ON THE NORTH CAROLINA LITERARY TRAILS PROGRAM

The North Carolina Literary Trails Program, when complete, will include sites related to literature across the state. Because new books and authors emerge constantly, it is impossible to be all-inclusive of North Carolina's literary treasures. The tours that make up the trails have been devised to represent the following priorities:

—historic sites where North Carolina authors have lived and worked;
—visitable sites that figure prominently in the published poetry, fiction, creative nonfiction, and plays of North Carolina writers and other writers who have spent significant time here;
—libraries with notable collections of manuscripts, books, and other literary artifacts related to North Carolina authors that are publicly accessible;
—bookstores and other venues where North Carolina authors take part in public programming or are represented in exhibits, events, performances, and other activities; and
—other local amenities related to each tour itinerary as recommended by contemporary authors familiar with the area who have, in some cases, been commissioned to write brief pieces for inclusion in these guidebooks.

PERMISSIONS

The following poems have been reprinted by permission of the author unless otherwise noted below:

Bathanti, Joseph: "House Hunting at Four Thousand Feet," copyright © 2002.

Byer, Kathryn Stripling: "Tuckasegee," from *Black Shawl* (Louisiana State University Press), copyright © 1998.

Chappell, Fred: "A Prayer for the Mountains," from *Source* (Louisiana State University Press), copyright © 1985.

Chitwood, Michael: "Looking for Horace Kephart's Grave, Bryson City, NC," from *Whet* (Ohio Review Books), copyright © 1995. "White Squirrels of Brevard," copyright © 2005.

Crowe, Thomas Rain: "The Saw Mill Shack," from *Nantahala: A Review of Writing and Photography in Appalachia*, copyright © 2004.

DiSanto, Grace: "You Salome! Are the Cloud Dancing on Grandfather Mountain," from *North Carolina's 400 Years: Signs Along the Way—An Anthology of Poems by North Carolina Poets to Celebrate America's 400th Anniversary* (Acorn Press), copyright © 1986, used by permission of Acorn Press, Durham, N.C.

Downer, Hilda: "Hills so beautiful they sting," from *Bandana Creek* (Red Clay Books), copyright © 1979.

Earley, Tim: "County Poem #11: Rapture," copyright © 2005.

Fitzgerald, F. Scott: "Oh Misseldine's, dear Misseldine's," from *Poems 1911–1940* (Bruccoli Clark), copyright © 1981, used by permission of Harold Ober Associates.

Foerst, Deborah: "Lights in the Smokies," from *Lights in the Mountain: Stories, Essays and Poems by Writers Living in and Inspired by the Southern Appalachian Mountains* (Winding Path Publishing), copyright © 2003, used by permission of anthology editor Nancy Simpson.

McFee, Michael: excerpts from "Grace" and "Pocket Watch," from *Sad Girl Sitting on a Running Board* (Gnomon Press), copyright © 1991, used by permission of Gnomon Press, Frankfort, Ky. "Linville Caverns," from *Colander* (Carnegie Mellon University Press), copyright © 1996, used by permission of Carnegie Mellon University Press, Pittsburgh, Pa.

Long or multiple prose excerpts from a single work have been reprinted by permission of the author unless otherwise noted:

Carden, Gary: "The Swinett," from *Mason Jars in the Flood and Other Stories* (Parkway Publishers), copyright © 2000.

Cornwell, Patricia Daniels: excerpt from *Ruth, A Portrait: The Story of Ruth Bell Graham* (Doubleday), copyright © 1997 by Cornwell Enterprises, Inc., used by permission of Doubleday, a division of Random House, Inc.

Daniels, Jonathan: excerpt from *Tar Heels: A Portrait of North Carolina* (Dodd Mead), copyright © 1941, used by permission of Lucy Daniels Inman.

Dargan, Olive Tilford: excerpt from "Serena and Wild Strawberries," in *From My Highest Hill: Carolina Mountain Folks* (University of Tennessee Press), copyright © 1998, used by permission of University of Tennessee Press, Knoxville, Tenn.

Dykeman, Wilma: excerpt from *The French Broad*, copyright © 1955, 1983 by Wilma Dykeman, used by permission of Henry Holt and Company, LLC.

Earley, Tony: excerpt from "Hallways," originally published in *Home: American Writers Remember Rooms of Their Own* (Pantheon, 1995); excerpts from "The Quare Gene," originally published in the *New Yorker*, September 28, 1998. Reprinted by the permission of Regal Literary as agent for Tony Earley. Copyright © 1995, 1998 by Tony Earley.

Ensor, Allison: excerpt from "'Wasted Monstrosity' or 'Divine Landscape': Henry James and Edith Wharton Visit Asheville's Biltmore House," copyright © 2004.

Frazier, Charles: excerpt from "Cold Mountain Diary," copyright © 1997.

Morley, Margaret: excerpt from *The Carolina Mountains* (Land of the Sky Books), copyright © 2004, used by permission of publisher Ralph Roberts.

Parris, John: excerpts from *Mountain Bred* and *Roaming the Mountains* (Citizen-Times Publishing Company), copyright © 1967 and 1982, used by permission of Susan Ihne for the *Asheville Citizen-Times*.

Reid, Christian: excerpt from *The Land of the Sky: Adventures in Mountain By-Ways* (Land of the Sky Books), copyright © 2001, used by permission of publisher Ralph Roberts.

Spencer, Elizabeth: excerpt from "Heading for the Hills," from *Close to Home: Revelations and Reminiscences by North Carolina Authors* (John F. Blair), copyright © 1996.

INDEX

Page numbers in italics refer to photographs and captions. Page numbers in boldface refer to maps.